FREEDOM OF ASSOCIATION IN CHINA AND EUROPE: COMPARATIVE PERSPECTIVES IN LAW AND PRACTICE

Freedom of Association in China and Europe: Comparative Perspectives in Law and Practice

edited by

YUWEN LI

Netherlands Institute of Human Rights, Faculty of Law
Utrecht University, The Netherlands

MARTINUS NIJHOFF PUBLISHERS
LEIDEN / BOSTON

A C.I.P. Catalogue record for this book is available from the Library of Congress.

Printed on acid-free paper.

Layout and camera-ready copy:
Anne-Marie Krens – Oegstgeest – The Netherlands

ISBN 90-04-14840-X

http://www.brill.nl

Printed and bound in The Netherlands

TABLE OF CONTENTS

FOREWORD

In the last few decades China has undergone a startling transformation, and nowhere is this more apparent than in the economic sphere. The decision to abandon a planned economy and embrace the process of internationalisation is one of the most striking aspects of this transformation. As third secretary at the Dutch embassy in Beijing from 1976-1978 and as ambassador to China for the Kingdom of the Netherlands from 2001 to 2005, I was able to witness these fascinating developments at first hand.

The aforementioned developments (and others) have had a major influence on the way civil society is organised in China. The Chinese government is starting to realise, with some reluctance, that it is not capable of identifying and addressing its citizens' every desire and problem. For this reason it no longer offers cradle-to-grave care ('the iron rice bowl'), increasingly entrusting that role to the private sector and NGOs. I believe this is a step in the right direction: NGOs (or 'social organisations' as they are called in China) can often devise faster, better and cheaper solutions to social needs and problems. It is quite understandable that the authors of this book were moved to examine their role in contemporary China.

The disengagement of the Chinese government and an increase in individual freedom has generated an explosion of desires and demands, which a growing number of NGOs are now trying to meet.

The onus is on the Chinese government to use legislation to create a nurturing environment for these NGOs. A legal framework must be established within which the NGOs can continue operating undisturbed, without coercive or restrictive interference from the government. It is only in this way that NGOs can reach their full potential and play a valuable role in society.

It is no surprise that the process of building a legal foundation for NGOs in China has been slow going. The Chinese government has had difficulty coming to terms with having to delegate some of its responsibilities to 'the free market'. In addition, the Chinese government has little experience with this process, and for that reason alone it has chosen to proceed with caution. It is hoped that intellectual contributions, from both inside and outside China, can further the debate on the position of NGOs and possibly accelerate developments in this area.

Since a visit to China by Minister for Development Cooperation Eveline Herfkens in 1998, the Dutch Ministry of Foreign Affairs has been allocating funds to activities aimed at bolstering the rule of law in China. In that spirit, between 2001 and 2004 the Dutch embassy in Beijing financed a study project run by the Chinese Academy of Social Sciences and Utrecht University that focused on the legal side of NGOs in China. One of the results of that project is this topical and fascinating book.

I would like to thank the authors for the courage and unflagging energy they have shown in writing this critical and forward-thinking book. I hope it will be a valuable contribution to the debate on the position of NGOs in China and an inspiration to many.

Dr. Philip de Heer

Ambassador of the Kingdom of the Netherlands
to the People's Republic of China

June 2005

PREFACE

This book, the outcome of collaboration between Chinese and Western scholars, is at long last ready for publication. When I read the familiar names and themes it contains my mind was cast back to a gathering some years ago in the garden at the back of the Royal Netherlands Ambassador's residence in Beijing. It was a lunch time in February 2002, the spring air still chilly; Ambassador de Heer and I had signed an agreement for a joint research project on legal aspects of social organizations in China. We took our drinks out into the back garden and both made some brief remarks for the occasion. I remember I said what a marvellous thing it was that the European nation that had seen the glories of the Dutch Republic and been home to Van Gogh should now be such an enthusiastic promoter of academic cooperation and exchange in the Far East; and to be seeking to further understand China's culture and society. Ambassador de Heer replied with a speech that displayed a broad-ranging knowledge of Chinese civilisation and that expressed his hopes for the further growth of governance by law and civil society here. The other Chinese participants in this event included my colleagues Professors Wu Yuzhang and Jiang Xiaohong and Wu Yan from the *Worker's Daily*, and of course also Dr Li Yuwen.

Dr Li began studying law in 1980 at China's most prestigious university, Peking University. After graduation she spent a short time working at the University before going to the Netherlands to take her doctorate study. In recent years she has acted as a coordinator for numerous influential projects and has been very active in promoting Sino-Dutch academic exchange. I recall that she was often joined in these endeavours by the equally enthusiastic and diligent Christine Pirenne from the Netherlands Embassy. The burdens of this work might well have served to stifle Dr Li's academic talents, but on the contrary she was a deeply engaged participant in all aspects of these collaborations on civil society organisation law, making scholarly contributions to the exposition of themes, survey work, translation, revisions to legislation and comparative studies. This book is the fruit of her many endeavours.

While I do not necessarily share all the conclusions of the studies presented here, I do nevertheless richly appreciate the research viewpoints and the spirit of openness on which they were based. In China, freedom of association is a political problem that has as yet no happy resolution and also a legal question that likewise has yet to be adequately addressed. In the China of antiquity, people did enjoy freedom of association in certain respects – a classic example would be Confucius gathering his disciples around him. Yet at the same time there were also severe restrictions on this freedom. Indeed the formation of associations was thought of most often in connection with secret societies and the underworld. The diversification of interests, the rising consciousness of citizens' rights and the dismantling and re-ordering of social structures that have accompanied market reform and the new ways of thinking have only added to the importance of association as a means of voluntary self-expression, collective pursuit of interests and social participation. Hence civil society organisations have been springing up in great numbers. In many ways the legal issues faced by civil society organisations in China are similar to those in Western countries; however, organisations here are quite different in terms of their social context and fundamental nature. The civil society organisations of today's China have come into being in a society formed by a proletarian revolution and shaped by a socialist collective economy. They are in concept not the same as Western NGOs and it is not easy to understand them using a model based on the Western premise of a bi-polar separation of government and civil society. It is equally important that Western scholars fully understand this about China and Chinese scholars fully understand this about the West. The great value of this book is that, with rich scholarship and abundant materials, it opens up a field for the separate research of these issues, where a variety of individual views on the matter are set forth, greater mutual understanding is possible and comparative study can be made.

Xia Yong

Professor of Law, Director of Institute of Law, Chinese Academy of Social Sciences, Vice President of Chinese Society of Law

Beijing, April 2005

ACKNOWLEDGEMENTS

As editor, I must firstly express my gratitude to two people without whom this book could never have been accomplished. Professor Xia Yong, Director of the Institute of Law of the Chinese Academy of Social Sciences (IOL), deserves credit for being the true architect of the study of legal issues concerning social organizations in China at the IOL. I remember vividly the summer of 2000 when we discussed the prospect of starting a cooperative project in the field of law for the first time. On that occasion he clearly pointed out that a precondition to the realization of the rule of law in China is the recognition and protection of human rights. While the human rights situation in China has improved in many respects in the post-Mao era, freedom of association remained a sensitive issue over which legal research and advocacy was yet to start. He anticipated that the emerging NGOs in China would persuade the government to enact new laws and it is the mission of Chinese legal researchers to involve themselves in the legislation process by leading the public debate and providing advice to the government based on comprehensive research. Professor Xia is a highly respected scholar who has published thoughtful and succinct essays on human rights in Chinese. He edited 'Towards the Age of Rights' in 1995, one of the first books to reflect the Chinese legal scholars' serious thinking and concomitant social responsibility in addressing citizens' rights in the reform period. Over the last three years Professor Xia's courage and commitment have stimulated his colleagues to delve into the problems, challenges and alternative solutions for constructing a legal regime which is conducive to facilitating the development of social organizations and consequently to maximizing the realization of freedom of association in China. The papers presented in this Book illustrate the success of the Chinese scholars' endeavours.

The second person I must mention is Mrs. Christine Pirenne who served as the first secretary at the Dutch Embassy in Beijing and was in charge of the rule of law program during 2001 to 2004. She left her beloved Africa to come and work in a totally different China. Thanks to her professional commitment and enthusiasm she soon adapted to the new environment. Impressed by the progress China has achieved during a relatively short period of time and the atmosphere of transition where 'everything is possible', she worked passionately with enthusiastic and responsible Chinese intellectuals. Of course, working with the Chinese in implementing various projects cannot be always straight-forward, but Christine's openness, comprehension, and patience enabled her with persistence to overcome many difficulties. I sometimes regret that because of the language barrier she was not always able to fully enjoy the outcomes of the projects she has supported. Hopefully, this book in English will bring her some gratification. My Chinese colleagues and I will always remember her major contribution to our work. It goes without saying that Christine's colleagues at the Dutch Embassy, Ambassador Philip de Heer, Karel van Oosterom, Paul Menkveld, and Rene Smullders have been the powerful backing for Christine's work. Their mutual trust and encouraging cooperation set an example of the most efficient and enjoyable team work. I thank them sincerely for their irreplaceable input to our work. Such heartfelt thanks also go to Job van den Berg, who is the successor of Christine, and has supported our project ever since.

Back at my Institute, The Netherlands Institute of Human Rights of the Faculty of Law of Utrecht University, my deep appreciation goes to Professor Cees Flinterman. As the Director of the Institute he has stimulated me to initiate cooperative projects in China, and his trust and vision in promoting human rights protection all over the world have been inspirational for me. Monienke Vergunst, a young but completely trustworthy, committed and hard-working student assistant has worked with me for nearly three years in all our China-related projects. I take this opportunity to extend to her my heartfelt thanks. Nathan Rasiah, my other student assistant, has worked diligently in helping me to complete the editing of this Book.

I would also like to thank all the contributors to this book, especially Professor Wu Yuzhang as the Project Manager who has not only showed his high quality of academic work but also skillful organizational capacity. His colleague, Dr. Jiang Xiaohong has also played an inestimable role. My thanks also go to Mr Richard Fries at the London School of Economics who carefully read and corrected all the manuscripts, and has always been very supportive to civil society research in China; to Jim Weldon, a highly qualified Sinologist, his linguistics talent and passion to NGOs work in China enabled him to translate accurately my Chinese colleagues' papers from Chinese into English. Last but not least my most grateful thanks to my husband Professor Nico Schrijver, and our lovely children Lineke and Kees, who inevitably suffered somewhat from my regular trips to China and busy job, but fully and enthusiastically supported me.

Yuwen Li, Editor, June 2005

LIST OF CONTRIBUTORS

CHEN Xinxin is an associate professor at the Institute of Law of the Chinese Academy of Social Sciences in Beijing, China. He obtained his Ph.D in Law at Renmin University in 1999 in Beijing, China, and was a visiting scholar at Oxford University and Lund University. His main publications include: *Legal Problems of One Country Two Systems*, (Dangjian Press, 2001); *Legal Protection of the Freedom of Expression*, (China Social Science Press, 2003). His main areas of research are press freedom, judicial review, international human rights law, and comparative study of legal theory and history.

Paul DEKKER studied political science at the Catholic University of Nijmegen, The Netherlands, and the Free University of (West) Berlin, and received his Ph.D from Utrecht University.

Currently he is head of the Participation and Government Research Unit of the Social and Cultural Planning Office. He is also Vice-chair of the Psychopolitics Research Committee of the International Political Science Association, a member of the editorial boards of the Journal of Civil Society and the Dutch Yearbook of Market Research, and the Dutch local associate for the Johns Hopkins Comparative Nonprofit Sector Project. He is also part time professor of Civil Society Studies at the University of Tilburg. He has done various research in the fields of public administration, environmental attitudes and behaviour, social attitudes and political participation; his research is often policy-oriented and in a trans-national comparative perspective. His present research focuses on political disaffection, social capital, volunteering and foundations.

Some of his recent publications concerning civil society and the nonprofit sector are: *Social Capital and Participation in Everyday Life* (with Eric M. Uslaner) (London/New York: Routledge, 2001); 'On the Prospects of Volunteering in Civil Society' (2002) 4 *Voluntary Action*; *The Values of Volunteering* (with Loek Halman, eds.) (New York: Kluwer Academic/Plenum Publishers, 2003); 'Civil Society, Social Trust and Democratic Involvement', (with Peter Ester and Henk Vinken) in: Wil Arts, Jacques Hagenaars and Loek Halman (eds.), *The Cultural Diversity of European Unity* (Leiden/Boston: Brill, 2003); 'The Sphere of Voluntary Associations and the

Ideals of Civil Society' (2004) 35 *Korea Observer*; 'Social Capital of Individuals', in: Per Selle and Sanjeev Prakash (eds.), *Investigating Social Capital* (New Delhi: Sage, 2004); 'The Role of the Third Sector in the Netherlands', in: Annette Zimmerman and Christina Stecker (eds.), *Strategy Mix* (New York: Kluwer Academic/ Plenum Publishers, 2004); 'The Netherlands' in: Adalbert Evers and Jean Louis Laville (eds.), *The Third Sector in Europe* (Cheltenham: Edward Elgar, 2004).

Richard FRIES has been involved with the legal, institutional and regulatory basis of civil society for 20 years. Since retiring as head of the English Charity Commission in 1999 he has been a visiting fellow at the Centre for Civil Society (CCS) at the London School of Economics and Chair of the Board of the International Center for Not-for-profit Law (ICNL).

Born in London in 1940, he studied philosophy at King's College, Cambridge and entered the British Civil Service in 1965. Serving 27 years in the Home Office, his career covered most aspects of that department's responsibilities, including criminal justice, policing, immigration, race relations and even horse racing! From 1987 – 1991 he was Under Secretary responsible for government policy on charity and the voluntary sector. This included developing proposals for the reform of the Charity Commission, the regulator of charities in England and Wales, including what subsequently became the provisions of the Charities Act 1993, strengthening the powers of the Commission. In 1992 he was appointed Chief Charity Commissioner (effectively Chair and Chief Executive). The role and responsibilities of the Commission are described in his contribution to this collection. As head of the Commission he was responsible for leading its reform from being an essentially legal body to being a broad-based organisation responsible for creating and applying an accountability framework for charities, providing support in meeting its requirements for integrity and good practice, and for investigating and remedying abuse and mismanagement. During his time at the Commission he initiated a comprehensive review of charity in fulfilment of the Commission's responsibilities for maintaining the Register of Charities. As Chief Commissioner he contributed to many conferences and discussions on charity law and regulation, including international discussions in Central and Eastern Europe and other parts of the world.

Since retiring he has continued to be involved in reform and development initiatives in charity and not-for-profit law in many parts of the world through the CCS and ICNL and personally. He has written extensively on these topics.

Yuwen LI is a senior researcher at the Faculty of Law of Utrecht University, the Netherlands. She obtained a Bachelor Degree in Law from Peking University in 1984 and a Master's Degree in International Law and International Relations from the Institute of Social Studies, The Hague, the Netherlands. In 1994 she received her Ph.D in International Law at the Law Faculty of Utrecht University, The Netherlands.

Dr. Li's main publications include: *Transfer of Technology for Deep Sea-Bed Mining: The 1982 Law of the Sea Convention and Beyond* (Dordrecht: Martinus Nijhoff Publishers, 1994); *Law-Making in the People's Republic of China*, (co-edited), (The Hague: Kluwer Law International, 2000); *Implementation of Law in the People's Republic of China,* (co-edited), (The Hague: Kluwer Law International, 2002). Her other publications cover Chinese business law, tax law, constitutional law, the court system, the lawyer system, and human rights.

From 2001 she has been the senior co-ordinator for China projects at the Netherlands Institute of Human Rights at the Law Faculty of Utrecht University, The Netherlands. In that capacity she has been involved in training Chinese judges, prosecutors, and correctional police on human rights as well as supporting civil society research and training in China. She has been one of the key speakers at the EU-China Human Rights seminars on freedom of association and presented several papers relevant to that topic.

LIU Peifeng is a post-doctoral researcher at the Faculty of Law of Tsinghua University, Beijing, China. He wrote his Ph.D thesis on freedom of association, and it discussed the topic from both Chinese law and practice and international perspectives. After receiving his Ph.D at the Post-graduate Institute of the Chinese Academy of Social Sciences, he has focused on research and teaching on NPO law, and training Chinese civil society organisations.

Dr. Liu's main publications include: 'Legislation Concerning Freedom of Association in European Countries', 2004 *Global Law Review*; 'Thinking on the Relevant Concepts Relating to NPOs', (2004) 10 *China Administrative Management*; *General Introduction to Civil Society Organizations* (co-authored) (Shishi Press, 2004). At present he is in charge of the research program on NGOs and Protection of the Labor Rights of Rural Immigrants. He is also involved in other research programs on topics including legal systems on freedom of association, NGOs' and citizens' participation in politics; legislation on NPOs and public policy on NPOs; the legal system relating to the development of Western China.

MO Jihong is a professor of Constitutional Law at the Institute of Law of the Chinese Academy of Social Sciences. He received his Bachelor Degree of Law at the Law Faculty of Peking University in 1986, and his Masters Degree and Ph.D in Law at the Post-graduate Institute of the Chinese Academy of Social Sciences.

He has published several books in Chinese, including: *The Logical Basis for Modern Constitutional Law* (Law Publishing House, 2001); *The New Conception of Constitutionalism* (Zhongguo Fangzheng Press, 1997); *General Introduction on Constitutional Trial* (China People's Public Security University Press, 1998); *The Legal Limitation of Freedom of Expression* (China People's Public Security University Press, 1998).

His recently published articles include 'Survey on Ought to Be – A Perspective of Constitutional Logic', in (2001) 6 *China Social Sciences*; 'The Relationship

Between International Conventions on Human Rights and Domestic Constitutional Law', in (1999) 3 *China Law*; 'The New Trend of the Relationship between International Law and Domestic Law', in (2001) 9 *World Economy and Politics*; 'Duties under the Two International Covenants on Human Rights and China', in (2002) 8 *World Economy and Law*. His main publications in English are: 'Legal Protection for Rights to Cultural Heritage', in 2003 *China Social Sciences* (English edition); 'The Globalization of Human Rights and International NGOs' Role', in (2002) *Korean Constitutional Review*.

Professor Mo's main research fields include constitutionalism and human rights, constitutional supervision and litigation, and comparative study on legal theory.

Rupert Graf STRACHWITZ has been involved with not-for-profit organisations for well over 30 years – as a volunteer, staff member, board member, consultant, researcher and lecturer. Since 1989, he has been managing director of Maecenata Management, a consultancy that specialises in foundations and associations, corporate citizenship and philanthropy, and since 1997, he has also been the director of the Maecenata Institute for Philanthropy and Civil Society, now affiliated to Humboldt University, Berlin.

Born in 1947, he studied Political Science, History, and History of Art at Colgate University, Hamilton, NY, USA, and Ludwig-Maximilians-Universitaet, Munich, Germany. He graduated as an M.A. in 1974 with a thesis on The Levellers, a 17th century English citizens' action group. After serving at the World Headquarters of the Sovereign Military Order of Malta (an international disaster relief and medical aid organisation) in Rome for 2 years, he became regional director for the Order of Malta Relief Service in Bavaria. Subsequently, he held a position in public life while serving on the board of a number of foundations as well as other NGOs, including German Caritas, where he was Vice-President in 1984/85. After becoming an independent consultant in 1989, he became increasingly involved with Third Sector research and chaired the German advisory committee of the Johns Hopkins Comparative Nonprofit Sector Project from 1995 to 2000. Today, while still occasionally acting as consultant, his main focus is on research and public policy to do with civil society and philanthropy. From 1999 to 2002, he served as member of the German Federal Parliament Commission on Civic Action. He chairs the European Policy Working Group of Europa Nostra, and sits on the board of the Fondazione Cariplo, Milan/Italy, and a number of other nongovernmental organisations at home and abroad.

He published numerous books and articles on foundation issues as well as cultural policy, the third sector, and civil society in German as well as in English, Italian, French, Japanese, and Polish.

Tymen J. VAN DER PLOEG studied Dutch Law at Leiden University 1965-1971, specialising in Civil Law. He worked as a lawyer at the bar of The Hague, and is now a professor of civil law at the Faculty of Law of the Free University of Amsterdam. In 1978 he defended his thesis on Civil Law and Voluntary Organisations in the new Book 2 of the Dutch Civil Code of 1976.

He has published several books and articles, especially in the field of association and foundation law and the relationship between voluntary organisations and the government, both according to Dutch law and from a comparative perspective and also in the area of the church and the law, including: 'A Comparative Legal Analysis of Foundations: Aspects of Supervisions and Transparency' in Helmut K. Anheier and Stefan Toepler (eds.) *Private Funds, Public Purpose: Philanthropic Foundations in International Perspective* (New York/Boston/Dordrecht: Kluwer Academic/Plenum Publishers, 1999); 'Foundations' (co-authored with F.W. Hondius) in Volume XIII of Detlev Vagts (ed.), *International Encyclopedia of Comparative Law*, (Dordrecht/Boston/Lancaster: Martinus Nijhoff Publishers, 2000); *Law of Associations, Foundations, Co-operative and Mutual Societies (Van vereniging en stichting, coöperatie en onderlinge waarborgmaatschappij)*, (4th ed., Gouda Quint: Deventer, 2002).

In 1989 he was senior fellow in International Philanthropy at the Institute for Policy Studies at the Johns Hopkins University in Baltimore, USA and since then he has been a regular contributor at international conferences about non-governmental organisations, as well as advisor and expert regarding legislation in this field in Central and Eastern Europe. In 1993 he co-established the interdisciplinary research group on government-NGO relationships at the Law Faculty of the Free University. He serves as chairman of the committee of experts of the Dutch Office for Fundraising.

WU Yuzhang is a professor of legal theory at the Institute of Law of the Chinese Academy of Social Sciences. He received his Master's Degree of Law at Peking University and was a visiting scholar at Harvard University. He is also the head of the Department of Comparative Law at the Institute of Law of the Chinese Academy of Social Sciences, chief editor of the journal, Global Law Review, and deputy chief editor of the prestigious academic journal China Social Sciences. His main books are: *Review the Conception of Rights of the Liberalism* (China People's Public Security University press, 1997); *Levels of the Rule of Law* (Tsinghua University Press, 2003); *Legal Issues on Social Organizations* (China Social Science Documents Press, 2004). He has also translated from English into Chinese the work of Robert Unger, R. Dworkin, Joseph Raz. His publications in English include: 'The Concept of Citizenship in the People's Republic of China', (with Li Buyun) in Alastair Davidson and Kathleen Weekley (eds.), *Globalization and Citizenship in the Asia-Pacific* (London: Macmillan Press Ltd., 1999). Professor Wu was the executive director of the implementation of the project on Chinese-Dutch Research Co-operation on the Legal Aspects of Social Organizations in China, funded by the Royal Dutch Embassy in Beijing from 2001 to 2004.

XIE Haiding is an associate professor at the Institute of Law of the Chinese Academy of Social Sciences and editor of Chinese Journal of Law. He received his Bachelor

Degree in Law from Anhui Normal University, his Master's Degree in Law from the Southwest University of Politics and Law in China, and his Ph.D from the Post-Graduate Institute of the Chinese Academy of Social Sciences. He edited the book *Women and Law* (China Foreign Trade and Economy Press, 1999). His recent publications include: 'Rethinking the Development of Rule of Law Theory in China' (2000) 6 *Chinese Journal of Law*; 'The Dilemma of Legitimacy Facing China's Civil Society Organizations' (2004) 2 *Chinese Journal of Law*; 'Hot Issues on Recent Research of Chinese Social Organizations' (2002) *Global Law Review*; 'Review and Future Prospects of Judicial Reform in China', (2002) *Global Law Review*; 'Legal Protection on Freedom of Academic Research: Chinese Case Studies' (2004) 6 *Case and Research*. His main research fields are freedom of association, academic freedom, and legal development in China.

LIST OF ABBREVIATIONS

ACWF	All China Women Federation
CASS	Chinese Academy of Social Sciences
CNY	Chinese Yuan
CPCC	Communist Party Central Committee
CPPCC	Chinese People's Political Consultative Conference
CSO	Civil Society Organization
ECHR	European Convention on Human Rights and Fundamental Freedoms
E-NGO	Environmental Non-Governmental Organization
FCF	Friends of China Foundation
FON	Friends of Nature
GONGO	Government Organized Non-Governmental Organization
GVB	Global Village of Beijing
ICCPR	International Covenant on Civil and Political Rights
IOC	International Olympic Committee
IOL	Institute of Law (of the CASS)
KMT	Kuomintang (Guomindang)
MCA	Ministry of Civil Affairs
NGO	Non-Governmental Organization
NPO	Non-Profit Organization
OECD	Organization for Economic Cooperation and Development
PRC	People's Republic of China
SARS	Severe Acute Respiratory Syndrom
SEPA	State Environmental Protection Agency
SOE	State-owned Enterprise
SONGO	State-owned Non-Governmental Organization
SORP	Statement of Recommended Accounting Practice for Charities

GENERAL INTRODUCTION TO THE BOOK

Yuwen Li

This book is the outcome of a three-year project of Chinese-Dutch Research Cooperation on the Legal Aspects of Social Organisations in China, funded by the Royal Dutch Embassy in Beijing from 2001 to 2004. The main aim of the project was to encourage Chinese researchers to deepen their knowledge and understanding of the current status of social organisations in China, and to allow them to explore possible ways of creating a friendly legal environment conducive to the exercise of the right to freedom of association. The book contains some of the best results of the Chinese researchers' work and papers presented by the European experts at the international seminars held in 2003 and 2004, organised jointly by the Institute of Law of the Chinese Academy of Social Sciences and the Law Faculty of Utrecht University in the Netherlands.

At the outset there was no intention to publish a book in English, one of the main reasons being that, at the time the project was designed, freedom of association was still a very sensitive political issue in China and academic discussion in legal circles was rather exceptional. There was uncertainty as to the capacity of Chinese legal scholars to adopt a critical approach in examining the existing legal system and to advance constructive suggestions. Indeed, during the first and second year of cooperation, we found that the research of the Chinese participants focused more on the historical aspects of associational life in China than on the potential for reform drawing on foreign laws and practice relating to associations, and international human rights standards concerning freedom of association. The furthest step taken was the occasional publication of short critical articles in Chinese newspapers.

Yuwen Li (Ed.), *Freedom of Association in China and Europe: Comparative Perspectives in Law and Practice*, © 2005 Koninklijke Brill NV, Leiden. Printed in The Netherlands, pp. 1-13.

However, by the end of 2003 it was evident that certain scholars participating had accumulated considerable knowledge based on their field studies and acquired a critical insight that they were willing to advocate publicly. Thanks also to the growth of academic freedom in general over the last few years, we felt that it would be a suitable time to publish the work of Chinese researchers in order to stimulate international understanding of the progress made and the dilemmas that China is facing, to facilitate international discourse and eventually to generate international support for the emerging new civil society organisations in China.

Of equal importance, the European experts who were invited to conferences in China were also enthusiastic about contributing to the book, resulting in an ideal combination of Chinese and European perspectives on law and practice relating to freedom of association in different countries. As far as we know this is the first book in English that offers systematic and critical research in this field.

One preliminary consideration concerns the difficulties posed by the choice of terminology. As with any subject, the terms used to refer to concepts in the field of freedom of association vary widely between countries and cultures, and they change over time. Choosing a particular term has consequences beyond simply whether or not the author is comprehensible to a particular reader; it also affects more subtly the message the author conveys, by, for instance, revealing his or her starting point of enquiry, and the assumptions and preconceptions upon which the work is premised. Although in a comparative study such as this, there is an understandable desire to adopt similar terminology for consistency and ease of comparison, it is of greater importance to respect the choice made by the author and retain the specific meaning that is imparted by that choice. In compiling this book, the problem of terminology was further exacerbated by the challenge of translation, especially when dealing with Chinese terms that escape a direct English translation. Hence the authors that have contributed to the book have each chosen from the variety of terms that exist – social organisations, non-governmental organisations, non-profit organisations, civic organisations, civil society organisations, the third sector, and so on.

The opening chapter by Dr Yuwen Li provides a comprehensive exposition of the tension that characterises the status of freedom of association in China. She highlights the existence of two antagonistic forces at play in today's China. On the one hand, the emergence of new social organisations and the evolution and transformation of old social organisations demonstrate the existence of a progressive social trend in China's associational life. At the same time, failing to acknowledge the new situation on the ground, the state continues to apply a constricting legal regime to social organisations, effectively hindering the free exercise by citizens of the right to freedom of association.

Dr Li explores China's gradually burgeoning civil society through a study of some empirical examples in which she charts the development of certain types of new organisations, such as women's organisations, environmental NGOs, trade associations, and non-governmental, non-profit, social welfare organisations. Although such organisations vary widely in size, capacity, and influence, together they represent a new social force which has emerged as a reaction to a pressing social need; as such, they demonstrate great potential to develop maturely in China. However, in spite of the promise they display, these organisations remain vulnerable, primarily because they face a powerful government and its agencies, which insist on applying a restrictive legal system.

Against this backdrop, Dr Li moves to address the shortcomings of the current law in detail, analysing the specific methods of control it deploys such as the dual administrative system, the system of registration, and the review system. Having come to the conclusion that a change in the law is unavoidable, the chapter proceeds to analyse the various possible options for change based on proposals for reform. Though aware of the contradiction between the gathering momentum of China's fledging civil society and the restrictive nature of the legal regime, Dr Li approaches the paradox with a healthy dose of legal circumspection. She concludes on a cautiously optimistic note.

> Obviously, it may be some time before a legal environment emerges that is bright and conducive to the development of NGOs and NPOs, or the third sector as a whole. It is the task of Chinese legal community to make efforts to bring out positive changes of the legal system relating to freedom of association; there are signs that they are doing so.

In the second chapter, Professor Wu Yuzhang's description of the 'model of government administrative control' forms the backbone of his exploration of the situation of social organisations in China. From the outset Professor Wu acknowledges that the study of social organisations proceeds from the starting point of enquiry of how better to protect the right to association that citizens enjoy under the law, an acknowledgment which foreshadows the critical approach of his paper towards the status quo in China.

Initially, he highlights the striking feature of the situation of social organisations in China that distinguishes them from their Western and non-Chinese counterparts – the high level of administrative control exercised by the government. He encapsulates the difference in perspective through his explanation of the two conflicting logics that exist: the logic of civil society and the accompanying understanding that freedom of association constitutes a vital component of civil society, which prevails in Western societies, as compared with the logic of governmental control, where government has the right to exercise control over the existence and development of social organisations. The author traces the roots of this notion back through the planned economy of the 1950s – 1970s, and further back to pre-revolutionary thinking, heavily influenced by the ideology of the Empire, where 'all the earth under Heaven was his Majesty's earth and all the land between the seas was administered by His Majesty's ministers'. This is a dogma that Professor Wu believes is still prevalent 'in the subconscious of many of the current governing class'.

The administrative model that exists in China has what he describes as a bipolar structure – the exercise of administrative control over social organisations, and the maintenance of consistency with central government policy. Under such circumstances, the structure is bound to err on the side of caution, taking 'the standpoint of the government ... as its point of departure and striving to avoid the development of social organisations getting out of control with the consequent dangers to overall social stability'. Thus, the existing model can be described as 'one of growth under restrictions and restrictions accompanying growth'.

He also reveals the way in which the principle of dual administrative control is advantageous to the Ministry of Civil Affairs on two fronts: it not only facilitates the control of organisations by the Ministry as final arbiter in the registration process; it also allows it to shift responsibility onto the sponsoring agencies if the need arises. Thus, the present model provides it with the power to control, without the burden of accountability.

Having surveyed the various shortcomings of the present administrative model as it stands, the author turns to address the use of legislation to apply the model, and the 'current dilemma of law'. The present legislation on social organisations faces problems that stem from the way the legislative process lags behind social development. He begins by exploring some of the main causative factors giving rise to the present need for reform. Such factors include the extremely rapid proliferation of social organisations matching the expansion in the socialist market economy, and the development of socialist democratic politics. Secondly, the development of Chinese society towards the 'small government, big society' paradigm necessitates a devolution of certain governmental functions to social organisations, also contributing to the need for a more dynamic administrative model.

Examining the 'real-world effects' of the model, the author notes that it only has a direct effect on a very limited number of social organisations. As a framework for analysis, Professor Wu considers the relationship between state and society in a broader context over a period of time. In the years following Liberation in 1949, the interpenetration of state and society was prevalent, but that relationship began to dissolve in the late 1970s. In the transitional period presently occupied, Wu offers the following judgement: '[t]he state can be characterised as proactive but not all-encompassing; society as passive but extremely vigorous'.

The author also places the relevance of the international human rights movement in the context of the state/society discourse, positing that in this era of globalisation, China would be naïve to assume that it can ignore the formidable momentum possessed by the human rights movement. Professor Wu concludes by calling on the government to strive for a 'win-win outcome', urging the government to loosen its control on the registration and management of social organisations; furthermore, in doing so, it need not view the change as a loss or a concession. The new distribution of power and responsibility should reflect the divergent roles to be played by different actors in society, and as such should be considered beneficial to all.

Dr Xie Haiding's contribution in chapter 3 also conducts a detailed examination of the relationship between civil society organisations and the law in China, probing both the effect of the law on the development of social organisations, and also the converse effect – the demands that the development of social organisations have placed on the law.

The Chinese concept of *hefaxing* forms a central component to Dr Xie's thesis. *Hefaxing,* he explains in his thorough analysis, has a dual meaning, meaning both 'legality' in the strict sense of conformity with the law, and also 'legitimacy' in the sense of appropriateness or reasonableness.

Turning first to what he describes as the 'dilemma of legality', Dr Xie observes that the arduous registration requirements imposed by the present legal order have resulted in a situation whereby 'more than 80% of CSOs lack 'legality' because they are unregistered, and have thus become illegal civil society organisations'. The second aspect of the 'dilemma of legality' manifests itself as the practical problems involved in implementation of the law – the inordinately high cost of implementation leads to its inevitable failure in actual practice. Furthermore, Dr Xie deduces, 'this indicates that failures of implementation are only the surface of the problem – its deeper cause lies in the inappropriate nature of current legislation'. A brief historical overview illustrates the correlation that exists between changes in legislation and the actual numbers of such organisations – evidence of the overly strict control applied.

The principal message of this contribution emerges when the author turns to address the ulterior meaning of *hefaxing* in an examination of the *legitimacy* of the current CSO regulations. His argument is straightforward and relies on the premise that the legitimacy of a law is dependent on 'a most fundamental precondition … that it will be obeyed by the majority of members of society'.

On considering whether the current state of affairs can be improved within the framework of the existing regulations, Dr Xie acknowledges that he approaches the question from the standpoint that 'a better future is one which further satisfies people's desire to form organisations', desires which constitute, in part, an expression of human nature. Analysing the question from this perspective reflects the same starting point for critical enquiry that Wu Yuzhang takes in adopting the 'logic of civil society'. Dr Xie concludes that the problem of legitimacy cannot be solved within the existing framework, opining that the prevalence of 'illegal' CSOs 'clearly announced the bankruptcy of this kind of restrictive legislation'. The contribution challenges the ideology underpinning the current legislative framework. A system that truly guarantees freedom of association will require the abandonment of the old ideology and the old habits that accompany it such as, for example, the tendency to attempt to 'plan' for the demand of CSOs.

Drawing from the lessons of his analysis he also briefly considers a few key features any new law should encompass, such as its ability to be applied in practice and the existence of inherent limits on its powers. In terms of policy, emphasis should be placed on providing standards and guidance, and an attempt made to balance the legislative tendency towards management with the protection of individual rights and freedoms, such as that of association.

Reflecting the author's progressive attitude is his use of the term 'civil society organisation'. He chooses this term out of a desire to address the singularity of the situation prevailing in China, and to avoid falling into the habit of either superimposing Western concepts and notions, or using the outmoded terminology that the Chinese legislation still adheres to.

Dr Liu Peifeng's paper, 'Approval and Non-interference in the Management of Social Organisations: A Critical Examination of Theory and Practice', approaches the issue from a alternate perspective and envisages a different solution. He explains at the outset that his critique is tempered with understanding:

> [a]lthough this paper will cast doubt on many aspects of the current registration system, it is written in a spirit of sympathy and understanding for the motives that put the system in place.

In examining the state of the current registration system, Dr Liu highlights some of the features that characterise the Chinese system, such as administration by level, and by the appropriate agency, and dual administrative control. In the same vein as other authors, Dr Liu identifies these features as by products of the excessive desire for state control of all aspects of social life, habits formed under the planned economy, and now the unwanted and unattainable relics of a past era. Despite recognising the evident shortcomings of the system, he is also able to understand the government perspective, and the rational justifications behind applying the system as it does.

Dr Liu is also acutely aware of the immense gulf that exists between theory and reality in China – while the government strives to control social organisations from the beginning through a complicated system of double approval, in reality, once registered, social organisations are free to do as they please. Additionally, the government expressly adopts a *laissez faire* attitude towards certain civic groups, such as hobby groups and book reading circles, which would be unable to meet the requirements for official registration.

The appearance of a strict registration and management process belies a system of law that in practice does not work: 'in reality the current state of administration of social organisations is still marked by a multi-polar division of powers and it is still impossible to give an accurate figure for the overall total number of social organisations …'. His examination of the possible modes of existence for social organisations in China reveals a complex matrix of organisations whose legal status and composition differ widely, and which the present system of registration is unable to keep an accurate record of.

This paper also undertakes various comparative studies of methods of social organisation administration, and the all-important relationship between state and social organisation. The author explicitly refers to social organisations in the context of individual freedom, and goes on to warn emphatically of the dangers of a government administration that is hostile to individual freedom: 'A totalitarian state that has this kind of replication in the forms of state and society is not only the enemy of individual freedom, it is also likely to be the source of corruption, paralysis and stagnation in that society'.

In spite of his comparatively sympathetic attitude he accepts that the current system of administration 'severely restricts the emergence of civil society, and prevents it playing a full role in social life' and that the system of dual control has been 'used to prevent groups from setting up, and are an obstacle to their achieving legal status'. He also understands that the conflict comes about in part because the government and public harbour different perceptions about 'what constitutes legitimacy'.

In suggesting a solution he departs from the approach of Dr Xie by suggesting action within the current legal framework. Dr Liu's field studies have infused him with confidence in the potential of local reforms, thus he champions local reforms and 'regional experiments to invigorate civil society'.

In the fifth chapter, Dr Chen Xinxin focuses on the position of one particular type of social organisation in China – environmental protection organisations. It is evident from the outset that in China, environmental organisations occupy a special position among social organisations, receiving comparatively favourable treatment from the government.

Dr Chen delves into some of the reasons for this disparity in treatment: environmental protection is in the fundamental interests of all sections of Chinese society, not merely one special interest group; educating the people of such a large and populous country is a steep challenge, for which the government needs the support of such organisations; and they are uniquely positioned for assisting the government in resolving the conflicts that may arise between short term regional economic development goals, and longer term environmental protection goals, due to their disinterested status. Perhaps the most significant reason for the government's supportive attitude stems from the strategy adopted by civic organisations in pursuing their goals: 'right from the start, China's civic environmental organisations defined themselves as inspirers and promoters of environmental awareness'. They relate to the government in a non-confrontational way, such that, 'not only will the activities of China's civic green organisations not have an impact on overall political stability, they in fact assist in the implementation of government environmental policy'.

Dr Chen reports favourably on the role played by these organisations in China, and their potential to continue in the same vein. They inspire public awareness of environmental issues; they develop and produce committed specialists, as well as motivated individuals who can take their expertise to other walks of life; they aid the resolution of actual environmental problems and issues; they can communicate with and assist the government on environmental issues, and inform it about public opinion; and they can contribute to improving China's image in the rest of the world.

Civic environmental organisations do face certain difficulties, but in contrast to the social organisations discussed by the other Chinese scholars in the book, they are not generated directly by the level of governmental interference. The main difficulties faced are the lack of funds, and the lack of a developed internal management infrastructure, for which Dr Chen is able to suggest possible solutions such as a system of tax incentives.

When Dr Chen's chapter is analysed in the context of the other contributions in the book, a question that arises is whether the position of civic environmental organisations in China could lead the way for a similar acceptance of other social organisations. Many of the beneficial features of environmental organisations are also present in other social organisations, to a greater or lesser extent, and it should be clear to the government that other organisations can be as helpful as environmental organisations in their respective spheres.

One fundamental question raised by this contribution is whether the *modus operandi* of environmental organisations as described by Dr Chen should form an acceptable prototype for social organisations in China. A key reason behind the preferential treatment accorded to environmental organisations in China is their tendency to avoid politicisation, and to limit their activities to practical initiatives, as opposed to 'political campaigns like those of environmental organisations in the West'. Dr Chen contrasts the strategy of Western Green organisations which seek to advance their cause through protest and publicly opposing government policy, with the cooperative and non-confrontational approach to lobbying adopted by the Chinese organisations. Whether such a difference in approach is symptomatic of the inherent restrictions on freedom of association in China, or whether it is merely reflective of cultural differences in preferring alternative strategies for achieving the same goal, is open to debate.

To close part I of the book, Professor Mo Jihong provides a detailed examination of the recently issued Regulations for the Management of Foundations in China. His contribution constitutes a detailed and timely introduction to the regulations which represent 'a complete redrawing of foundation legislation'. After a brief overview of the historical development of foundations in China – their emergence, and the previous legislative solutions for dealing with them – Professor Mo embarks on a thorough analysis of the substance of the Regulations.

He observes the positive nature of the guiding principles of the new Regulations: to foster the development of foundations, and promote their growth, and then goes on to examine eight of the key characteristics of the legislation in greater depth. One such characteristic is the importance of a public welfare orientation for foundations – the feature that distinguishes them from ordinary businesses and enterprise. Another characteristic that builds on the notion of promoting public welfare activities is the principle of 'management by type' which reflects the desire to encourage all sectors of society to take part in public welfare activities. The author also writes approvingly of provisions in the legislation for improving the financial position of foundations, such as increasing the value of assets, encouraging fund-raising and creating a virtuous mechanism for the flow of funds.

The inclusion in the Regulations of provisions to supervise international foundations is a novel development – at present they exist unrecognised and unsupervised. Professor Mo is positive about the development and confident that it will contribute to the 'further opening up to the outside world and fuller realisation of the principle of the rule of law'. Others may take a more cynical view of the extension of governmental control to international foundations.

In spite of the Regulations' provision for tax incentives, and the use of tax instruments to support foundations, Professor Mo believes there are still shortcomings in this area. Despite his generally supportive attitude towards the regulations, the author admits that aspects of government interference in foundations remain problematic, such as the inherent biases that exist in government policy towards certain foundations. Similarly, though the Regulations do encourage the adoption of principles of transparency and openness, Professor Mo believes more should be done to oversee asset management.

The second part of the book contains contributions from some of the leading experts on associations in Europe. In the first paper of this part, Paul Dekker illustrates the Netherlands' long history of social organisations that are active in the public sphere and work to fulfil collective needs. They are often referred to as 'private initiatives', emphasising their origins, and as the 'societal midfield', drawing attention to their intermediary functions between the state and individual citizens. In comparative perspective, the Netherlands is a country with a large and well established non-profit sector and civil society. The Dutch non-profit sector turned out to be the largest out of 22 national non-profit sectors compared in economic terms in 1995, mainly because of the many private organisations that deliver welfare state services. Its dependency on public funding is substantial, but smaller than in some other countries with a large non-profit sector, and voluntary work is not pushed aside by paid professionals.

The modernisation of civil society seems to be taking place more quickly in the Netherlands than anywhere else. Old mass organisations (churches, trade unions and political parties) are withering away and relatively new organisations in the areas of human rights, international solidarity, and the environment are enjoying massive support. The successful development of Dutch social organisations has led to a civil society with huge numbers of members and supporters but limited associational life, and to an economically significant nonprofit service sector, with limited private initiative left.

The literature suggests many positive effects of social organisations on the development of social capital and political democracy. Statistical evidence for positive effects of individual participation in the organisations is, however, rather weak in the Netherlands. This might be the case because the organisations have been bureaucratised and because associational life has spread into other spheres of society. However, social organisations and private non-profits remain important as an infrastructure of a democracy and as means to deal with cultural diversity and to attract additional voluntary resources for public causes.

In his chapter on law and associational life in Britain, Richard Fries describes the distinctive nature of civil society in Britain, and the common law basis on which it operates. He describes the long evolution of the voluntary sector and the extensive and important role it plays in British life. It forms, in effect, a 'third sector', as it is sometimes called, alongside the public and market sectors.

The growth of voluntary action, and its institutional forms, is based on the principle of freedom of association, now underpinned in British law by the European Convention on Human Rights, enforced by the European Court of Human Rights in Strasbourg, and since the enactment of the Human Rights Act 1998 also directly enforceable in domestic courts. In principle, associational activity within the law is not subject to any legal or administrative process. For that reason the estimate that there are perhaps three-quarters of a million voluntary bodies can be no more than an estimate, since most are unregistered with any legal or administrative authority.

The key distinction in British associational law is between bodies pursuing essentially private ends and those serving the public interest. Charity, a long established legal form as well as a colloquial expression for philanthropy, is the key legal basis for organised voluntary action. The fundamental element of charity is public benefit. Any organisation whose purpose is in the public interest (as determined under the common law of charity) has charitable status regardless of its institutional form.

In addition to having a public benefit purpose, charities must be independent of the government or any outside organisation or individual (for example a founding company or benefactor), as reflected in the law which gives a charity's trustees absolute responsibility for its activities. It must also be non-profit-distributing – that is, while a charity may make a surplus, for example through enterprise activities, that surplus must be devoted to its activities (it cannot, for example, be distributed to board members).

Charity law and regulation have developed in parallel. The chapter describes the basis for the registration and accountability of charities by the Charity

Commission – a balance between the right of anyone to establish an independent organisation to pursue the public interest, and the need for such an organisation to be accountable in exchange for the privileged legal and fiscal status it has as a charity. The distinctive nature of the Charity Commission is that it is a public body operating independently in the public interest to maintain public confidence in charities.

In his contribution Rupert Graf Strachwitz assesses the legal framework for charity in Germany, exploring some of the deficiencies of the present system and offering suggestions for reform. In charting the development of this area of the law over time, it is evident that charity has long featured as an aspect of German life and culture; though he believes this also explains why the legal framework at present is 'exceedingly traditional and no longer corresponds to a systematic approach to the definition of the role of government, the business community, and civil society within a modern political order'.

In describing the legal nature of a charity, the first point of reference is fiscal law – legal entities are granted tax exemption by the tax authorities if they meet the detailed conditions for charitable activity found in the general tax law. The chapter enumerates the various forms charities can take – associations, foundations, mixed charities and charitable companies – and locates them within the matrix of law that applies to them – fiscal law, the Civil Code and the Constitution, which protects the right to associate.

Strachwitz concludes that a drastic revision of the legal framework for charities is inevitable and overdue. The Parliamentary Commission on Civic Engagement has highlighted the pitfalls in the present system, and suggested a range of amendments to the existing regulations, as well as entreating the adoption of a new outlook. Strachwitz specifically invites reform on a host of pivotal issues, such as deductibility of donations, and the primacy of the motivation of an organisation over its utility to the state, and so on. He concludes, 'whether a different systematic approach will be introduced in Germany … remains to be seen'.

Tymen van der Ploeg provides an overview of the legal implementation of freedom of association in the Netherlands and other Western European countries, countries which for the most part are governed by the legal regime of the European Convention on Human Rights, which restricts the competences of the states to curtail the freedom of association unnecessarily. In most countries freedom of association is enshrined in a law on associations and foundations.

Van der Ploeg traces firstly the historical development of the law on associations and foundations in both the Netherlands, and other countries in Western

Europe. In most countries, associations are free from governmental control both at the point of establishment and subsequently, because they are considered democratic, membership organisations, in which the management board is controlled by the general meeting of members. However, in many countries, the government is involved in the establishment and supervision of foundations. In the Netherlands only the public notary is involved in the process of establishment, and subsequently the public prosecutor and the court have supervisory powers over them. In many countries the rules about the establishment and supervision of associations and foundations predate the European Convention on Human Rights. Until now, citizens of Western European countries have not challenged these laws as being incompatible with the right to freedom of association. An important feature of the law pertaining to NGOs are the rules that apply to registration, accountability and transparency. Most countries apply a system that requires the public registration of associations and foundations. The rules concerning transparency and accountability tend not to be elaborated in any great detail.

An important and unavoidable theme for NGOs is their relationship to the State, and whether the State is involved in their establishment or not. A survey of the different ideologies that are expressed in Dutch politics reveals that they all place NGOs in a favorable position, albeit for differing reasons. In practice this has led to a flourishing civil society in the Netherlands. Within the European Union as a whole there is a positive attitude towards NGOs as important agents in society, and different ways are used by government to accommodate NGOs as advocates or service providers – among them, collective litigation, taxation, subsidies and fundraising. By these means, NGOs can be given an important place in society alongside government.

In the Netherlands the situation is liberal, as the government is not involved in the establishment of associations and foundations as legal persons. Of course, the state should maintain its supervisory task and combat the abuse of NGOs and criminal activities. The experience of the Netherlands proves that government should not feel threatened by the existence of NGOs: a democratic state functions optimally with lively NGOs, just as NGOs can operate optimally within a democratic and stable state.

PART I

CHINESE PERSPECTIVES

1

A CRITICAL EXAMINATION OF THE LEGAL ENVIRONMENT FOR SOCIAL ORGANISATIONS IN CHINA

Yuwen Li

1 INTRODUCTION

The right to freedom of association is a fundamental human right, and has been recognised as such by a number of international and regional human rights instruments. Article 22 of the International Covenant on Civil and Political Rights (ICCPR),[1] states:

> 1. Everyone shall have the right to freedom of association with others, including the right to form and join trade unions for the protection of his interests.

While recognising freedom of association as a right, the restriction of which is generally prohibited, Article 22 explicitly recognises qualifications which, if fulfilled, would justify a restriction:

> 2. No restrictions may be placed on the exercise of this right other than those which are prescribed by law and which are necessary in a democratic society in the interests of national security or public safety, public order (ordre public), the protection of public health or morals or the protection of the rights and freedoms of

1 United Nations General Assembly Resolution 2200 A (XXI) of 16 December 1966, entered into force on 23 March 1976. See also Article 20 of the Universal Declaration of Human Rights, United Nations General Assembly Resolution 217 A (III) of 10 December 1948; Article 11 of the European Convention on Human Rights.

Yuwen Li (Ed.), *Freedom of Association in China and Europe: Comparative Perspectives in Law and Practice*, © 2005 Koninklijke Brill NV, Leiden. Printed in The Netherlands, pp. 17-69.

> others. This article shall not prevent the imposition of lawful restrictions on members of the armed forces and of the police in their exercise of this right.

The importance attributed to freedom of association in international law and politics determine that it is politically perilous for any government to ignore or severely curtail the existence of the right to freedom of association, or to impose burdensome legal rules to restrict its exercise. International law makes general provision for the principle of freedom of association, but the specific degree to which this right can be exercised in a given country depends largely on the country's domestic legal system. In practice, national laws relating to the registration and administration of associations, foundations, charities, and any self-governing, private organisations, and the tax laws relating to all kinds of non-profit and non-governmental activities determine the practical possibilities for the formation and operation of associations.

The modern notion of freedom of association, as understood in most Western countries, is a new phenomenon in the People's Republic of China that only emerged in the 1980s and expanded in the 1990s. In line with the administrative reforms that moved towards the goal of 'small government, big society', the government has begun to devolve certain functions to society at large, for example by allowing new trade associations to regulate and coordinate business operation in various sectors. A combination of domestic exigencies and external pressures has contributed to the government permitting, for example, environmental non-governmental organisations and women's organisations. In addition, economic reform has resulted in inevitable social and cultural changes. At grass-roots level, many organisations have emerged simply to meet the needs of society. Since they are small-scale, and not politically motivated groups, local government does not usually acknowledge their existence. Thus, one might assume that nowadays in China there is a space for private initiatives to organise themselves. However, the government has been applying a strict registration system, and administrative measures which forbid or limit organisations that it deems might cause social unrest or political instability. For instance, privately-initiated human rights organisations and religious organisations cannot be officially registered, and without registration their existence is 'illegal'. Thus, in China, which kind of social organisations can flourish and which cannot depends largely on government policy. The official parlance is that social organisations are the 'bridges' between the government and society. This has also led to the situation whereby most associations, from their formation, do not enjoy the sort of autonomy enjoyed by associations or NGOs operating in the Western world. Although, over the last two decades, associations have expanded rapidly, their legal as well as social status remains fragile and vulnerable in the face of a powerful state, and the increasingly powerful market sector. Many associations have to fight for survival and development in society, and are forced to cooperate carefully with government departments in order to avoid dissolution by administrative decisions.

The reality is that, on the one hand, the Chinese social organisations initiated by the government have been metamorphosing into more autonomous organisations, and even more significantly, many privately initiated social organisations have emerged and expanded – both trends which seem to typically reflect the 'associational revolution' that is underway at the global level, as depicted by Western scholars;[2] on the other hand, however, China was, and remains a powerful Party-state centered political regime, which restricts the pace and scale of the expansion of social organisations. This article focuses on these two countervailing trends that characterise the right to freedom of association in China – on one hand there has been a rapid expansion of associational life since the 1980s, but on the other hand, militating against this expansion, is the tightened legal regime that has excessively restricted citizens' rights to freedom of association, and has hindered the healthy development of the non-governmental and non-profit sector in China. First, it provides some explanation of various terms used in a Chinese context to describe associations, such as 'social organisations', 'NGOs', 'NPOs', 'the third sector', and 'civil society'. Secondly, I will discuss some major types of social organisations which have expanded not only numerically, but also in terms of their scale and influence over the last two decades. Their strength, and the dilemmas they face illustrate the general situation of social organisations as a whole. Thirdly, the paper will scrutinise the antagonistic legal regime that regulates social organisations in China, which is a characteristic illustration of the government policy of limiting and controlling social organisations by law. However, it will also be shown that such a legal design is both impractical and ineffectual, and has resulted in approximately 50% of social organisations in China operating without official registration. Such a situation not only undermines the authority of the written law and that of the relevant government organisations in charge of registration, but also impedes the development of social organisations and the support of Chinese and international society for them. As a result, new law or the improvement of existing law is indispensable.

2 Lester M. Salamon, 'Introduction', in: *The International Guide to Nonprofit Law*, (New York: John Wiley & Sons, Inc., 1997), at p. 1.

2 Clarification of concepts

Although new organisations or groups beyond the domain of government or market emerged in China only in the reform period (since 1977), they have proliferated rapidly in various fields. Academic associations, trade associations, environmental NGOs, women's organisations, learned societies, sport and hobby clubs, have emerged and expanded over the last two decades. Consequently, research on these organisations has extended since 1990s. As at the international level, various terms are commonly used by Chinese scholars, practitioners and the media to describe privately initiated, non-profit organisations including: 'non-governmental organisations' (NGOs), 'non-profit organisations' (NPOs), 'the third sector', 'civil society'. Meanwhile, in law the government continues to use the term 'social organisations' despite the fact that such organisations have undergone a considerable change and the old concept can no longer represent the newly emerged social organisations or even the changed 'old' ones. It should be noted that at the present time, no one term can encompass all social organisations – the different terms used place a different emphasis on the nature or characteristics of particular organisations, and the differences in terminology can also reflect differences in basic concepts about what this set of organisations really includes. However, despite differing terminology and the various perspectives that exist on the proliferation of new, and more autonomous social organisations, there is a general consensus that, today, private initiatives to set up organisations enjoy an unprecedented level of space and opportunity, and a civil society is emerging in China.[3]

Social organisation is the term most similar to 'association', as used in the Western world and in international human rights instruments. Even though in recent years, new terms, such as 'NGO' and 'NPO' have been used increasingly by Chinese scholars and sometimes also by government officials, in Chinese legal documents 'social organisation' remains the term used to represent the term 'association'. A social organisation is defined in law as a 'voluntary group formed by Chinese citizens in order to realise a shared objective, conducting activities according to its charter for non-profit purpose.'[4] The voluntary nature of social organisations distinguishes them from governmental organisations. However, under Chinese law a social organisation must be affiliated with a

3 Jude Howell, 'Women's Organisations and Civil Society in China', (2003) 5 (2), *International Feminist Journal of Politics*, at p. 192.

4 Art. 2 of the 1998 Regulations for Registration and Management of Social Organisation. See Appendix I of this book for the English text.

government institution. This unsurprisingly gives rise to doubts among Western observers, including many in the international aid community, as to whether there are any genuine NGOs in China.[5]

According to official classification, social organisations include academic organisations, professional organisations, trade associations, cultural and art organisations, sport organisations, religious and social welfare organisations. Academic analysis can lead to a different classification. Social organisations can be distinguished, for instance, into three types: official, semi-official and semi-civic, and civic, according to the method of formation, the selection and background of the key leading posts within the organisation, and the sources of funds. All of them are undergoing a dynamic change in China's transition towards a market economy and a more politically and culturally diversified society. Under this trend, official social organisations are shifting in a direction in which they are becoming more self-supporting and independent. Semi-official organisations are gradually becoming self-regulating civic organisations. The grassroots civic organisations, though not specifically promoted by the government, are finding their own space to act and advocate their ideas. Government policy is to foster the development of social organisations that are conducive to economic reform and social harmony, while strictly controlling and forbidding social organisations that, in their view, may constitute a challenge or potential threat to the unity and stability of Chinese society. This explains why the number of trade associations and professional associations has flourished, while human rights organisations and religious organisations remain sparse. In addition, unlike most of the Western European countries, political parties and trade unions are *not* considered social organisations. Consequently, Chinese citizens cannot form a political party or an independent trade union.

Non-Governmental Organisation. In 1995 when the Fourth World Conference on Women and the Non-Government Forum were held in Beijing, they brought with them the concept of an NGO to China. In order to participate in

5 Nick Young, 'Searching for Civil Society', in: *250 Chinese NGOs, A Special Report from China Development Brief*, (Beijing: China Development Brief, 2001), at p. 18. Nick Young takes the view that NGOs do exist in China. In his words 'there is a significant community of autonomous organisations, that it is probably growing (although, given the lack of previous surveys of this kind, this can only be a speculative judgement), and that it will probably continue to grow. Government policy and action will undoubtedly be a very important factor in whether and how this community develops in the future, but it is by no means the only factor. The imagination and energy of the people involved will count for a great deal; and international organisations may also have a significant role to play.'

the Non-Government Forum, the Chinese government encouraged some mass organisations to set up NGOs. Influenced by this grand event, many Chinese scholars and media started to use the term 'NGOs' to describe both the newly emerged social organisations, and the old ones in their then changing state. Chinese NGO experts commonly distinguish between 'top down' and 'bottom up' NGOs. The former are created by the government, and supported by government funding and preferential policy; and in consequence their activities and management are also subject to government control. The latter are set up by citizens' own initiatives. They usually do not receive preferential treatment from the government; consequently the government exerts less control over them. They are the grassroots organisations that have close contact with citizens. Their funds, information and volunteers come either from Chinese citizens or foreign NGOs.

In some countries 'NGO' is a somewhat restricted term that often refers only to the 'subset of non-profit organisations involved in development work'.[6] In China there is no such restriction about when the term of NGO is used, though recently, as Chinese scholars learned the limitation of the concept of NGOs in some countries, they have preferred to use the term 'non-profit organisation', or 'non-profit sector', or the 'third sector', or the 'non-governmental public sector'.

Generally speaking, NGOs is a broad term used to describe all kind of social organisations. For instance, the book '250 Chinese NGOs', includes many local social organisations that are either government or privately initiated. It also contains four mass organisations (All China Women's Federation, All China Youth Federation, China Association for Science and Technology, and China Disabled Persons' Federation), and a number of national organisations in the fields of education and development, poverty alleviation, environment, welfare service, religion – all of which are Government Organised Non-Governmental Organisations (GONGOs), or known as State-Owned Non-Governmental Organisations (SONGOs). As explained, the reason for including such organisations as NGOs, is among others, that '[m]any of these organisations are steadily acquiring a more independent identity, and developing a sense of themselves as belonging to a distinctive, non-government community.'[7]

6 Lester M. Salamon, *supra* note 2, at p. 4. This has been stated in the chapters in this book by Richard Fries and Paul Dekker referring to the cases of Great Britain and The Netherlands.

7 Nick Young, *supra* note 5, at p. 13.

Non-profit organisation is a term largely used in the USA. It has been pointed out that the term 'NPO' is not an ideal expression since it emphasises what these organisations are not, rather than what they are. However, it is more precise than the term 'NGOs' or 'civil society' since it highlights the most common essential feature of these entities throughout the world, namely the prohibition on their distribution of profits to owners or shareholders.[8] Influenced by the US-led study of NPOs, in the most recent research work by Chinese scholars the term 'NPOs' is increasingly used. Differences exist in various countries on what organisations are referred to as NPOs. For instance, in the Netherlands the term 'non-profit organisations' refers to those in the fields of health, culture, the arts and social services, as well as to special interest groups, trade unions, sports clubs, and organisations dealing with humanitarian, human rights and other social or public interest issues.[9] In China, there has been no suggestion of including trade unions as NPOs, but most scholars tend to agree that NPOs include all sort of social organisations, non-commercial institutions (*shiye dangwei)*, and popular non-enterprise work units (*minban feiqiye danwei*).

The third sector is a relatively new concept in social science theory. The US-led comparative empirical research by the Johns Hopkins Comparative Nonprofit Sector Project suggests the entities within the third sector share five common defining features: (1) organised, they have an institutional presence and structure; (2) private, namely they are institutionally separate from the state; (3) non profit distributing, they do not return profits to their managers or to a set of 'owners'; (4) self-governing, they are fundamentally in control of their affairs; (5) voluntary, membership in them is not legally required and they attract some level of voluntary contribution of time or money. According to them, entities that share these five features include: associations, foundations, mutual-benefit organisations, service-providing agencies such as hospitals, universities, and day care centers, advocacy groups, grassroots development agencies, self-help groups.[10]

8 The author also admits that 'non-profit organisations' is an ambiguous term in the English language – they are also referred to as 'voluntary organisations', 'charities', 'associations', 'tax-exempt organisations', and the 'independent sector'. See Lester M. Salamon, *supra* note 2, at pp. 3-4.

9 Ary Burger and Paul Dekker, *The Nonprofit Sector in the Netherlands,* (The Hague: Social and Cultural Planning Office, 2000). Available at: www.scp.nl/english (Last visited March, 2005).

10 Lester M. Salamon, Helmut K. Anheier *et al.*, *Global Civil Society,* (Baltimore: The Johns Hopkins Center for Civil Society Studies, 1999), at pp. 3-4.

A difference between the US-led research and some European scholars is that the latter disagree with the exclusion of cooperatives and mutual aid societies from the third sector on the grounds that mutuals and cooperatives can distribute some of their profits to members. According to the European experts, some cooperatives have never distributed their profits. Those that do distribute their profits do so to a very limited degree. Cooperatives and mutual aid societies 'are a product of the same philosophy as associations; that is, they are created not for maximising return on investment but for meeting a general or mutual interest, contributing to the common good, or meeting social demands expressed by certain groups of the population.'[11] In European countries, the distinguishing criterion is the existence of limits on profit distribution.

Research work on the third sector was one of the most challenging topics in the 1990s in China. Some Chinese academics advocate the idea that governmental organisations, for-profit organisations, and non-profit organisations are the main organic forms in the fields of politics, economy, and society, and that an effective market economy and democratic political system cannot be left without the support of a developed third sector. It is argued that Chinese economic reform has proved that the market economy is the most efficient and effective way of economic operation. However, the market economy has also resulted in many new problems, which cannot be resolved by market rules. If these problems cannot be addressed in a timely and proper manner, they will constitute barriers for further economic development and cause social instability. Thus, apart from economic and political reforms, social reform is also needed. Social reform is actually a redistribution of power, and specifically requires that some of the power at present exercised through the political process and the market should be transferred to society at large.[12] Some Chinese believe

11 Adalbert Evers and Jean-Louis Laville, 'Defining the Third Sector in Europe', in Adalbert Evers and Jean-Louis Laville (eds.), *The Third Sector in Europe*, (Cheltenham: Edward Elgar, 2004), at p. 12. In their view, 'a US-led debate whose parameters, though they often pretend to be universal, are characterised by the specific context in which they have developed. [...] The specific features of a European approach to the third sector can be summarized on the basis of three parameters: the type of organisations involved, the intermediary nature of the third sector within a "welfare pluralism" or a plural economy, and a sociopolitical dimension that is as important as the economic dimension.', at p. 11.

12 Xu Yongguang, 'The Current Situation of the Third Sector in China and Our Tasks' (*Zhongguo disanbumen de xianshichujing yu woumen de renwu*), in China Youth Development Foundation and Committee on Development Research on Foundations (eds.), *Chinese Social Organisations at a Crossroads (Chu yu shizilukou de Zhongguo shetuan)*, (Tianjin, Tianjin renmin chubanshe, 2001), at pp. 109-110.

that the third sector includes three main types of social groups: social organisations, non-commercial institutions, and democratic parties. They explain that social organisations are typical third sector organisations. It is debateable whether democratic parties are governmental or semi-governmental organisations. Non-commercial institutions were a part of the governmental organisations, but in recent years many popular non-enterprise units have emerged, such as kindergartens, schools, research centers, and hospitals.[13]

In view of the fact that all types of social organisations, including NGOs and NPOs, are undergoing rapid development in China, use of the general and broad concept of the 'third sector' can cover a wide range of social organisations and facilitate a forward-looking approach to studying the status, functions and development trend of social organisations. Moreover, using the 'third sector' as the opposite to government and market is conducive to strengthening the significance of the third sector in China.

Civil society emerged in the 18th century in the context of the rapid commercialisation and industrialisation, associated with the rise of capitalism. When those who controlled capitalist production were seeking access to political power, a new relationship between society and the state developed. The business people's demand for a voice in state affairs created a space between business, families and the larger realm of the state. In that space, members of the bourgeoisie and their allies negotiated a shared identity and common political purpose.[14] While the term 'civil society' was popular in the 18th and 19th centuries, it was long in disuse. Only in the late 20th century did the collapse of communist regimes in central and eastern Europe bring the topic of civil society back into currency in the West, not only in the context of the market economy, but also of political democracy. 'Most of the recent discussion of civil society has centered on the linking and mediating role that civil society is deemed to perform between state and society, primarily to control or provide a counterpoise to the state.'[15]

13 Gao Bingzhong, 'The Concept of Legitimacy – Understanding the Emergence of the Third Sector' (*Hefaxing de gainian –lijie disanbumen de xingqi*), in Su Li *et al* (eds.), *The Regulatory System and Development – The Legal Environment for the Third Sector* (*Guizhi yu fazhan-disan bumen de falu huanjing*), (Hangzhou: Zhejiang renmin chubanshe, 1999), at p. 306.

14 Timothy Brook and B. Michael Frolic, 'The Ambiguous Challenge of Civil Society', in Timothy Brook and B. Michael Frolic (eds.), *Civil Society in China*, (Armonk: M.E. Sharpe, 1997), at p. 8.

15 *Ibid*, at p. 9.

It is quite obvious that the Western conception of civil society has been formed and developed in Western ideology, culture and capitalism. When studying civil society in China a fundamental issue is whether civil society actually exists there. Generally speaking three different opinions can be identified. One is that China 'either historically or at present, contains clearly defined elements of civil society.'[16] The opposite view is that 'in China little more than the political-cultural continuity of a system alternately fragmented into narrow and parochial shards of familial power or dominated in an authoritarian manner by the elite at the center.'[17] The third view is that at present a state-led civil society is emerging in China; the new system of village elections, the rise of NGOs, and business associations could prove this. According to Frolic, there are two kind of civil society in China. One is the type, 'which emphasises the opening up of the political system, limitation on state power, and the advancement of the rights of autonomous groups and individuals. This civil society is still poorly developed and is struggling to maintain itself in China. The second civil society is the so-called 'state-led civil society', which refer to 'the recent creation by the state of literally hundreds of thousands of organisations and groups that serve as support mechanism to the state.'[18] He further pointed out that state-led civil society,

> is based on a number of assumptions. First, the new associations and groups are not against the state but a part of it. Second, they serve as training grounds for the development of civic consciousness. Third, they function as intermediaries between state and society. Fourth, state-led civil society is not riven by conflict between its civil society components and the state. It is a marriage of convenience rather than a catalyst for citizen resistance. Finally, mutual perception of strength and weakness plays a key role. Elements in the state perceive the need for change and regard social organizations as functionally useful, without threatened the state's hegemony. Those within the social organization perceive a slightly weakened state, but are more interested in short-term economic gains than individual autonomy at the expense of state power. Neither wants the state to collapse.[19]

16 Paul Nesbitt-Larking and Alfred L. Chan, 'Chinese Youth and Civil Society', in Timothy Brook and B. Michael Frolic, *supra* note 14, at p. 152.

17 *Ibid* , at pp. 152-153.

18 B. Michael Frolic, 'State-Led Civil Society', in Timothy Brook and B. Michael Frolic, *supra* note 14, at p. 56. See also his article, 'Reflections on Civil Society and Human Rights', in: Errol P. Mendes and Anik Lalonde-Roussy (eds.), *Bridging the Global Divide on Human Rights, A Canada – China Dialogue* (Aldershot: Ashgate, 2003), at pp. 15-38.

19 *Ibid*, at p. 58.

Many Chinese intellectuals take the position that civil society is emerging in China by looking at the changing relationship between the state, market and new social organisations. In their view, as a result of administrative reform and building market economy, semi-autonomous social organisations, such as trade associations, service providing organisations and NGOs have emerged and are expanding. These new organisations have separated themselves from the government. In addition, since they provide public goods, or semi-public goods and social welfare goods, they are also different to the typical market sector organisations (companies). Thus, these new organisations have the nature of civil society, or at least their development should contribute to the building of civil society. However, there are some concerns at the development of such organisations in a country in which the government continues to wield unchallenged power, and in which there is a significant imbalance between the state, the market, and the newly emerged social organisations.[20] The changes occurring in China represent positive developments, and defending the view that a civil society is emerging in China is a positive way of observing that development. While recognising that the emerging civil society in China is currently state-led, far from mature, and that its future also depends on the further shrinking of state power, it is still constructive to acknowledge this newly emerged civil society, and to promote its expansion and strength, rather than to deny its existence or relevance merely because its formation and ideology do not fully match the Western model. Frolic pointed out:

> We see a transformation in process, but it is difficult to visualize its path and velocity. In the short term, the state has the capacity to muffle or harness any concerted pressures for autonomy, and it is fair to say that no one has the capacity or the will to challenge that state by means of conventional forms of civil society. In the long term, this social formation could change, with a restructuring of state-society relations and the appearance of an effectively functioning civil society. For the present, however, expectations of the imminent emergence of Chinese civil society in the Western sense are premature if not misleading.[21]

20 Tao Chuangjin, 'China's Civil Society in the Field of Market Economy' (*Zhongguo shichang jingji lingyu lide gongminshehui*), in Wang Ming *et al.* (eds.), Chinese Non-government Public Sector (*Zhongguo fei zhengfu gonggongbumen*), (Beijing: Tsinghua daxu chubanshe, 2004), at pp. 34-58.

21 B. Michael Frolic, *supra* note 18, at p. 67.

3 The Expansion and Constraint of Social Organisations in Post-Mao China

Since the founding of the People's Republic of China, social organisations have always been marginalised and strictly controlled by the government. It is reported that, in 1965, there were about 100 national-level social organisations and 6000 local-level social organisations. During the 1966 to 1976 'Cultural Revolution' all social organisations were eliminated. From the end of the 1970s social organisations were re-established and entered into a period of explosive growth in the 1980s and 1990s. A rough estimation is that now there are about 220,000 registered social organisations in China. However, due to the strict registration system, it is estimated that a similar number of unregistered social organisations exist in China. Generally speaking, the number as well as the influence of these social organisations is linked with the level of economic development in a region. In costal and economically relatively developed areas the figure of social organisations is higher than inland and remote areas.[22]

Using the criterion of 'organisations that carry out social organisation activities', one can identify four different types of social organisation:

(1) Those registered with the civil affairs department of the government, and having the status of legal persons.
(2) Those affiliated with registered social organisations. In order to avoid the registration system provided in law, some social organisations choose to be affiliated with registered social organisations. In exchange such social organisations remit a certain amount of money to their sponsoring organisations. Their independence depends on the personal relationship between the leaders and the sponsored organisations. However, such social organisations are usually more active than the sponsoring organisations.
(3) Those engaging in activities as social organisations, but registered as enterprises with industrial and commercial bureaux. Such organisations either do not want to follow the registration procedures, which require them to find a government institution as sponsor, or are not able to find an institution to be its sponsor. This is the case for many environmental NGOs.
(4) Finally, those organisations that are not registered at all but clearly engage in activities by way of association with others. There are all kinds of grass-roots organizations in rural and urban areas, such as various farmers associ-

22 Wu Zhongze and Chen Jinluo (eds.), *Social Organisations Management Work* (*Shetuan guanli gongzuo*), (Beijing: Zhongguo shehui chubanshe, 1996), at p. 7.

ations, salons, forums, clubs, bird associations. Under current Chinese law, unregistered social organisations are 'illegal' social organisations.

However, many Chinese scholars particularly stress that 'illegal' social organisations should be understood as meaning that they are not registered in accordance with the procedures provided by the law, but this does not mean there is a lack of legitimacy for their existence, or they are guilty of anything.[23]

The widening of associational life in post-Mao China is complex, and deserves wide ranging interdisciplinary study. In general and simple terms, three main factors are crucial. The first is the change and relaxation of government policy. At the end of 1970s the Chinese government decided to launch economic reform by allowing different economic actors to participate in economic construction. Foreign investment was encouraged and private business was gradually recognised. Economic reform also resulted in the changing government's role in the economic field; slowly but surely the government has allowed more and more scope to enterprises to independently carry out their activities. Reform of administrative organs has shifted the government's role from direct and micro-control of the economy to indirect control and macro-planning. As a result numerous trade associations were set up by the government. Although these associations are semi-official organisations, they are moving towards more independence and autonomy, and moreover they are supposed to develop into fully self-regulated trade associations. At a local level, private business gave the owners independence and flexibility. However, in facing the powerful state and big state-owned enterprises, private business is also vulnerable and isolated, thus they have the incentives to set up associations to strengthen their position.

Secondly, the expansion of social organisations is a natural reaction to social needs. Economic development has caused profound influence on people's life. For instance, there is an increasing demand for better care of the elderly and disabled. Services provided by local government could not meet the demand, which has led to the emergence of many non-profit service providers, and such service providers possess a degree of moral authority. Another such instance is that people who have the same or similar beliefs, interests, hobbies, age, home-town, or occupation consider associations to be a vehicle for them to be able to interact, enjoy and support each other. In recent years, the government has taken a relaxed attitude to political control over such needs. In addition, economic growth has had a negative effect on the environment. More and more

23 See Xie Haiding's chapter in this book.

people are becoming sensitive to the protection of nature and animals, which has led to the expansion of environmental NGOs.

Thirdly, international support for the non-government and non-profit sector in China has resulted in the establishment of many NGOs. The Ford Foundation, Asian Development Bank, the World Bank, and other such institutions, all have programs for promoting the third sector in China. In addition, international NGOs' activities in China also give inspiration, and established good practice for Chinese NGOs. Most international NGOs work in the fields of poverty alleviation, education, health, environmental protection, HIV-AIDs prevention, and protection of women's rights. As China is driven into the global economy, the impact of international NGOs and civil society movement on Chinese civil society is sure to increase.

In order to provide a more concrete impression of the activities, influences, strengths and weakness of social organisations in various fields in China, I will discuss below four types of social organisations: women's organisations, environmental NGOs, trade associations, and non-government social welfare organisations. These organisations are chosen mainly because they represent both the traditional and the most recently emerged social organizations, they share some similarities as well as differences with similar types of associations in other countries, and their further development may reveal the existence of a broad space for the non-government and non-profit sector in China.

(1) Women's organisations

When studying women's organisations in China one has to first consider the All China Women Federation (ACWF) that is the largest national women's organisation in China, founded in 1949 by the Central Communist Party to promote equality between men and women. The ACWF has local branches at every administrative level and in some cases, women workers' committees in non-commercial institutions, factories and mines are also affiliated with the ACWF. Since the 1980s the ACWF has undergone a gradual reform towards a direction of focusing more on women's interests and rights. While having the task of performing a bridging role, between the Party and women in the society, the 1995 Fourth World Conference on Women in Beijing, profoundly reshaped ACWF in its relation to women and the central government. Preparations for this event provided ACWF cadres at both national and provincial level opportunity to gain knowledge of international feminist debates and to witness the dynamism and commitment of non-governmental women's organisations. From 1995 the ACWF 'began to refer to itself publicly as a non-governmental organisation, so as to legitimize itself internationally, to facilitate international fund-raising and to distinguish itself from government organs.'[24]

The status of the ACWF as an official, central level women's organisation constitutes both a strength and a weakness of the ACWF. Its official position has enabled it to participate in introducing legislative and policy changes in favour of women. However, its influence is very much carried out through informal connections and channels, and is largely dependent on the gender awareness of the political establishment.[25] The ACWF is supposed to communicate the interests of the Party to its constituency of women; on the other hand it should also reflect the interests of women up to the Party. This dual purpose leaves it with the dilemma of deciding which interests to prioritise when there is a conflict of interests. In this respect it has been observed that: '[t]hough historically the ACWF has tended in the last instance to prioritize the Party's interests, it has increasingly articulated and fought for the interests of women and negotiated further room from the Party to do so.'[26] While recognising this positive development, the fact that the ACWF is an organisation under the direct leadership of the Party cannot be underestimated, and its work to serve women is necessarily limited for political reasons. For instance, in the Major Tasks of the ACWF in 2005 issued on 16 January 2005, it was clearly pointed out that the ACWF and its all level women organisations:

> must study and carry out seriously the spirit of the Party's Fourth Meeting of the 16th Session, follow the strategic plan of the Party to strengthening the Party's capacity of leading the country, taking into account the reality of women's development and women organisations' work, enhance recognisation of the importance, necessity, and urgency of strengthening women organisations' capacity, to take capacity-building as a long-lasting basic task, to play its role as the bridge between the Party and mass women and as the important social pillar of the State power, to take strengthening women's organisations at basic level as the core task, to serve the overall situation and serve women, especially women at basic level, to continually provide women's organisations with capacity in organizing women, promoting women's interests, educating women, and serving women, to a maximum degree to unite women around the Party, and to act as the propagandist of the Party's policy, as the link between the Party and the mass of ordinary women, as the servant

24 Jude Howell, *supra* note 3, at p. 195.
25 *Ibid*, at p. 202.
26 *Ibid*, at p. 202.

> of the mass of ordinary women, and contribute to expanding social support to the Party and consolidating the governing position of the Party.[27]

Despite the fact that the ACWF and its branches enjoy a dominant position in women's affairs in China, since the 1990s a new group of women organisations has emerged and expanded. They enjoy more autonomy than the ACWF and its branches, and are fully dedicated to women's interests and gender issues. There were about 7300 such registered women organisations by the end of 1999.[28] The emergence of these organisations was essentially influenced by the NGO Forum in Beijing in 1995, and many of them are supported with foreign funds. In general, the new organisations can be divided in three sorts: service-oriented, occupational, and research-oriented.

Service-oriented women's organisations provide services to meet various needs of women. One example is the Maple Women's Psychological Counseling Center in Beijing, whose predecessor was the Women's Research Institute of the Chinese Academy of Management Science established in 1988. The Center has conducted research on women's employment and political participation, domestic violence, sexual harassment and family problems. In 1992, the Center started the first Women's Hotline in China to provide free services to women, which was funded by Ford Foundation. In 1998 the Center set up the 'Ark' Family Center to provide psychological and social service to single parent families. In 2001, the Center, in cooperation with Tianjin Women's Federation, started a project on 'family problems and community intervention' in a district in Tianjin to help vulnerable women in community.[29] Another women's organisation, which focuses on rural women, is the Cultural Development Center for Rural Women, registered in 2001. Its predecessor is the Rural Women Knowing All Magazine, created in 1993 under the sponsorship of the ACFW. In 1995, influenced and encouraged by the United Nations Fourth World Conference for Women, they started to learn new concepts from foreign NGOs, and received international support for organising projects to promote rural women's development, such as literacy, micro-credit, encouraging women's participation in politics, reproductive health, and life crisis intervention. In 1996 the magazine initiated the Migrant Women's Club – the first organisation

27 See www.women.org.cn/allnews/01/44.html (Last visited March, 2005.)

28 Du Jie, 'Gender and Governance: The Rise of New Women's Organisations', in Jude Howell, (ed.), *Governance in China*, (Lanham: Rowman & Littlefiled Publishers, 2004), at p. 178.

29 See www.maple.org.cn. (Last visited March 2005.)

dedicated to supporting migrant women. In 1998, the magazine set up the Practical Skills Training Center for Rural Women, which provides rural women opportunities to participate in a variety of training and education. In 2001 it registered with the industrial and commercial bureau, the Beijing Cultural Development Center for Rural Women.

Occupational organisations provide information and support for career women. At national level such organisations include the China Women Mayors' Association, the Chinese Women's Association for Science and Technology. At local level, examples are the Capital Women Journalists Association and the Shanghai Women Engineers' Federation.[30] It is interesting to note that both at the central and local levels there are women entrepreneurs' associations – they are led by successful businesswomen and are typical outcomes of economic reform.

Research-oriented organisations, institutes and centers have been established in universities, the ACWF, and the social science research academies.[31] Apart from research on women's rights and gender issues, some of these centers also provide legal aid to women. One such well-known organisation is the Center for Women's Law Studies & Legal Services at Peking University, established in 1995 by the Faculty of Law, and funded by the Ford Foundation. The Center gathers together a highly committed and professional team of professors, researchers, post-graduates and part-time lawyers. It has represented women in high-profile litigation cases concerning labour rights, personnel and property rights, and divorce cases. Some of the cases were reported by the media and generated wide social attention. For instance, they represented 25 female migrants *pro bono* in a collective lawsuit of labor payment disputes against a garment factory in Beijing. The case lasted for more than two years, was reported by numerous newspapers, and was finally settled fairly by the court. The Center also provides free legal advice to clientele through a telephone hotline, and sometimes also provides in-person consultations on cases relating to domestic violence, sexual abuse, employment discrimination, divorce, child custody and child support.[32] The Center's achievement on legal aid to women has received a prodigiously positive reception in society, and many women beneficiaries have shown their appreciation by writing articles, letters and

30 Du Jie, *supra* note 28, at p. 178.

31 *Id.* See also for instance, Gender Window- Beijing Normal University, Women's and Gender Research Center of Zhongshan University, Women's Studies Center of South China Normal University, in *250 Chinese NGOs*, *supra* note 5, at pp. 95, 142, 143.

32 *250 Chinese NGOs*, *supra* note 5, at p. 88.

sending silk banners. Based on their practical experiences the Center has published books and reports to generate legislative, judicial and social attention to women's rights. As with many of the grassroots women's organisations, despite its current success, the Center faces uncertainty over its sustained development. The Center has been funded by the Ford Foundation, and from 1995 to 2002, the Foundation provided USD 630,000 to the Center. That nearly all its funding comes from one source is a cause for concerns for its continuity and future.[33] The uncertainty of funding is a common problem for most of the centers engaged in gender studies in China.

Unlike the ACWF, the new independent women's organisations do not have direct influence upon policy and legislation change. Many of them focus on service delivery and do not aim to influence policy. Those groups that seek some influence on policy, in addition to their other goals, are small in scale, with extremely limited networks and lack legitimacy in the eyes of the government. In addition, new women's organisations are financially heavily dependent on foreign donors, and their reliance on volunteers for some of their work constitutes also a restraint on their activities and the extent of continuity.[34]

Chinese women constitute about one fifth of the women in the world. In China's long history of feudalism, the rule that the male is superior to the female has dominated the society. Influenced by old conceptions and tradition, the infringement of women's rights remains a serious problem in China today; women are considered as a weak and disadvantaged group. It is difficult to estimate exactly how many women's organisations operate in China. Some cannot be registered at all, such as the Lesbian and Gay Beeper Hotline.[35] Some of the smaller women's organisations that are mainly service providers do not need to be registered in the eyes of local governments. There are also many second or third-level women's organisations affiliated to large registered organisations. Whatever the number may be, one can be sure that there are too few rather than too many women's organisations in China, especially organisations fully dedicated to gender issues. Consequently, there is plenty of room for women's organisations to develop.

33 Wang Ming *et al.* (eds.), *Case Study on China's NGOs* (*Zhongguo NGO yanjiu*), *UNCRD Research Report Series No.38*, (Beijing: UNCRD, 2000), at pp. 194-205.

34 Jude Howell, *supra* note 3, at p. 204.

35 *Ibid*, at p. 196.

(2) *Environmental NGOs (E-NGOs)*

Environment degradation as a side effect of economic development has caused increasing concern both inside and outside China. As people's consciousness regarding the environment has risen, environmental protection has entered various aspects of people's life. A number of environmental NGOs have emerged, and are actively involved in environmental protection. Generally speaking there are four types of E-NGOs in China.[36] First, the 'top down' ones; they are registered, partly funded by the government, and consequently their operations are in varying degrees dependent on the government. Such organisations constitute the majority of the E-NGOs, for example the Chinese Society of Environment Science, Chinese Society of Animals, Chinese Society of Natural Resources, Chinese Society of Environmental Industry, China Green Foundation, and so on. It is debatable whether such E-NGOs are in fact NGOs. In the normal sense, NGOs must be non-governmental and independent from the government. However, some Chinese argue that they are the 'top down' type NGOs developed out of the realities of China. They are independent legal persons established according to law, they have some characteristics of civic and autonomous organisations, and are thus quite distinct from governmental departments. Moreover, under the current situation in China, such organisations could obtain the trust of both the government and society and use the resources from the both.

The second type is the 'bottom up' E-NGOs, which are established by private initiative, enjoy autonomy and independence in carrying out their activities. It would not be an exaggeration to state that the emergence of such grassroots environmental NGOs since the 1990s constitutes an innovation in the environmental field in China of revolutionary proportions. Such E-NGOs usually keep a certain distance from the government, they are self-reliant in funding, human resources, management and policy, or they rely on project funds from foreign sources. Even though they sometimes stress the significance of cooperation with the government, and intend to create an impression of active collaboration with government policy, they usually resist direct administrative interference or control. They usually keep close contact with citizens, stimulate and use social forces through their members and volunteers. Despite their small numbers, such NGOs are increasingly valued both inside China and abroad.

36 Zhao Xiumei, 'Investigation on Environmental NGOs in Beijing' (*Guanyu Beijing huanbao NGO de diaocha fengxi*), in Wang Ming *et al.*, (eds.), *supra* note 33, at pp. 39-40.

For instance, the Friends of Nature was established by Liang Gongjie in 1994, and has become one of the best-known Chinese E-NGOs. It has more than 1000 members from all walks of life, with intellectuals as the main force. The organisation set out with its mission to promote environmental protection and sustainable development by raising environmental awareness, and initiating a 'green culture' among the public. It has also been active in environmental education, helping to save the Tibetan antelope, organising bird watching groups, and it runs an environmental magazine and so on. Several international agencies, such as the Ford Foundation, Shell, Save Our Nature, Hong Kong Caritas, have given funds to Friends of Nature, and the organisation has also generated moderate domestic funds.[37] Another famous Chinese E-NGO is the Global Village of Beijing (GVB), founded by Liao Xiaoyi with her own money in 1996. In 2001, the organisation had 12 full-time employees and nearly 4000 volunteers nationwide. They are pioneering the production of television programmes on environmental issues, and have successfully developed a regular ten-minute programme on 'Time for Environment' that has been broadcast by a national television channel. To generate the media's interest in environment, the GVB organises an Annual Forum on Journalists and the Environment. It also has its own environmental training center in Yanqing County, 50 km from central Beijing. They have promoted 'green communities' in Beijing to educate citizens adopting an environmentally friendly lifestyle, and to monitor their local environment and to participate in policy-making. The GVB has partnered with the United States EPA in its attempt to reduce the global mercury, coal and oil-fired power plants. It has published the first environmental guidebook for the Chinese public – 'The Citizen's Environment Guide', it also publishes a monthly newsletter called 'Voices of Grassroots' that articulates the opinions and activities of E-NGOs in China.[38]

The third type is 'the environmental volunteers groups', which refers to those groups that did not follow the legal procedure for establishment or do not possess legal personality, but exist and function as *de facto* 'bottom up' E-NGOs. They have their names, promoters or founders, and they organise regular as well as irregular activities; thus, they do not appear as individuals, but as organisations. For instance, Friends of Green in Hebei province is a truly grassroots organisation without registration, but has managed to voice and realise

37 *250 Chinese NGOs*, *supra* note 5, at p. 92, and the organisation's website: www.fon.org.cn (Last visited March 2005).

38 *250 Chinese NGOs*, *supra* note 5, at p. 96, and GVB's website: www.gvbchina.org (Last visited March 2005).

its ideas. From 1993, Zhang Zhongmin, a teacher at the Hebei Economy and Trade University, started to lead a group of students in investigating, promoting and making suggestions for saving water. In 1996, he set up a student association called 'The Son of Nature' to focus on environmental education work. Although according to governmental regulations, student associations do not need to be registered at the relevant civil affairs department of the government, they are also not allowed to carry out activities in society at large. In 1998, Zhang Zhongmin together with a few environmental activists set up an 'Environmental Association of Friends of Green'. In 2000 the Association publicised itself as 'Friends of Green'. In 2001, the Friends of Green was included in the book of '250 Chinese NGOs', and in the same year received funding from Oxfam Hong Kong for a project on environmental campaigning and building the capacity of news journalists. Managing this project enabled the organisation to learn how to apply for funding, manage, and monitor projects and strengthened its organisational capacity. The organisation has jointly set up green schools, produced television programs, and provided training programs for enterprises that are interested in environmental issues. The Friends of Green, though without registration, has developed good relations with the local government and got their support, as well as the support of local enterprises and many volunteers.[39]

The fourth type is the student E-NGOs. They are founded by students and registered at universities. A number of universities have their own environment organisations, such as Green Association of Tsinghua University, Green Life Association of Peking University, Environment and Development Association of Peking University and so on. The students E-NGOs have expanded quickly. They either organise activities by themselves, or jointly participate in E-NGOs activities.

Environmental NGOs are the most successful NGOs in China. This is due to the fact that, for the time being, the environmental issue is less politicalised. The central government has decided to make environmental protection one of the basic policies of the country, and it has recognised that E-NGOs could play a special role in educating people. Thus, relatively speaking, environmental NGOs have better access to government information, funds and other support, while they also easily command public support. It has rightly been observed by Peter Ho:

39 Tong Lei, 'The Way of Grass-roots Organisations' Cooperation – 'Friends of Green'' (*Caogen zuzhi de hezuo zhidao*), in: Wang Ming *et al.* (eds.), *supra* note 20, at pp. 132-147.

> environmentalism in China also has a distinct feature that sets it apart from the West and the ex-socialist states in the Eastern bloc: it lacks both the opportunity and the immediate urgency to openly confront the central government.[40]

Even those small numbers of grassroots E-NGOs prefer to cooperate with the government, than to oppose them. Liao Xiaoyi, the founder of the Global Village of Beijing once pointed out that:

> We still adhere to our principles: guide the public instead of blaming them and help the government instead of complaining about it. This, perhaps, is the "mildness" referred to by the media. I don't appreciate extremist methods. I'm engaged in environmental protection and don't want to use it for political aims. This is my way, and my principle too.[41]

In the Charter of the Friends of Nature (FON), it states that the FON supports all policy, measures and activities carried out by the government, social organisations and individuals which are in favour of environmental protection and sustainable development of society, and is willing to cooperate with them. Meanwhile, they make efforts to supervise, critisise, reveal and appeal to relevant parties to prevent and stop anything that is contradictory to environmental protection and sustainable development.[42]

(3) Trade associations

Strictly speaking, trade associations are established by economic entities that work in the same sector, for the protection of their common interests and rights. Trade associations should be set up voluntarily, and they should enjoy self-regulation and autonomy. In China however, many trade associations were established by the government, as part of an initiative aimed at reforming

40 Peter Ho, 'Greening Without Conflict? Environmentalism, NGOs and Civil Society in China', in (2001) 32 (5) *Development and Change*, at p. 897. This assessment mirrors the general relationship between social organisations and the government in China. In Beijing, investigation shows that 87.5% of NGOs took the view that they need governmental support for their activities and expansion; only 4.8% expressed no such need; 7.7% do not want to answer such a question. 66.3% of them indicated they need governmental financial support and project funds; 64.4% hope that the government could provide legal and policy information. See Wang Ming *et al.* (eds.) *supra* note 33, at pp. 34-35.

41 Quoted by Peter Ho, *ibid*, at p. 916.

42 Art. 5 of the Charter of the Friends of Nature, available in Chinese at: www.fon.org.cn.

governmental administrative organs and reducing the responsibility of the government for managing economic actors in the 1980s. As a result, many trade associations in China are 'top down' organisations, closely linked to the government. For instance, it was reported that, in 1986, when reform of administrative organs in Shenzhen took place, administrative bureaus for all industrial sectors were abolished, and eighteen industrial trade associations were established to assist the government in managing various sectors. Initially, the government sent civil servants to work at the associations while remaining paid by the government, and provided funds for the associations' operation.[43] However, it is also true that over the last decade such trade associations have undergone certain changes whereby they have begun to acquire a degree of independence from the government. In Shenzhen, it is stated that in the ten years after their establishment, the trade associations grew to a certain scale and the government stopped allocating money to them. At present, all industrial trade associations are self-funding, they hire their own personnel, and they enjoy autonomy.[44]

The 'top down' trade associations exist at national as well as local level. In 2000, there were about 480 national level trade associations in industrial and commercial fields. [45]At local level no statistics can be found on the total number of trade associations. The general situation is that in economically developed areas, there are a greater number of trade associations, and also they command a greater influence than in the economically less developed areas. A study of trade associations in Guangdong province illustrates that by the end

43 Zu Yuqin, 'Analysis of the Current Situation of Social Organisations' Development in Shenzhen' (*Shenzhenshi shehui tuantie fazhan de xianzhuang fenxi*), (Summer 2002) *Global Law Review*, at p. 177.

44 Although 'top down' trade associations are initiated by the government, it is also the interest of enterprises to have this new form of organisation to protect their interests. It is rightly observed that: 'More and more economic actors are now outside the old protective shells of the work unit, be it a state enterprise or an agricultural collective. But separation brings isolation, and decreased dependence brings increasing vulnerability. This generates both a greater consciousness of individual interests and greater awareness of the need to protect them in the context of pressures from both the state and the market. Since the individual economic agent is powerless against both the market and a still powerful state, there is a trend toward a recognition of a group interest (*quntide rentong*) and, in turn, pressure for a social organisation (*shetuan*) to act on behalf of this group interest.' Gordon White, 'Prospects for Civil Society in China: A Case Study of Xiaoshan City', in (January 1993) (29) *The Australian Journal of Chinese Affairs*, at p. 72. Available at: www.jstor.org (Last visited March 2005.)

45 Jia Xiejing, 'Trade Associations in Wenzhou' (*Wenzhoushi de hanye xiehui*), in Wang Ming *et al.* (eds.), *supra* note 20, at p. 244.

of 2000 there were 112 provincial trade associations, 99 of them were founded on government initiative, while 13 associations were set up by enterprises' own initiative. Among the 112 associations, 9 of them have been financially self-sufficient, able to hire their own personnel, and enjoying autonomy for their operation, while 39 of them are affiliated to the relevant government departments in respect of personnel, finance, and office facilities, and 64 associations are affiliated to the main founders (enterprises) in respect of personnel, finance and office facility.[46]

Apart from 'top down' trade associations, many 'bottom up' associations have also emerged and they play a significant role in providing services and formulating standards for quality control and market order for enterprises producing the same products. Such associations are mostly set up by private enterprises because of their practical need. The case of Wenzhou city is one such example. The city of Wenzhou is well known in China for its developed private business. As more private entrepreneurs appeared, it also became difficult to maintain a healthy market order. Many fake products were thrown into the market, prices were disturbed by unfair competition, and some poor quality goods damaged the reputation of private business, all of which had a direct impact on the interests of businessmen. Local government tried to put the market in order, but felt incapable of dealing with the mounting problems. Against such a background, many private businessmen in the same sector gathered together to institute trade associations with the hope that the associations could help them to regulate the market. Usually the chairmen of the associations are the 'powerful' entrepreneurs, elected by the members of the associations. The funds of the associations are raised through the membership fee, service fees, and some donations of enterprises. Local government has provided sufficient administrative support to the trade associations.[47]

The 'top down' trade associations usually get special support from the relevant departments of the government in terms of finance, personnel, and other resources. Not surprisingly, this support costs them their independence from the government. Many such organisations have experienced or remain at the stage of 'two names, one team', which means that while the organisation has its own name, it is staffed by the same personnel of one department of government. Using the above-mentioned case in the Guangdong province as an example, the 112 trade associations have 392 full time staff, 303 of them are hired by the professional leading units (sponsoring agency); 79 out of the 112

46 *Id.*
47 *Ibid.*, at p. 255.

trade associations use offices provided by the professional leading units or enterprises. Some governmental departments continue to take trade associations as their internal organs, and arrange for retired personnel, or soon to be retired personnel, to work at the trade associations. Lack of independence is also reflected in the ways the leading positions of associations are elected. In the case of Guangdong, among the 112 trade associations, 29 of them were elected through procedures provided in the charters of the associations; in 32 of them the candidate names were given by their professional leading units and election was only a formality; in 43 of them the candidate names were given by main founders (enterprises); and in 8 of them the leading positions were directly appointed by their professional leading units.[48] However, it is interesting to note that affiliation with the government does not mean that the associations are financially dependent on the government. Most associations collect fees from their members and charge fees for their services. In the case of Guangdong, the 112 trade associations had a total income of CNY 25,570,000. Service charges account for 41.55% of the association's income, membership fees account for 35.87%, other income derives from government subsidy and allocation, and enterprises donation. This shows that trade associations are capable of supporting themselves financially.[49]

For the time being 'top down' trade associations have to serve two interests: the interests of the government, and the interests of their enterprise members. The government represents the general public interest, while a trade association represents the specific interests of its members. When conflicts between such interests occur, 'top down' trade associations intend to give priority to the government's interest.

Compared to the 'top down' trade associations, the 'bottom up' ones are more independent from the government, thus enjoy more autonomy in their operations. Of course, the negative impact may be that their influence on government policy is very limited, and moreover they may be vulnerable to government intervention. For whatever purpose, they are compelled to maintain a good relationship with local government so as to avoid conflict or confrontation, which would surely have a negative impact on the trade associations. 'Bottom up' trade associations are more concerned with providing various services to their members so as to enhance sector development. In addition, they give priority to maintaining fair competition and protecting the interests

48 Li Jianjung, 'The Trade Association of Guangdong Province' (*Guangdong shengde hangye xiehui*), in Wang Ming, *supra* note 20, at p. 233.

49 *Ibid*, at pp. 224-227.

of member enterprises. For instance, they organise negotiation among the enterprise members on product prices and ensure that the agreed price will be followed by the members so as to prevent some enterprises from applying a lower price, resulting in disorder of the market.

It is increasingly recognised in China that trade associations play a significant role in providing services for enterprises; in self-governing, collaboration, supervision and holding legitimate rights and interests of enterprises; and in assisting government in reinforcing the administration of the sector. Thus, some Chinese experts have proposed that trade association should be treated as economic-type social organisations with different registration procedures to other social organizations being registered with the civil affairs department of the government, without the need to affiliate with a professional leading unit.[50] Such a suggestion may be helpful in promoting the growth of trade associations, and enhancing their independence. However, in the wider context, considering that all social organisations should be treated equally no matter whether they operate in the economic sphere or in the political, cultural, religious or social welfare spheres, it is right not to treat trade association differently. All types of social organisations are supposed to be set up by individual (both citizen and enterprise) initiatives for various purposes, and there is no justification for prioritising one type of organisation merely because it enhances economic development. Social organisations in the fields of politics, culture, social welfare, religion and human rights are as important as trade associations. In connection with this, we may draw from the internationally recognised interpretation of freedom of association under Article 22 of the International Covenant on Civil and Political Rights.

> [The Article] does not expressly list the possible *purposes* of an association (ideological, religious, political, economic, labour, social, cultural, sport or other), it is also to be assumed here that the protective scope is broad. Religious societies, political parties, commercial undertakings and trade unions are as protected by Art. 22 as cultural or human rights organizations, soccer clubs or associations of stamp collectors.[51]

50 See Sheng Hongchao and Wang Ming, 'Low Voltage Electrical Apparatus Association of Yueqing City' (*Yueqingshi diya dianqi hangyexiehui)*, in Wang Ming *et al.* (eds.), *Case Study on China's NGOs, UNCRD Research Report Series No.43*, (Beijing: UNCRD: 2001), at p. 149.

51 Manfred Nowak, *U.N. Covenant on Civil and Political Rights: CCPR Commentary*, (Kehl am Rhein, Strasbourg, Arlington: Engel, 1993), at p. 386.

The essence of freedom of association is to provide legal protection for people to form all sorts of associations, not one particular type of association. Furthermore, a different registration procedure for trade associations may reduce the urgency for relaxing the dual registration system for other social organizations and the continued strict state control of other organisations acceptable.

(4) Non-governmental social welfare organisations

Under the planned economy, social welfare organisations were fully run by the state and financed by local government. Due to the limited funds of local government, social welfare services have fallen far behind social needs. Parallel with the economic reform, the government started to reform the social welfare system by adopting a new policy of socialisation of social welfare services. State resources, market resources, and the resources of local communities, families, and individual citizens have been mobilised, allowing the previous single state system to be replaced by multiple actors participating in the social welfare system. Various non-governmental social welfare organisations emerged against this background in the 1990s. Most of them provide services for disabled children, elderly people, orphans, mentally disabled people, and other vulnerable groups.

Since very limited government financial support and business donations are available to non-governmental social welfare organisations, most of them have to charge fees for their services. This excludes people from receiving such services if they cannot afford to pay. For those who can pay, the prices of these services have to be kept low, since the government does not provide any subsidies for people with special needs. This forces non-governmental welfare organisations to set the standard of their services at a very modest level so as to make them reasonably priced for the average client.

Although they have existed for a very short period of time, non-governmental social welfare organisations have contributed significantly to the needs of special groups in society, and some of them have developed smoothly. For instance, the Hetong Elderly Welfare Association was established in 1995 by a doctor of traditional Chinese medicine who had worked in Austria and Germany. He was inspired by the quality of social services for elderly people in those countries, and decided to devote himself to social welfare service to elderly people in China. They have set up a few 'Hetong Homes for the Aged', receiving relatively low fees (about CNY 300 per month, which is about EUR 30). They have also established a school to train nurses for the aged. The Association's activities are mainly focused in Tianjin, but it hopes to expand to other cities in China. Moreover, the Association is quite successful in obtaining government subsidies and private donations, besides the fees collected from residents of Hetong Homes.[52] Another example is the Xiang Yan Center for the Development of Children in Jiangjing city. It was established in 1995 with the help of a substantial contribution by a Taiwanese couple with a lot of experience in the education of mentally disabled children. The Center started by providing education for mentally disabled children from the age of 3 to 16; it has expanded by setting up a library with children's toys, a welfare farm for mentally disabled adults, and a center for mentally disabled people to meet each other and relax. Thus, the Center has developed into a project providing education, employment, and daily relaxation activities for disabled people.[53]

However, the path of many non-governmental social welfare organisations has not been smooth since they are a relatively new phenomenon in China; they have faced a number of daunting problems, and continue to do so. Firstly, despite the fact that central government policy encourages private initiatives in social welfare services, some local government may hesitate to support such organisations. The example of the well-known Guangzhou Zhi Ling School for disabled children provides an insight into the problems faced in reality. The School was founded in 1985 by a former trade union employee, Meng Weina, a few people committed to public welfare work, and parents of disabled children. Since there was no precedent for such a school for mentally disabled children run by ordinary people, neither the local education department nor the civil affairs department wanted to register it. Meng Weina went to press the Deputy Mayor to have the school registered, but was disregarded. She then followed the legal procedure in organising a demonstration with parents and disabled children in front of the local people's congress. With local media supporting, the local government issued a document approving the School a year later. Following this experience Meng Weina founded the Guangzhou Hui

52 *250 Chinese NGOs*, *supra* note 5, at p. 259. I met a senior staff member of the Hetong Elderly Welfare Association at an international conference in Beijing in 2003 and was told that the association has received financial and professional help from German institutions. The Association has sent their staff to Germany to study the German experience in running houses for aged.

53 It should be noted that even though the Center provides free of charge education for disabled children, they could not enrol the number of children they want. This is mainly because many parents of disabled children do not want their children to go out in public, despite the fact that study has proved that early education for disabled children can improve their life ability. Deng Guosheng and Wang Ming, 'Xiang Yang Children Development Center', in Wang Ming *et al.* (eds.), *supra* note 50, at pp. 55-67.

Ling Service for the Disabled and Beijing Hui Ling in 1990 and 2000 respectively. Although the Hui Ling Service has now expanded to include a kindergarten, special schools, and training centers for nurses, a long-term residential center and an autism research center, a lack of understanding and support from local government has detracted from the expansion. According to Meng Weina, this is the biggest frustration they have had in developing their undertakings.[54]

Secondly, even though local government as a whole supports a social welfare organisation, a specific department of local government may be hostile to the organisation because of a conflict of interests. The experience of the 'First Aid Association for Traffic Accidents' in Huludao city demonstrates this. This Association was founded by a private entrepreneur, Li Shuwen. In 1993 he set up a private enterprise, the Qianjin Motor Repair Shop. The Shop is located near the 102 national highway, which carries approximately 20,000 vehicles from across China every day. The Shop's main business consists of repairing vehicles damaged in accidents. Through his work Li Shuwen has witnessed many serious traffic accidents which have caused death and injury as well as loss of property.[55] Usually after an accident occurs, the parties involved or people who witnessed the accident call the office of the local traffic police. The office should send officers to the spot instantly to rescue the injured, ensure their property is protected, and restore the normal flow of traffic. However, for various reasons, such as a lack of human resources and equipment at the office of the local traffic police, injured people and their property could not be helped promptly in practice, causing irreversible harm to the people involved,

54 *250 Chinese NGOs*, *supra* note 5, at pp. 80, 133, 135. I met Meng Weina in an international conference in Beijing in July 2004, and was deeply impressed by her dedication to providing services for disabled children and their families. She has ample experience with local government officials who have not only ignored or neglected her organisation's work, but also abused their administrative power, imposing obstacles in the way of the organisation, and resulting in the organisation having to fight hard for its existence, causing a huge human and material loss for the organisation.

55 The rapid construction of highways and roads, the increasing levels of motor vehicle traffic on roads, combined with the absence of safety measures and a general consciousness for safe driving, have led to the high number of traffic accidents in China. It was reported that in 2001, the number of deaths due to road traffic accidents reached more than 100, 000, while in the USA it was 40,000 and in Japan it was 10,000. See Deng Guosheng and Gong Huixian, 'Volunteer Help, Civil Charity: First Aid Association for Traffic Accidents in Huludao City', in Wang Ming *et al.* (eds.), *supra* note 20, at p. 331.

their families and enterprises.[56] In mid-sized and small cities in China this problem is quite serious, and local government appears to lack the capacity to tackle it. Civil affairs departments and hospitals also seem unable to deal with the problem that injured people brought to hospital may not be able to afford the medical costs. Li Shuwen witnessed all these problems and took the initiative to provide first aid following traffic accidents in Huludao city. In 1998 he bought three rescue cars and equipped each with a stretcher, oxygen cylinder, tourniquet and other emergency treatment apparatus; he employed three drivers and twelve rescue personnel to patrol the 102 national highway and the main streets of the city 24 hours a day. Within one year this first aid team has participated in traffic accident relief work on 80 occasions and rescued 166 injured people. In 1999 Li Shuwen founded the 'First Aid Association for Traffic Accidents'. This initiative received support from both local government and the media. The Association not only provided first aid for the injured but also negotiated with hospitals to ensure that the injured receive treatment promptly. However, for some reason the Association was disliked by the local traffic police. Since the members of the rescue team are often first to arrive at the scene of the accident, sometimes they are asked to provide eyewitness evidence by the police, and sometimes the evidence they gave did not match that collected by the police. Thus from time to time Li Shuwen received threatening letters demanding that the Association's work be stopped, and his business also suffered because people did not dare to bring cars and trucks to be repaired there knowing that he had a bad relationship with the local police. Thus, a privately initiated association, aimed at providing humanitarian help to people in need, faces the real challenge to survive.[57]

Thirdly, private non-profit welfare organisations have to compete with state welfare institutions and for-profit organisations; indeed, the former are disadvantaged in many respects. Nowadays, state welfare homes are still heavily subsidised by the government, so they are able to charge less from self-financing clients than private welfare homes.[58] This results in unfair competition with non-government institutions. In addition, since these organisations are new,

56 Sometimes after accidents involving large lorries local people would take the opportunity to steal the goods that were being transported, which caused a loss of goods to the relevant enterprises.

57 Deng Guosheng and Gong Huixian, *supra* note 55, at pp. 330-349.

58 Yiyi Lu, *The Limitations of NGOs: A Preliminary Study of Non-governmental Social Welfare Organisations in China,* (London School of Economics: 2003), at p. 4. Available at: www.lse.ac.uk/collections/ccs/publications/iwp/iwp13.htm. (Last visited March 2005).

and they cannot offer competitive salaries and other social security guarantees comparable to those enjoyed by public sector employees, they cannot recruit many highly trained, experienced staff. Most of them employ migrants from rural areas and laid-off workers. This certainly has an impact on the quality of the services they provide. Research has shown that 'well-off families choose not to use NGO service because they are not satisfied with the qualifications of their staff.'[59] In addition, in recent years private investment in welfare services for commercial purposes has increased. Some of them provide a very low standard of services, hiring fewer staff so as to charge lower fees, hence attracting some low-income clients. This puts pressure on NGOs, which try to maintain certain basic standards. In addition, some private businesses also invented the so-called lifelong care arrangement, allowing parents to pay a non-refundable lump sum when they send their children to a residential home. Some parents worry about their children's future and opt for lifelong care. However, since the payment is non-refundable, even if the parents are not satisfied with the services their children receive, they cannot afford to withdraw and lose what they have paid. The lack of regulation on quality control and financial supervision results in unfair competition between non-profit and for-profit organisations.[60]

Social welfare services have a big market in China. In view of the severe financial constraints on the government and its inability to meet fast-growing needs, one would expect that non-profit social welfare organisations would be encouraged to fill the gap. However, this does not mean that the government should bear less responsibility for the support of welfare services. Rather, the government should provide both financial and administrative support to non-profit welfare service organisations, and provide regulations for fair competition between these and for-profit organisations so as to expand and upgrade social welfare services.

4 The Shortcomings of the Current Law

4.1 Legal System Featured with Strict Government Control

Like many European countries, the Chinese Constitution provides that citizens of the People's Republic of China enjoy freedom of speech, press, assembly,

59 *Ibid.*, at p. 11.
60 *Ibid.*, at pp. 10-11.

association, procession and demonstration.[61] Thus, one can be certain that freedom of association is recognised as a constitutional right. However, this general constitutional provision is not sufficient to ensure that individual citizens can exercise the right. Unlike most Western European countries, the Chinese government has issued a number of specific regulations that legitimise strict government control over associations. These include: the 2004 Regulations for the Management of Foundations; the 1989 Interim Regulations on Administration of Foreign Chamber of Commerce, the 1998 Provisional Regulations for Registration and Management of Popular Non-Enterprise Work Units, and the 1998 Regulations for Registration and Management of Social Organisations. These laws have the common characteristic of strict government control on associations and foundations. Since the 1998 Regulations on Registration and Management of Social Organisations (hereafter the 1998 Regulations) is the most important piece of law relating to freedom of association in China, it will be discussed in depth below.

4.2 The Main Limitations of the 1998 Regulations

There are four main aspects to the 1998 Regulations: a 'dual administrative system'; clauses imposing excessive restrictions on the establishment of social organisations; a broad discretionary power of the registration department to refuse approval to a social organisation; and an annual review system (annual inspection).

4.2.1 Dual Administrative System

According to Article 6 of the 1998 Regulations, from its establishment to its operation, a social organisation should be administered under both the civil affairs department of the government and professional leading units. The Ministry of Civil Affairs and local civil affairs departments at and above county level are the departments concerned with the registration and administration of social organisations (hereafter registration department, which is also commonly referred to as registering agency). The relevant departments of the State Council and local government at and above county level, and organs empowered by them, are the relevant professional leading units (*yewu zhuguan danwei*, hereafter

61 Art. 35 of the P.R.C. Constitution.

'leading unit', which is often referred to as sponsoring agency) of social organisations in relevant sectors and professions.[62] The registration procedure is that a candidate social organisation first needs approval by a leading unit; the unit then makes a preliminary application to the registration department (Article 9). Within six months of the approval of the preliminary application by the registration department, the candidate social organisation must hold members' assemblies, pass its charter, elect its executive organs, responsible officers and legal representatives and apply to the registration department for final registration (Article 14). Obviously, this is a three-step approval procedure.

The dual administration system was mainly designed to facilitate the management and control of social organisations by the government. It ensures that any registered social organisations meet the criteria of need determined by the government. Consequently it results in the phenomenon of government and social organisations being tied together (*zhengshe bufen*). The official view is that the dual administration system reflects the Chinese reality, since such administration must implement government policy and serve professional and social needs, which cannot be done by one government department. Professional leading units are familiar with the professional activities of social organisations, which gives them the ability to undertake various tasks of administration and control. The combined work of the leading unit and registration department should increase the efficiency of management.[63]

62 According to the Announcement of the Ministry of Civil Affairs concerning Re-confirmation of Professional Leading Units for Social Organisations (February 2000), professional leading units include: all ministries of the State Council and its offices, and relevant departments of local governments at and above county level; all departments of the Central Communist Party and the relevant departments of the Party at and above county level; the General Office of the National People's Congress Standing Committee, the General Office of the National Political Consultative Conference, the Supreme People's Court, the Supreme People's Prosecution Office and the relevant departments of all these organs at and above county level; organisations entrusted by the Central Communist Party, the State Council or local Party Committees and governments. The Announcement lists 22 organisations entrusted to be leading units of social organisations at a national level, such as the Chinese Academy of Social Sciences, the All-China Federation of Trade Unions, the All-China Federation of Women, the Communist Youth League, China Disabled Persons' Federation, etc.

63 See the information given by the Guangdong government – the Guangdong Folk Organisation Information at the Guangdong local government Civil Affairs Department website: www.gdmjzz.gov.cn (Last visited March 2005). However, scholars' work has proved that the dual administration system has serious drawbacks, see chapters in this book by Wu Yuzhang, Xie Haiding, and Liu Peifeng.

The 1998 Regulation imposes a wide range of supervisory and management responsibilities on leading units (Article 28). They include:

i) investigating the social organisations' preliminary application for establishment, its modification or cancellation;
ii) supervising and guiding social organisations to ensure that they obey the relevant laws, regulations and national policy, and undertake activities according to their charters;
iii) conducting the preliminary stage of the annual examination;
iv) helping the registration department and other relevant departments to investigate and deal with illegal activities of social organisations;
v) acting with other relevant departments in guiding the process of winding up social organisations.

It seems that, in addition to requiring leading units to assist the registration department in following the procedures of registration and administration of social organisations, this Article also gives leading units some political responsibility for social organisations, namely that leading units should ensure that a social organisation's purpose and activities are politically correct. In view of the rapid expansion of social organisations over the last twenty years in various fields, it is understandable that some governmental institutions are either not willing to take on these heavy responsibilities, especially the political risks, or are incapable of doing so and thus refuse to be leading units for social organisations. In the Announcement on Several Questions concerning Rectification and Examination of Social Organisations issued by the Ministry of Civil Affairs in 1999,[64] it was stressed that if, due to a change of functions (among other reasons), a leading unit does not want to be the leading unit of a social organisation, the social organisation should look for a new one. If necessary, the original leading unit should assist the social organisation in finding a new leading unit. After a social organisation has completed its procedure with the registration department concerning the change of leading unit, the former leading unit can then end its relationship with the social organisation. In circumstances where a social organisation cannot find a new leading unit, the original leading unit should continue to act as its leading unit and must not force the social organisation to operate as a body without an institutional link with the govern-

64 This document is contained in the *Collection of Laws and Regulations on Social Organisations in China*, compiled by the Research Center on NPO Law at the Law School of Peking University, 2003.

ment. Although the 1998 Regulations impose heavy responsibilities on leading units, in practice some leading units hardly do anything other than collecting administration fees from social organisations.

In practice, the requirement for affiliation with a leading unit means that every registered social organisation has a link with a governmental institution. This may prevent some organisations from being registered because of the impossibility of finding institutional support[65] – though one option for them is to exist secretly. It may also impose a heavy burden and delay the setting up of the social organisation.[66] It may also decrease the independence of a registered social organisation since it has to get the approval of its leading unit on significant activities and appointments to leadership posts. Indeed, this has led some social organisations to decide not to register themselves as such; instead, they register themselves with the industrial and commercial bureaux as enterprises.[67] However, the purposes and activities of such enterprises are

65 One such example is the non-governmental and non-profit organisation Guangzhou Hui Ling Service for the Mentally Disabled. It is the first Chinese grassroots educational organisation devoted to the mentally disabled. It owns five service branches: a kindergarten, a school, a vocational training center, a residential facility and a research institute. These branches are under the jurisdiction of various governmental organs: the residential facility is registered with the local civil affairs department; the kindergarten and the school are affiliated with the educational bureau of local government; and the vocational training center is affiliated with the association for disabled people. However, the Guangzhou Hui Ling Service for the Mentally Disabled has not been able to find a governmental institution to be its leading unit; consequently it has not been registered with the Civil Affairs Department as a legally registered social organisation. Its establishment was based on an approval document of the Guangzhou government after demonstration and petition to the Local People's Congress and media support. See Wang Ming *et al.* (eds.), *supra* note 50, at pp. 68, 79.

66 For instance one of the most widely known environmental NGOs, Friends of Nature, first applied for registration with the National Environmental Bureau in 1993 and was rejected. In 1994, it found the Ministry of Culture as its leading unit and was finally registered with the Ministry of Civil Affairs. Since most of the activities of the Friends of Nature are environmentally linked, it does not have much to do with the Ministry of Culture; the latter mainly receives administrative fees and ensures that the Friends of Nature does not cause any political problems. See Wang Ming *et al.*, *supra* note 33, at pp. 162, 168.

67 For instance, the Global Village of Beijing is a typical 'bottom up' environmental NGO registered with the Beijing Bureau of Industry and Commerce as an economic entity (company), rather than with the civil affairs department as a social organisation. Its founder has openly stated that since Chinese law requires a social organisation to be affiliated with a governmental institution which inevitably diminishes the autonomy of the social organisation, the Global Village values the significance of its autonomy,

typically those of social organisations, and some of them are very well known grassroots NGOs in China. Since the Ministry of Civil Affairs and its local departments do not have the power to supervise the activities of enterprises, there is hardly any control over the activities of enterprises, which are, in practice, NGOs.

The attachment to a leading unit creates a great disparity between Chinese social organisations and Western NGOs. Thus, as a Chinese scholar observed, no truly autonomous and legitimate NGOs exist in China; the NGOs that are truly independent from the government can only exist illegally and their influence is extremely limited.[68]

4.2.2 Excessive Restriction Clauses on the Establishment of Social Organisations

According to Article 10 of the 1998 Regulations, a social organisation must meet the following six conditions. As will be illustrated below, some of them are formulated in such a general way that it leaves a wide discretion to the registration department to interpret them, which is a disadvantage to social organisations when making an application.

(i) Number of Members

It is required that an organization must have more than 50 individual members or 30 institutional members, or a total of more than 50 members if a social organisation consists of both individual and institutional members. The number of founders required is quite high compared to that required in other countries. In most Western European countries, a minimum of two founders is necessary. Of Central and Eastern European countries and the Newly Independent States (the former Soviet Union), a number require two to five founders; a few countries require 15 (e.g. Poland), 20 (e.g. Romania), or 30 (e.g. Bosnia and Herzegovina). It is claimed that 'requiring a number of founders so high that it is very difficult to form legally registered associations could be inconsistent with

although as an economic entity they incur other obligations, such as having to pay tax. The Green River is another example of a 'bottom up' environmental NGO registered as an enterprise.

68 Xie Haiding, 'Several Hot Issues on Studying China's Social Organisations in Recent Years' (*Jinqi Zhongguo shetuanfa yanjiu zhong de jige redian wenti*), in (Summer, 2002) *Global Law Review*, at p. 181. His conclusion is based on some profound research by Chinese experts.

international law.' It is recommended that the minimum number of founders should be 10 or less.[69]

(ii) A standardised name and corresponding organisational structure

Article 10, paragraph 2 states that a social organisation's name must comply with the relevant law and regulations and must not offend public morality. The name must reflect the social organisation's activities, character and areas of operation. Where national social organisations use 'Chinese' and 'All China' in their titles, local social organisation must not use these phrases. As to the meaning of 'corresponding organisational structure', one cannot find a direct explanation in the 1998 Regulations; however, Article 14 refers to a general meeting of members, an executive body, responsible officers (*fuze ren)* and legal representative (*fading daibiao ren).*

(iii) A fixed domicile

The 1998 Regulations do not provide any details about the meaning of a fixed domicile. It is generally understood that a social organisation as a legal person must have a fixed office as its daily site of operations, where all legal documents and correspondence will be sent, and the domicile also determines the court whose jurisdiction the social organisation is under. However, based on the practical experience of a senior civil servant at the Ministry of Civil Affairs a fixed domicile is interpreted as meaning that a social organisation should possess the right to use the domicile independently, must not share it as an office with other organisations, and it must not be located in a private house.[70]

(iv) Full-time staff with qualifications appropriate to the professional activities of the organisation

The requirement of full-time staff seems unnecessary since the question of whether to hire full-time or part-time employees should really be decided by the social organisation itself, in accordance with its financial situation and other circumstances. As to 'qualifications appropriate to the professional activities of the organisation', one would imagine that all social organisations desire

69 *Freedom of Association: The Question of NGO Registration, OSCE Human Dimension Implementation Meeting, October 1998, Background Paper 5,* (Warsaw, Poland: OSCE/ODIHR, 1998), at para. 6.1.1 and X.

70 Chen Jinluo and Wang Jianqin, *Theoretical and Practical Research on Chinese Social Organisations (Zhongguo shehui tuanti lilun yu shiwu yanjiu),* (Beijing: Research Centre on NPO Law at the Law School of Peking University, 2003), at pp. 172-173.

professionally qualified staff. However, such a requirement under the 1998 Regulations is useless since the 1998 Regulations do not and indeed cannot provide any criteria for a 'qualification appropriate to ... the organisation'. This phrase is explained by a Chinese expert to mean that a social organisation should be representative within its professional area. The responsible persons or key members should therefore enjoy authoritative status in their professional area and be of a sufficient standard to be respected in foreign relations. For instance, for an academic social organisation the participation of leading academic experts is necessary.[71] This is a rather restricted interpretation, but it seems to reflect how the relevant government departments judge a social organization.

(v) Lawful assets and sources of funding

A national level organisation must have a minimum of CNY 100,000 as its business fund and a local level or a trans-administrative-district organisation must have a minimum of CNY 30,000. It is not entirely clear what the term 'business fund' means. It has been explained that this provision 'mainly concerns the minimum value of the property that a social organisation should have. Although the amount is not very high, it sometimes creates a difficulty for many organisations.'[72]

(vi) The ability to bear civil liability independently

According to Chinese civil law every legal person enjoys civil rights and bears civil liability independently. The Regulations state that social organisations are legal persons, thus they must be capable of bearing civil liability independently. The real purpose of this requirement seems to highlight the fact that a social organisation should bear civil liability under its own name and with regard to its own property and must not depend on its leading unit,[73] and consequently it should not depend on the government.

71 *Ibid.*, at p. 175.

72 Ge Yunsong, 'On the Establishment of Social Organisations Under Chinese Law', 3 (2), 2000 *International Journal for Not-for Profit Law*, at p. 2. Available at: www.icnl.org/journal/vol2iss3/ar_chinalaw.htm (Last visited March 2005). See also Xie Haiding's paper in this book, footnote 38.

73 Chen Jinluo and Wang Jianqin, *supra* note 70, at p. 173.

4.2.3 The Broad Discretionary Power of the Registration Department to Refuse Registration to Social Organisations

Under the 1998 Regulations, meeting the aforementioned six conditions does not guarantee that a candidate social organisation will automatically be approved by the registration department. The 1998 Regulations entrust the registration department with the broad power to reject an application if one of five situations occurs (Article 13):

(i) Existing evidence proves that the purposes or the scope of the business of a proposed social organisation are contradictory to Article 4 of the 1998 Regulations

Article 4 provides that social organisations must follow the Constitution, laws, regulations and State policies, that it must not reject the basic principles confirmed in the Constitution, must not cause danger to the unification and security of the State and the solidarity of all nationals, must not cause harm to State interests, public interests and the legitimate interests of other organisations and citizens, and must not contravene public morality. Social organisations may not engage in profit-seeking activities.

There is no doubt that social organisations must follow laws the same as all individual citizens. However, the required observance of State policy can cause problems from time to time. State policy can be decided on, and issued by various government organs in various forms. They can be general or specific, open to the public or closed as internal documents, and moreover, they can be easily changeable due to shifts in government priorities. The lack of transparency of State policy leaves registration departments with a flexible discretionary power to refuse registration to a social organization, and the latter has difficulty defending itself due to the lack of information.

As to the other extremely general expressions used in Article 4, such as 'State security', 'State interests', 'public interests' and 'public morality', one could take the view that this leaves broad scope for a registration department to interpret them in any given case if it decides to refuse registration to a social organisation.[74]

With regard to the requirement that a social organisation should not engage in profit-seeking activities, it should be interpreted as requiring that a social organisation may not use its own name to do business. In 1995 the Ministry

74 For more extended discussion on this provision, see Ge Yunsong, *supra* note 72, at pp. 6-8.

of Civil Affairs and the National Bureau for Industry and Commerce jointly issued an Announcement concerning Several Issues on Social Organisations Engaging in Business Activities. It provides that a social organisation engaging in business activities may set up an enterprise as a legal person, or may also create a business organisation without legal personality, and they would be allowed to obtain business licenses. However, the social organisation may not engage in business activities using the name of the social organisation. In practice, however, the government, especially at a local level, encourages social organisations to become involved in business so as to be self-funding. For instance, it was reported that at the end of 1996 social organisations in Shenzhen had established about 86 varied commercial companies and 117 public interest entities – making a profit of more than CNY 10 million and paying more than CNY 2.5 million taxes to the government. While contributing to State revenue, they also increased income for the social organisations, which is essential for their own development.[75] Though the issue of social organisations making profit through business is very controversial, it is now largely recognised by Chinese academics that social organisations may engage in business for profit-making purposes, but may not distribute profit among its directors and members.

(ii) There is no need to establish a new organisation if there is already a social organisation active in the same or similar field in the same administrative area

This is the so-called 'non-competition principle'. Its rationale was explained by the Ministry of Civil Affairs as being that the establishment of too many social organisations without planning leads to development without order, the overlapping of functions among social organisations, and repeated admission of members, thus giving them a heavy economic burden. In dealing with foreign entities, it could also easily cause blind competition, resulting in a harmful social effect.[76]

'No social need' is one of the most frequently used arguments by registration departments to refuse registration or to dissolve a social organisation. Since it is the governmental organs that determine social need, it places the existence of a candidate social organisation or an existing social organisation completely in the hands of the government. Recently, some Chinese scholars have raised the question of whether such a choice should be left to the market, and hence

75 Zu Yuqin , *supra* note 43, at p. 178.

76 Ge Yunsong, The System on the Third Sector (Disanbumen de faluzhidu), in Su Li *et al.* (eds.) , *supra* note 13, at p. 47.

to let the market determine the life and death of a social organisation based on whether there is popular demand for it.[77]

In connection with the argument of social need, it is certain that to a large extent it is government policy to allow limited use of social organisations to attain governmental goals. As discussed above economic reform and reform of government organisations have led the government to abandon some management and social functions, and the government has been supporting social organisations in taking over those functions. As one government official has stated:

> When nurturing and developing NGOs, the government will adapt its efforts to local conditions and provide support selectively to those NGOs which merit it most. It is most important to nurture those NGOs which can take on those functions which will be relinquished by the government – disciplining, coordinating, managing and supervising trade and business associations – and to support a group of public interest foundations and charities.[78]

With government support trade and business associations have been the fastest expanding set of social organisations over the last two decades. It was said by the government source, that in 2000 there were approximately 165,000 NGOs in China: about one-third of them were trade associations; another third were academic groups; and the last third public welfare and community organisations.[79]

Article 19 of the 1998 Regulations is relevant to the no-competition principle, providing that social organisations may not establish regional branches. The official explanation is that if one social organisation sets up its branch in another administrative area, this could result in a repetition of work with a local social organisation, and is also not convenient for the administration of social organisations. Actually, the core concern of the government is that the growth of individual social organisations could make their supervision difficult. This

77 *Ibid*, at p. 51. See also Wang Ming, *et al.*, Reform of China's Social Organizations – from a Government Choice to a Social Choice (*Zhongguo shetuan gaige – cong zhengfu xuanze dao shehui xuanze*), (Beijing: Shehui kexue wenxian chubanshe, 2001).

78 See the speech of Guangyao Chen at the World Congress of Association Executives on 12th August, 2000. The speech is published in the *International Journal of Not-for-Profit Law*, available at: www.icnl.org/journal/vol3iss3/ar_guangyao.htm (Last visited March 2005).

79 *Id.*

means that social organisations only have a limited local nature, which restricts their capacity to develop into large organisations.

Obviously, the non-competition principle has a monopoly nature which aims to protect those existing social organisations, mostly established under government initiative, while preventing registration of those promising new social organisations that are emerging under private initiative. In the long run this is harmful for the expansion and capacity building of Chinese NGOs.

(iii) Founders or proposed responsible officers who are currently, or who were once under the criminal penalty of deprivation of political rights, or without full capacity for civil conduct

According to Chinese Criminal Law (Articles 54 to 58), deprivation of political rights include deprivation of the right to freedom of association. Thus, if a person is under the criminal penalty of deprivation of political rights, he or she cannot be the founder or the proposed responsible officers of a social organisation. However, the 1998 Regulations provide that a person who was punished with deprivation of political rights can *never* be a founder or responsible officers of a social organisation, which goes demonstrably beyond the scope of the Criminal Law. In fact it changes the Criminal Law by extending the time of the punishment. It is quite certain under the Chinese legislative order that only the highest legislature, namely the National People's Congress and its Standing Committee, are competent to amend the Criminal Law. Accordingly, the Regulations' restriction on persons who were punished with the deprivation of political rights is invalid.

In practice, the Ministry of Civil Affairs has issued guidelines that have set a high political standard for the responsible officers of social organisations. For instance, in the Model of the Statute of Social Organisation, Article 24 provides that the chairman, deputy chairmen and secretary-general of a social organization must hold the Communist ideology and policies, and must possess good political ethics.[80] The department in charge of social organisations in the Ministry of Civil Affairs also gives guidance that the responsible officers of a social organisation should exclude those who were the legal representatives of social organisations that were dissolved due to a violation of the law, or those

80 The Model of the Statute of Social Organisation can be found on the website of the Ministry of Civil Affairs: www.mca.gov.cn (Last visited March, 2005.)

who were the responsible officers of illegal organisations that have been banned.[81]

(iv) If falsification occurred in the application

According to Article 11 of the 1998 Regulations, in applying for the establishment of a social organisation, the founders must submit the following documents to the registration department: an application form; an approval document by the leading unit; a capital certificate report and the certificate for the right to use the site; basic background and identification of the founders and proposed responsible officers; and the draft charter. Clearly falsification of any documents mentioned here can be used by the registration department to reject an application.

(v) Any other situations prohibited by laws and administrative regulations

In China, the National People's Congress and its Standard Committee are authorised to enact laws, and the State Council is competent to issue administrative regulations. If situations prohibited by laws and administrative regulations occur, refusal by the registration department is consistent with the rule of law principle. The importance of this provision should be understood as restricting any other government organs, such as ministries, local governments and local legislature, from imposing any limitations on the establishment of social organisations.

4.2.4 Annual Review System

Article 31 of the 1998 Regulations provides that social organisations must submit their annual work report to their leading units by 31st March each year. After preliminary approval by the professional units, the report must be submitted to registration departments by 31st May for the annual examination. The work report should contain details of the social organisation's compliance with laws, regulations and State policy; details of its compliance with the registration procedures provided in the 1998 Regulations, and whether it has been carrying out its activities according to its charter; and any issues relating to a change of staff, internal structure and financial management.

81 See Working Guideline, section 13, under the title of 'what are the concrete requirements for responsible officers of social organisations', available at: www.chinanpo.gov.cn (Last visited March 2005).

The annual review can lead to two results: a pronouncement that the social organisation is qualified or disqualified. To be qualified a social organisation must meet the following conditions: observation of laws, regulations and State policy; carrying out activities according to its charter and no conduct in violation of the law or discipline; having sound financial management, income and expenditure following the relevant State regulations; prompt compliance with the procedures concerning change of registration and organisational structure; being managed according to democratic procedures; and to have accepted the annual examination within the required period. A social organisation will be disqualified if one of the following ten circumstances occurs. (1) It did not carry out any activities within a year. (2) There is a lack of funds to support on-going operations. (3) It carried out activities beyond its charter. (4) It breached financial regulations. (5) Internal management showed serious problems and major decision-making failures of democratic procedure. (6) There was a violation of relevant rules by collecting membership fees incompetently. (7) It did not follow the procedure for change of registration and organisational structure. (8) Without special reason, it did not accept annual examination within the required period. (9) It produced falsified documents during the annual examination. (10) Any other violation of relevant regulations.

Some Chinese view the annual review as an important means for governmental supervision of social organisations. Not only is it conducive to social organisations developing according to the law, but it also allows the government to discover problems in the implementation of the law and stimulate the improvement of the law.[82] However, the system is quite burdensome for the registration departments. In view of the fact that registration departments at all levels have very limited staff and there are an increasing number of social organisations, it is practically impossible to conduct the annual review as provided for above. In practice some registration departments carry out the annual review as a simple procedure of passing documents.

82 Chen Jinluo and Wang Jianqin, *supra* note 70, at p. 251.

4.3 Main Systems Used in Control of Social Organisations

4.3.1 Reporting System

The preceding analysis of the key features of the 1998 Regulations may give a general impression of a legal framework for social organisations in China which is strict and state-controlled. However, in practice, governmental organs have developed even more severe control measures that bear the same legally binding effect. One such measure is the 'reporting system for significant activities'. For significant and large-scale activities, such as organising a large-scale seminar or holding an exhibition, social organisations must seek the approval of the relevant government department.[83] It is reported that the Shanghai Provisions on Management of Social Organisations require social organisations to report to the registration department and leading units 15 days before they hold the general assembly to set up the organisation, an election meeting regarding the change to a leading post, organise activities across provinces, or any other activities that may have a significant social impact. The Chungqing Provisions on Management of Social Organisations request social organisations to report in advance to the relevant registration department or the leading units if they are going to organise significant activities. According to a Chinese study these reporting systems were first initiated by local government, and were supported by the Ministry of Civil Affairs. Up to now there is no unified reporting system in China and local practice can therefore vary in nature and extent.[84]

4.3.2 Rectification

Over the years the Chinese government has used the technique of 'purging' to pursue its aim of controlling social organisations. Since 1989, two nationwide comprehensive rectifications have been launched – the first was in 1990, and the second was in 1997. The Ministry of Civil Affairs stated that there were major problems within social organisations, which gave rise to the first rectification at that time. The problems alleged were that some social organisations were influenced by thoughts of bourgeois freedom; some engaged in profit-making activities; some were operating without registration, or engaged in activities beyond the scope of their charters; the work of different social organisations

83 Ge Yunsong, *supra* note 76, at p. 67.
84 *Ibid*, at pp. 67-68.

overlapped with each other; some collected fees arbitrarily that increased the burden on enterprises.[85] Consequently, the rectification focused on:[86]

(1) Abolition of social organisations that opposed the Four Cardinal Principles,[87] and advocated bourgeois liberal thoughts, especially those which showed serious wrongdoing during the June Event in 1989.
(2) Postponement of registration, or revocation of registration of social organisations whose target was profit, or who were engaged in business activities that were irrelevant to the purposes of the organisations, or engaged in activities that were contrary to the charters of the organisations.
(3) Dissolution or merging of social organisations that were not needed by society, duplicated, or did not meet the basic conditions for carrying out activities.
(4) Rejection of or orders to dissolve social organisations that were established without official registration. As to those social organisations that were really needed for society and met the conditions prescribed by law, they had to be re-registered.
(5) Clarifying the relationship between social organisations and their leading units.
(6) Strengthening supervision, promoting social organisations' management according to their charters and law.

This rectification lasted for more than a year. After the rectification the number of national level social organisations was reduced from 1600 to 1200, and local social organisations dropped from about 200,000 to 180,000.[88]

The second rectification lasted from 1997 to 2000. After this rectification, a number of social organisations were dissolved, and the number of local social organisations was reduced to about 136,000.[89]

85 *Ibid*, at p. 70.

86 Wang Ming, *supra* note 77, at pp. 101-102.

87 The Four Cardinal Principles were added to para. 7 of the Preamble of 1982 Constitution as: 'The Chinese people of all nationalities will continue to be led by the Communist Party of China, guided by Marxism-Leninism and Mao Zedong Thought, adhere to the people's democratic dictatorship and follow the socialist road.' For a discussion of the principles, see Jianfu Chen, *Chinese Law: Towards an Understanding of Chinese Law, Its nature and Development*, (The Hague: Kluwer Law International, 1999), at pp. 68-72.

88 Ge Yunsong, *supra* note 76, at pp. 70-71.

89 Wang Ming, *et al.*, *supra* note 77, at p. 102.

Apart from the two nationwide comprehensive rectifications mentioned above, from time to time small-scale adjustments in certain locations and certain fields were also occasionally undertaken. For instance, in 2000 as a part of the repression of *FaLun Gong*, the government instigated rectification of Qigong associations.

Rectification characterised the approach of the Chinese government to administrative management. During the rectification, each social organisation must submit all the documents required by the registration department, and undergo a strict review. If a social organisation could not pass this stage it would be dissolved. The review is based on the government policy at the given time, rather than a law or regulation. In addition, during the rectification process hardly any new social organisations were approved.

Rectification is viewed by some Chinese scholars as contradictory to the rule of law. It is argued that the duties of the relevant government organs in supervising social organisations should be fulfilled according to the law, and not beyond the law. Moreover, it is argued that the fact that governmental organs do not strictly follow the law in their daily work is the major reason for the need for rectification. According to the 1998 Regulations, annual review of social organisations should be exercised by registration departments. However, in practice some departments do not show enough interest in the work of social organisations and the annual examination is only a formality involving examinination of some documents. In some cases this has led to the situation that some social organisations deviate from the purpose the government designed and envisaged.[90]

5 THE PROSPECTS FOR A CHANGE IN THE LAW

In recent years, some Chinese legal scholars have taken a critical approach to studying the legal system relating to freedom of association in China. They have challenged the dual administration system, and appealed for the creation of a liberal legal environment conducive to the development of NGOs and NPOs. Some governmental officials were in agreement with the academic critics. For instance, a senior official of the Ministry of Civil Affairs in charge of social organisations once stated:

90 Ge Yungsong, *supra* note 76, at pp. 71-74.

> The legal system is unsound. Regulations for running non-profit organisations are not yet perfected. A disconnect exists between policies and regulations and the objective, practical requirements. The legal system is lagging behind and that definitely affects the smooth development of China's NGOs.[91]

While acknowledging that the current legal framework concerning social organisations in China can no longer meet the present social needs, a number of different proposals have been put forward to change the legal system. First, it has been suggested that a basic law on association should be enacted by the National People's Congress. On this view, the current legal framework that contains one provision in the Constitution and administrative regulations issued by the State Council is not sufficient in providing a legal guarantee for citizens to form and join associations. Between the Constitution and administrative regulations there should be a law to clearly guarantee the right of citizens to freedom of association as provided in the Constitution, and it should be compatible with obligations under the international conventions that China has ratified. This basic law would then be supplemented by separate laws on special types of social organisations (such as the regulations on foundations), other relevant regulations and ministerial rules. This approach would lead to a unified and multi-level legal system for social organisations.[92]

The second approach is to revise the 1998 Regulations. The proponents of this view do not think that a favourable political climate exists to enact a law that promotes and protects citizens exercising freedom of association. However, they suggest that some improvements can be made to the 1998 Regulations so that the current legal system can match the reality.

The third approach is to keep the 1998 Regulations as they are, and wait for the momentum necessary for political leaders to be prepared to enact a new law that places citizens' right to freedom of association as the purpose of the law. In their view since the 1998 Regulations contain many loopholes, and are practically impossible to implement at every local level, they allow many grass-roots social organisations to operate free of their constraints. Based on field studies at county and district levels, some Chinese scholars have contended that under the current political climate any revised administrative regulations

91 Guangyao Chen, *supra* note 78. At that time he was the Deputy Director of the Bureau of Civic Organization Management of the Ministry of Civil Affairs.

92 Chen Sixie, 'The Current Situation and Future, A Comment on the Current Legislation concerning Social Organisations in China' (*Xianzhuang yu weilai: wugou shetuan lifa zhuang kuang shuping*), (Summer, 2002) *Global Law Review*, at p. 176.

may tighten registration procedures for social organisations at all levels, with the consequence that unregistered social organisations at local level will be 'illegal', and forced to close down.[93]

Knowing the remaining political sensitivity concerning freedom of association in China, one has to admit that such concerns are not without foundation. Alternatively however, it could be argued that the 2004 Chinese Constitution includes, for the first time, provision to protect human rights, China has ratified the International Covenant on Economic, Social and Cultural Rights, and it is predicted that China will soon ratify the International Covenant on Civil and Political Rights – perhaps the political momentum exists to advance a new law that will in fact make the exercise of freedom of association by citizens easier rather than harder. Nowadays, when drafting new laws, central government faces a host of pressures from home and abroad, and must take into account public opinion. Academics should make a concerted effort to prevent the new law or revised administrative regulations from regressing, and to secure progressive legislation.

Viewed from the perspective of enhancing the protection of citizens' right to freedom of association, it would be ideal to see the enactment of a new law as outlined above. The voices of academics, NGO practitioners, civil servants and the general public should be heard. Whether or not such voices would result in a new law is uncertain, but certainly without them there would be no prospects for such a law. A glance back at the legislative history concerning social organisations could lead to the conclusion that the passing of a new law may require more time, but this cannot diminish the significance of advocacy work at present. In 1987, when the Ministry of Civil Affairs started to be in charge of the work of social organisations after the Cultural Revolution, a committee on drafting a law on social organisations was established. However, it was decided eventually that the conditions were not ripe for making a law, and since at that time there was a need for the governmental administration of social organisations, the Regulations for the Registration and Management of Social Organisations were issued in 1989, and were amended in 1998. During the 1990s some investigation and drafting work was conducted by the Ministry of Civil Affairs, but due to various reasons the work on drafting a law was not

93 I have heard such views from several Chinese scholars during the conferences organised by the Institute of Law of the Chinese Academy of Social Sciences in 2003 and 2004 in Beijing.

persevered with, nor was it concluded.[94] It seems advisable to let the Committee on Legal Works of the National People's Congress take a leading role in drafting the new law, rather than the Ministry of Civil Affairs. The Ministry is an administrative organ of the central government – its main mission is to manage social organisations. The management function of the Ministry determines its limitations in envisaging the essence of freedom of association as a fundamental human right of individuals. Thus now, and in the coming years, support and cooperation should be given to the legislative authority to encourage them to put the drafting of a law on associations on its legislative agenda.

At present, the Ministry of Civil Affairs is consolidating opinions in revising the 1998 Regulations. It is difficult to predict whether any substantive improvement will be made, or whether some setback will occur. In the words of a Chinese NPO expert:

> in the short term one cannot expect that a comprehensive and liberal legal system charged with promoting NGO development and standardising their activities will appear in China. The existing and forthcoming regulations and policies, no matter how detailed and logical their contents are, the control and restrictive nature and the more and more complicated procedure and framework, constitute an element of limiting China's NGOs growth for a long time to come.[95]

Obviously, it may be some time before a legal environment emerges that is bright and conducive to the development of NGOs and NPOs, or the third sector as a whole. It is the task of the Chinese legal community to make efforts to bring out positive changes of the legal system relating to the freedom of association; there are signs that they are doing so.

6 Conclusion

In Western countries, the right of citizens to freedom of association has a long history. The legal system has gradually developed to facilitate the easy exercise of this freedom, as well as to make associations accountable. In China, such freedom has never flourished, and moreover in the 1960s and 1970s it was

94 See conference paper presented by Chen Jinluo at the seminar on Basic Theoretical Issues concerning Freedom of Association, organised by the Research Center on NPO Law at the Law School of Peking University, September 2003, (paper with author).

95 Wang Ming, *supra* note 33, at p. 21.

virtually totally prohibited to set up any associations. Over the last two decades as a consequence of opening up and reform in the economic, political, and cultural spheres, privately initiated social organisations have proliferated quickly, and those governmental-initiated social organisations have also undergone considerable modification towards focusing more on serving their constituency. This positive development has been recognised both inside and outside China, and has encouraged many Chinese and international NGOs to make their contribution to this process.

In facing the explosive growth of social organisations, the Chinese legal system governing social organisations has shown an obvious inefficiency, and moreover is viewed widely as constituting a barrier in the way of the healthy development of civil society. From a human rights perspective, such a legal system excessively and disproportionately restricts citizens' right to freedom of association.

There are different legal models for regulating associations. For instance, the Dutch legal model is an extremely liberal one that grants any association the right to decide whether or not it wants to be registered, and registration is with the Chamber of Commerce, which is a non-government organisation itself. Once registered, the association's rights and duties are regulated by the Civil Code. In England and Wales, only charity organisations need to be registered, and the Charity Commission acts independently in registering and providing all sorts of services to charity organisations.

A common feature in these countries is that there exists no compulsory registration that applies to all kinds of association. These legal systems proceed on the realistic assumption that it is neither possible nor desirable to impose compulsory registration on all associations. In contrast, the current Chinese law makes all unregistered associations 'illegal' and under it they face a possible crack down by the government. Furthermore, in Western countries the laws respect the independence and autonomy of associations, and there is no requirement for any affiliation between associations and governmental institutions. In this respect the Chinese law is widely critisised as it requires all social organisations to have a governmental sponsor. This system has not only prevented many privately initiated social organisations from surfacing, compelling them to operate 'secretly', but has also forced registered social organisations to be dependent on a government sponsor, and even to be abused by it.

Thus the priority in China, is first to abolish the sponsoring system and secondly to eliminate compulsory registration for all social organisations. Chinese experience has demonstrated that it is neither possible nor necessary to register all grassroots social organisations. The criteria for registration should not be based on the type of organisations, such as economic-type, political-type, or cultural-type; the right to freedom of association should be enjoyed regardless of the field in which the organisation operates, and the government should not be allowed to discriminate against the type of organisation to which it objects. The rationale for registration should be based on accountability, namely to hold those registered accountable for themselves and to the society at large. Chinese lawmakers should seriously consider solutions based on the experiences of other countries, such as for example, confining registration to associations with a public utility function. Since such associations collect public funds and serve the public interest, the public have the right to know that they are legally registered and their activities and financial record should be publicly available.

One cannot be very optimistic when studying the current legal system governing social organisations. Strictly speaking, it reflects a highly unbalanced relationship between the government and social organisations. The government enjoys a position of absolute dominance: it has the power to make the law, to interpret the law, as well as to enforce the law. Moreover, it can take measures that go beyond the law, such as calling for rectification of social organisations at anytime and any place, if such measures accord with the wishes of government. It is not an exaggeration to presume that, in essence, the power to decide over what kind of social organisation can exist, what kind of activities they can engage in, and other crucial issues rests ultimately with the government. However, the question is whether such a strict control system really works and what will be the consequences in the long run. At local level one can already witness the relaxation of local government in implementing the regulations, and also the large number of social organisations that exist and operate beyond the legal framework. If the market economy is the choice that the Chinese government has to make for saving the country's economy as well as political unity and stability, then tolerance and support for citizens' initiatives for associational life may prove to be another choice that the government should take for maintaining social cohesion and harmony. The government's policy of excessive control over social organisations has hindered the development of social organisations, and created the feeling of constraint within such organisations. The use of social stability as an instrument to impede the growth of social organizations is state action which can only generate a social revulsion that will eventually undermine the government's authority.

Despite Chinese social organisations' short period of history, shortage of funds and lack of transparency in management, and so on, it is undeniable that they play a pivotal role in transitional China. The government and the market simply cannot meet all social demands, or reduce or solve all social problems.

A third sector is needed not only to provide people the opportunity to act in their own interests or the public interest as a whole, but also to play a supplementary role to support the government in tackling social needs, especially neglected ones. The energy, creativity and potential that Chinese social organisations, NGOs and NPOs have shown over the last twenty years, and the increasing support they have received both domestically and abroad, and the huge space for them to develop in China, give one a sense of certainty that as a new social force, it will continue to grow and extend. Of course, its pace of development also depends to a large extent on government policy and the law. In this context it should be pointed out that the government and social organisations have different missions, and play different roles in society, but it does not mean that they are against each other. It is quite normal that in a concrete situation they hold different opinions merely because they have different concerns. The government and the third sector should build up a kind of cooperative relationship though such cooperation cannot prevent the occasional confrontation. For some organisations, such as human rights NGOs, it is unavoidable that they often challenge government decisions. It is their mission to act as a 'watch dog' to monitor that human rights are respected and protected by the government. Many surveys on Chinese social organisations have illustrated that social organisations prefer to cooperate with the government and a good relationship is conducive to realising their ideas. It seems the linchpin of the problem lies with the government, and whether it can fully trust the social organisations, especially those privately-initiated ones, to exercise self-regulation; and on all level of governmental institutions whether they could treat social organisations as an independent and autonomous group rather than an extension of government or second or even third class 'citizens'. Consequently, it is also important that the government adopts a respectful and trusting policy towards social organisations, and fosters a relationship of mutual trust. This may not be easily achieved, but if the government is committed to modernising China, and embracing a progressive understanding of the role of associations in a pluralistic society, it will choose to cooperate and support social organisations rather than to restrict them. It goes without saying that as the government has its role to play in facilitating the development of social organisations, it is also incumbent on the social organisations themselves to mature healthily, enhance their capacity, retain accountability and pursue good practice. China would be on a good track if a balanced relationship between the government and social organisations can be maintained, and each can perform its functions according to law.

2

GOVERNMENT ADMINISTRATION OF SOCIAL ORGANISATIONS – ITS MODEL AND EFFECTS

Wu Yuzhang

1 INTRODUCTION

Were one to say that in China, people are generally unfamiliar with Western rights, this would not be quite so true of the right to freedom of association, since social groups – organisations formed by voluntary combination – have existed throughout history with the exception of a few specific periods. Of course, Chinese people in ancient times did not share contemporary Western 'rights' concepts, but they did tacitly regard freedom of association as something perfectly right and proper. For them it fell into the category of what was justified and reasonable, and was something any individual should be able to do. In this sense, to say that historically Chinese people have enjoyed the right to freedom of association may not be true in strict terms of certain aspects of rights theory but is nevertheless a statement not without merit. In the years since the founding of the People's Republic of China, and especially in the reform period, the number of social organisations has grown apace. Statistics from 2002 inform us that there were 1,712 registered national or intra-provincial level social organisations. Nationwide there was a total of some 130,000 social organisations, as well as 110,000 popular non-enterprise work units.[1] We already have available related research by Chinese scholars into the phenomenon of social organisations, research that offers clear confirmation of the existence

1 Statistics from the Ministry of Civil Affair's website: http://www.mca.gov.cn/statistics/index.html.

Yuwen Li (Ed.), *Freedom of Association in China and Europe: Comparative Perspectives in Law and Practice*, © 2005 Koninklijke Brill NV, Leiden. Printed in The Netherlands, pp. 71-101.

of an individual's rights of association and a similarly clear picture of the state of China's social organisations.[2]

Today, when we study the phenomenon of social organisations, no matter what discipline we approach the question from, we all proceed from the standpoint of how better to protect the right to association that citizens enjoy under the law. For this reason, the first part of this paper is a description of the model of government administrative control of social organisations that currently obtains.[3] We will see that one fundamental reality in the existence and development of social organisations is the control exercised by government. In the 21st century, when we compare the differences between Chinese and foreign social organisations (not just Western but also those of some developing nations), this is one feature that stands out, indeed is very striking. Looking at social organisations or freedom of association in Western societies, although there are regulatory controls, they take place within the logic of civil society as a given, and the understanding that freedom of association is an essential component of civil society. The logic we follow in China is different, one where government has the right to exercise control over the existence of social organisations. It is no exaggeration to say that the government has a complete monopoly in deciding what kind of social organisations can exist, what kind

2 Notable publications include: Wang Ying *et al., An Intermediate Level of Society – Reform and China's Social Organisations (Shehui zhongjian ceng – gaige yu Zhongguo de shetuan zuzhi),* (Beijing: Zhongguo fazhan chubanshe, 1993); Wang Ming *et al.*, *Reform of China's Social Organisations – from a Government Choice to a Social Choice (Zhongguo shetuan gaige – cong zhengfu xuanze dao shehui xuanze),* (Beijing: Shehui kexue wenxian chubanshe, 2001); Kang Xiaoguang, 'Chinese Social Organisations in the Era of Transition' *(Zhuanxing shiqi de Zhongguo shetuan)* in: *Chinese Social Organisations at a Crossroads (Chu yu shizilukou de Zhongguo shetuan),* China Youth Development Foundation and Committee on Development Research on Foundations (*eds.*), (Tianjing, Tianjing renmin chubanshe, 2001); He Zengke (ed.), *Civil Society and the Third Sector (Gongmin shehui yu disan bumen),* (Beijing: Shehui kexue wenxian chubanshe, 2000); Zhang Jing (ed.), *State and Society (Guojia yu Shehui),* (Hangzhou: Zhejiang renmin chubanshe, 1998); Chen Jinluo, *Legislation for and Administration of Social Organisations (Shetuan lifa yu shetuan guanli),* (Beijing: Falü Chubanshe, 1997); Bureau of Civic Organisations Management of the Ministry of Civil Affairs (*ed.*), *Handbook for Administrative Work on Social Organisations (Shehui tuanti guanli gongzuo shouce),* (Internal Document, 1996).

3 Professor Wang Ming holds that for most purposes we should recognise two models of control of social organisations, a government choice model and a social choice model. See Wang Ming *et al.* (2001), *supra* note 2.

of activities they can engage in, and when they can be subject to investigation.[4] I would go so far as to say that our understanding of social organisations is located too often within a framework defined by this government control. The second part of this paper looks at how that control increasingly takes place through legislation, in line with the ongoing process of reform in China, and the strengthening of the rule of law. The third part locates the model of control in a framework where the state and society are in a relationship of both opposition and interaction, and analyses the successes and failures of the model, or we could say, its real-world outcomes. Although this model of government control now operates through legislation, it does not stand alone and cannot escape the constraints of the bipolar relationship between state and society.[5] My basic theoretical premise is that given this context of opposition and interaction, a successful model for government administrative control of social organisations will be one that sees a balance between the forces of government and of society.

2 Discussion of the Model

Ever since the founding of the People's Republic of China, the Party and government have paid close attention to the question of social organisations. As early as 1949, the 'Joint Guidelines for the Chinese People's Political Consultative Conference' stated clearly that the people of the People's Republic of China had the right to free association. In 1950 the State Council (*zhengwuyuan)* promulgated China's first administrative regulations on this matter, the 'Temporary Measures for the Registration of Social Organisations' *(Shehui Tuanti Dengji Zanxing Banfa).* The same year saw the Ministry of Internal Affairs *(neiwubu)* issue its 'Detailed Regulations for the Implementation of the Temporary Measures for the Registration of Social Organisations' (*Shehui Tuanti*

4 This view is shared by Kang Xiaoguang: 'Government both exercises control of social organisations through laws, and has the final right of interpretation of those laws. This is apparent not only in that government can at any time ignore legal provisions to rectify or close down social organisations and moreover also retains a monopoly on the process of legislating concerning social organisations.' See Kang Xiaoguang, *supra* note 2, at p. 8.

5 State and society are two parts of a framework or analytical tool used by scholars in recent analyses of social organisations. Several viewpoints have emerged around this analysis, including pluralism theory, statutory body theory and Chinese specialness theory. It will suffice for our purpose to note that these differences exist.

Dengji Zanxing Banfa Shishi Xize). Of course, at the same time as the Party and government were taking positive steps to concede the people's right to free association, they were instituting a crackdown on all kinds of reactionary social organisations left over from pre-revolutionary society, including secret societies with religious background (*huidaomen*). Although the 1949 Measures and their accompanying regulations were not at all complex, they did 'establish the guiding thought and administrative system for managing social organisations at the national level'.[6] Using this approach, the People's Government effected a rapid turn-around in what had been a chaotic situation as regards social organisations, and brought both the very existence and the future development of social organisations into a pathway delimited by government. However, as early as 1964, social organisations were beginning to act independently in their own interests. For example, some legally registered social organisations began to form associations with one another, and sought to find work units to act as their sponsors. This goes to show that the registration measures set out in the early years of new China were no longer adequate to meet the needs of the development and management of social organisations, because they lacked rules that could be applied in the real world.[7] After the Cultural Revolution began in 1966, government, to all intents and purposes, fell into a state of paralysis. Consequently those social organisations operating under government administration ceased to exist in anything but name. At the same time, organisations not under government control, the various Red Guard groups and Struggle Factions sprung up at a ferocious rate. If the protection of rights and interests is the standard by which we measure such social organisations and other organisations, we find a variety of circumstances. Some did indeed protect the safety of some citizens and their property; there were also organisations that harmed the personal and property interests of certain citizens. The majority of organisations at this time engaged in both protection and harm. This is hardly surprising, as the standard by which social organisations' activities were measured at that time was not 'human rights'. After the end of the Cultural Revolution, Chinese society once more set out on the road to modernisation. Keeping pace with the progress of reform and opening and following the rapid growth of the market economy, social organisations became increasingly active once more. The 1982 Constitution gave a clear affirmation of citizen's right to association. Article 35 states that citizens of the People's Republic of China have freedom of

6 Chen Jinluo, *supra* note 2, at p. 19.

7 Bureau of Civic Organisations Management of the Ministry of Civil Affairs, *supra* note 2, at p. 104.

speech, press, assembly, association, procession and demonstration. In 1989, the State Council promulgated the 'Regulations for the Registration of Social Organisations' (*Shehui Tuanti Dengji Tiaoli).* Almost a decade later, with the aim of making administration of social organisations more effective and in the light of accumulated experience, in 1998, the State Council issued revised Regulations. The Party and government had garnered valuable experience through long and complicated years managing China's social organisations. Increasingly, administration of organisations' activities could be effected by following set rules and in a framework of established law.

As ordinary citizens we are the ultimate subjects of a variety of administrative measures of both the Party and government. We do not know how any policy concerning social organisations comes into being; all we have are a certain number of actual policies in this regard laid down at different points in history. However, at the same time as seeking to understand these policies, if we contemplate what has gone before, perhaps we can both sense and even conclude that a model of government administrative control of social organisations does indeed exist as the background to the variety of types and tenor of policy measures. Although this model can only be deduced implicitly, the reality is that it guides and delimits administrative policy. So despite the lack of any complete written account of such a model or of any full statement in this regard in any official document, I am convinced of its existence as the logical inference to be made. In the various research conducted into social organisations to date, little attention has yet been paid to such a model, which is regrettable because this administrative model is both settled and fundamental. Actual policies may be applied loosely or strictly at different times, administrative institutions may or may not act on a given issue, but behind this flexibility we find that the basic principles of administration, that is to say this model, have always stayed the same. With this in mind we can say that such policy as exists for administering social organisations and potential changes to it will only be such as this model supports or permits. The most prominent question concerning this model is naturally 'What is it?' and this, in my opinion, ought to be the starting point for our research into this issue. Only once we have answered this can we get into how we ought to approach the wider questions.

2.1 The Implications of the Government's Administrative Model

By 'government's administrative model', I mean the fairly fixed methods adopted by responsible government agencies when overseeing the creation, activities or disbanding of social organisations.[8] The key point here is that decisions about the existence and development of social organisations are made by government. We know of officials responsible for the administration of social organisations who admit that 'management of social organisations is an important part of overall state management.'[9] This model has at least two identifiable characteristics. First, the model controls the whole life-cycle of Chinese social organisations 'from the cradle to the grave'. During some periods in history, government agencies exercised a very detailed control. For example, establishing a social group required staff to be assigned under official administrative regulations, and disbanding the group required first finding new placements for the people who worked there. Second, the model has not only existed for a considerable period of time; thanks to continued practical application and learning from accumulated experience, it can now be said to have been perfected to a high degree. It encompasses the fundamental principles of government control, its objectives and the structure and policies through which that control is exercised. The model has little place for individual initiative or spur of the moment decision making. That is to say, changes to the model by and large do not happen due to internal factors or at the inspiration of an enlightened official, but as a consequence of external factors and of the Party and government's conception of the core aims of their work. Changes to the model only come when there are changes to those core aims. This is because the model is at base a product of the need to implement the core tasks of Party and government.

We should be aware that the model for government administrative control of social organisations which currently applies has a historical pedigree. It is intimately connected with planned economy implemented by the Chinese government from the 1950s lasting through until the 1970s. Indeed it can be called a by-product of this period of intense centralism, because the underlying thinking of the model – of the control and organisation of everything by the state – is entirely of a piece with the planned economy strategy. And it goes without saying it is also consistent with centralisation of power that was also the policy advocated in China at that time. Of course, the administrative model was also influenced by the legacy of pre-revolutionary Chinese society where 'all the earth under Heaven was His Majesty's earth and all the land between

8 Professor Wang Ming calls this 'government-chosen', meaning that it is the agents of government who have the final decision in the establishment, activities and disbanding of social organisations. Wang Ming *et al.*, (2001), *supra* note 2, at p. 64.

9 Chen Jinluo, *supra* note 2, at p. 23.

the seas was administered by His Majesty's ministers', a dogma that still exists in the subconscious of many of the current governing class. This subconscious understanding serves to some degree in sustaining the government's monopoly status in terms of all decision making in China. The end result of a combination of these various factors is that for all practical purposes government administration of social organisations can be equated with total government control of social organisations. They are organised according to the principles of government logic, they are subject to government administrative control and, in certain ways, themselves serve as an extension of that control.

2.2 Observing the Development of Social Organisations in China

When we consider the lessons that can be drawn from the development of social organisations in China since 1949, certain features command our attention. First, the conceptual framework associated with Western NGOs 'is not an entirely effective analytical tool'.[10] This is to say, since social organisations lack any genuine independence, and since there was no other possible way for them to develop, they are and have always been one of the numerous subjects of government administrative control. It also means that the internal logic of the development of social organisations in China is entirely subsidiary to that of the government. For this reason, among China's social organisations, all those that have properly registered legal status are either fully or partially government-organised, whereas the majority of popular grassroots organisations remain unregistered. Second, the various ways in which government exercises administrative control over social organisations do not operate in isolation – they are interconnected and can be regarded as an essential component of quite a comprehensive model. If we do not understand this model we cannot say anything of any value regarding current administrative practise, and the best we can do is merely apply a piecemeal approach to the consideration of a series of issues. Third, by explaining this model we also explore and discover the actual relationship between laws and society in China. In one sense, an explanation of this model represents a cross-section through which we can observe society, where we can see how the operation of an actual administrative framework impacts social organisations' own ability to exist and thrive. We can also see to what extent the law can actually be effectively implemented in China. Indeed, in considering this ques-

10 Kang Xiaoguang, *supra* note 2, at p. 6.

tion we may find out a great deal about phenomena that legal textbooks are unable to explain.

2.3 The Basic Substance of the Government Administrative Model

2.3.1 The Government's Basic Concept Toward Social Organisations

In official formulations social organisations have a variety of functions: they represent an actualisation of the masses' role in the New China as 'masters in their own house', and serve as helpers to Party and government.[11] Later, as social organisations developed over time, there came a change in the way that the above formulations were interpreted. The currently prevailing interpretation is first, that since social organisations exist to represent the interests of a given section of the population, the government can use such organisations as a medium for learning what the people are thinking, and likewise the people can use social organisations as a means of expressing their opinions to the government or some functional part thereof.[12] Second, social organisations should engage in activities designed to promote public welfare. The bottom line is that social organisations serve as a bridge and a link between the Party and government and the popular masses. Within the confines of this basic understanding, there are specific functions for social organisations to perform, for example they can invigorate the market economy, they can play a positive role in the construction of socialist modernisation, they can promote the traditional moral values of the Chinese nation, they can promote international exchanges, and so forth.

One feature of the government's concept of social organisations is the emphasis placed on their playing a positive role in society, for example what they can do to help the Party and government achieve their stated goals and

11 Chen Jinluo lists as features of social organisations that 'they act as a bridge and connection for mutual interaction between the Party and government and the broad masses'; that they 'are the main way in which the people exercise their role as masters in their own house'; and that they 'are helpers for Party and government'. Chen Jinluo, *supra* note 2, at p. 5.

12 Duoji Cairang, 'Actively Foster, Improve Management, Promote the Healthy Development of Civil Society Organisations', in Bureau of Civic Organisations Management of the Ministry of Civil Affairs, *A Selection of Recent Regulations and Policies Concerning the Administration of Civil Society Organisations (Youguan minjian zuzhi guanli zuixin fagui zhengce zhaibian)*, (internal document, 1998), at p. 73.

the part they can play in the protection of citizen's rights. Put another way, defining an entity by reference to its function usually means that one is not considering the intrinsic nature of the entity itself but merely drawing conclusions by external observation. In the normal course of affairs the nature of a something is taken to be some quality inherent to it, and this is the essence of what distinguishes it from some other thing. Functions, on the other hand, are merely the external manifestations of that nature. Since this is the case, it seems we must then consider the actual nature of social organisations. So what is it? It is an autonomous collective formed voluntarily by citizens or non-citizens (foreigners) for the purpose of pursuing some joint objective. In most cases social organisations are the result of exercising the right to free association granted to them by the constitution and protected by the law.

2.3.2 The Guiding Thought Behind the Administration of Social Organisations

In line with this view of the function of social organisations, the guiding thinking of the government's administration of them follows four objectives. The first is the objective of a standardised administration of social organisations. This objective can de defined as ensuring that the existence and development of social organisations is beneficial to national economic growth and social stability. One could even go so far as to say that all, and only, social organisations that are beneficial to these latter two goals are the ones allowed to grow, whilst naturally all those who cannot promote prosperity and stability are subject to restrictions. Wen Jiabao, speaking in 1994, said 'Grasping opportunities, deepening reform, expanding openness, promoting development, maintaining stability – this is the big picture of the work for the Party as a whole.'[13] He went on to express the hope that social organisations in China, including the China Association for Science and Technology whom he was addressing at the time, would have a clear understanding of this big picture and align their own work to be of service to it. Secondly, government officials emphasise both social organisations fully and actively fulfilling their perceived functions, and also the strengthening of administrative control. Current parlance expresses this as 'an equal emphasis on development and supervision'. However it appears that the trend is in fact to stress the administration and supervision side of this equation. The third objective is to make clear the current tasks of

13 Speech by Wen Jiabao on the 27th February 1994 to the Fourth Plenary Session of the China Association for Science and Technology. Quoted in Bureau of Civic Organisations Management of the Ministry of Civil Affairs, *supra* note 2.

administrative control. The government wishes to establish mechanisms for administrative management, including a legal and regulatory system and associated policies; but at the same time in order to improve its administrative control the government is planning to adopt a number of measures. The first of these is to draft development plans for social organisations, and bring the existence and growth of social organisations in line with the plans for economic growth and social development and also the realities of their local situation. The second is to improve capacity building for organisations so that they reduce dependence on government as far as is possible. The third is to place the administration of social organisations within a legislative framework. The fourth is to enhance the overall effectiveness of supervision and control. Lastly, the government wants to modernise the administration of social organisations, computerising records and other relevant information and improving speedy communication amongst social organisations and between organisations and government agencies. But it has to be said that for a long time now there have in fact been 'two different kinds of guiding thinking'[14] behind government administration of social organisations. Is the goal to protect citizen's right to association or to limit it? Many contradictory factors add to the complexity of this question – there is a general acceptance of the need to protect and even extend the right to free association, but also constant calls for limits to be placed on it; also while there is official approval of the exercise of the right of association it is paradoxically coupled with consistent resort to measures which limit and curtail that right.

2.3.3 Re-examining the System of Control

In terms of a social group's official license for achieving of legal status, China implements a system summed up as 'registration by the appropriate agency, dual administrative control, and administration at the appropriate level'. 'Registration by the appropriate agency' means that only the Ministry of Civil Affairs or its line agencies at county level and above can register social organisations (no other agency has this power). On completion of the approval process the Ministry agency will issue a 'Certificate of Registration as a Legal Person for Social Organisations'. 'Dual administrative control' describes how, in the process of establishing a social group, approval must first be sought from a sponsor agency (*yewu zhuguan danwei*), only then can a group proceed to

14 Chen Jinluo, *supra* note 2, at p. 20.

registration with the Ministry or one of its agencies at county level or higher as stipulated in the 'Regulations on Administration of Registration of Social Organisations'. 'Administration at the appropriate level' refers to the stipulation that social organisations which operate on a national level will register with the central Ministry, whereas local organisations will register with line agencies of the Ministry at the appropriate county or higher level, which is a means of making clear the scope for organisations' recruitment of members and conduct of activities. National level organisations can recruit members and conduct activities countrywide, local organisations only in their local area.

If one considers the practice of Western nations, one can discern two different general strands of thinking concerning the establishment and activities of social organisations: a 'preventative system' and a 'punishment system'. The former requires organisations to register with the appropriate agency upon formation; the latter doesn't require this but allows for governments to penalise or punish organisations should they violate law or regulation after they have been formed. The rules for registration of social organisations in China can be called the basic system by which the issue is dealt with here. The key is that through the mechanism of registration the government can keep a constant check on the overall state of social group activity and place them under the purview of state control. In this sense the registration system is a major component of the model for the administrative control of social organisations. If we attempt a summary we find that although the Ministry of Civil Affairs has the various administrative mechanisms outlined above, underlying them are just two consistent objectives. One is standardisation and limitation, seeking to make social organisations develop in a way stipulated by government; the other is protection and service, that is creating the conditions for organisations to exist and grow, and providing various services to help them carry out their activities.

As well as acting as gatekeepers of whether or not a group can be set up, government sponsor agencies can have a group's registration revoked if they are found to be engaging in activities that are illegal or not expressly allowed; moreover they may at any time instigate clean-up and rectification campaigns which strip organisations of their legal status. Naturally these campaigns serve to illustrate the government's status as controller of social organisations and final arbiter of matters concerning them. Figures show that since 1949 there have been four large-scale rectification campaigns, in 1951, 1990, 1997,[15] and

15 Wang Ming *et al.* (2001), *supra* note 2, at pp. 100-103.

most recently in June of 2003, when 63 national level social organisations were closed down.

2.3.4 Administrative Personnel

Of course, the implementation of an administrative model needs the existence and activities of administrative personnel. A document from 1992 states that:

> [c]urrently, each of the 30 provinces, autonomous regions and directly administered cities that make up the country have established departments or offices for the administration of social organisations with a total assigned staff of 217 cadres. 270 prefectural cities or districts of directly administered cities and 700 counties or county level cities have also established agencies for administering socials organisations, with 605 and 726 full or part-time staff respectively.[16]

These figures show that provincial-level agencies for administration of social organisations had on average only around seven staff; at prefectural level there were something less than two staff per office, whilst at county level the average number of staff was just above one person. Staffing levels like this were definitely out of step with the level of growth of social organisations. However, we are certain that today the staffing level has doubled. To take Shanghai as an example, prior to 1999 there were only 60 cadres responsible for administering social organisations in the county-level districts and divisions of the city. That year the municipal Party Committee and government approved the establishment of a sub-departmental level Bureau of Social Group Administration with a staff of 50, which nearly doubled the total administrative staff in Shanghai.[17]

At the same time we can see that not only does government administration of social organisations require administrative personnel, it can also not escape the prioritisation of that personnel's own interests. These administrators have undoubtedly worked very hard and achieved a great deal, but it has to be said that in their interpretation and implementation of policy they always seem to place their own interests if not first, at least very high up the list of priorities.

16 Bureau of Civic Organisations Management of the Ministry of Civil Affairs, *supra* note 2.

17 Bureau of Civic Organisations Management of the Ministry of Civil Affairs, *Collected Recent Regulations and Policy Concerning the Administration of Civic Organisations (Minjian zuzhi guanli zuijin fagui zhengce huibian)*, (internal document, 2000), at p. 141.

This means that the implementation of policy, and indeed the exercise by citizens of their constitutional rights comes to depend on the existence of this bureaucratic class. Take as an example the principle of dual administrative control. This is not, of course, something that social organisations want; quite the contrary, it is one of the administrative practices they are most eager to see reformed. It is of course a great advantage to officials of the Ministry of Civil Affairs. Such a policy not only gives them the role of final arbiters in the registration of social organisations, it also exposes them to the least possible risk in exercising their power, because prior to even applying for registration a social group must first be checked and approved by a so-called sponsoring agency.

2.3.5 Inseparable Twins: Support and Restriction

Like Chinese society as a whole in the current period of transition, the administrative model for the control of social organisations is bipolar in structure. Specifically, since the model is asked to simultaneously exercise administrative control over social organisations and to maintain a constant consistency with central policy, it unavoidably displays features aimed at satisfying these two requirements. The guiding principle of such a structure is to place controls on the development of social organisations. It takes the standpoint of the government or its agencies as its point of departure and striving to avoid the development of social organisations getting out of control, with the consequent dangers to overall social stability. At the same time, from time to time another secondary principle is seen accompanying this core imperative, though it is not always apparent: an encouragement of the development of social organisations based on an understanding of what they actually are and a respect for citizen's legitimate rights. In the normal course of events this secondary principle cannot be separated from the core task. The prevailing situation is one of growth under restrictions and restrictions accompanying growth. However, this secondary principle is not always obscured in the shadow of the core imperative of control. Quite the reverse, there is always the opportunity for this secondary principle to redirect the objectives of the administrative model such that it can more fully reflect social demand. There are even times when the secondary principle can take on a guiding role.

The administrative model outlined above of course has its own theoretical premise or assumption and it is this that explains how such a model comes to be. The presumption is that the state or government is the final arbiter of all social life and the government must as far as possible exercise complete control over all aspects of it. Put another way, the work of social organisations is part of the overall work of the Party and government and hence it should be an embodiment of the relevant policy directives. The common perception is that social organisations are almost without exception actually officially run and agencies of either the Party or the government. China has operated under the principle of the leading role of the Party for such a long time that we all accept that 'the Chinese Communist Party is the core force guiding our endeavours'. For both historical and pragmatic reasons, the Party and government enjoy enormous popular prestige and they have many great accomplishments. So comrades responsible for social group work should have a full understanding of the relevant policies of the Party and government and carry them out in their day-to-day work, making that work subject to adjustment by policy directive. This is moreover something the Party and government require. 'Civil Affairs agencies must establish the principle that their social organisations work, follow and serve the Party's overall task and goals'.[18] From this perspective, the development and achievements of social group work result from the leadership of the Party and government. Thus the generally held belief in Civil Affairs agencies is that the organs responsible for registering and administering social organisations should facilitate the growth of social organisations as an extension of the core work of the Party and enable social organisations to have the best possible effect on and role in social development. Seen another way, if some aspect of social life is not administered and managed then the government is failing in its duties. On a deeper level this is connected to a political theory of the all-encompassing state. However, social praxis in the post-reform era has shown that this presumption no longer holds. For one, the government has already publicly admitted that in the past it controlled many aspects of society it should not have, and moreover did it badly. Now the government's public stance is that the goal of reform of its role is 'small government and big society'. Deputy Minister for Civil Affairs Fan Baojun, in a speech given on the 16th September, 1992 stated 'Small government and big society is an inevitable trend of historical development'.[19] Subsequently, then member of the State Council, Chen Jun, said 'One of the important directions of our reform of the political system is towards small government and big society. The growth of social organisations is an important part of that big society.'[20] This means

18 See the speech by Chen Junsheng quoted in Bureau of Civic Organisations Management of the Ministry of Civil Affairs (*ed.*) *supra* note 2, at p. 99.

19 *Ibid.*, at p. 105.

20 *Ibid.*, at p. 99.

that one of the goals of the change in government's role is the creation of a state that is no longer all-encompassing, and the return to wider society of many of the powers government had formerly taken over. Seen in this light, the evident abdication of powers and privileges that are a part of government reform go not only to the individual citizen but should also go to various types of social collective. Exploring this question more deeply, we find that as well as the common understanding that social organisations are something the government should be controlling there is also a perception that organisations not subject to government control are not to be trusted. Taken to the extreme they are considered anarchic elements. We should however recognise that in everyday life we encounter social organisations of all kinds, some that are closely associated with the government, some that are neutral in this respect, and some that cause the government significant discomfort. The nature of organisations will doubtless change frequently as society continues to develop. Any attempt to force social organisations to develop in one particular way will have little chance of success. Moreover, the problem is that one or other of the various types of social organisations are not dispensable since their existence *in toto* constitutes the natural order of civil society. Mutual interaction between the various types of organisations has a naturally limiting effect that creates an atmosphere which prevents the emergence of really extreme organisations. The reality is that so long as those organisations which do not entirely accord with government expectations conduct their activities in accordance with the existing laws then they should be allowed to exist, because in the end social organisations are independent entities with their own developmental logic.

3 Using Legislation to Apply the Government Administrative Model

The use of legislative measures to administer the activities of social organisations has been a process that has developed gradually in China. While it was the case in the early days of New China that there were the temporary measures governing the registration of organisations and also detailed stipulations for their implementation, for various reasons despite the part the measures played in establishing the framework under which social organisations have been administratively controlled in China, for an extended period of modern history the administration of social organisations in China has been flexible and subsumed into overall government administrative control. Hence it can be said that this happened without reliance on laws or regulations. In everyday practice the government relied on overall policy in this regard, since it was these policies that enabled administrators to resolve the specific problems they were faced with. Later, during the Cultural Revolution, as normal government ground to a halt, so too administrative control of social organisations was largely absent.

3.1 The Process of Legislation and its Key Characteristics

There have already been two occasions when legislative measures were introduced in the period since reform and opening. The first came in 1989 when the State Council issued its Regulations for the Registration and Administration of Social Organisations (*Shehui Tuanti Dengji Guanli Tiaoli*). The second came in 1998, when the State Council revised the 1989 Regulations. These have also been called the 'new Regulations'. These two legislative actions share some common features worthy of our attention. First, the Regulations represent a fairly full embodiment of the core principle of government administrative control, namely placing restrictions on social organisations. More specifically, restrictions were placed on the number of social organisations and also the activities they could undertake.[21] The 1989 Regulations drawn up by the State Council may be considered to be an expression of their understanding of the political unrest of that year; however, the fact that the same core spirit is upheld in the 'new Regulations' issued in 1998 after the changes in the role of government that came in response to the growth of the market economy, and with social organisations now invested with new powers passed on to them in the government reform, could lead one to the conclusion that 'the words no longer fit the picture'. Second, the legislation is both a summation of past administrative practice and an attempt at innovation. On the one hand, the Regulations are of course a summary expression of accumulated experience in the practice of administering social organisations, as can be seen in a number of the clauses; on the other hand, we must be aware that certain of the stipulations in the Regulations have no precedent in prior praxis and are innovations. Of these, the system of dual administrative control is the most obvious example. Although the general belief is that the Temporary Regulations of 1950 formed the basic legislative framework for the administration of social organisations in the years that followed, there is no mention of the dual control system to be found in

21 It has been noted that 'from the 1990s the overall tenor of government administration of social organisations was an emphasis on restriction'. See Kang Xiaoguang, *supra* note 2, at p. 18.

them. That is to say there was no regulation requiring social organisations to find a sponsoring agency. It was the 1989 Regulations that required Chinese social organisations to have two overseeing agencies, their sponsoring agency and their registration agency. This situation was continued in the 'new Regulations' of 1998. In fact this requirement caused quite a number of problems between social organisations and their registering and sponsoring agencies. This came in part because when seeking to set up a new group, gaining the approval of a sponsor was no guarantee of gaining the approval of the registrar. This meant that a sponsor's approval was merely a precondition, but the system served to divide the risk formerly entirely undertaken by the Ministry of Civil Affairs. Should Civil Affairs register a group that later caused problems, the sponsoring agency would be the ones to bear the brunt of any criticism that resulted from the mistake. Furthermore, since the question of social organisations is politically sensitive and since potential sponsors have neither the ability nor the desire to administer them, many already extant social organisations are hard pressed to find an appropriate agency willing to act as their sponsor. This then means they achieve legitimate registered status. In sum, in this kind of administrative model legislation does have a role, and we may expect that role to expand in the future. If we agree that this is so, then perhaps one day when the core work of Party and government is not simply economic growth but instituting the rule of law in all aspects of social life, then we may expect the administrative model to also embody that same goal and to play a part in its realisation. But as we have noted, in everyday practice government officials are most likely to follow policy rather than the letter of the law.

3.2 The Possibilities for Administration through Legislation

As reform has progressed and with the gradual strengthening of socialist democracy we have seen legislation become a part of the administrative model. Put another way, the administrative model has already assumed a legislative basis through the introduction of various laws and regulations concerning the administration of social organisations. This shows that the model we described above does not in itself completely preclude the existence of legislation. The problem I would like to address now is under what circumstances a move to administration through legislation would be possible. Of course there are a number of factors that affect this. There are the instructions given by senior national leaders, though of course in terms of our model despite their provenance these are still external factors. Are there factors inherent to the model that can allow it to move from excluding legislation as a means of administration to its acceptance? The reality is that if an administrative model is fundamentally opposed to working through law then even if external intervention tries to force the issue it will not necessarily be effective. In my view the main reason that the prevailing model has been able to incorporate new legislation is that space already existed within it thanks to the administrative methods and tools already employed. The government has taken the laws to be a way of improving its administrative toolset. This is to say changing to administration through legislation encounters no obstacles in terms of pre-existing government thinking on the matter. As long as it is seen as improving administrative control, a new measure would be acceptable be it legislative, economic or administrative in form; moreover it can be happily employed at the same time as measures of other types. The deeper problem is that, although legislation can find its place in the prevailing administrative model and even by its presence give rise to a new openness, at the same time the nature of the model will be what determines the ultimate fate of the law as it is applied.

3.3 The Actual Nature of Administration through Legislation

Because of the prevailing fundamental realities in China, the increasing use of legislation to implement the model of control has by no means meant that the law has been seen as a set of rules for both government and social organisations to follow. On the contrary – and perhaps this can be seen as quite normal – it has meant that the law has become a tool that serves the administrative model. Or we could say that the prevailing model would only allow the law as a tool not a law that prescribes the goals of administration. Or else that administration through legislation results in the law becoming another tool for the government to control social organisations with. There are complex reasons for this. First, this kind of legislative practice is related to our accustomed definition of what the law is. For a long time we have seen laws as embodiments of the will of the state: they are tools through which the state governs. In reality, although this understanding did at one time serve a purpose, it has been out of date for quite some time. The experience of other countries, and our own in the reform era, tells us that the true nature of laws is that, apart from the instrumental aspect, they also serve to mediate between various interest groups in society – that is, to serve as a way of balancing those competing interests. If the law serves merely as a tool for the administrative control of social organisations and does nothing to limit and restrain the power of government, not only is it completely at odds with the spirit of reform and mobilising popular enthusiasm, but it will also cause social organisations to do everything they can to avoid legal limits on their activities and rely instead on the protection of administrative powers or individual prestige. When this is the case, administrative control or control by legislation is helpless and ends ultimately with legislative control existing in name only. But the law is not a static tool; it tends to grow and gradually expand its role. As the socialist market economy and democratic politics develop, the law will no longer be content to serve as a mere tool; it will seek to set limits on both social organisations and the government's control over them. It will seek to aid not only government in exercising control, but also to assist citizens in exercising their rights. It will limit both the controlled and the controller, but should most of all protect citizens' rights. In the final analysis the law encourages a spirit of equality and seeks to protect the freedoms of citizenship.

3.4 The Current Dilemma of Law

In response to the demands of social development and political change, after hard struggles, and despite countless obstacles, we have gradually moved towards a model of administrative control of social organisations based on law. However, since the legislative process lags behind social development, new problems have arisen which have left the legislation already in place facing problems of reform. A great number of causes gave rise to this situation, some more important than others. First, as the socialist market economy has grown and socialist democratic politics developed, so the expansion in social organisations has been extremely rapid. The prevailing administrative model has not been able to keep pace with this, meaning that quite a number of social organisations, especially the 'grassroots' organisations, are left outside the ambit of registered legal status. Moreover, for a variety of reasons, these organisations which, as the law stands, should be considered illegal are able to openly conduct their business and avoid any legal limit to their activities. So we have on the one hand a model of administrative control that encompasses legislation, and on the other, a considerable number of organisations operating beyond the law. Second, Chinese society is developing towards a 'small government, big society' model. This makes the rapid rise of social organisations to take over what were previously government functions an important goal. But problems caused by the administrative model make such development painfully slow and far from achieving its goal. Various social organisations show a tendency to develop along the model of government-run organisations. This will mean that government will remain 'big government' seemingly in control of everything and society will remain weak and underdeveloped. Third, the current level of legislation in the overall legislative order is low. In China according to Chinese laws on legislation, the Constitution is the highest law, below that there are the basic laws, then laws, then administrative regulations and measures. For a variety of reasons, at least at the time of writing, laws in China concerning social organisations are at a legislative level equivalent to administrative regulations. They are quite some way below the power of the relevant provisions in the Constitution. They are of a lesser type, and moreover there is little in the way of intermediate legislation between these two extremes. Only with intermediate legislation would we have something appropriate to the important status that the activities of social organisations have in social life. Hence, in terms of a legislative programme, we need to draft a 'Law on Association' or a 'Popular Organisations Law' as a means of implementing the provisions of the Constitution and guiding the drafting of measures covering the specific issues of social group administration.

In China, laws do not occupy a central place in the government's administrative model. First, for a long time now, the government's administration of social organisations has been based on policy decisions, even to the point that the decision as to whether or not to draft regulations on social group administration and when to draft them was a result of policy. In the minds of many comrades, especially those actually responsible for its implementation, the administration of social organisations is work that falls into the category of politics and policy. Second, when compared to the exponential growth of social organisations and their activities, China's regulations concerning their regulation seem pitifully few and hard to actually implement. This leaves a lot of blank areas. Third, although these regulations do exist government still exercises management of social organisations through administrative measures.[22] This can be seen not only in the constant calls from government officials for increased staffing of administrative agencies, but also in the fact that the existing regulations have yet to be given judicial force and the courts have as yet no role in deciding disputes concerning social organisations. Consequently we hardly have case precedents as regards social organisations, and moreover this also means that

22 Some leading comrades have stated clearly that the agencies responsible for administration of social organisations are part of the government and their work is an important part of state administrative work. See Bureau of Civic Organisations Management of the Ministry of Civil Affairs, *supra* note 2, at p. 128.

government administrative agencies have little choice but to exercise total oversight over social organisations, with little means for outsiders to understand what difficulties such work presents. At one point in time, the Bureau of Civic Organisations Management of the Ministry of Civil Affairs *(Mingjian zuzhi guanliju)* had only 20 staff responsible for overseeing 1,810 organisations.[23] Of course, the problem may not be quite so simple. Perhaps we also suffer from another tendency – we attach importance to legislating but not to implementing the resulting laws. To put it even more starkly, we attach importance to the drafting of laws and regulations but relatively little importance to their implementation, especially their implementation by judicial agencies. This also shows that the laws currently permitted have limited space in which to play an effective role. The currently existing laws are only 'legislative law', laws on paper only, not living laws. I even feel that, for some comrades, laws and regulations are merely a framework and are even in a certain sense dead, whereas policy provides detailed rules for day-to-day implementation and is alive. Policy can change the essential meanings of laws and regulations, broadening their scope or narrowing it. This makes policy extremely important. It is said that a new law on social organisations is currently being drafted. We ought to think about the prevailing government administrative framework. If we do not, even if we use a new vocabulary and bring out some new rules and regulations, what will it actually mean?[24] In the end, if there is no change in how we understand this issue, social organisations will still not have the space they require to develop in.

23 *Ibid.*, at p. 133.

24 In speeches made by officials charged with administering social organisations we can perceive the following logic: they encourage everyone to get going under the rules as they presently stand and then look forward to future legislation. We may perhaps admit such a logic serves the purposes of day to day administrative work, since it speaks to practical experience and the pattern that can be inferred from the random phenomena of past practice. However, for one thing, most unregistered social organisations are in fact actively carrying out activities, albeit we can call these 'rootless' activities that may be forbidden at any time. Also, this kind of thinking goes against legal logic. Legal logic says that we first recognise a principle and then after intense critical consideration express that principle in concrete terms and give it a written form. More importantly still, legal logic requires that we respect the law, not that we attempt to break it or find loopholes in it, doing what we please because we find it convenient.

4 The Real-world Effects of the Administrative Model

If, however, we consider the real-world effects of this kind of administrative model then it is indeed far from ideal. Related documentation shows that this model has a direct effect only on a limited number of social organisations, something less than a fifth, or maybe a tenth of the current total of social organisations.[25] The enormous number of social organisations that are not registered with the Ministry of Civil Affairs have carried on doing their own thing regardless.[26] This is a phenomenon worthy of further analysis. This is a classic example of group behaviour used to get around formal state controls. It is also widespread. For example, the self-same tactic is used, whether consciously or unconsciously, by individual traders trying to get around Bureau of Industry and Commerce regulations governing the renting of commercial premises and counter space.[27] This further shows that, so far as social organisations or individual traders are concerned, formal state norms of behaviour are not an authority to be overly worried about. If a social group or a trader can get the support, be it active or tacit, of some authority (individual or institutional) it doesn't matter what state norms allow, so long as one proceeds with caution and doesn't do anything too out of the ordinary. It is worth noting that the period in which the administrative model was taking shape also saw large-scale growth of social organisations in terms of both total number and types,[28] and also a growth in the size of individual organisations and their social impact. For this reason there emerged an obvious disparity between the model as it

25 Scholars have noted that in 1996 there were 44, 000 social organisations in China with the status of legal persons, which means that of the social organisations recognised and registered by the Minister of Civil Affairs, only about a fifth have the status of legal persons. (See Kang Xiaoguang, *supra* note 2.)

26 *Id.*

27 Xiang Biao points out that in the period of transition from an old system to a new one, one coping strategy adopted by people who find some regulation inconvenient is not directly to seek its reform but just to get around it somehow. Such behaviour may not necessarily lead to a change in the written rules, but can cause them to be a great deal less effective. See Xiang Biao, 'Mobilisation, the Marketisation of Traditional Networks, and Non-state Spaces' *(Liudong, chuantong wangluo shichanghua yu feiguojia kongjian)*, in: Zhang Jing (ed.), *State and Society (Guojia yu shehui)*, (Hangzhou: Zhejiang renmin chubanshe, 1998), at p. 146.

28 Here I am assuming that all social organisations share the same basic nature. Although something of a simplification, it has no bearing on the credibility of the reasoning and explanation presented in the main text.

was conceived to be, and its actual ability to limit social organisations, which is something worthy of further investigation.[29] The common belief is that if an administrative control model is established, it ought to be able to play a part in limiting the real-world activity it has been set up to restrict and make it operate within the norms prescribed by the model. Put another way, government's logic of control is that the more total and direct that control is, the better it should be capable of ruthlessly suppressing anything. From this perspective, any gaps in administrative control or any areas of life that cannot be directly controlled represent a failure of government management. However, in a real-world situation where state and society are both in opposition and mutually interact, the government does not always have the final say in everything. As well as the government's logic there is also a logic of social development which says that the more freedom there is the better, and the less control exercised the better. This social development logic can limit the absolute implementation of government control. Government logic in its turn limits social development, preventing its full and free flourishing.

4.1 State and Society

For a considerable time after Liberation in 1949 there was no division between the state and society, social collectives were swallowed whole by the state and the state controlled all aspects of society. Administrative control penetrated down to the most basic units of Chinese society, including even family life. However, this interpenetration of state and society began to be broken up beginning in the late 1970s. The reforms instituted under government leadership since that time have been characterised as a 'loosening of restrictions'[30] guided by a principle of 'abdicating powers and benefits.'[31] By maintaining this guiding principle in reform, various elements of society were successfully mobilised allowing for the 'Chinese economic miracle' that followed. The government's

29 This is quite a common phenomenon in China. A similar situation can be seen in the development of Zhejiang Village, a migrant trader community in southern Beijing. At certain periods of the Village's development the government chose to turn a blind eye to a number of practices there, giving them tacit support and sometimes even encouragement. See Zhang Jing (ed.), *supra* note 27, at p. 146.

30 Xia Yong, (ed.), *Towards An Age of Rights (Zou xiang quanli de shidai)*, revised and expanded edition (Beijing: Zhongguo zhengfa daxue chubanshe, 2001).

31 Some scholars characterise the past decade or more in China as one where this 'abdication of powers and benefits' was the guiding principle. See Wang Shaoguang and Hu

'abdication of powers and benefits'[32] encouraged the sudden upsurge of social forces. For example social organisations and new media enterprises rushed in to fill the spaces left by a retreating government and the newcomers met with the public's approval. But at the same time it also gave rise to a number of difficulties for the government, in terms of imposing its decisions and desires. Some scholars took to considering these problems as part of an insufficiency of government capacity.

The relationship between state and society is one kind of analytical tool or framework. That is to say, it can be used as a way of explaining certain current issues in Chinese society, for example the issue of rights, which naturally includes the right to free association. Of course, scholars differ in their views about this.[33] As an analytical framework, the emphasis is on explaining an issue or phenomenon in the context of the interactive relationship between the state and society, and thus arriving at a truer and more fundamental understanding. Although many scholars are talking about this relationship these days, and

Angang, The Decline and Consequence in Capacity of the Chinese Government's Ability to Derive (Zhongguo zhengfu xiqu nengli de xiajiang jiqi houguo) in Zhang Jing, *supra* note 27, at p. 4.

32 This process was marked by the following characteristics: first, since this was an area of life formerly subject to government control, the 'abdication of powers and benefits' amounted in reality to a complete withdrawal from the sector. Although directives from the Party and government had already made the scope and limits of this abdication clear, for a complex of reasons the old administrative thinking, mechanisms and model remained as part of the make-up of those cadres who had served under the old system. They also had a lingering influence on popular ideology, limiting the thinking and behaviour of both officials and ordinary citizens. Second, an abdication of this kind could only take place in stages. When the government withdrew it did so gradually, avoiding a 'shock therapy' approach and making the process reasonably orderly. Natural this method of withdrawal was decided upon by the government, and was undertaken in accordance with the government's assessment of prevailing trends. Third, an abdication of this kind can often be a case of wanting to withdraw but actually entering further, or a combination of retreat and advance at the same time. Even as it withdrew from various sectors the government kept itself ready to re-enter them at any time if it deemed that necessary. Indeed the government planned and deliberately undertook further controls in new areas periodicly. This was of course a complicated and confusing process. Fourth, as government abdicated powers, citizens began to exercise their rights. Of course, in the prevailing conditions this too happened in small stages, in a trial and error fashion and in different ways for different people, indeed even in ways that were actually repeated.

33 Professor Ji Weidong believes that a bipolar schema of society and state in opposition is not suited to the situation in China. See Ji Weidong, 'The One Inevitable Error of the Critics' *(Pipanzhede qianlü yuyishi)*, in Zhang Jing, *supra* note 27, at p. 40.

using it as an analytical framework, they often lack the supplementary concepts or judgements required to sustain such an approach. Without these, any such analysis is empty and ultimately disingenuous. Indeed, without support of such concepts, no such analysis is even possible. For this reason, I want to offer two judgements on the state and society respectively made in the light of the relationship between the two in the transitional period. The state can be characterised as proactive but not as all-encompassing; society as passive, but extremely vigorous. For the former, the state had a guiding role in reform but for a variety of reason was not always able to fully realise its objectives. As to the latter, although society or social elements were not progenitors, once mobilised they were extremely vigorous and were difficult to completely extinguish. Some may say that judging the relationship to dovetail so neatly, seeing the state and society to be so mutually complementary, is overly simplistic. It is of course to some extent a simplification and it ignores some of the complexities of the state-society relationship. But analysing the issues in the light of these extreme conditions is likely to reveal certain special characteristics that are influential even in a complex environment and is thus worth the attempt. Looking at the state, firstly we can see that a thorough implementation of the model for administrative control of social organisations demands a lot of resources or capacity; for example, it requires administrative staff at the various levels of government throughout the country with access to an appropriate level of resources. However, the abdication of powers and benefits has left the government short of capacity and it finds it hard to apply the model to the very deepest levels of society as it desires. Second, since control now operates on a legislative basis it shares the general characteristics of Chinese law as it stands at the present time, one of which is that it is hard to implement. Moreover, its new legislative basis means it is no longer the only rational and authoritative model prevailing in society. The reality is that the government's abdication of powers and benefits has created a number of new social demands and new social forces. In certain social environments and at certain times their power and influence can compete with that of the government's administrative model in some respects. Examples include the growth of the market economy, the deepening of democratic reforms, traditions or customs unique to certain areas,[34] a degree of local autonomy,[35] or the personal prestige of certain indi-

34 Writers as far back as Weber have observed that the power of patriarchal organisations could often be more effective than that of state laws and even at times be able to contest the operation of those laws. Ji Weidong, *id.*

35 Some scholars note that when local forces are well resourced they are emboldened. First

vidual leaders; any of these may be decisive factors in the growth and flourishing of a social group. Viewed in this light, we probably need to say a little more about those unregistered social organisations which are 'doing as they please'; since they are indeed carrying out activities without being registered they can be accused of pleasing themselves, but not really in the fullest sense. In the current social environment these organisations can only be operating with the support or tacit approval of some authoritative agency or personage outside of the normal legal framework; otherwise there is no way they could carry on. Third, as reform has progressed, as social forces have grown and as the government no longer has sufficient resources to support endless numbers of public officials, the concept of 'small government, big society' has been made one of the goals of reform. Chen Junsheng, then a member of the State Council, said as early as 1992 'One of the important directions of our reform of the political system is towards small government and big society. The growth of social organisations is an important part of that big society.'[36] We can say that the setting of this goal had a negative impact on government's implementation of its own administrative control model.

Turning to the impact on society, we can say that the government's 'abdication of powers and benefits' and 'loosening of restrictions' have made individual rights clearer and promoted a rise in rights consciousness and have also led to the formation or revival of social forces. This is apparent to anyone who cares to look. But this is not the end of the matter. These individuals and social forces, invigorated by government's abdication of powers and benefits, are gradually forming their own logic: they are no longer willing to be pitiable creatures at the government's beck and call. Quite the contrary, as social organisations emerge they explore every possible avenue for continuing their existence, and argue a case for their right to that existence through the positive role they play in society. Perhaps we can say that they emerge as a result of government policy, but they grow and develop because of social transition. Moreover, although these social forces and organisations produced by govern-

they pay lip service to the central authorities whilst secretly disregarding directives, which may then develop into a power contest with the centre and eventually to a completely empty respect for central power stopping just short of open resistance. I however see another side to this issue which is not quite so dark as Wang and Hu paint it. At least in the Chinese experience, local initiatives are often the testing ground and seedbed for policy innovations which are eventually adopted at national level. See Wang Shaoguang and Hu Angang, *supra* note 31.

36 Bureau of Civic Organisations Management of the Ministry of Civil Affairs, *supra* note 2, at p. 99.

ment abdication of power must accept the reform polices set by that government, they are quite likely to take whatever measures they are permitted to lobby against some specific reform policy that is not to their liking. There is of course also another possibility. In today's China when someone finds a policy not to their liking, or that it prevents their pursuit of some interest or advantage, their tactic will not be to oppose authority directly. They will not make a direct call for the relevant government agency to revise or revoke the disliked policy. They will seek out some other authority and by exploiting the fissures and rivalries that exist between various lines of authority give legitimacy to their own opposition to the policy. In this case, it appears that no actual harm has come to the policy whereas in fact the policy has been recreated. Where once it was the only authority on a given matter, it has now become merely one of a number of competing authorities. Also, in a time of increasing globalisation, China must pay close attention to the international human rights movement, and avoid coming into conflict with it as far as possible. Internationally the trend is to protect citizen's right to free association and to oppose government interference in the activities of social organisations. If the Chinese government wants to create a favourable impression on the international stage, it cannot interfere too much in the affairs of social organisations. This means that even as the government enacts restrictions of social organisations' activities it is careful not go too far and bring unwanted opprobrium on itself.

4.2 The Result of Reforms

Despite the above, a reform carried out under government guidance naturally leaves the government still largely uncontested as final arbiter of policy issues. This finds concrete expression in the government's ability both to control social organisations through laws and regulations, and also to have legal recourse to institute clean up and rectification campaigns whenever it sees fit. The government controls the creation of legislation for social organisations and also the interpretation of the administrative application of that legislation.[37] Consequently, although the government and the Ministry of Civil Affairs have begun to emphasise their service role and have drafted numerous documents to this effect, since the Ministry retains the powers outlined above – not as yet fully restrained by legislative measures – it can not only impose rectification on legally

37 Kang Xiaoguang, *supra* note 2.

registered organisations, it can also shut down at any time as illegal any of that great number of unregistered organisations – organisations which the Ministry is especially suspicious of to begin with. Although the government is gradually withdrawing from the social organisations sector, this withdrawal is in fact very different from a military retreat. It takes only a single order for a well-trained army to pull out completely from a battlefield, even one it perhaps occupied at the cost of much blood and sweat. The government's withdrawal is hardly the same. Each backward step seems to happen only as a result of pressure from society and with careful and detailed planning. In contrast, citizens exercising their right to free association are much more reactive. Each forward step taken under the model of administrative control takes a citizen into uncharted territory. This is because we can never fully know what exactly are the boundaries and scope of government withdrawal or where the limits to government administrative control of social organisations lie. Because of this confusion, every experiment citizens make in exercising their right to association can appear revolutionary, each freedom enjoyed cause all manner of disturbance. Although this is the case, for the reasons outlined above, and also because social forces are growing in power all the time, the Ministry of Civil Affairs handles problems of this nature with extreme caution, fearful of making trouble for itself. In the end neither the state, nor society is happy with the way things are. From the state's point of view the inability to fully implement the administrative model is a major failing; society finds it cannot yet fully enjoy autonomy in this regard and what freedom it has comes with no guarantee. However, the struggle between these two mighty forces does lead to a kind of balance or accommodation, whilst neither side is happy with it both accept in its own best interest. A further result of the struggle between these two opponents is that the administrative model has slowly evolved to become one that controls only some of China's social organisations but by no means all of them or all of their many types. Likewise this struggle means that those parts of the model that now have a legislative basis cannot be fully implemented, nor have the courts yet handled cases concerning social organisations. In short, government administrative control of social organisations is only partially effective, and a great number of existing social organisations have no legal status. It is a curious form of accommodation. In fact the situation has benefits for each of the three parties involved. When they compare themselves to the great mass of unregistered organisations, those organisations that have achieved legal status can feel very pleased with themselves, even somewhat arrogant, and can feel they are better in some way. The unregistered organisations are not interested in registration as such; all they want to do is get on with their chosen activities. The government agencies feel that on the one hand the existence of so many unregistered organisations makes something of a mockery of standards and norms, but on the other appears almost to deliberately protect their continued existence, as they serve as a threat to the development of those organisations that have already registered. Put simply, if the unregistered organisations all gained legal status then some of the privileges enjoyed by the present legal organisations would lose any real meaning when diluted in a greatly expanded mass of registered organisations.

We should say here that the current model of administrative control for social organisations once functioned very well but I doubt there is anyone who would say that it cannot be changed. The reality is that the model does not exist in isolation; changes to the structure of wider society will inevitably lead to changes in this model. This change will happen regardless of whether we want it to or not, it is an objective necessity. In fact, a combination of factors is driving forward reform of or change in the model. Important among these factors are:

(1) Developments in Chinese society require such a change

We all know that government administration of social organisations is of necessity directly affected by the actual practise of management. China is in a period of transition; the market economy is developing apace, changes in the structure of the economy are creating various different interest organisations. This diversification of interest organisations calls for a concomitant diversity of social organisations and also for more communication and exchange between the various interest organisations. Social change is giving birth to new social organisations, and their diversity is not something we can avoid.

(2) International pressure is in favour of a change

Since China's signature and accession to international human rights accords, and its undertaking the responsibilities of membership of the WTO, government administrative control of social organisations will be held to new international standards. Moreover compliance will have to be reported regularly and will be subject to evaluation. These international commitments mean that the Chinese government will have to take its administration of social organisations very seriously.

(3) Conceptual issues

For a long time China's administrative control of social organisations has had its own unique guiding principles. But as society has developed these principles have come more and more under assault by Western civil society theory. The key issue is the need to recognise social spaces, that the state or government is not the same thing as society, society is something much broader. This is to say, people have become aware of, and have indeed begun to accept, civil society theory.

(4) The government's own goals for reform

In the period of reform and opening the government has already recognised that previously it managed many things it should not have, and managed some of them quite poorly, putting itself to a great deal of trouble for little appreciable benefit. The government has long sought to streamline its agencies and create a 'small government' in a 'big society'. If we are to achieve this latter goal there will have to be a change in the model for administrative control of social organisations. I am convinced that by a process of reforming in step with the times the Chinese government will gradually bring its administrative control of social organisations into line with international standards, and that that control will happen with a proper legal framework.

5 CONCLUSION

I believe it is unavoidable that the compromise solution described above will persist for some time to come. This is to say that, in terms of the relationship between society and the state, the standard by which a good administrative model will be judged will no longer be one that considers solely one party's interests alone, but will rather seek to satisfy both sides at the same time. The future direction of reform should look to create a 'win-win outcome', allowing unregistered organisations to gain legal status and giving administrative agencies the authority they need.[38] This calls for both sides to not only maintain their

38 Some overseas observers believe that future reforms in China will not come about through some interest group wresting greater autonomy from the state, but will be 'a question of coordinating the interests of different sectors'. See Zhang Jing, *supra* note 31, at p. 4.

own standpoints and protect their own interests but also to understand and respect those of the other. At the same time, we must be clear that the retreat of government will be accompanied by the extension of citizen's rights. Of course, here this means rights in the broad sense. Both historical experience and current actualities show us that wherever a government withdraws from some area of social life that it previously controlled there will be a corresponding increase in the free space enjoyed by the people. On the surface it appears that the government has retreated but this is not so. In fact this means that a government and its citizenry have reached a mutual understanding of one another's activities. This means that the relationship between government management and popular freedom has moved away from the abnormal situation of the past that was seriously unbalanced in favour of the government, and has returned to a proper and more normal footing. This alone is the highest expression of governance in a modern society.

3

THE DILEMMA OF LEGITIMACY FACING CHINA'S CIVIL SOCIETY ORGANISATIONS

*Xie Haiding**

1 INTRODUCTION

Research on civil society organisations in China has expanded exponentially since the mid 1980s. Contemplating why this should be so, one can identify factors which fall into three broad categories. First, the period of 'reform and opening' has seen an explosion in the total number of civil society organisations. The extent of the positive and negative impact of the rapidly growing ranks of civil society organisations on both society and the state has attracted increasing attention. The healthy development of such organisations is an issue of ever greater importance for decisions made by both state and non-state actors. From this arises the increasing desire for description of that development process, investigation of the positive social functions of civil society groups, analysis of their activities and exploration of appropriate policies and legislation concerning them. Second, in the late 1980s and early 1990s Western civil society theories reached Chinese academia, encouraging the comparative study of the phenomena in Chinese and overseas societies. This process allowed certain of

* This paper was written for the project on 'Chinese-Dutch Research Co-operation on the Legal Aspects of Social Organisations in China'. It draws on insights gained from the author's surveys of civil society organisations in Shenzhen and Anhui. The preliminary versions of the conclusion presented in detail here were published in the Chinese Newspaper, *Legal Daily,* 19th March, 2003 and 17th April, 2003. Dr Yuwen Li of Utrecht University was kind enough to offer comments on a draft of this article. I offer sincere thanks for her constructive criticism.

Yuwen Li (Ed.), *Freedom of Association in China and Europe: Comparative Perspectives in Law and Practice*, © 2005 Koninklijke Brill NV, Leiden. Printed in The Netherlands, pp. 103-149.

the unique features discernible in actual civil society practise in China to be explained. These included the basic nature of the organisations; the reasons for the increase in their number; the role they played in political, economic and cultural life; and their legal status. This in turn led to the formation of a normative model for civil society research intellectually grounded in and deriving its ideal models from Western civil society theory. Lastly, the formal political acceptance in China of human rights and rule-of-law discourses that came in the 1990s opened new avenues for research into civil society organisations to address questions of freedom of association and the construction of a state governed by law.

Overall, this research has been able to identify numerous barriers to the development of civil society organisations and to indicate a healthier direction that China might take. The deficiencies of the research to date are, however, quite obvious. For example, there is a confusing plethora of terms: 'social organisation', 'non-profit organisations', 'non-governmental organisations', 'civil society organisations', and they are applied seemingly at random. Sociological research into organisations' development lacks depth and has been for the most part restricted to mere descriptive accounts. Explorations of the legal context have ignored real world experiences and have thus been unable to show the real relationship between the two. There has been a failure to break down the key impediment to the healthy growth of civil society – that it is stifled by the tendency in the laws, regulations and policies under which it is managed to exert control. These have led to the present abnormal state of civil society organisations. This article will concentrate on two major aspects of the relationship between civil society organisations and the law: how the rules have affected civil society organisations' development and, in turn, what demands that development has placed on the law. A secondary focus of analysis and discussion will be on the contributing systemic factors that led to the abnormality of civil society organisations' development and the appropriate remedies to it. We will begin by noting an important truth about China's civil society organisations: more than 80% of them exist outside the law. At the same time, legally registered groups exhibit problems of poor internal management, shoddy accounting and even sometimes outright criminality. With these facts in mind, I will offer an analysis of structural factors contributing to this from both a legislative and an enforcement perspective. From this I develop a discussion of the wider questions of legitimacy and legality as they relate to the laws on civil society organisations. This then forms the basis for further exploration of the need to frame a unified civil society organisations law and the principles under which such a law should be drafted. However, to avoid as far as possible any epistemological confusion, I think it is necessary to first discuss and define two key concepts before we proceed – 'civil society organisation' (*minjian zuzhi*) and 'legitimacy' (*hefaxing*).

2 Defining the Concepts: Civil Society Organisation and Legitimacy

2.1 Civil Society Organisations

The bodies studied in this paper are known by a variety of terms in today's China, including 'social organisations', 'popular non-enterprise work units', 'civic organisations', 'non-profit organisations', 'non-government organisations', and 'the third sector'. The meaning of these terms or the particular aspect of civil society organisations that they emphasise varies with the theme and the intellectual and actual context of the formulations they are used in. Sometimes they all mean something very similar, sometimes their meanings are quite far apart.

For a considerable period of time the terminology employed in Chinese laws and regulations followed that of the 'Temporary Measures for the Registration of Social Organisations' (*Shehui tuanti dengji zanxing banfa*) issued by the State Council (*zhengwuyuan*) in 1950.[1] For example, the 'Regulations for Registration and Management of Social Organisations' (*Shehui tuanti dengji guanli tiaoli*) issued by the State Council in October 1989 stipulated that they were designed to regulate social organisations organised within the territory of the People's Republic of China such as associations, academic associations, federations, research associations, foundations, friendly societies, promotional bodies and chambers of commerce.[2] Beginning in the 1990s as a result of

1 Prior to this, regulations such as the 'Method for Registering People's Organisations in the Shaanxi -Gansu – Ningxia Border Areas' (1942) and the 'Method for Registering People's Organisations in the Shaanxi -Gansu – Ningxia Border Areas' (1949) had used such terms as 'Popular Organisations' (*minzhong tuanti*) and 'People's Organisations' (*renmin tuanti*). The relevant regulations can be found in Wu Yuzhang (ed.), *Legal Aspects on Social Organizations (Shehui tuanti de falu wenti)*, (Beijing: Shehui kexue wenxian chubanshe, 2004).

2 Art. 2 of the Regulations. The Regulations is contained in Bureau of Civic Organizations Management of the Ministry of Civil Affairs (ed.), *Handbook for Administrative Work on Social Organizations* (Shehui tuanti guanli gongzuo shouce), (Internal Document, 1996).

reform, especially the reform of the work unit system,[3] some of the institutional work units that had previously been entirely state-run were turned over to private individuals or otherwise funded from non-government sources. This meant the emergence of 'popular non-enterprise work units' which were distinct from 'social organisations' and also under the direct control of neither government nor market. In 1996 the Party's General Office and the State Council jointly issued a 'Notice concerning strengthening the work of managing social organisations and popular non-enterprise work units.' It was from this point that the practice of calling this type of organisation 'popular non-enterprise work units' began and that the term began to appear alongside references to social organisations.[4] In 1998 the State Council promulgated the 'Temporary Regulations for the Registration and Management of Popular Non-Enterprise Work Units'[5] and also revised the 1989 Regulations on social organisations. The full definition of popular non-enterprise work units is 'social organisations run by enterprise or institutional work units, social organisations or other social forces, or by individual citizens, using non-state assets, and engaging in social service activities of a non-profit nature.'[6] Social organisations are 'social organisations of a non-profit nature formed voluntarily by citizens to realise some common purpose of their membership and conducting their activities in accordance with their constitutions.'[7] At the same time, the Ministry of Civil Affairs re-designated its 'Social Organisations Administration Department' as the 'Bureau of Civic Organisations Management'.[8] Likewise, local governments renamed their

3 Yang Xiaomin, Zhou Yihu, *China's Work Unit System (Zhongguo danwei zhidu)*, (Beijing: Zhongguo jingji chubanshe, 2000), see especially Chapters 4 to 6.

4 Xu Ruixin, 'Explanation on a Few Key Issues Relating to Administration of Social Organisations', in Bureau of Civic Organisations Management of the Ministry of Civil Affairs (ed.), *A Selection of Recent Regulations and Policies Concerning the Administration of Civil Society Organisations (Youguan minjian zuzhi guanli zuixin fagui zhengce zhaibian)*, (Internal document, 1998).

5 The English document is contained in the Appendix II of this book.

6 Art. 2 of the Regulations.

7 Art. 2 of the Regulations for Registration and Management of Social Organisations, see Appendix I of this book.

8 Professor Yu Keping contends that, 'prior to reform, civil society had only minimal legitimacy, ever since 1949 'civic organisation' and 'civic society' have been extremely sensitive terms'. The change in name in government offices means that civil society organisations have received formal government and official approval and have achieved official legitimacy. This is related to the strong growth of civil society organisations, profound changes in the political, cultural and academic debates about civil society. Yu Keping, 'The Rise of Chinese Civil Society and its Significance for Governance', in Yu Keping *et al.*, *The Rise of Chinese Civil Society and Changes in Governance*

offices as civic organisations management offices or sections; or they newly established such bodies. 'Civic Organisation' gradually came to be used as a concept encompassing both 'social organisations' and 'popular non-enterprise work units.' In the 'Temporary Measures for Suppressing Illegal Social Organisations,' issued by the Ministry of Civil Affairs in April 2000, the term entered use in the language of official regulations.[9]

In academia, since the various terms mentioned above were the terminology employed in official regulations, they still appear regularly in scholarly works. However, with the increase in international academic exchanges, especially the acceptance of and enthusiastic debate about Western civil society theory that began in the early 1990s, new concepts such as 'non-profit organisations', 'non-government organisations' and 'the third sector' began making frequent appearances in both formal and informal academic discourse and research. Overall the specific vocabulary chosen or preferred by different participants in these discussions was a function of their understanding of certain Western civil society concepts, their judgment of the state of development of social organisations in China and the direction they hoped such development would take, and whether or not the subject under discussion was in the West or in China. For example, some scholars hold that the definition given by the Johns Hopkins Comparative Non-profit Sector Project of what constitutes an a Non-profit Organisation (NPO) – 'any organisation that meets the five criteria of being organised, popular, non-profit, self-governing and voluntary is regarded as an NPO' – is the most widely accepted, and although continuing to refer to 'social organisations' in their discussions of the Chinese past and present, when turning to future reforms will speak rather of 'the third sector.'[10] Other scholars hold that the term NGO first referred to international NGOs recognised by the United Nations and later came to include those organisations in first world countries working for third world development, and that now it mainly refers to organisations in developing nations working to promote economic and social

(Zhongguo gongmin shehui de xingqi he zhili de bianqian), (Beijing: Shehui kexue wenxian chubanshe, 2002), at pp. 204-205.

9 The document is contained in Bureau of Civic Organizations Management of the Ministry of Civil Affairs (ed.), *Collected Recent Regulations and Policy Concerning the Administration of Civic Organizations* (*Minjian zuzhiguanli zuixin fagui zhengce huibian*), (Internal document, 2000).

10 Wang Ming *et al.*, *Reform of China's Social Organisations – from a Government Choice to a Social Choice (Zhongguo shetuan gaige – cong zhengfu xuanze dao shehui xuanze)*, (Beijing: Shehui kexue wenxian chubanshe, 2001.) See especially chapters 2 and 20.

development, especially grassroots organisations;[11] hence scholars of this view are careful to avoid the term when discussing groups in China, especially their future prospects. Still other scholars hold that although organisations meeting the strict definition of NGO are extremely rare in China, if one accepts a standard of 'existing outside the state and market systems' then a vigorous growth of social organisations in all shapes and sizes can be discerned.[12] Another academic view is that NPOs can be referred to collectively as 'the third sector', that the state of the social sector is largely decided by the state of the third sector and more specifically by the state of the non-profit sector, and that the healthy development of the third sector is a precondition for China's market reforms and the construction of socialist democracy; hence they refer to research into NPOs as 'third sector research'.[13] Of course in reality 'the West' is not

11 Ibid, at pp. 12-13 and also chapter 20. See also Wang Shaoguang, 'Theory and Practice – An Overview of the Third Sector in Different Countries' in China Youth Development Foundation and Committee on Development Research on Foundations (*eds.*), *Chinese Social Organisations at a Crossroads (Chu yu shizilukou de Zhongguo shetuan)*, (Tianjin: Tianjin renmin chubanshe, 2001), at p.383. One Western scholar has observed, 'In a more fundamental sense, NGOs are usually believed to be opposed to the activities of the state and profit-seeking organisations. The source of NGO's legitimacy is their criticism of state and private sector actors. The tasks and practical activities of NGOs are extremely radical and are very different from those of the state and private sector. However the arena in which NGOs can operate is set by the state, and their activities are limited by various laws and regulations', Jude L. Fernando, and Alan W. Heston, 'NGOs Between States, Markets and Civil Society', in He Zengke *ed.*, *Civil Society and the Third Sector (Gongmin shehui yu disan bumen)*, (Beijing: Shehui kexue wenxian chubanshe, 2000), at p. 274.

12 Jia Xijin, 'Theory and Practice of Civil Society in China', in *supra* note 1, at p. 107.

13 Xu Yongguang, 'Foreword to the "China Third Sector Research Yearbook"' in China Youth Development Foundation and Committee on Development Research on Foundations (*eds.*), *supra* note 11. Professor Qin Hui based on a view of the Third Sector in the West grew up in already modernised societies proposes that 'the way forward for China's Third Sector and civil society' lies in 'organisations with a civil society consciousness' and 'NGOs': 'if we say that the significance of the Third Sector in the Western world is not limited to ordinary charitable and public welfare activities, but that it also implies a new understanding of citizen's rights and obligations, then this is even more the case in terms of the significance of the development of China's Third Sector, because the reality is that it must begin from fighting for the most basic right to citizen participation and the creation of a space where that can happen'. Qin Hui, 'From Tradition Civic Public Welfare Organisations to a Modern "Third Sector" – Certain Questions in the Comparative History of Public Welfare in China and the West', in China Youth Development Foundation and Committee on Development Research on Foundations (*eds.*), supra note 11, at p. 54.

a unitary whole and these concepts cannot have a single definition even there. Nevertheless because they arrive at an understanding of Western concepts from a different background, and due to the inevitable distortions of the process of translation, scholars in China still show a marked degree of confusion in their selection of conceptual terminology. Indeed, the same scholar in the same paper will often use different terminology as if it were interchangeable.

This paper will follow the usage of 'civil society organisations' (CSOs). There are three reasons why I choose to do this. First, since my intention is conduct an exploration of the relationship between CSOs, and the law rooted in the actual prevailing situation in China with little reference to the Western experience, keeping to the terminology that has developed in Chinese legal usage is more helpful to the exercise at hand. Second, the future development of China's CSOs will be guided by certain standards or tendencies, and these are already basically those contained in the definitions employed in existing regulations – 'organised', 'non-profit', 'popular' and 'voluntary'. Third, although the terms NPO and NGO are understood and have entered common parlance in the West, their direct translation into Chinese makes it hard to understand why institutional work units that do not seek to make a profit are not considered NPOs, or why market bodies such as enterprises cannot be considered NGOs. Also the set of terms positing a 'third', and the expression 'sector' can lead to mistaken impression of what the actual situation is, and the question as to whether social organisations can be divided into government, market and what is considered a 'third sector' still needs further research.

However, while 'CSO' certainly does not merely refer just to 'social organisations' and 'popular non-enterprise work units', it happens to be the case that current regulations places both such types of organisation under this same larger category. Whether used as a legal or an academic term, CSO needs to be kept as an open term so that it can reflect effectively the intentions of actual organisations and the reality of their future development. These latter will enrich and extend its meaning. Based on this understanding, and extracting the essential shared characteristics defined in current legislation concerning 'social organisations' and 'popular non-enterprise work units', in this paper a CSO is understood to be: a social organisation formed voluntarily by Chinese citizens and engaged in non-profit activities. Here, 'voluntarily' means 'neither compelled to participate in nor prevented from participating in'; 'non-profit' means that an organisation does not have making a profit as an objective and its members do not directly share in any profits it may make; 'formed voluntarily by citizens' makes clear that it is unofficial and thus of a popular nature.

2.2 Legitimacy/Legality

The Chinese word '*hefaxing*' combines two main meanings: the first is similar to that of the English word 'legality' indicating that an action or the existence of some thing meets legal requirements; the second refers to 'appropriateness' and 'reasonableness' and expresses the notion that an action or thing accords with the values set by some human entity or process as well as certain other non-enforced factors, that people approve of or agree with it and are willing to accept or follow it, a meaning similar to the English word 'legitimacy.'[14] For example, if we speak of the '*hefaxing*' of a law, by the first of these two meanings we are saying that some group or type of specific legal standards are in accord with the provisions of higher laws or the constitution; in the second sense we are saying that those particular legal standards meet certain human standards (justice, equity, rationality, freedom) or accord with people's ideals and expectations, and are thus considered reasonable and proper, and are followed voluntarily.

The standards by which the 'legality' of an action or thing is judged are the rules set down for it in actual laws. So if one is able to clearly ascertain what that law says, it is quite easy to decide whether something is 'legal'. The standards for measuring whether an action or thing is 'proper' are certain values held in people's minds. Since values are various, subjective and highly abstract, assessing something's 'propriety' is relatively complicated. Thus within the traditions of political philosophy we find that the basis for determining 'legitimacy' (in the sense of proper) changes from hard-to-fathom 'natural laws' into 'common aspirations', then from the impossible to prove 'common aspirations'

14 Since the character '*fa*' in Classical Chinese had no special meaning beyond actual laws, the two major meanings of the word '*hefaxing*' are the result of academic and philosophical exchanges between China and the West. Professor Lin Yusheng once suggested that the English word 'legality' should be translated as '*hefaxing*' (here I translate it as '*hefalüxing*') and 'legitimacy' as '*zhengdangxing*' in a speech at Peking University on 6th May, 1999, see Gao Bingzhong, 'The Rise of Social Organisations and their Problem of Legitimacy', in China Youth Development Foundation and Committee on Development Research on Foundations (eds.), *supra* note 11, at p. 77, footnote 1, which is obviously thinking based on consideration of how we are used to the word '*hefaxing*' being used in Chinese in the past. But many other scholars also translate 'legitimacy' as '*hefaxing*'. This has meant that the existing Chinese word '*hefaxing*' now has two meanings, 'legality' in the sense used in legal positivism, and 'legitimacy' in the sense used in political philosophy.

to 'representative democratic process', and then from symbolic democratic processes to the 'effective acceptance' posited by functionalism.[15]

Since the standards for determining 'legality' and 'propriety' are different, we are left with four logical possibilities when determining the '*hefaxing*' of a given action or thing: it is both legal and proper; it is legal but not proper; it is considered proper but is not legal; or that it is neither legal nor proper. In the first case we have full legitimacy, in the second and third cases we lack sufficient legitimacy, and in the last case we find a severe lack of legitimacy: all but the first case present dilemmas of legitimacy. If we develop this further we can say that should some situation regulated by law fall entirely into the second case it would show that although that law was effective in practice[16] it was lacking in propriety. For example if thievery became a widespread practice because the law encouraged it, its prevalence would attest to the effectiveness of the law but there would be an obvious lack of propriety. If it was the third case that obtained we would find that the law was neither proper nor effective and we would be facing a serious crisis of legitimacy. For example, if the law forbade citizens from intervening personally to prevent criminality, but many of them frequently still did so, that law would be severely lacking in legitimacy.

It is not my intention to explore every one of the diverse aspects of the legitimacy of Chinese CSOs in this paper, I merely seek to start from the dilemma of legality that existing CSOs find themselves in, relate it to the

15 We could say that the two meanings of '*hefaxing*' belong to two different academic traditions, legal positivism and political philosophy. In the latter tradition, although a clear understanding of the concept of 'legitimacy' began with Rousseau, and was connected to ideas about 'the common will', prior to this the tradition of natural laws had in fact given a clear account of the essential meaning contained in the concept. After Rousseau, Schumpeter once advocated a concept of legitimacy that could be described as 'the process of representative democracy', whereas Weber posited 'effectively obeyed' as the standard by which to judge legitimacy. Debates on the question of legitimacy in modern political philosophy mostly relate to the relationship between legitimacy and effectiveness. See David Beetham, *The Legitimation of Power*, (London: MacMillan Education Ltd, 1992); William Connolly (ed.), *Legitimacy and State*, (Oxford: Blackwell Ltd, 1984); Jurgen Habermas, *Legitimation Crisis*, (London: Heinemann Educational Books, 1976).

16 The 'actual effect' *(shixiao)* and 'effectiveness' (*xiaoli)* of a law are different concepts. The latter refers to a law's ability to limit, to say 'a legal standard has *xiaoli*' implies that those the law addresses should obey the standard; the former refers to whether or not the law's ability to limit actually happens in reality, to say 'a legal standard has *shixiao*' implies that those the law addresses do in fact obey the standard and that the limits set by the standard are realised.

'Regulations for Registration and Management of Social Organisations' and the 'Temporary Regulations for the Registration and Management of Popular Non-Enterprise Work Units', and show the major causes of that dilemma. From this I will examine the dilemma of legitimacy that faces the current system of laws governing CSOs. With the preceding as a foundation I will then further explore how the actual problems of legality attending CSOs can be solved by new legislation.

3 THE DILEMMA OF LEGALITY FACED BY CIVIL SOCIETY ORGANISATIONS

There has been an explosion in numbers of CSOs in China in the years since reform.

> By early 1989, China had seen a sixteen-fold increase in the number of national-level social organisations compared with the situation on the eve of the Cultural Revolution; then there were just under 100 such organisation, in 1989 there were more than 1,600. Local groups over the same period increased thirty-threefold from a total of 6,000 to over 200,000.[17]

Statistics on the Ministry of Civil Affairs' (MCA) website say that in 1991 there were 836 national-level social organisations and 116,000 local ones. By 1996 they report 1,845 national organizations (including inter-provincial organizations), and 187,000 organizations registered at county level or above. The corresponding figures for 2002 are 1,712 and 133,000 respectively, with 111,000 popular non-enterprise work units also listed.[18]

However, the figures above tell only a part of the story of the growth in CSOs in China. As well as these formally registered organisations there are also a large number of unregistered groups. Survey work I conducted in the early parts of 2002 and 2003 in areas of Shenzhen and Anhui suggested that registered groups represented only between 8% and 13% of the total number

17 Fan Baojun, Deputy Minister for Civil Affairs, 'See the Trend Clearly, Liberate Thinking, Open up a New Situation in our Country's Social Organization Work – Speech to the National Conference on Social Organisation Work', in Bureau of Civic Organisations Management of the Ministry of Civil Affairs (ed.), *supra* note 2, at p. 104.

18 Available on the Ministry's website at: www.mca.gov.cn/statistics/index.html.

of CSOs.[19] If we also include temporary organisations formed to address specific problems or for entertainment or celebratory purposes, such as mutual aid organisations formed by farmers in flood-affected areas, or temporary alliances of migrant workers formed to redress problems with unpaid wages, then this proportion becomes smaller still. The results of my study are broadly in line with estimates given by scholars researching CSO issues: there as yet exist no formal figures for the number of CSOs below county level but conservative estimates say there are at least three million.[20] Also, according to an official from the Ministry of Civil Affairs speaking in November 1998 their preliminary estimate of the number of popular non-enterprise work units was 700,000,[21] yet the number of such organisations officially registered with the Ministry at the end of 2002 was only 111,000. Thus if we estimate that there are at least ten times as many CSOs in existence as are officially registered we should not be too far from the actual situation.

Article 3 of the current 1998 'Regulations for Registration and Management of Social Organisations' stipulates that the establishment of a social organisation should be examined and approved by its sponsoring agency *(yewu zhuguan danwei)* and then registration should be conducted in accordance with the provisions of these Regulations. But the following organisations do not fall within the scope of the registration provision of these regulations:

1. people's organisations participating in the Chinese People's Political Consultative Conference;
2. organisations that are exempt from registration having been ratified by the State Council's body for the management and staffing of institutions and having been approved by the State Council;

19 Statistics for surveys conducted by some local civil affairs departments in 2002 and 2003. My thanks go to the comrades there who made these available to me. I have also previously conducted small surveys based at township level. The statistical results of these surveys suggest that registered social organisations account for only between a twelfth and a twentieth of the total number of social organisations. In the case of popular non-enterprise work units, registered organisations account for between a tenth and a twelfth of the total. These proportions are even lower than those revealed by the local Civil Affairs surveys.

20 'At a conservative estimate, there are at least three million social organisations at township or village level, counting both registered and unregistered organisations, in the country as a whole'. Yu Keping, *supra* note 8, at p. 200.

21 Duoji Cairang, 'Actively Foster, Improve Management, Promote the Healthy Development of Civil Society Organisations', in Bureau of Civic Organisations Management of the Ministry of Civil Affairs (ed.), *supra* note 4, at p. 71.

3. organisations established and active internally in agencies, organisations, enterprises.[22]

Article 35 of the 1998 Regulations states that:

> If a social organisation engages in preliminary activities without approval, or if it carries out activities as if it were a social organisation without being registered, or if a social organisation whose registration has been cancelled continues to carry out activities as if it were a social organisation, then the registration and management agency will close the organisation down and confiscate its illegal assets; in criminal cases, criminal penalties will be applied in accordance with the law; in non criminal cases, a public security sanction (*zhi'an guanli chufa*) may be imposed in accordance with the law.

Article 39 stipulates that all social organisations must re-register within a year from date of the Regulations taking effect, that is, before the 25th October, 1999. Organisations that do not re-register cannot carry out activities as a social organisation.

Article 3 of the 'Temporary Regulations for the Registration and Management of Popular Non-Enterprise Work Units' states that 'the establishment of a popular non-enterprise work unit should be examined and approved by its sponsoring agency and then registration should be conducted in accordance with the provision of these Regulations.' Article 27 states:

> Popular non-enterprise work units that carry on activities as such an organisation without being registered, or those whose registration has been revoked but continue to carry on activities as a popular non-enterprise work unit will be closed down by the registration and management agency and have their illegal assets confiscated; in criminal cases, criminal penalties will be applied in accordance with the law; in non criminal cases, a public security sanction may be imposed in accordance with the law.

In Article 2 of the 'Temporary Measures for Suppression of Illegal Civic Organisations' issued by the Ministry of Civil Affairs in April, 2000 it states:

22 The 1989 'Regulations for Registration and Management of Social Organisations' did not make clear which social organisation did not need to register, merely stipulating the principle that those to whom 'other laws and regulations apply' were exempt.

> Where any of the following situations is the case a civic organisation is considered to be illegal: 1. where it conducts preliminary activities without being approved; 2. where it conducts activities as if it were a social organisation or a popular non-enterprise work unit without being registered; 3. where it continues such activities after its registration has been revoked.

The 'registration' referred to in the regulations and administrative orders quoted above means that the formal registration with one of the various branches of the Ministry of Civil Affairs has followed the application and approval process outlined in either the 1998 'Regulations for Registration and Management of Social Organisations' or the 1998 'Temporary Regulations for the Registration and Management of Popular Non-Enterprise Work Units'. Thus groups registered with other departments or state agencies will not be regarded as registered civil society organisations.

In the light of the regulations outlined above, CSOs not registered with the Ministry of Civil Affairs (with the exception of those excluded by Section 2, Article 3 of the 'Regulations on the Registration and Management of Social Organisations', i.e. people's organisations participating in the Chinese People's Political Consultative Conference (CPPCC), those approved directly by the State Council, and purely internal groups within enterprises or organisations) will in future be 'illegal civil society organisations'.[23] As we have no statistics on either the number of organisations that are exempt from registration or total numbers of CSOs in China, we cannot say what proportion of CSOs in China are thus 'illegal'. However, we can offer a comparative example in the case of popular non-enterprise work units. As we said above, in 1998 there were some 700,000 such organisations, but at year end 2002 only 111,000 were

23 However there are uncertainties in this understanding of the law because it may depend on whether or not an unregistered organisation is presenting itself as a 'social organisation' or a 'popular non-enterprise work unit'. In practice there are very many civil society organisations that do not find themselves simply regarded as 'illegal' by civil affairs agencies, rather they fall into a space between 'legal' and 'illegal' organisations; they could be termed 'extra-legal civil society organisations'. For example, the majority of the enormous number of rural technical associations are not registered with civil affairs agencies and are not required to comply with the two major laws on CSO registration. Their legality is unclear and they have no specific legal status. There is, however, no clear line showing where 'extra-legality' ends and 'illegality' begins and the distance between the two states is similarly an unknown. When the state's implementing agencies run a crackdown campaign, 'extra-legal' can very quickly turn out to be 'illegal' after all. For this reason, in this paper I include these organisations in the conceptual category of 'illegal CSOs' for the purposes of discussion.

actually registered. This would mean that even if the total number of popular non-enterprise work units had not increased in the intervening years, at least 84% of existing groups are 'illegal' according to the stipulations of the 'Temporary Regulations for the Registration and Management of Popular Non-Enterprise Work Units' and the 'Temporary Measures for Suppression of Illegal Civic organisations'.[24]

Put this way, more than 80% of CSOs lack 'legality' because they are unregistered, and have thus become 'illegal civil society organisations'. Of course registered groups may also lose their legality or at least lack sufficient legality if they engage in activities that break existing laws and regulations. Articles 32, 33 and 34 of the 'Regulations for Registration and Management of Social Organisations' and Articles 24, 25 and 26 of the 'Temporary Regulations for the Registration and Management of Popular Non-Enterprise Work Units' list ten types of situations that would be illegal for registered organisations:

1) if a social organisation engages in deception while applying for registration, or if within one year of receiving the 'social organisation legal entity registration certificate' it does not engage in any activities;
2) the 'social organisation legal entity registration certificate' is obliterated, hired out or lent, or the social organisation's official seal is hired out or lent;
3) activities go beyond the principles and area of work as defined in the charter;
4) supervision and reviews in accordance with the regulations are refused or not accepted;

24 Because the 'Temporary Regulations for the Registration and Management of Popular Non-Enterprise Work Units' had only just been promulgated in 1998 it is impossible to base a calculation on the number of such organisations registered at that date. According to Article 31 of the 'Temporary Regulations', organisations already in existence prior to the regulations coming into effect had one year from that date (i.e. until 25th October 1999) to apply for registration. Also, the 'Opinion Concerning the Carry Forward of the Work of Re-registering Popularly Non-Enterprise Work Units' (see *supra* note 9) issued by the Ministry of Civil Affairs on the 30th December 1999 required that starting in January, 2000 re-checking and re-registration of existing popular non-enterprise work units should be carried out, and this should be completed by 'the end of December 2000 at the latest'. Even considering the complexity of the re-registration process and the large amount of time it must have required, the figure for popular non-enterprise work units registered at the end of 2002 should be a reliable one.

5) modifications of registration are not carried out in accordance with the regulations;
6) branches or representative agencies are established without approval, or where poor management of branches or representative agencies has serious results;
7) engaging in profit seeking activities;
8) the organisation's capital, public contributions or donations are seized, secretly divided or diverted;
9) national regulations are contravened in the charging of fees, collection or receipt of financial resources, donations or contributions;
10) other laws or regulations are broken.

However, the reality for registered CSOs is that:

> in the vast majority of social organisations their internal structure, administrative systems, decision-making processes, financial systems, bonus arrangements and monitoring mechanisms are all inadequate; moreover it is generally the case that their staff are aging, funding is inadequate and finances are chaotic...almost all social organisations are engaged in profit-seeking activities. Some social organisations collude with their sponsoring agencies to use their administrative powers to seek illegal advantages.[25]

> At year end 1995 there were 1,810 national-level social organisations...my preliminary figures reveal that of these only 20% were able to conduct actual activities in line with their stated missions, that is only about 400 of them. A further 20% either conducted no activities at all or were riven by internal problems and divisions.[26]

When Jiangsu Province conducted a rectification of provincial level social organisations in 1996 some 3,000 organisations of various types were forcibly combined or closed down, reducing the total number by about 20%.[27] Also

25 Kang Xiaoguang, 'Chinese Social Organisations in the Era of Transition' *(Zhuanxing shiqi de Zhongguo shetuan)*, in China Youth Development Foundation and Committee on Development Research on Foundations (eds.), *supra* note 11, at p. 5.

26 'Speech given by Deputy Minister Xu Ruixin at a discussion forum with leading comrades from certain social organisations (21st May, 1996)', in Bureau of Civic Organisation Management of the Ministry of Civil Affairs (ed.), *supra* note 2, at p. 132.

27 Zhang Lianzhen, 'Actively Explore Social Organisation Reform, Work Hard in the Service of the Whole Province's Economy and Society', in Bureau of Civic Organisations Management of the Ministry of Civil Affairs (ed.), *supra* note 9, at p. 139.

in 1996, Guangdong Province conducted a rectification of 'the problem of illegitimate sponsorship' in 317 provincial level foundations and some friendly associations. The campaign revealed 70 friendly associations with irregularities and 71 foundations behaving illegally.[28]

When one considers the present limited ability to enforce the law we can be certain that the above figures reveal only a part of the problem. The dilemma of legality amongst civil society organisations will in reality be even more serious. What are the causes of this dilemma? The rapid growth in the desire to form organisations encouraged by the process of reform and opening, the distribution of some government functions to social actors attending the reforms of government as part of a trend to 'small government, big society', rising living standards accompanying market reforms providing the economic wherewithal for the formation of organisations, pursuit of private interests, a general lack legal consciousness amongst China's citizenry – all these can in part explain the phenomenon. However, some of these reasons can only explain the growth in overall numbers of CSOs, and some are normative deductions that are impossible to prove. They are not able to offer a fundamental explanation for the causes of these organisations' dilemma of legality and thus cannot provide either policy or legal solutions to redress the actual problem. In what follows I will seek to investigate this from the perspective of the law, especially at the level of both implementation and legislation.

4 The Dilemma of Legality Facing CSOs: Implementation

According to current regulations, China's system for the management of CSOs can be characterised as 'registration with the appropriate agency, dual responsibility and management according to administrative level'. 'Registration with the appropriate agency' means that all CSOs except those specifically exempted by law should be registered with the Ministry of Civil Affairs. Those whose registration is with other state agencies or departments will be regarded as not having an effective registration. 'Dual responsibility' means that the administration of CSOs comes through the cooperative efforts of both the registration agency and the sponsoring agency, who jointly exercise a management and

28 Ou Guangyuan, 'Explore a New Way of Managing Social Organisations for a New Era, Serve Social Stability and the Construction of the Two Civilisations', in Bureau of Civic Organisations Management of the Ministry of Civil Affairs (ed.), *supra* note 9, at p. 126.

supervisory role over CSOs. 'Management according to administrative level' means that in line with the size of a CSO, national level organisations will be administered by the registration agency of the State Council and a sponsoring agency at the corresponding level; local organisations will be handled by local registrars and sponsors.

According to Article 6 of the 'Regulations for Registration and Management of Social Organisations', and Article 5 of the 'Temporary Regulations for the Registration and Management of Popular Non-Enterprise Work Units' the agencies implementing the management of CSOs are primarily the CSO management agencies of the Ministry of Civil Affairs at various levels and the individual CSO's sponsoring agency. Specifically, the Ministry of Civil Affairs under the State Council, and its line agencies at county level and above are the registration and management agencies of the People's Government for CSOs and popular non-enterprise work units at that level. The relevant ministries under the State Council and their line agencies at county level and above, and organisations empowered by the State Council or the People's Government at county level and above, are eligible to be sponsoring agencies for CSOs and popular non-enterprise work units within their relevant industry, scientific discipline or area of work.

Article 27 of the 'Regulations for Registration and Management of Social Organisations' and Article 19 of the 'Temporary Regulations for the Registration and Management of Popular Non-Enterprise Work Units' stipulate the supervisory and management responsibilities of registering agencies: (1) registration and record keeping with respect to establishment, modification and closure of social organisations and popular non-enterprise work units; (2) conducting an annual review of the organisation; (3) supervision and review in cases where organisations fail to comply with the relevant regulations, and for applying disciplinary sanctions in such cases.

Article 28 of the 'Regulations for Registration and Management of Social Organisations' and Article 20 of the 'Temporary Regulations for the Registration and Management of Popular Non-Enterprise Work Units' stipulate the concomitant responsibilities of sponsoring agencies: (1) investigating social organizations or popular non-enterprise work units' preliminary application, establishment, modification or cancellation of registration; (2) supervising and guiding social organisations in compliance with the Constitution, laws, statutory regulations, national policy, and in carrying out activities in accordance with their charter; (3) conducting the preliminary stage of the annual review; (4) assisting the registration and management agency and other relevant departments to investigate and deal with any illegal activities of organisations; (5) in cooperation with other relevant departments, guiding the process of winding up social organisations or popular non-enterprise work units.

These are just the normative regulations concerning the responsibilities of implementing agencies set down in two major pieces of legislation; in actual practice those agencies' responsibilities greatly exceed these alone. Article 3 of the 'Temporary Measures for Suppression of Illegal Civic Organisations' states that 'registration agencies for social organisations and popular non-enterprise work units are responsible for investigating illegal civic organisations, collecting related evidence, issuing decisions for their closure in accordance with the law and confiscating their illegal assets'. Apart from the responsibilities listed above, sponsoring agencies are also responsible for day-to-day administration of registered social organisations. Such work mainly consists of:

> Responsibility for the education of leading figures and full-time staff of social organisations about the overall situation, about their tasks and about political ideology, making them familiar with state laws and policies and ensuring that they follow them; responsibility for oversight of the election and taking and leaving office of social organisations' leadership, and also for managing the establishment of Party organisations amongst full-time staff, their assignment to posts, adjustments to their pay and fixing of job titles; responsibility for checking and managing social organisations' major activities in the sphere of work (including the holding of research forums), their financial activities, their receipt of donations and their external and overseas activities; responsibility for checking and offering suggestions concerning changes to the internal structure of organisations or their expansion or contraction and also encouraging the organisation to go to the registering agency to change or cancel their registration. At such times they are also responsible for such post dissolution work as assisting a social organisation in settling its debts and providing documentation that outstanding debts have been paid off.[29]

From the above we can see that the administrative and supervisory responsibilities of implementing agencies cover pretty much everything from the preparation for and establishment of organisations, their day-to-day activities, to their dissolution, as well as also the crackdown on and suppression of illegal organisations. Theoretically the system of management and supervision by 'registration with the appropriate agency, dual responsibility and management according to administrative level' ought to be able to prevent or effectively

29 Wu Zhongze, Chen Jinluo (eds.), *Social Organisations Management Work (Shetuan guanli gongzuo)*, (Beijing: Zhongguo shehui chubanshe, 1996), at p. 31; See also Kang Xiaoguang, *supra* note 25, at p. 11.

reduce the problems of legality attending CSOs. So what, after all, is it that causes their dilemma in this respect? The following will look at an example of setting up and operating a social organisation in accordance with the relevant laws and see what supervisory and management services implementing agencies would be providing under normal circumstances.[30]

(1) Subjecting itself to the checking and approval of its sponsoring agency (Article 9). Those aspects of a social organisation checked by its sponsoring agency include: the need for and viability of that particular social organisation; checking up on the political circumstances and how authoritative and representative within their given industry, discipline or speciality the proposed chairpersons, deputy chairpersons or general secretaries of a social organisation in the preparatory stages of establishment are; checking on a proposed social organisation's scope of activities, the localities those activities will be conducted in and what form they will take; checking whether its source of funding is legal and stable; and checking whether the proposed organisation meets the various conditions stipulated for acting as a legal person.

(2) Application by the founders of an organisation to the registering agency. The founders should submit to the registering agency their preliminary application document, the contents of which should include the need for and viability of the organisation; its mission and scope of activity; the location and type of activities it will conduct; the funding for those activities and its sources of funding; what type of membership it hopes to attract and where they will be. They should also submit their letter of approval from their sponsoring agency, financial documentation, proof of rights to use their place of business, a list of proposed officers of the organisation, details of their and the founders' identities and personal circumstances, and a draft constitution (Article 11). The registering agency will, within 60 days of receipt of a full set of documents, carry out a check of the documents provided and make a decision to approve or deny the preliminary application (Article 12). Organisations that have their

30 For the relevant regulations see sections 3 (establishment and registration), 4 (changing and cancelling registration), and 5 (supervision and management) of the 1998 'Regulations for Registration and Management of Social Organisations'. The 'Regulations' contain no unitary provisions concerning sponsoring agencies' checking and annual review duties, but in practice these are conducted in broadly similar ways with slight local variations. Here I have followed the stipulations of the Guangdong regulations available on the website of the province's CSO Information Network at www.gdmjzz.gov.cn (Last visited March, 2005).

preliminary application approved should then submit their application to register their establishment after holding their first full members' meeting or meeting of members' representatives (Article 14). The registering agency will, within 30 days of receipt of documents relating to the application to register, check those documents again and will register those organisations that meet the set conditions. Registration includes such items as an organisation's name, address, mission, scope and locality of activities, legal representative, funds for activities and sponsoring agency (Article 16). Organisations approved for registration should file documentation with the registering agency within 60 days of the date of approval. The registering agency will then issue a 'Social Organisation Legal Entity Registration Certificate' within 30 days of the filing of documents. Filed documentation should include all the items provided during registration, the letter of approval from the sponsoring agency, the style of its official seal and its bank account details (Articles 17, 18).

(3) The organisation should submit an annual work report to it sponsoring agency before the 31st of March each year. Once this has been approved by the sponsors, it should be submitted to the registering agency prior to the 31st May, and the organisation should submit to an annual inspection. The annual work report should include details of how the social organisation has upheld the laws, regulations and state policies, how it has conducted any processes concerning registration as laid down in the regulations, how it has conducted activities in accordance with its constitution, any changes to its staff or organisational structure and financial information (Article 31). Materials to be provided in the course of an annual inspection normally include: a 'Social Organisation Annual Report Document'; audited accounts for the preceding year; an evaluation of the preceding year's work and plans for work in the coming year; a copy of the 'Social Organisation Legal Entity Registration Certificate'; as well as any other materials relating to information reported. The registering agency carries out its inspection by checking the provided materials and through other measures, confirms that the organisation has followed the laws, regulations and relevant policies and has carried out activities within the scope of activities and in accordance with its mission as set out in its constitution, and that it has not done anything illegal or violated standards of discipline. It also checks that the organisation's financial system is healthy, that its income and expenditures are in line with state mandated regulations, that it has promptly submitted any documentation resulting from changes to its registration or organisational arrangements and that it has submitted itself for annual inspection within the stipulated time limit. If all the above conditions are met, the

organisation passes its annual inspection. Should it be discovered that any of the following conditions exist, then it will fail its annual inspection:

- the organisation has carried out no activities in the preceding year;
- its funds are insufficient to support its normal activities;
- it has carried out activities that violate its constitution;
- it has violated financial regulations;
- there are serious internal problems in the organisation or a serious failure of democratic decision making;
- it has levied excessive membership fees in violation of regulations;
- it has not had a fixed place of business for more than a year;
- it has not registered organisational changes or provided the documentation that it should;
- it has not submitted to annual inspection within the proscribed time limits and there are no special extenuating circumstances for this;
- it has committed falsification in the annual inspection process; or
- it has violated other regulations.

(4) An organisation wishing to alter its registration or its filed documentation should first apply to its sponsoring agency for checking and approval of such action. If this is given, it should then apply to the registering agency within thirty days. If an organisation revises its constitution, it should also report this to the registering agency within thirty days of its approval by the sponsoring agency (Article 20).

(5) Organisations that seek to disband, divide or combine with other organisations because they have fulfilled the mission stated in their constitution, or who wish to cease activities for some other reason, must first have this checked and approved by their sponsoring agency. The sponsor will, in cooperation with other relevant agencies, guide the work of winding up the social organisation, after which the registering agency will cancel the organisation's registration and revoke its filed documentation (Articles 21, 22, 23, 24).

The first four groups of services outlined above must be provided to pretty much any legally registered social organisation. Let us consider again the other responsibilities of the implementing agencies, such as oversight of the day-to-day activities of social organisations, punishment of illegal activities, suppressing and sequestrating the assets of unregistered or illegal groups, and also occasionally conducting general surveys of CSOs within their administrative jurisdiction as and when higher authorities request, indeed even needing at one point to re-register already legally registered social organisations. From this we can suppose that if all of China's three million CSOs registered legally, submitted to annual inspection and reported their major activities for approval, for the staff of implementing agencies to provide effective supervision and management (especially in China where such skills are not yet up to the most modern standards) would require an incredibly large CSO management system and also an incredibly large budgetary allocation.

In September 1992, a senior official at the Ministry of Civil Affairs made public the organisational structure and staffing of the then extant CSO management agency within the Ministry:

> To date, 30 provincial level administrations have already established social organisation management departments or offices, with a total staff of 217 cadres. 270 district level or directly governed municipalities and also 700 county level administrations have done likewise, the former having a full and part-time staff of 605, the latter of 726 persons.[31]

Later, as the state became more aware of and improved its administration of CSOs there were some changes to this situation. In 1999,

> Beijing and Shanghai established social organizations management agencies at sub-departmental (*futing*) level. The Beijing agency was assigned a staff of 140 in 9 sections including 50 people in a supervision team (*jiancha dadui*). The agency in Shanghai had a staff of 50 in 5 sections. Provinces such as Qinghai and Hubei have also established CSO management departments this year.[32]

31 Fan Baojun, *supra* note 17, at p. 107.

32 'Speech by Minister for Civil Affairs Douji Cairang to the Forum on Improving the Management of CSO (6th December, 1999)', in Bureau of Civic Organisations Management of the Ministry of Civil Affairs, *supra* note 9, at p. 137. The original urban divisions of Shanghai (county-level sub-districts) had a total of 60 cadres responsible for CSO management. The 50 members of staff mentioned here were additional recruits added in 1999 when the Municipal Party Committee and Government approved the establishment of sub-departmental level Social Organisations Management Bureau. See 'Summing up by Deputy Minister for Civil Affairs Xu Ruixin Delivered to the Forum on Improving the Management of CSOs' (8th December, 1999). Elsewhere, staffing levels at the Tianjin Municipal Social Organisations Management Agency increased from an original 7 to 17, and the city's county-level and district division also set up specific agencies for this work, assigning a staff of 5. In 1998, Tianjin set up a 'Social Organisations Management Network' made up of 27 Party and government agencies. See Deputy Mayor of Tianjin, Xia Baolong 'Serve the Overall Situation, Support Reform, Vigorously Explore New Ways of Conducting Social Organisations Work' in Bureau of Civic

Improvements to the staffing and funding of implementing agencies should have a positive impact on solving the dilemma of legality facing CSOs and a direct manifestation of this was seen in the results of a national crackdown on illegal CSOs. For example Beijing investigated and dealt with over 400 illegally established social organisations; on a 'Day of Implementing Administrative Management of Social Organisations' in successive years on the 27th of May in 1994 and 1995, Tianjin cleared up a total of 51 unauthorised social organisations. Between 1994 and 1998 Guangdong advised 223 illegal social organisations to voluntarily disband, cancelled the registration of another 150, suppressed a further 14 in accordance with the law and ordered another 22 to disband.[33] However, these achievements were at best only a small help in resolving the overall dilemma of legality for China's CSOs. The increase in staff and funding of implementing agencies did see the closure, cancellation or absorption of a number of registered CSOs. For example, in the case of social organisations the total number of registered organisations for the six years inclusive 1996 to 2001 was respectively 185,000, 181,000, 166,000, 137,000, 131,000 and 129,000[34] a steady fall of significant proportions year on year.

I conducted a survey in certain districts in the first six months of both 2002 and 2003. Although the scope and subjects of my survey were extremely limited and the methodology left a great deal to be desired (due to circumstances the sample consisted of 'asking whoever I could find') meaning that no general conclusions can be drawn from the results, at the very least they do reflect a part of the situation. There were three types of respondent to my survey: Civil Affairs departments, sponsoring agencies and some CSOs. Survey respondents who were comrades working in CSO management agencies all raised the

Organisations Management of the Ministry of Civil Affairs, *supra* note 9, at pp. 163-165. In Shandong 'just after provincial institutional reform had been completed in 1996 and with agency staffing levels effectively frozen, a provincial 'Social Organisations and Popular Non-enterprise Work Units Management Office' was established with the approval of the provincial government. The originally approved staff of ten was increased by the addition of a further five persons and funding for the office was also increased'. Deputy Governor of Shandong Lin Yansheng, 'Keep our Eyes on Stabilising the Overall Situation, Improve Management and Guidance, Promote the Healthy and Orderly Development of Civil Society Organisations' in Bureau of Civic Organisations Management of the Ministry of Civil Affairs, *supra* note 9, at p. 200.

33 Ou Guangyuan, 'Explore a New Way of Managing Social Organizations for a New Era, Serve Social Stability and the Construction of the Two Civilizations', in Bureau of Civic Organisations Management of the Ministry of Civil Affairs, s*upra* note 9, p. 107.

34 From the Ministry of Civil Affairs' website: www.mca.gov.cn/news/news2002032501.html.

problem of their understaffing. Indeed some counties where organisational restructuring had not yet been carried out had no full-time staff responsible for CSO management at all. Around 2001, as the state attached increasing importance to CSO issues, the government at various levels made corresponding improvements to their capacity for CSO management in the course of government restructuring – county level authorities would usually establish a CSO management section or office with one or two full time members of staff. Some civil affairs officials working in CSO management further pointed out that inadequate staffing was not their only problem. Other difficulties included: high levels of expenditure, low levels of legal understanding amongst the citizenry, a lack of clarity in the laws and regulations themselves which made them hard to fully comprehend, and also a divergence between the apparent directions of law as against overall policy. Of the score or more sponsoring agencies surveyed none had a dedicated member of staff or agency responsible for the supervision and management of CSOs. The impression gained from the CSOs surveyed was that there existed a general resentment of the ineffectiveness of registering agencies, whose demands were regarded as excessively strict; also they found it hard to find willing sponsoring agencies and some that could be found expected excessive payment or some other favours in return.

For the civil affairs agencies at various levels implementing management, lacking adequate staff and funding, and faced with the rapid growth in the desire to form civil society organisations, it is already impossible to fully carry out their responsibilities in accordance with the laws outlined above, and still less to regularly do as higher government levels demand and allocate staff and resources to clean up and rectification campaigns. At the same time, although the regulations have stipulated broad responsibilities for sponsoring agencies, they have made no hard provisions saying exactly who should undertake such a role, nor have they outlined any specific legal sanctions for sponsors who are lax in discharging their duties – meaning that, in practice, on the one hand, the vast majority of agencies with the necessary legal status to act as sponsors are not willing to do so, and on the other, those that do find it hard to perform their duties properly.[35] This all serves to increase the burden on the registering

35 Since potential sponsoring agencies have a choice as to whether or not to assume such a role, if we accept the assumption of economic theory that they will make decisions on a rational basis, then an agency meeting the legal requirements to act as a sponsor would be expected to consider the potential implications of so doing in terms of their own interests. A 'sponsoring agency' has wide-ranging legal obligations and unless there were obvious benefits for so doing, a rational actor would not choose to undertake such a role. If the benefits accrued from the CSOs it oversees exceed the burden of responsib-

agencies. In the light of this situation, short of manpower, materials and money, registering agencies are not only forced to allow a large number of unregistered CSOs to continue existing, they are not even able to exercise the management role set down by the rules and regulations over those CSOs that are legally registered. This means that the more illegal CSOs there are, the more there is a need for 'clean-up and rectification', but since those campaigns add to the everyday operating costs of implementing agencies, those agencies are less and less able to fulfil their duties.

Government reforms on themes of 'streamlined government' and 'small government, big society' mean that there is no possibility of expanding management agencies in terms of staff levels. The budgetary deficits of both central and local government disallow an increase of resources. If we consider the whole range of functions of China's government, and also the many other problems the state must solve in the preliminary stage of socialism, management of CSOs cannot, and should not be treated as a special case in terms of the manpower and financial resources allocated to it. Looked at in this way, a capacity to implement the law that falls short of what the law requires, and thus leads to an inability to implement the law, must be one of the main causes of the dilemma of illegality facing civil society organisations.

5 The Dilemma of Legality Facing CSOs: Legislation

The analysis of the implementation of the law given above makes it clear that the current regulations governing the management of CSOs make the costs of implementation too high, leading to a failure of implementation in actual practice. This indicates that failures of implementation are only the surface of the problem – its deeper cause lies in the inappropriate nature of current legislation.

ilities, then any other responsibility shirked or fulfilled in a less costly fashion will create a consequent increase in benefit to the sponsor. Also, shirking one's responsibilities can benefit the CSO you should be supervising and thus in turn increase your potential to get something back from them, to the point that aiding and abetting a CSO in illegal activity can be in line with maximising one's own benefit.

5.1 Coincidences of Alternations in Legislative Approach and Changes in Total Numbers of CSOs

The proliferation of CSOs is not just a phenomenon of the post-reform era. Already in the early years of the 20th century, China saw the establishment of all kinds of political, economic and social organisations. By 1911, there were 193 politically radical or revolutionary groups alone, such as Sun Yat-sen's *Tong Mengjun*. By 1913 there were 1,076 chambers of commerce. Between 1912 and 1921 in Jiangsu Province alone the total number of social organisations reached 1,403.[36] In the years prior to the establishment of the People's Republic of China there was a time when CSOs were quite numerous and widespread. After 1949, first the State Council issued its 'Temporary Measures for the Registration of Social organisations' in 1950, then the Ministry of Internal Affairs issued the 'Detailed Regulations for the Implementation of the Temporary Measures for the Registration of Social organisations' in 1951, and after this came the first rectification campaign aimed at social organisations. In 1965, there were close to 100 national level social organisations on the Chinese mainland, and around 6,000 local groups. During the ten years of the Cultural Revolution social organisations across the country fell into a state of effective paralysis. With the revival of their activities in 1976, the overall number of social organisations began to rapidly increase, and a second period of proliferation began. By 1989, the number of national level social organisations in China had reached around 1,800, and there were close to 200,000 local organisations. Related to this was the fact that in the period between reform and opening and the issuing of the 'Regulations for Registration and Management of Social Organisations' in 1989 China's CSOs were operating in an environment where effectively there was no law for them to abide by because the 1950 'Temporary Measures' had fallen into abeyance during the Cultural Revolution, apart from a few 'Notices' and 'Decisions' issued internally by the Ministry of Civil Affairs.

In 1989, the State Council issued the 'Regulations for Registration and Management of Social Organisations', which was followed by another clean-up and rectification of CSOs. According to figures given by the Ministry of Civil Affairs for registered groups, by the end of 1991, there were 836 national level

36 Tao Heshan, *Civic Groups and Innovations in the Political System – Research into the Main Actors in China's Modernisation* (*Shimin qunti yu zhidu chuangxin – dui Zhongguo xiandaihua zhuti de yanjiu*), (Nanjing: Nanjing daxue chubanshe, 2001), at pp. 75, 80, 88.

social organisations and 116,000 local organisations. In 1996 the total number of social organisations in China reached a historical high point, with 1,845 national level or inter-provincial organisations and 187,000 organisations at county level or above. Beginning in the latter half of 1996, the Ministry of Civil Affairs was appointed by the State Council to revise the 'Regulations for Registration and Management of Social Organisations'. The revised law was approved and came into effect on the 25th October, 1998. This was followed by a period of reregistering and reconfirmation for existing organizations, and there was a downward movement in the total number of social organisations. In 2000 there were 1,528 national level organisations and a total of 130,768 organisations in the country as a whole.[37]

We can see from this brief historical outline that there is a coincidence between changes in legislation governing CSOs, and rises and falls in the total number of such organisations. After almost every new law is promulgated, there is a rapid fall over the short term in the total number of legally registered CSOs.

5.2 The Control-oriented Management Tendency of the Current Legislation

Article 10 of the 1998 'Regulations for Registration and Management of Social Organisations' stipulates that:

> To establish a social organisation the following conditions must be satisfied: 1. An organisation must have more than 50 individual members or more than 30 institutional members or, if it has both individual and institutional members, a total of at least 50. 2. It must have a standard name and a corresponding organisational structure. 3. It must have a fixed location. 4. It must have staff with qualifications appropriate to the professional activities of the organisation. 5. It must have lawful assets and a source of funds. National level organisations must have a minimum of CNY 100,000 to cover their activities; local social organisations and inter-area social organisations must have a minimum of CNY 30,000. 6. It must be capable of assuming legal liability in its own right.

Article 13 stipulates that:

> The registration agency will not approve the preliminary registration in any of the following cases: 1. There is documented proof showing that the objectives and area of work of a social organisation applying for preliminary registration do not comply

37 Ministry of Civil Affair's website: www.mca.gov.cn/statistics/index.html.

> with Article 4 of these regulations. 2. If in the same administrative area there is already a social organisation active in the same or similar area of work, there is no need for a new organisation to be established. 3. If the applicant or the proposed officers of the organisation have ever been subject to the criminal sanction of being deprived of their political rights, or do not possess the capacity to assume full civil liability. 4. If deception is employed in the preliminary application. 5. There are other circumstances prohibited by law or administrative rules and regulations.

Article 11 of the 'Temporary Regulations for the Registration and Management of Popular Non-Enterprise Work Units' states that:

> In the following circumstances the registration agency should not allow registration, the reason for any refusal should be explained to the applicant: 1. There is documented proof showing that the objectives and area of work of a popular non-enterprise work unit applying for preliminary registration do not comply with Article 4 of these regulations. 2. There has been falsification during the application process. 3. There is an existing popular non-enterprise work unit in the same administrative district with the same or similar scope of activity, and thus no need to establish a new one. 4. The proposed legal representative is currently or has previously suffered the criminal sanction of removal of political rights, or does not possess the capacity to assume full civil liability. 5. There are other circumstances prohibited by law or administrative rules and regulations.

Since other articles in current legislation stipulate that a CSO 'must register', organisations that do not meet the above conditions are not only ineligible to register, in legal terms they have no right to exist. Considered from the current national situation of being in the preliminary stage of socialism there are still enormous disparities between not only the countryside and the cities, and between the East and the West, but also between different industries, different social orders and in terms of economic and educational attainments. Different people have different abilities to meet the cost of forming organisations. For citizens at the bottom of the social ladder, disadvantaged groups and poor residents of mountainous areas, the regulations concerning membership and funds for activities without doubt place a formidable barrier to the exercise of their right to free association – and in terms of what forming organisations means, and can achieve, they are precisely the people who most need to be able to do so.[38]

38 Especially in the case of marginalised groups, such as farmers in poor areas and migrant workers and laid-off workers in the cities, the legal requirements for minimum amounts

The stipulation requiring a CSO to 'have staff with qualifications appropriate to its professional activities'[39] should only apply to some social organisations as in reality many have no need for such staff. It is hard to understand the requirement that an organisation 'possess the capacity to assume full civil liability'[40] since the regulations have already set a lower limit of the amount of funds for activities, it seems to serve as an emphasis on the seriousness of establishing a social organisation. On the face of it the stipulation requiring 'documented proof showing that the objectives and area of work of a social organisation … do not comply with Article 4 of these regulations', that is, 'social organisations must observe the Constitution, state laws, regulations and state policy; must not oppose the basic principles of the Constitution, harm the unity, security or ethnic harmony of the state, or interests of the state and society, or the lawful interests of other organisations or citizens, or offend social morality...social organisations may not engage in profit-seeking activities'[41] seem reasonable enough, but regarding the 'documented proof' we are left ignorant of who should provide such proof, who judges it and what the evidentiary standards are. Then there is the stipulation that if there is another social organisation 'in the same administrative district with the same or similar scope

of funds are in effect for most of them the forcible removal of their right to establish civil society organisations. I learned in the course of my survey that recently some counties and towns have taken an interpretation of higher level instructions on promoting the growth of CSOs as the basis for a policy of allowing new groups which do not yet meet membership or funding requirements to first 'place themselves on file', and then complete formal registration procedures once they have grown sufficiently to fulfil statutory requirements. However, in terms of the intention of the legislation, these clauses were designed to limit the formation of grassroots groups. This is clearly revealed in the 'Notice issued by the Ministry of Civil Affairs concerning issues related to the re-checking and re-registration of social organisations' (*supra* note 2) issued in April 1991: 'social organisations at or below street committee or township level, when applying for registration, should submit to the registering agency an evaluation of their suitability given by the appropriate government or Party agencies of the district in which their area lies, or their county or municipal Party or government where there are no intermediate levels of administration'. Clearly, this is a great deal stricter than the requirements for other CSO applying for registration.

39 Art. 10, Regulations for Registration and Management of Social Organisations.

40 Art. 11, Temporary Regulations for the Registration and Management of Popular Non-Enterprise Work Units.

41 Art. 4, Temporary Regulations for the Registration and Management of Popular Non-Enterprise Work Units.

of activity, and thus no need to establish a new one'.[42] The connection between the existence of a similar group and the need or otherwise of establishing a new one, and indeed the whole concept of necessity here, is very unclear from a legislative point of view. The stipulation that persons who have previously been stripped of their political rights cannot found or serve as officers of social organisations is hard to justify in legislative terms.[43] The above regulations are broadly the same as those contained in the 1989 'Regulations for Registration and Management of Social Organisations'. However, since the latter legislation did not insist that an organisation 'must register or it is illegal' it follows logically that those that did not meet these conditions were merely ineligible for registration, and their right to exist at all remained an unresolved question.

Current legislation has affirmed a system of 'registration with the appropriate agency, dual responsibility and management according to administrative level'. Officials from the Ministry of Civil Affairs in explaining this system have indicated that 'registration with the appropriate agency' is significant in two ways: it helps regularise the way in which social organisations are managed; and it also strengthens that management.

> For a certain period of time in the past, because any government agency had the right to set up social organisations, there was over-rapid growth in numbers of organisations and a loss of overall control, and complete chaos in the work of granting legal person status to civil society organisations. To avoid this state of affairs occurring, it was proposed that the Ministry of Civil Affairs should handle matters concerning social organisations.[44]

The 'dual responsibility' system was established in the 1989 'Regulations for Registration and Management of Social Organisations' and was reinforced in the regulations covering social organisations and popular non-enterprise work units issued in 1998. The system in operation was first seen in the early 1990s and was the object of criticism from CSOs, academics and even some officials in implementing agencies. The reasons it was so widely denounced can probably

42 Art. 11, Temporary Regulations for the Registration and Management of Popular Non-Enterprise Work Units.

43 For a discussion of the suitability of these stipulations see the critique given by Ge Yunsong, The Legal System on the Third Sector (*Desanbumen de faluzhidu*), in Su Li *et. al.*, *The Regulatory System and Development – The Legal Environment for the Third Sector (Guizhi yu fazhan – disan bumen de falü huanjing)*, (Hangzhou: Zhejiang renmin chubanshe, 1999), at pp. 33-50.

44 Xu Ruixin, *supra* note 4, at pp. 88-89.

be reduced to three main aspects: firstly, during the process of establishing and registering a social organisation it sets up a threshold, and organisations which meet all the other legal requirements but are unable to find a sponsoring agency find that they are still doomed to an illegal existence; secondly, when an organisation conducts activities it is subject to two separate strands of checking and supervision, which may be working to the same agenda or may be at cross purposes or duplicating one another – only those organisations able to satisfy two different supervisory 'tastes' at the same time are able to carry out the work they want to; thirdly, in the process of implementing this system of management often the sponsor and registering agency try to pass off their work to the other agency, they may harbour resentment of one another and even accuse one another of failing to perform their mandated responsibilities. Now why was such a widely disliked system not only not abolished, or watered down when the laws were revised, but was in fact actually further strengthened? The legislative agencies felt that the functions of the sponsoring agencies in checking and approving registration applications and in supervising staffing arrangements were important.

> Checking and approving registration applications include checking applications to establishment, their alteration or cancellation. That is, you can approve the establishment of an organisation, approve changes to its application and approve the cancellation of its application, and you may also deny approval. Once an organisation is established, after a time a sponsoring agency may find that the organisation's activities exceed the scope that the sponsor is competent to oversee, or perhaps because of structural reforms the sponsor no longer has the same capacities it once had and cannot continue as a sponsor, or perhaps a social organisation does not submit to the sponsor's guidance; in these cases a sponsor may well propose to the registering agency that it no longer acts as sponsor of that social organisation. If the organisation cannot find a new sponsor within a set period of time the registering agency will, as the regulations stipulate, cancel the organisation's registration as it no longer meets the necessary legal requirements. A major part of a sponsor's management of staffing is their interference in the selection of senior officers of organisations. The choice of leading figures in social organisations from general secretaries on up must be based first on the assessment and recommendation of the sponsoring agency, and only then is it submitted to the board or membership for a democratic election. Sponsors can make suggestions concerning the reassignment and removal of leading figures in social organisations, but the final decision will be made democratically within the organisation.[45]

45 See, Xu Ruixin, *supra* note 4, at pp. 90-91.

We have called the above situation the control-oriented management tendency of the current legislation. Control-oriented management is like the way a parent treats a child, it is based on the authority the manager holds over the managed, it seeks to prevent problems from arising; through strict supervision and the methods of control it seeks to avoid the managed organisation doing something that would harm the state, society, others or itself. It is because of this tendency that current legislation has set the requirements for registration relatively high; that is has established a 'dual responsibility system' that is simultaneously strict yet riddled with loopholes; and that it has drawn a clear demarcation line between legal and illegal which says in effect if you don't meet the legal requirements to register then you are an illegal organisation. This legislative tendency also supplies a credible explanation for the changes in the total numbers of social organisations following the promulgation of new regulations and also makes it easy to see why legislation has provided implementing agencies with such broad-ranging and unlimited powers and yet saddled them with such exceptionally high implementation costs.

Control-oriented management is based on a distrust of the managed, and finds its justification in their supposed 'immaturity and ignorance'. At the same time, the implementation of this kind of management is also predicated on the actual immaturity of the managed. As they grow, the costs of that management increase and even exceed the limits of the possible, leaving managers incapacitated and opening the way for a slide into effective *laissez faire*. The current legislation once sought to control the rate of growth of the total number of CSOs, but its practical application led to unforeseen results. One of these is that although the number of legally registered CSOs has indeed been controlled, this free-for-all caused by the impossibly high costs of implementing effective management means that organisations which cannot meet legal requirements have 'gone underground' and continue as illegal organisations, whilst legal organisations take advantage of the weaknesses in management to seek private advantages or even engage in outright illegal activity. Another unforeseen consequence is that the increase in the number of illegal organisations has strengthened citizens' belief that they can get away with not legally registering their organisation, which sets up a vicious circle feeding the growth in illegal CSOs.

6 The Problem of Legitimacy in Current CSO Regulations

The preceding discussion makes clear that not only is the serious dilemma of legality facing CSOs a direct reflection of the lack of effectiveness of the current regulatory system governing them, but also that there is a causal relationship between the two, that is, the dilemma of legality is, to a great extent, the product of the inappropriateness of the current legislation. We know that for a law to be worthy of the name, a most fundamental precondition is that it will be obeyed by the majority of members of society. In these terms the current system of legislation governing CSOs has severe problems of legitimacy.

6.1 The Contrary Nature of CSOs' Legality and Propriety

The current CSO legislation uses an organisation's status as registered or unregistered as the standard by which the 'legal' are distinguished from the 'illegal', which has the effect of stripping any legal status from the great majority of CSOs that are not registered. But this can only show that the existence of these organisations is not legal, it does not prove that their existence is not right and proper.

Scholarly research since the 1990s has confidently affirmed the enormous significance China's CSOs play in our political, economic and social lives,[46] and that research very rarely considers only the role of legally registered CSOs. The percentage of grassroots rural CSOs that are legally registered is relatively low, but research on these groups has shown that overall they play a major role

46 For example, the essays by Kang Xiaoguang, Qin Hui and Gao Bingzhong, *supra* note 11; Yu Keping's two pieces, 'The Rise of China's Civil Society and its Significance for Governance', *supra* note 8, and 'China's Rural CSOs and Changes in Governance', in *Zhonguo gongmin shehui de xingqi he zhili de bianqian,* (Beijing: Shehui kexue chubanshe, 2002); Chen Jinluo, *Legislation for and Administration of Social Organisations (Shetuan lifa yu shetuan guanli)*, (Beijing: falü chubanshe, 1997); Qi Bingwen (ed.), *The Management, Building, and Development of Civil Society Organisations (Minjian zuzhi: guanli, jianshe, fazhan)*, (Jinan: Shandong daxue chubanshe, 2001); Wang Ming *et al.*, *supra* note 10; Ma Changshan, 'Brief Discussion of the Legal Status of China's Social Organisations and how to Restrain the Tendency for them to Become Instruments of Official Administration', (1992) (3), *Politics and Law* (*Zhengzhi yu falü*), and 'A Discussion of the Right to Freedom of Association in China' in (1993) (5), *Politics and Law* (*Zhengzhi yu falü*); Sun Bingyao, 'Township Social Organisations and China's Grassroots Society *(Xiangzhen shetuan yu Zhongguo jiceng shehui*)' in (1994) (9), *Chinese Journal of Social Science* (*Zhongguo shehui kexue jikan).*

in village self-governance, social welfare activities such as care for the elderly and disabled, and in the provision of economic services to rural residents. 'They have fundamentally changed the structure and actuality of governance in the Chinese countryside, and overall have been a force promoting rural democracy and good governance'.[47]

Take the example of farmer's self-help organisations.[48] They have been the major social organisations seeking to provide self-help services to farmers in the years following the rural reforms and the establishment of the market economy. Mindful of the role played by farmer's self-help organisations, and their potential impact on the rural development over the long term, right from the 1980s through to the present day state agencies have expressed their approval and support for these groups in numerous official documents. For example, the Communist Party Central Committee (CPCC), Document No.1 from 1983, 'Certain Economic and Policy Questions Presently Concerning the Countryside' says: 'There are many skilled craftsmen, able producers, intelligent young people and demobilised servicemen in the countryside. We should give full play to their special talents and support them in establishing technical service organisations.'[49] In January, 1987, a consultation document put out by the General Office of the State Council said, concerning rural specialist producers associations, that 'they are a new kind of specialised technical service organisation that display unique Chinese characteristics'.[50] In 1989 the State Council's 'Decision Concerning Relying on Scientific and Technological Progress to Stimulate Agriculture and Strengthening Work for the Dissemination of Scientific and Technological Achievements' stated:

> We should actively support specialist technical associations and research organisations that draw their membership mainly from farmers, and have farmer technicians and science and technology workers as their key actors, progressing towards the formation of a national agricultural technical extension network composed of existing

47 Yu Keping, 'China's Rural CSOs and Changes in Governance', *supra* note 46, at p. 57.

48 This draws on Zhang Xiaoshan *et. al.*, *Linking Farmers and the Market – Research into Chinese Farmer's Intermediary Organisations* (*Lianjie nonghu yu shichang: Zhongguo nongmin zhongjie zuzhi yanjiu*), (Beijing: Zhongguo shehui kexue chubanshe, 2002), at p. 240 ff.

49 People Daily, 10 April 1983.

50 See Zhang Xiaoshan, *supra* note 48, at p. 240.

> extension organisations, mass organisations for promoting agricultural science and farmer's specialist technical associations.[51]

In 1991 the CPCC's 'Decision Concerning Further Improving Agriculture and Rural Work' said 'We should attach importance to promoting the development of all types of civic specialist technical associations, research organisations and technical service organisations, and give full play to their role in popularising applied technologies and opening up new productive industries'. The 1993 'Certain Measures Concerning Present Day Agriculture and Rural Economic Development' issued by the CPCC and State Council stated:

> the various types of people run specialist technical associations and research organisations in the countryside are a new force in the socialised agricultural services system. Governments at all levels should improve the guidance and support given them so that as they provide services they can grow into technological and economic actors and move down the route of self-development and self-service.[52]

Document No. 2 issued by the CPCC in 1998 said:

> the various specialist associations and groups and other forms of cooperative association formed by farmers on their own initiative are for the most part collective economic entities where farmers pool their labour and capital. They are beneficial for bringing farmers into the market economy and for improving the agricultural socialised service sector and they should be actively encouraged and vigorously supported.[53]

However, surveys of these farmer's organisation show that only a very few of them have registered with civil affairs agencies, and thus the great majority are not legal organisations.[54]

51 http://www.nj110.com.zcfg/53.htm.

52 http://www.china.org.cn/chinese/zhuanti/jd/493907.htm.

53 See Zhang Xiaoshan, *supra* note 48, at p. 240.

54 Some farmer's self-help organisations are not in fact run on a 'not-for-profit' basis, but their social impact is ultimately similar to genuinely non-profit self-help groups. This leads to a further criticism – for-profit groups can quite easily register as such with the Bureau of Industry and Commerce and achieve a fully legal status, whereas non-profit organisations fulfilling the same social role find it hard to achieve such legality precisely because they are not trying to make money. This is another example of the contradictions inherent in the present situation.

Also, although properly registered 'legal CSOs' have attained the legal right to exist they do not necessarily become right and proper as a result. A good example of such organisations is those CSOs that do little actual work and exploit their organisational status, or even exploit administrative powers, to seek illegal benefits. The standard for assessing the legality of a CSO is determined by the rules and regulations, but its propriety will be ascertained from its actions, and the actual social impact that it has. This is why the divide between legality and illegality that depends only on whether or not an organisation is registered has led to the contrary nature of how the legality and propriety of a CSO is ascertained.

6.2 The Potential of the Current Legislation Governing CSOs

The current CSO laws have problems of legitimacy because they are ineffective and have led to contradictions between a CSO's legality and propriety. Nevertheless if they still have the potential to change this current state of affairs and become part of a better future then those problems of legitimacy can be solved within the existing framework.

When I say, 'change the current state of affairs', I mean the question as to whether they can achieve the kind of outcomes that a law should. The most important of these would be resolving the problem that ten times as many CSOs exist illegally than are registered. Looking at the existing legislation we can see a logical possibility for changing the current state of affairs: since that legislation grants broad powers to implementing agencies and also has strict provisions for the punishment of illegal CSOs, then perhaps these illegal organisations could be abolished at a stroke through some sort of campaign to apply the law. And indeed, this kind of logical possibility has been fully recognised and applied in actual practice. Since the 'Regulations for Registration and Management of Social Organisations' came out in 1989 there have been at least three such campaign style enforcement activities. However, logic is after all only logic. The rectification campaign that followed the promulgation of the two regulations in 1998 was probably the largest scale and longest lasting instance of such activity, but still today we have yet to see any outcome from it and it was far from ideal. Although there was a large drop in the number of legally registered organisations after the clean up campaign, viewed from the long term we will probably see an increase in the number of illegal organisations. Because if we suppose that people's desire to form organisations has not changed, but registration is difficult, then legalised organisations will become fewer and unregistered, illegal ones will proliferate. Moreover, rectification campaigns are a very costly way of implementing the law. Since these organisations have not registered, implementing agencies must first conduct a great deal of investigative work before they can enforce the law and they need to get hold of a great deal of solid evidence on a whole range of matters. At the same time rectification campaigns are by nature periodic occurrences. If illegal CSOs are rational actors then they will surely just lie low during these periods and this again greatly increases the enforcement costs for implementing agencies. Again, as state material, financial and personnel resources are limited, such high-cost enforcement strategies cannot be employed as the norm. Also, over the course of a long running contest with the implementing agencies, the illegal CSOs will naturally accumulate an ever richer repertoire of tricks to deal with their opponents. Couple this with the overall increase in the number of CSOs attending overall social development, and the costs of enforcement can only continue to rise, and the possibility of employing this method becomes less and less.

When I say the law can become part of a better future I mean it can satisfy people's desire to form organisations. Citizens' desires to form organisations are in part an expression of human nature.[55] One scholar described this human nature aspect of the desire to form organisations as the 'water ladle principle' – you can push down on the fishing float until it is completely submerged and temporarily hidden under water, but relax your hand for just a moment and it will bob up to the surface again.[56] The desire to form organisations is also in part a result of the social, economic and political environment. In the post-reform era, China has carried out a major process of reform, separating government from enterprises and government from society. There has been a steady movement away from the government controlling all aspects of social life and many functions formerly the preserve of the government require new social actors to come forward and undertake them. As the process of modernisation continues we have also seen the appearance of a host of new social problems. Neither government, nor business is able or willing to resolve these problems, and thus there is a widespread demand for civil society organisations. At the same time, the increase in social production has not only brought changes to

55 Liu Zuoxiang, 'The Roots in Basic Human Nature of the Right to Freedom of Association', paper presented at the Conference on Legal Aspects of Social Organisations held by the Institute of Law of the Chinese Academy of Social Sciences in 2002 (the paper is with the author).

56 Wang Ming *et al., supra* note 10, at pp. 89 ff.

citizens' modes of living and mindsets, it has also provided the economic basis for the formation of CSOs. These changes in the social, economic and political environment ensure that the demand for CSOs will not only not weaken, it will in fact continue to rise to ever new heights. A comparison has been made between the numbers of NPOs per ten thousand people in 15 different countries. The results show that in mainland China there are only 1.45 NPOs per ten thousand people, which is only 1.3% of the figure for France, 1.5% of the figure for Japan, 10% of the figure for Singapore and even when compared to the figures for our own Taiwan it is only 15.5%.[57] From this we can see that the demand for CSOs can only continue to rise in China.

It has been the tendency of several previous CSO regulations to attempt to use legislation to suppress citizens' desire to form CSOs. The result has been what we have seen above; the existence of vast numbers of illegal CSOs has clearly announced the bankruptcy of this kind of restrictive legislation.

Our legislation and administrative practice for CSOs should adopt a different approach towards the ever increasing demand to form organisations – perhaps we can seek to 'plan' that demand. Legislatively, both the 'Regulations for Registration and Management of Social Organisations' and the 'Temporary Regulations for the Registration and Management of Popular Non-Enterprise Work Units' stipulate that if in the same administrative area there is already an organisation active in the same or similar area of work, there is no need for a new organisation to be established and the registering agency should reject an application to register. In practice, a minority of CSOs have monopoly status: the state only allows citizens to participate in one certain organisation and forbids the establishment of new similar bodies; indeed sometimes the state demands that citizens must participate in certain organisations. 'Planning' could be a way of responding to the demand for CSOs, seeking to satisfy that demand through already established organisations that people actually participate in, or are encouraged to participate in. However, let us first not discuss whether the demand for CSOs can in fact be 'planned' for. Looking at the existing organisations that people have to choose from, their partial monopoly status is based on their dependence on the government. In most cases, they were in fact directly or indirectly established by the government. The reason the government is willing for people to participate in these organisations is that the government has complete control over them. In practice these organisations are exactly

57 *Id.*

what sociologists call 'secondary vertical channels of communication'[58] or are simply tools through which government controls society. There are both theoretical and practical doubts as to whether participation in these organisations can be considered 'freedom of association'. More importantly these doubts are not just held by me, but by almost all the respondents to the survey I conducted, who were similarly perplexed. Indeed officials in implementing agencies frankly admitted that joining these organisations differed from the strict sense of 'freedom of association'. That the demand for CSOs cannot be met through 'planning' is a function of the basic nature of that demand. Freedom of association implies a voluntary and independent choice. Where that choice is not free, the concept of freedom of association is an empty one.

6.3 The Problem of Legality in Current CSO Regulations

The preceding discussion has been conducted on the assumption that current CSO legislation has legality. But if such a law does indeed have legality, does this not say that China's whole legal system, and not merely that part of it governing CSOs has a problem of propriety?

According to the provisions of Article 89 of the Constitution and Article 56 of the 'Legislative Law' (*lifa fa*) the State Council has the right to draft administrative regulations concerning CSOs.[59] Taking just this as our starting point, not only is current CSO law in accordance with the provisions of higher laws, it is also constitutional. However, the Constitution and Legislative Law only grants 'the functional power of administrative management'. Do the current laws exceed the bounds of a 'limitation to management'? Specifically, does the current law have the right to assert that unregistered CSOs are illegal? Does it have the right to place substantive limits on citizens' constitutional rights to freedom of association?

It is difficult to offer a clear definition of the scope of administrative management. If we make a simple comparison with marriage registration, which

58 Wang Ying *et al., An Intermediate Level of Society – Reform and China's Social Organisations (Shehui zhongjian ceng – gaige yu Zhongguo de shetuan zuzhi),* (Beijing: Zhongguo fazhan chubanshe, 1993).

59 Item 8, Art. 89 of the Constitution states that the State Council exercises its powers 'to direct and administer civil affairs, public security, judicial administration, supervision and other related matters'. According to Art. 56 of the Legislative Law, administrative regulations can regulate 'items of the administrative and management powers of the State Council as laid down in Article 89 of the Constitution'.

also falls under the aegis of the Ministry of Civil Affairs, we find that, of course the law on the management of marriage registration can set conditions for the registration of a marriage and the process for registration, but if we seek an answer to the question of whether living as man and wife without registering is illegal we must look in the Marriage Law and not in registration regulations. The regulations governing the registration of CSOs can set conditions and procedures for registration and what aspects of a CSO's operations will be subject to supervision, but can it really use an organisation's registration status to determine whether or not it is legal or illegal? Citizens' right to freedom of association is one of the basic rights clearly outlined in our Constitution. The exercise of this right will of course need to be exercised in accordance with the specific provisions of laws and regulations, and in this process it will of necessity be subject to the procedural restrictions contained within them. The current laws both set strict requirements for registration, and declare all unregistered CSOs to be 'illegal'. This is not just a procedural restriction on the constitutional right to freedom of association; it also places substantive restrictions on that right. This turns an ordinary constitutional right into a special privilege and thus exceeds the effective scope of administrative management. So although the current CSO laws are not entirely without legality, at the very least, their legality is not entirely satisfactory.

7 Legislative Suggestions for Promoting the Development of CSOs

7.1 Draft a 'Civil Society Organisations Law' – Progress Towards a Complete System of CSO laws

In terms of the actual requirements of civil affairs work in China, there is of course a need for a system of regulations covering the registration of CSOs. But as we saw in the simple analysis outlined above, it is also clear that we have no legislation at the intermediary level of 'law', between the Constitution above, and the administrative regulations below. Citizen's right to freedom of association is a basic right. The important part of what this right involves is not a question of the administration of CSOs, it involves every citizen and in all likelihood it also involves almost every sphere of their social life – political, economic, cultural, educational and environmental. It is also intimately interconnected with the other rights and freedoms granted to citizens in the Constitution. In the present state of affairs, the lack of legislation at the level of law has led to an inability of the legislation at administrative level to support the heavy burden thus placed upon it. It not only appears to exceed the bounds of what it has the power to legislate about, it is also powerless in the social reality brought about by the rapid changes following reform and opening. The drafting of a 'Civil Society Organisations Law' and the redrafting or revision of administrative regulations will make progress towards a complete system of CSO laws, something that the situation demands and the rule of law requires.

In fact, the 13th Congress of the CPC already saw a clear proposal setting out the legislative task of drafting an 'Association Law' (*jieshe fa*), and moreover entrusting the Ministry of Civil Affairs with drawing up a preliminary draft of such a law. Beginning in 1987 the Ministry of Civil Affairs, in line with the instructions of the State Council, began the work of drafting association legislation. Over the course of the next five years they produced a variety of very different drafts, before reporting back to the State Council in 1993.[60] Although this substantive law on CSOs, the 'Association Law', was not brought forward at the expected time, this makes abundantly clear that the necessity of a unitary law covering CSOs has been recognised for a long time. Compared to 1987, the current level of development of CSOs makes the necessity for such a law to be introduced even more pressing.

I have already briefly explained why I would call such a law the 'Civil Society Organisations Law' in the introduction to this paper. Here I will restrict myself to a general outline of some issues of principle in such a piece of legislation. A detailed discussion of these issues must wait for another paper.

First, the new law must fully reflect its ability to be applied in practice. This means that full consideration must be given to the implementing capacity possible under the current national political framework, the implementing costs that implementing agencies are able to support, the likely level of approval that the standards set by the law can be expected to garner from the citizenry and where the major problems of existing CSOs actually lie. Of these, the implementing cost is the most important and the most crucial factor.

Second, the new law must set clear limits to its enforceable powers, especially limits on powers to legislate concerning the implementation of the law. That the current law assigns such broad powers to implementing agencies that it has become basically unenforceable is in a large part due to the fact that the legis-

60 Speech by Yang Yanyin, Deputy Minister for Civil Affairs at the 'Third Beijing Municipality Working Forum on Social Organisation Management', in Bureau of Civic Organisations Management of the Ministry of Civil Affairs (ed.), *supra* note 2, at p. 122.

lators and the implementers are in fact one and the same people. Moreover, since there is no judicial process for resolving disputes that arise in the implementation of the regulations, the people who set the rules are also the people who enforce and interpret them. The very real problems attending this situation where one body drafts, enforces and interprets legislation are abundantly clear. In the light of this, the drafting of the 'Civil Society Organisations Law' should be carried out under the auspices of the Standing Committee of the National People's Congress. They should arrange for academic specialists and implementing agencies to conduct broad-ranging social surveys, draw up a draft, and consult widely with all sectors of society, especially with CSOs themselves, as laid down in the Legislative Law.

Third, the emphasis of the new law should be on providing standards and guidance for CSOs. The law, administrative regulations and local ordinances must provide clear information as to what behaviour is forbidden, what behaviour is limited by the law, what behaviour the law encourages, and also what different punishments different violations of the law will attract. Whether or not a CSO provides services to society in line with its mission statement will be apparent mainly from the activities it undertakes. It is these actions (and not status) that the law should seek to regulate, and only then decide whether a CSO is 'legal' or 'illegal'.

Fourth, the new law must achieve a balance between the two legislative tendencies towards, on the one hand 'management', and on the other 'protection of rights'. Freedom of association is a citizen's constitutional right, and is moreover an internationally accepted basic human right. When deciding between the effective management of CSOs and a citizen's right to free association, there is no need to pick only the one or the other, 'freedom of association' addresses violations of the right to associate as one wishes, management addresses the misuses of that right. The new law should pursue a harmony between these two.

7.2 Promote a Change to the System of Management – Move from a System of Control to an Enabling, Service-oriented Management

We should also use the opportunity provided by drafting a 'Civil Society Organisations Law' to promote a change to the system of management, moving from a system of control to an enabling, service-oriented management. This would be an essential step if we are to genuinely implement the political reform goal of 'small government, big society', promote and consolidate the achievements of the construction of a democratic rule of law, and put into practice the ideal of 'good governance'.[61]

The current system for the management and registration of CSOs is, in effect, a system of management by strict control. The rationalisation for such a system is that the managed are 'not mature' and the possibility for its successful use also depends on the premise that the managed are 'naive'. As the managed have grown to maturity the implementing costs of such a system have grown ever higher, gradually exceeding the possible limits that management agencies can expend, leading ultimately to a failure of the manager's capacity to manage, and deteriorating into a situation of effective *laissez faire*. The opposite of a control-oriented management would be an enabling, service-oriented management. 'Enabling' means that, although this system would still consider the level of maturity of the managed organisations and would also still consider what likely harm any inappropriate action they take would have for the state, society, others or themselves; it would not adopt a general attitude of distrust towards managed organisations. Rather it would proceed from an assessment of needs of the managed organisations for growth and development, and allocate rights of self-governance appropriate to its maturity, always as far as possible respecting and encouraging the managed organisation's sense of itself as an independent actor. At the same time active government support would be given to those CSOs playing a vital role in political, economic or cultural fields and meeting pressing social needs (such as environmental organisations), thus promoting the growth of public interest CSOs. By 'service' I mean that the main aim of such a model would be the provision of government services, promoting CSOs' sense of responsibility and raising their public credibility – for example, by publicly disseminating information about CSOs to allow the general public access to knowledge about the real situation of CSOs whenever they want it. As managed organisations grow and mature, the implementation costs of an enabling, service-oriented management system would decrease, escaping the vicious circle into which control-oriented management has fallen.

To move from control-oriented management to enabling, service-oriented management, the first thing that must be done is to get rid of the 'dual responsibility' system. Not only can it not achieve the goals it was originally set up for – assisting Civil Affairs departments in carrying out effective management

61 For a discussion on the relationship between the development of CSOs and 'good governance' see Yu Keping, *supra* note 8, and also the same author's, *Governance and 'Good Governance'* (*Zhili yu shanzhi*), (Beijing: Shehui kexue wenxian chubanshe, 2000).

of CSOs – in practice it has also given rise to a large number of unforeseen problems, such as obstructing citizens' exercise of their right to free association and collaboration between sponsoring agencies and the CSOs they oversee for mutual benefit and illegal gains, or protecting and abetting a CSO to engage in illegal activities.

The change to enabling, service-oriented management would also require a reform of the current system of registration. Worldwide, we can probably identify the following various types of registration system:

- requirement that all CSOs register and also setting strict conditions (control-oriented) on their being able to register, such as in Singapore and Thailand;
- requirement that all CSOs register but setting no substantive limits preventing registration, such as in Indonesia;
- requiring that only certain special types of CSO need register, such as the UK where only charities need register;
- a system of voluntary registration, but preferential policies and tax breaks available to groups meeting certain requirements, such as the US, Canada and South Africa;
- and lastly no requirement for registration at all, such as in Italy.[62]

The first two kinds of registration system are helpful for control but have high implementation costs and are only appropriate for countries with small populations or an underdeveloped civil society. The third system achieves savings in the cost of implementation, but the decision as to what types of organisations need register must be taken in the light of overall social development. The fourth system uses laws to encourage compliance in a CSOs' own interests and is the classic model of an enabling type of management. The last type, requiring no registration and relying entirely on punishing illegal activities as a method of management is appropriate in countries where civil society is mature and CSOs exercise good self-discipline and ought to be the ultimate form that management models eventually take in all countries. Considering the demands placed on implementing agencies by the recent government reforms here in China, our large population and great number of CSOs and also the requirements for political stability that exist in this period of reform and opening, in this paper I advocate a system resembling that in the third and fourth of my examples, stipulating that certain types of organisation and those of a certain size must

62 Chen Jinluo, *supra* note 46, at pp. 127 ff.

register and that all others may register voluntarily should they wish to, with an accompanying system of tax incentives. In this system, even those groups not actually legally required to register can do so and become legal persons and thus if they find themselves in dispute with any other social actor, be it civil, criminal or administrative, they can enjoy the rights and undertake the responsibilities such a status carries with it. Members of unregistered organisations can only enjoy individual rights as citizens. Should there be a requirement to assign legal responsibility this can be done by adopting joint liability or some other method.[63]

As well as moving to this new system of management, we should also establish a mechanism for social monitoring and one for self-regulation by CSOs. This would see an end to the unitary control and management of CSOs by the government and the transition to a diversified system of socialised management where government manages, society monitors, and CSOs exercise self-discipline. Many of China's present CSOs have problems with their internal organisational structure, management systems, decision-making processes and financial systems; organisations have serious problems with chaotic finances, and shortage of funding meaning they rarely carry out any activities and in some cases even abuse their status as CSOs for private material ends. None of these problems will be completely resolved by government control. The basic way to solving these problems is by means establishing a CSO operating mechanism through the setting of legal standards, compelling CSOs to be open and transparent. This will establish trust between CSOs and the general public and help attract public donations that will ameliorate funding difficulties. In fact the basic reason that CSOs are well developed in many Western nations and that very few of them engage in illegal activities is that there is a process of virtuous mutual interaction between CSOs and wider society. For example, anybody can go to the CSO registration organisation and read whatever files on a given CSO that she wishes to.[64] If CSOs' activities, funding and employment of staff are all highly transparent and every penny of public donated money can be accounted for at any time, then the public will naturally be able to trust CSOs and they will no longer have insurmountable problems in finding sources of

63 Joint liability would be appropriate for responsibility under civil law; under the administrative and criminal codes responsibility can be assigned according to each individual's specific actions as in, for example, the way that the criminal code deals with joint crimes or criminal gangs.

64 Chen Jinluo, *supra* note 46, at p. 147.

funding. Moreover when they operate in such a genuinely transparent way how will they be able to engage in illegal activities or to seek personal gain?

8 Conclusion

In summary, in this paper I contend that there is a serious problem of legality attending the development of China's civil society organisations, and that this is the direct result of the incapacity of the agencies responsible for the supervision of CSOs, and ultimately the product of inappropriate legislation. The current regulatory system covering CSOs is seriously ineffective and is caught in a dilemma where it has neither propriety nor legality. Solving the problems faced by China's CSOs requires that we draft a 'Civil Society Organisations Law' as soon as possible, and promote a change in the management system from one that is control-oriented to one that is enabling and service-oriented.

In recent years, as CSOs have played an ever more prominent role in China's national and social development, there has been a great deal of research into civil society issues. This has been carried out not only by academics but also by the official agencies charged with managing China's CSOs, and they have also been active participants in discussions of related issues with their counterparts in academia. One of the most important outcomes of this process has been the formation at different levels – central and local, of parts of the system and as a whole – of legislative and policymaking decisions concerning the supervision of CSOs. However, whether it be in terms of the ever growing number of legal documents or the proposals made by academics, neither the dilemma of legality facing CSOs nor the problem of basic legality that many face has attracted the attention they deserve. The rectification campaigns continue unabated. Experiments made by certain local governments, of implementing a system where a CSO merely has to 'place itself on file', were for the most part in fact originally tactics employed to make the work of rectification easier, and they have not been able to turn into a new model for management that can address the legality dilemma. There are still major disagreements amongst scholars concerning the question of whether a CSO's legality ought to be defined by its registration status. Overall, the idea that management should be control-oriented is still deeply rooted in many minds.

The work of managing civil society organisations is related to citizen's ability to exercise their right to freedom of association and to the promise of that right as contained in the Constitution. The healthy and diverse development of civil society is not the result of applying the rule of law, but is in fact one of the preconditions under which a society with the rule of law needs to arise. If the laws governing civil society organisations have no legitimacy then the dilemma of legality of China's CSOs will not be resolved. Seeking to 'build the rule of law' without attaching importance to the legitimacy of enacted laws will not only fail to deliver any positive outcome, it is in fact quite simply unimaginable.

4

APPROVAL AND NON-INTERFERENCE IN THE MANAGEMENT OF SOCIAL ORGANISATIONS: AN EXAMINATION OF THEORY AND PRACTICE

Liu Peifeng

1 INTRODUCTION

China employs a system of strict control over the registration of social organisations. Both the 'Regulations for Registration and Management of Social Organisations', promulgated in a revised form in 1998, and the current 'Temporary Measures for the Registration and Management of Popular Non-Enterprise Work Units' stipulate that approval by a sponsoring agency (the *zhuguan danwei* or 'professional leading unit') is a precondition for establishing a non-governmental, not-for-profit organisation. Only then may it proceed to registration with the registration agency. This is despite the fact that the latter agency itself adopts a policy of giving permission to register only where it deems it appropriate, as opposed to automatically registering all applicants who meet the specified criteria: it carries out very strict checks on applicant social organisations. The 'Temporary Measures for Suppressing Illegal Social Organisations' promulgated by the Ministry of Civil Affairs in April 2000 reiterated this rigorous approach: social organisations and other civic groups which had not been granted permission to set up and register were deemed to be illegal organisations that should be closed down. This strongly controlling tendency is evident in the government's administrative activities as well as in these rules and regulations, with frequent crack-downs and rectification campaigns and re-registrations of existing organisations.

The use of a system requiring prior approval before a social organisation can be established is not something peculiar to Chinese or indeed Asian practice;

Yuwen Li (Ed.), *Freedom of Association in China and Europe: Comparative Perspectives in Law and Practice*, © 2005 Koninklijke Brill NV, Leiden. Printed in The Netherlands, pp. 151-188.

it was previously employed in the former Soviet Union and Eastern Europe. In the transition of those latter states from socialism to democratic systems the old social organisation registration system was one of the first social control measures to be abandoned. The realignment of political power in those countries had its beginnings in the recognition of the legitimacy of what had previously been considered illegal organisations and the fact that they indeed represented certain social forces and interests, and in 'round table' meetings and dialogue between government and civic organisations.[1] The system has been employed in many Asian nations, achieving the hoped-for effect in some, such as Singapore; in many other countries actual practice has been a mix of this strict requirement for explicit permission and a certain amount of *laissez-faire*: whilst unapproved social organisations are able to be socially active, they occupy an extremely tenuous position in terms of their legality.

In China, this system has been the subject of continual dispute from its very inception and there has been constant debate about and experiments in putting into practice other theoretical or practical models. In recent years, as social organisations have grown in influence and as the overall social system in China has undergone change and popular opinion has called for reforms, outright rejection of the social organisation registration system has grown. In certain respects this system restricted the development of social organisations and other civic groups. This makes it necessary to conduct a thorough critical examination of the current state of the social organisation registration system, attendant theoretical debates and the various alternative systems on offer and to explore directions for future development that are both realistic and geared to the long term.

This paper will offer some practical and theoretical analysis of the management of social organisations based on the current state of the registration system in China. The paper is divided into three sections: the present state of the registration system; an analysis of the theory behind the administrative management of social organisations; and a look at alternative systems and the objections to them. Although this paper will cast doubt on many aspects of the current registration system it is written in a spirit of sympathy and understanding for the motives that put that system in place.

1 Yang Hua (ed.), *Documentary Account of the Dramatic Changes in Eastern Europe (Dong Ou jubian jishi)*, (Beijing: Shijie zhishi chubanshe, 1991), at pp. 7-15; *Freedom of Association East and West: Current Law and Practice in Helsinki Signatory Countries*, Report of US Helsinki Watch Committee, (New York: Helsinki Watch, December, 1989).

2 The Present State of the Registration System

China's current system for registering social organisations came into being after the founding of the People's Republic and was further developed both by regulations on the management of social organisations, laid down in 1989 and revised in 1998, and in its practical implementation. Its historical roots can be traced back to the early years of the 20th century: the provisions in the 1908 Constitution granting the people of Tsing Empire freedom of association were the beginnings of modern legislation on social organisations; subsequently the 1914 'Public Security and Police Law' made regulations on this issue. However, the system of requiring approval for registration began with the management practices of the Nationalist government and with measures adopted in the revolutionary base areas in the same era. According to the law in the period of the Republic of China, the right of citizens to freedom of association was protected by law; but according to instructions issued by the party office of the KMT concerning people's organisations, the establishment of all professional and popular organisations required the prior checking and approval of the party office, and it retained the power to oversee and guide organisations after they had been set up. Special legal provisions were made concerning the various professional bodies, such as the Chambers of Commerce Law, the Industrial and Commercial Associations Law, the Trade Union Law and the Peasants' Associations Law. Such organisations needed both permission from the KMT's party office to set up and the approval of their local government authorities. Social organisations that met the conditions for a legal entity as laid down in civil law would assume that status after registering themselves with the relevant agencies.[2] In the revolutionary base areas different methods were used to achieve the same ends. The 1942 'Method for Registering People's Organisations in the Shaanxi – Gansu – Ningxia Border Areas' stipulated that all popular organisations in the border region had to apply to their local government authorities for registration, and they would pass on the request to the Civil Affairs Bureau (*minzheng Ting).* Thus in one sense the present approval-based system of registration can be seen as a continuation of similar systems of administrative management prevailing in China's recent history. This choice is based in part on consideration of the historical impact of popular organisations, especially religious organisations, on social stability and is also a reflection of the general abnormality apparent in Chinese society in recent years.

2 Wang Shijie, Qian Duansheng, *Comparing Constitutions* (*Bijiao xianfa*), (Beijing: Zhongguo zhengfa daxue chubanshe, 1997), at p. 113.

Of course, historical precedents can only serve as an explanation of how a certain reality or system came to be; they are not proof that this is rational or right.

2.1 The Current Registration System and its Characteristics

Currently, China implements a strict approval-based system governing the registration of social organisations. Its main features and characteristics can be summarised as 'registration with the appropriate agency, dual administrative control and administration at the appropriate level'.

2.1.1 Registration with the Appropriate Agency, Dual Administrative Control, and Administration at the Appropriate Level

'Registration with the appropriate agency' means that all social organisations must register with the Ministry of Civil Affairs or its local line agencies at county level and above. No other agency has the power to register social organisations or issue them a registration certificate. Legally registered social organisations have legal status and are considered as independent actors under civil law, enjoying the rights and duties such a status entails. 'Dual administrative control' means that every social organisation is subject to the administrative control of both the registration agency and its 'professional leading unit' or sponsoring agency. According to the 'Regulations for Registration and Management of Social Organisations', the Ministry of Civil Affairs and its line agencies are the organs of a given level of government responsible for registering social organisations and popular non-enterprise work units; organisations which operate across administrative boundaries should register with a government agency at a higher level that covers all the areas they operate in. Sponsors – the professional leading units – in the particular industry, scientific discipline or social sector in which a social organisation works must be agencies of the State Council or of local government authorities at county level and above, or organisations empowered by those agencies. The registration agency is responsible for:

(1) registering or keeping on the record the establishment of a social organisation, changes in its status and its winding-up;
(2) annual inspections of registered organisations;

(3) oversight and investigation of any violations of regulations and the application of administrative sanctions to any organisations found to be in breach.

Sponsoring agencies are responsible for:

(1) checking and approving preliminary applications from an organisation to register and any subsequent changes or requests to close down;
(2) monitoring and guiding social organisations' compliance with the Constitution, laws, regulations and national policy and checking that they carry out the activities stipulated in their charters;
(3) preliminary stages of the annual inspection;
(4) assisting the registration agencies and other relevant bodies in investigating illegal activity and imposing sanctions; and
(5) collaborating with the relevant agencies in guiding the winding-up process for social organisations that have closed down.

'Administration at the appropriate level' means that national social organisations are registered with the Ministry of Civil Affairs and administered by the relevant agencies of the State Council. Local organisations are registered with the Civil Affairs line agency and find their sponsoring agency at the appropriate level. This administration at the appropriate level does not imply any concomitant ranking by level of social organisations; it just reflects the geographical scope of the organisation's activities and membership. Once they are registered social organisations have the status of independent legal entities and can develop horizontal relationships with their peers but no vertical relationships of superiority and subsidiarity. There is no difference in the rights enjoyed by different social organisations due to their size; they are all civil actors of equal status.

This administrative system can be said to be something particularly marked by 'Chinese characteristics'. It is both a continuation of the habits of governance formed under the planned economy and a response born of the lack of alternatives to the present state of development of social organisations in China. 'Administration by level' and 'by appropriate agency' certainly smack of the administrative practices of the era of economic planning; 'dual control' shows all the hallmarks of a desire for state control of all aspects of social life. Overall the state is seeking to fix the status of social organisations, to place each peg in its correct hole, to ensure that organisations' activities do not overstep prescribed boundaries. Hence we can say that our system for administering social organisations is still caught up in the patterns of the planned era. While the wish to release social forces is evident there is fear about the directions they may choose to go . However, looked at another way this system is not without its rational justification. First, in a country as big as China, with the vast differences between cultural and economic development found in different regions and the generally low level of administrative capacity, administration at different levels is inevitable. The key problem is that 'administration at different levels' should not mean 'restrictions at different levels'. Restricting the activities of social organisations to the locality in which they are registered and brooking not even the slightest overstepping of those bounds is patently 'restriction at different levels' and not just administration. The flaws in such a practice are obvious. It severely restricts competition between different social organisations and prevents the formation of a national market in public goods, creating a set of petty fiefdoms and thus greatly diminishing the effectiveness of the allocation of social resources. Second, in a situation where the development of social organisations has been disorderly, where they lack effective means for self-regulation and where there is only weak social oversight of their activities, 'administration by appropriate agency' is not bad as a temporary measure to make up for these deficiencies. Relying on the Ministry of Civil Affairs alone it would not be possible to carry out such an enormous administrative task: 'administration by appropriate agency' creates the conditions that allow society to play a mediating role – the key is the method that such administration employs. At present that can be seen to be overly strict and controlling to the point of suppression; administrative agencies often exceed their powers, and indeed at times social organisations become a tool used by official agencies to resist reform, fight changes in their status and to protect their vested interests.

2.1.2 Simultaneous Requirement for Approval and Laissez-faire

Looked at in terms of existing regulations, in China achieving the status of a legitimate social organisation is controlled by a strict system of approval. Social organisations that are established without such approval are illegal organisations; they enjoy no legal protection for their activities and may be closed down. In reality we operate a system requiring dual approval that is much stricter than other countries which also have systems requiring approval. Usually these countries will have a system where the administrative agency carries out a check on an organisation applying for registration. If this is approved the process of formal registration becomes a formality. In China both the sponsoring and registering agencies carry out strict checks. During those checking processes both agencies employ strict measures of control which restrict the development of social organisations. For the government this dual administration serves as a double guarantee. The government can easily exercise control over social organisations and has the widest possible powers to control the establishment of social organisations that are not in full accord with the government. However 'for the people this affect is an enormous frustration. Not only is the process far too elaborate and excessively time-consuming, the standards applied by the two agencies involved in their checking and approval can also be different (especially as they have wide-ranging powers of independent decision making which often lead to conflicts of opinion over specific issues) which is a source of great inconvenience for an applicant.'[3] The opportunity costs for both the inspection agencies and the applicants under this dual approval system are very high and represent a significant burden on both the government and the applicant. A further potential problem lies in the variety of forms and substance of civil society organisations – what are they to do if they cannot find a sponsoring agency? The result of this is a restriction on the emergence of social organisations and an encouragement to the formation of illegal organisations, because when social organisations cannot find sponsors, or when official agencies are unwilling to act as sponsors in the hope of avoiding any potential problems the role may bring, it becomes difficult for social organisations to become properly legally registered.[4]

The counterpart to this system of strict requirements for approval is the attitude of *laissez-faire* adopted by the government towards some civic organisations based on joint interests – hobby groups, temple fair organisations, book reading circles, salons and discussion forums and even house churches. By the standards of the current regulations such organisations would have no

3 Su Li *et al.*, *The Regulatory System and Development – The Legal Environment for the Third Sector (Guizhi yu fazhan – disan bumen de falü huanjing)*, (Hangzhou: Zhejiang renmin chubanshe, 1999), at p. 180.

4 Guangzhou Huiling, a civil society service provider is an example of this problem. Huiling was China's first civil society provider of special needs education, running a kindergarten, a vocational training centre and a community home. Huiling's different branches each had different sponsoring agencies; the community home was registered with the local Department of Civil Affairs, the kindergarten and another school with the Education Department and the vocational training centre with the Disabled Association; the general organisation however remained unable to register for a long time. Huiling has continuously worked hard to register as a social organisation but to date without success. Its legal status relies on a government document issued after Huiling petitioned NPC meetings and mobilised the support of the media and public opinion. See Wang Ming *et al* (eds.), Case Study on China's NGOs (*Zhongguo NGO yanjiu*), UNCRD Research Report Series No. 43, (Beijing: UNCRD and Tsinghua University NGO Research Centre, 2001), at pp. 68-83.

way of meeting the requirements to apply for official registration or simply have no hope whatsoever of ever being registered and are in fact illegal organisations that ought to be suppressed. In reality the government is often either supportive of the aims of these organisations or chooses to turn a blind eye to them. Of course, these organisations' legal status is a sword constantly hanging over their heads, meaning that they often only have a temporary existence. The moment there is some outbreak of insecurity in a related social area, or an organisation of a similar type becomes problematic, these organisations can be closed down and sanctions can be imposed on the people involved.

Another example of this conflation of strict approval and *laissez-faire* can be seen in how tightly the government controls registration, but how lax by comparison it can be in its oversight of the activities of social organisations. We can see that the regulations set a high threshold for the achievement of legal status by social organisations but that there is little interference in terms of monitoring and management of their activities after that. In truth, by their very nature it is important for social organisations' development that their activities have appropriate transparency and that their internal organisational structures are rational, but the laws are found wanting in these respects. The government makes an implicit value judgment, relying on status to determine its attitude to the behaviour of a given social actor, just like the old revolutionary notion that 'if its roots are red then its offshoots will surely be correct', or put another way 'if he's not one of us then he must have different intentions'. Thus they feel that the fundamental of watertight control is to keep tight control over admission into the charmed circle of the approved, and this will be enough to solve the problem. Actual circumstances provide proof of this. To take an example, Guangzhou Huiling, an organisation providing services for disabled people, applies every year to the government and foundations for financial support but usually receives no response. Between 1990 and 1999 Huiling received a total of CNY 410,000 in government support, a mere drop in the ocean for a civic service provider that spends millions every year. By contrast, agencies directly under government control or under official welfare agencies receive substantial support. For instance, a governmental disabled association set up a rehabilitation centre using CNY 18 million of official funds that was designed to be serving 600 clients in the first two years, though in reality it only served 80 people, resulting in an enormous waste of resources.[5]

5 *Ibid,* at p. 80.

In China, the original intent was to have administration of social organisations by strict control of approvals, but what has actually happened is the parallel existence of both that system and also a degree of *laissez-faire*. This can lead us to consider a number of points about the relationship between social organisations and the state. Can the state ultimately succeed in exercising total control over social organisations? What are the dimensions in which we should seek to understand the relationship between social organisations and the state? Let us consider the first question first. The establishment of modern bureaucratic structures greatly increased the ability of the state to manage and control social life. However, in an open and diverse society, the diversity and complexity of popular society in both structural and quantitative terms far exceeds the complexity of state structures for governance, hence the state lacks the capacity to exercise total social control. In an open society, hoping to set and achieve far-reaching general social objectives is merely an exercise in fantasy. The limitations of resources and administrative capacity under which the state operates are an unavoidable reality. Second, social organisations are not undesirable just by their very nature. In the broad sense they come into being to satisfy some existing desire of the populace. The variety and diversity of social organisations is a reflection of the diversity of popular desires. Placing restrictions on social organisations is in one sense to restrict the diversity of popular desires and to restrict human development. Also, social organisations and government agencies are both types of organised social actors and both are essential in the highly organised societies of the modern world. Government relies on its monopoly position in its provision of public goods, whereas social organisations act voluntarily and compete in a market place to provide their public goods. The former uses compulsory methods to realise public welfare objectives, the latter relies on voluntary actions to realise public or private ends. The two are to an extent complementary; the public services provided by social organisations can compensate in areas where government is failing. In terms of overall governance, that exercised by government and that exercised by non-governmental organisations can both be said to be essential ways of achieving that whole. The government, by holding a monopoly on violence, upholds overall social stability and prosperity; social organisations are an important way in which grassroots public will is given expression in an orderly fashion. Complex modern societies call for self-organisation and self-provision of services by the general populace.

2.1.3 Restrict Competition, Restrain Growth

The existing regulations governing social organisations display a basic overall strategy in China of restricting competition between and restraining the growth of social organisations. Article 13 of the regulations governing social organisations and Article 11 of those governing popular non-enterprise work units state that there is no need for two such organisations working in similar fields to exist in the same administrative area and thus applications to establish new organisations where ones already exist should be rejected. More than this, administrative agencies often take it upon themselves to close down or forcibly combine social organisations they deem to be replicating work or that they think have no need to exist.[6] The underlying values of such methods are a desire to limit competition between social organisations and thereby to get rid of the destabilising effects of such competition on overall social stability; there is also the fear that if there are too many social organisations government will find it harder to control them. Competition can lead social organisations to adopt different means of securing their existence and winning access to resources which can easily lead them outside the limits government would like to set for their activities. Article 19 of the social organisations regulations also makes provision concerning branch and representative organisations, stating that branch organisations cannot have independent legal status and forbidding the establishment of local branches. Popular non-enterprise work units are forbidden to establish branch organisations. Even representative organisations should usually only be set up in the place where the parent organisation is registered.[7] As to allowing various different departments to approve the establishment of social organisations, this is also rejected by the registering agency with the basic

6 In the basic document that governed the 1991 clean-up reform of social organisations, the 'Request for Instructions from the Ministry of Civil Affairs Concerning the Clean-up and Rectification of Social Organisations' (as passed on by the General Office of the State Council), it was proposed that social organisations that did not meet the requirements of society or which replicated existing organisations should be closed down or combined. The document is contained in Bureau of Civic Organizations Management of the Ministry of Civil Affairs (ed.), *Handbook for Administrative Work on Social Organizations (*Shehui tuanti guanli gongzuo shouce), (Internal Document, 1996).

7 The 'Ministry of Civil Affairs Notice Concerning Questions Related to the Re-checking and Re-registration of Social Organisations' issued in 1991 states that national and inter-provincial social organisations should not normally establish representative agencies or offices outside the region in which they have their headquarters. The document is contained in Bureau of Civic Organizations Management of the Ministry of Civil Affairs (ed.), *supra* note 6.

reason given that 'this will be disadvantageous to controlling the over-proliferation of organisations...if not correctly coordinated, every department and administrative system setting up organisations in this way will lead to a great increase in the number of national level social organisations whose functions will overlap or replicate one another. This will then be copied by their line agencies in every province, district and county so that the number of organisations will be impossible to control.'[8] These laws and policies had certain positive outcomes from an administrative point of view, because from a purely negative perspective the most effective way to resolve a problem is to stop it at source, even though this is bad for the activities and development of social organisations. The disadvantages that result from restricting competition, or from what could be called a monopoly, are already evidenced in numerous real-world examples. Limiting the expansion of an organisation also directly affects its ability to undertake activities, as its scope and capacity for the latter are closely connected to the former. In the documents it issued concerning clean-up campaigns, the Ministry of Civil Affairs set another standard by which social organisations are to be judged: 'meeting the requirements of society'. This is an exceptionally specious standard. What are the 'requirements of society'? By whose standards will they be decided? Do social organisations exist to meet the requirements of society or the requirements of individual citizens? In ideological terms questions such as these are easily answered: the government represents the broad interests of the people, thus the government's standards are society's standards and the people's standards. However, the objective reality is far less simple: standards like this only serve as a justification for governmental control of social organisations, and they leave something unanswered. It requires a more detailed analysis to see whether they are beneficial to the overall development of social organisations.

2.2 The Registration and Management System – The Real Situation

Despite the strict registration system and the existence of a dedicated registration agency, in reality the current state of administration of social organisations is still marked by a multi-polar division of powers and it is still impossible to

8 Ministry of Civil Affairs Notice Concerning Questions Related to the Re-checking and Re-registration of Social Organisations Established by Different Departments' issued in 1992. The document is contained in Bureau of Civic Organizations Management of the Ministry of Civil Affairs (ed.), *supra* note 6.

give an accurate figure for the overall total number of social organisations; nor is there as yet one single form which the administration of social organisations takes. The reason for this is that a large number of social organisations exist as illegal organisations or at least lack legal status. This uncertain legal status naturally affects the ability to conduct an accurate count of them. There are also a large number of social organisations established internally in official agencies or by exercise of special *fiat* which fall outside the remit of the registration agencies. Figures given by the Bureau of Civic Organisations Management of the Ministry of Civil Affairs say that in total there were 130,768 social organisations at year end 2000. Of these 40,152 were academic organisations, 36,605 trade organisations, 34,849 were specialist organisations, 16,361 were associations, and 1,273 were foundations. But these figures are only for organisations registered with the Ministry of Civil Affairs, not a total of all extant groups in China or even all legal organisations. This is because although since the late 1980s the official system has appointed the Ministry of Civil Affairs as the agency in charge of administering social organisations, the multipolar state of management has not been entirely ended. At the same time, as a result of certain historical or systemic factors, there are a number of long-standing social organisations that have a special status and do not need to register to achieve legal status. There are also many social organisations which cannot register and operate on the boundaries between legal and illegal status. Officials of the Ministry of Civil Affairs have stated frankly that there are numerous social organisations in China that do not fall under the Ministry's administrative control and that those organisations registered with the Ministry only represent a part of the total number of social organisations and other civic groups. A careful examination of the situation shows that there are eleven different ways for a social organisation to exist in China:

(1) Social organisations that are registered as per the 1998 Regulations, the figures given above being a count of such groups;
(2) Social organisations set up internally in a work unit, such as campus student organisations, work unit staff clubs, alumni associations and so on; such organisations have the approval of a sponsoring agency but do not register with the Ministry of Civil Affairs; the activities they conduct internally within their parent organisation have legal approval and they may maintain relationships with other similar groups;
(3) Those organisations which the law does not require to register with the Ministry of Civil Affairs such as Chinese Red Cross Associations, Lawyers' Associations, Accountants' Associations and so forth – some

of these organisations are registered at agencies of the Bureau of Industry and Commerce;

(4) Social organisations that participate in the CPPCC (Chinese People's Political Consultative Conference), that is the eight 'democratic parties', the All-China Federation of Trade Unions, the Communist Youth League, the All-China Women Federation, the All-China Association for Science and Technology, the All-China Overseas Chinese Association, Taiwanese Compatriot's Association, the All China Youth Association, and the All-China Trade and Industry Association, and local branches of these organisations. These organisations enjoy a special political and legal status in China so that although they share a similar nature with social organisations they are not under the administrative oversight of social organisation management agencies;

(5) Social organisations appraised by the relevant department of the State Council and exempted from registration, such as the All-China Art and Literature Association, the All-China Writers' Association, the All-China Federation of Disabled People, Song Qing Ling Foundation, etc;

(6) Community-based social organisations such as homeowners' groups or community elderly associations;

(7) Rural social organisations. The vast majority of social organisations in China's countryside are not registered. Rural social organisations can be divided into two types: traditional social organisations such as clan and kinship organisations, temple fair associations, and associations of worshippers at a particular temple or shrine; and modern social organisations such as mutual aid groups and technical associations (growers' associations for some particular crop or product);

(8) Social organisations registered with agencies of the Bureau of Industry and Commerce – under the prevailing administrative system in China some organisations which cannot find sponsoring agencies chose to register as if they were commercial enterprises; many representative agencies of foreign organisations adopt this approach;[9]

9 Save the Children UK was the first international NGO to register as a commercial enterprise with the Bureau of Industry and Commerce in Yunnan. Subsequently a large number of other international organisations came to work in Yunnan and used the same approach to achieve legal status. See Wang Ming (ed.), *supra* note 4, at p. 51. The main reason such a situation came about is that most foreign organisations were unable to find a Chinese sponsoring agency and were thus unable to register as social organisations. This means that these organisations are unable to benefit from some of the preferential policies covering social organisations such as tax breaks and also

(9) Organisations set up by Chinese citizens abroad that then become active within China, for example groups set up by overseas Chinese who later move back to China and then continue to provide social services to members in the name of that organisation;

(10) Social organisations that exist as subsidiary to other top-tier social organisations. Because of the restrictive nature of registration requirements and other factors attributable to the administrative system many groups find it difficult to register independently and thus can only exist as subsidiaries of larger organisations leading to a situation where social organisations are administering other social organisations – this situation is especially prevalent in academic and trade organisations. Many social organisations are marked by the conceptual framework inherited from the all-pervasive state and also seek to benefit from economies of scale and a comprehensive management approach, meaning that they end up with needlessly complex stratified internal organisational structures. The Ministry of Civil Affairs sometimes also appoints top-tier associations or similar social organisations to act as sponsor agencies for other social organisations; for example, the China Association of Science and Technology is usually appointed to act in this role for scientific and technical social organisations. The All-China Association for Research into Staff Ideological and Political Work is the national body in charge of similar organisations in various industrial sectors; the All-China Federation of Trade Unions acts as sponsor to employees' technical associations, and so on;

(11) On-line social organisations. Access to the internet has also had an impact on the existence of social organisations, with the emergence of on-line social organisations such as forums and internet environmental protection organisations. Existing as they do in the virtual world of the internet, such organisations have no possibility of applying to register, much less succeeding in doing so.[10]

As we can see from the above, China's social organisations can exist in a complex variety of ways: some are registered, others are not; some have special

of course keeps them outside the oversight of the Ministry of Civil Affairs which can make it easy for such organisations to engage in inappropriate activities.

10 These observations are based on a speech made by Li Yong of the Ministry of Civil Affairs at the Conference on Legal Aspects of Social Organisations held by the Institute of Law of the Chinese Academy of Social Sciences, in Beijing, May 2002.

legal status, others do not; there are traditional groups, such as those based on kinship, and there are very new types of organisation such as the on-line communities; some organisations are registered with agencies of the Ministry of Civil Affairs, some are registered with other agencies; some organisations are legal, some are illegal.[11] In such a situation it is naturally impossible to say for certain how many social organisations there actually are. The Ministry of Civil Affairs itself admits that registered groups account for only about a fifth of all social organisations.[12] Nor does the largely unknown reality of social organisations make clear the inadequacies in state management; to a certain degree it also shows how complex the issues concerning social organisations are. However the available statistics for social organisations do have value for comparative purposes. They show that Chinese society is undergoing a transformation from a monolithic state, where all aspects of society are under state control, to a situation where there is separation between the state and society and an increase in the space in which citizens can autonomously allocate their resources and act independently. Just as democracy is not a function of some statistical relationship, nor is civil society measured by the total number of social organisations. What matters is the nature of those social organisations, namely whether they exist independently or merely as dependents of the government. In the latter case all we can say is that the government is exercising its powers

11 Differentiating between legal and illegal organisations is a very tricky affair in China. The normal understanding is that any organisation that has not registered with the Ministry of Civil Affairs and its local departments is thus illegal and this is the stance taken by the official 'Regulations' on registration. However this presumption does not stand up to close inspection, many organisations exist happily without any need to register, such as students' organisations which need only to register with their campus authorities. In many cases a social organisation makes its establishment or existence legal by inviting senior officials from its sponsoring agency or some government department to participate. Irregular application of administrative powers and rule by personal *fiat* are also factors affecting whether or not – or how – some social organisations exist. At the same time, what are here then illegal social organisations are not by nature general violators of the law; many organisations which cannot register for one reason or another still play a positive social role. In China, the legitimacy and legality of social organisations is not always the same thing, a situation which gives rise to many difficulties both for government administrators and of course the organisations themselves. For a discussion of these questions see Gao Bingzhong, 'The Rise of Social Organisations and their Problems of Legitimacy', (*Shehui tuanti de xingqi ji qi hefaxing wenti)* in: *Chinese Social Organisations at a Crossroads (Chu yu shizilukou de Zhongguo shetuan)*, China Youth Development Foundation and Committee on Development Research on Foundations (*eds*.), (Tianjing: Tianjing renmin chubanshe, 2001), at pp. 75-91.

12 Li Yong, *Supra* note 10.

in a new way, not that there is a fundamental realignment of the way government controls society. Only when social organisations exist independently of government, when they follow different modalities and concepts of behaviour from government, when they are able to exert pressure on government and restrain the unbridled exercise of its power, only then can we say that we have an independent civil society.

In terms of how social organisations exist in the real world with regard to registration and legal status, groups can be divided into registered organisations, organisations dependent on an official agency and purely civic groups.[13] These organisations have access to their own legitimate resources and have space in which they can exist in Chinese society. They are in some respects a part of the general social order and in line with the legal order, but in some ways come into conflict with these. Purely civic organisations, because they are not registered, do not have a legal existence; that they therefore come into conflict with the legal system goes without saying. Registered organisations may also come into conflict with the general social order in terms of their values or because of the way in which they act. Overall, however, social organisations are a positive and healthy force in society. If we consider social organisations in terms of their relationship with civil society and with government we can also see three broad types: non-governmental organisations; semi-governmental organisations; and government-organised organisations. Although we have seen the formation of a basically multi-polar situation, it is still heavily marked by corporatism: government-led organisations or organisations with government involvement are still the main type of social organisation in China. Social organisations serve as an intermediate layer in Chinese society or as a 'second-tier government'. Independent groups have also developed and they represent the direction in which future development will go in China but we cannot yet say that civil society has formed, or at least not a mature civil society.[14]

13 Su Li *et al.*, *supra* note 3, at pp. 307-308.

14 Kang Xiaoguang has offered the following judgement on the way in which social organisations have developed: 'in today's China there is a limited level of liberal democracy and popular participation and overall control of society exercised by a ruling elite. Social organisations that are able to exist because they have special permission to do so from the government play a mediating role between government and the public and serve as a channel for interaction. The government uses these organisations to limit or control the independent activity of different interest organisations. Legal social organisations have a monopoly status in representing the public and combine their representative functions with administrative functions. The state exercises monopoly control over representation and the right to participate in policy decision-making, a state

2.3 Measures that Support the Registration System

An inevitable accompaniment to a strict registration system is measures to crack down on and clean up illegal social organisations. The history of the development of social organisations in China is also a history of regular government rectification campaigns. In the years since the founding of the People's Republic of China there have been three major clean-up campaigns, in 1950, in 1990 and in 1997. The campaign of 1950 was aimed mainly at cracking down on reactionary social organisations and achieving the socialist reform of civic groups. In terms of consolidating the power of the newly established socialist regime this crack-down had some positive significance. Yet there were also negative outcomes – the campaign effectively, completely suppressed the nascent and as yet still fragile civic society that had begun to emerge in the last years of the Qing Dynasty and during the Nationalist era. It also contributed to the centralisation of power and the emergence of a totalitarian society. The chaos of the Cultural Revolution can in part be attributed to the attenuated state of civil society. Social problems and conflicts lacked any systematic mechanism for resolution and amelioration, leaving the adoption of abnormal means the only option; this led ultimately to the extremes of behaviour seen in that decade. The lack of means for the formation of autonomous civic organisations meant that the power crisis at the top was accompanied by disorder and chaos at grass-roots level of society. The second major crack-down began in 1990. This time the focus of the campaign included organisations that opposed the 'Four Cardinal Principles', long-term advocates of bourgeois liberalisation, groups that 'society had no need for' and those that replicated the work of existing organisations. A vast swathe of social organisations were closed down and by applying the policy of annual inspections more were de-registered. In all 400 national level organisations were de-registered or closed down – for local level groups the number exceeded 20,000.[15] The crack-down continued at this pace – in 1992 6.2% of the total number of groups were de-registered, in 1993 a further

which is the decisive power in the formation of public policy and in the outcomes of collective activities: these are the basic characteristics of the standard corporatist state.' See Kang Xiaoguang, 'Chinese Social Organisations in the Era of Transition' *(Zhuanxing shiqi de Zhongguo shetuan),* in: *Chinese Social Organisations at a Crossroads*, *supra* note 11, at p. 9.

15 Fan Baojun, 'See the Trend Clearly, Liberate Thinking, Open up a New Situation in our Country's Social Organisations Work' *(Renqing xingshi, jiefang sixiang, kaikuo woguo shetuan guanli gongzuo xin jumian), supra* note 6, at p. 108.

7.3% and 4.7% in 1994.[16] The third major campaign began in 1997. By year-end 2000 the campaign had seen the reduction of the total number of groups in China from some 200,000 to a remaining 136,000. Of the missing groups 47,000 had been de-registered and 12,000 had been closed down altogether. There was a reduction in the number of national organisations from 1,849 to around 1,500.[17]

Such large-scale crack-downs had a major impact on the way in which social organisations developed in China. The campaigns were a process by which the government could filter civil society in a way that naturally entailed an imposition of the government's own values and views, resulting in a kind of state control of civic organisations. Officials from the Ministry of Civil Affairs were quite clear about their macro-control objectives in documents they wrote on this: 'by drafting and implementing a registration policy that encourages and guides, by using a system of approvals and whatever necessary legal intervention we can vigorously foster a body of social organisations that are beneficial to economic construction and make full use of their positive impact in encouraging productive forces to carry forward a sustained rapid and healthy economic growth. We should foster an appropriate social intermediary level adapted to our situation, concentrate on developing trade and industry organisations that can act as arbitrators and instruments of self-regulation and develop such social organisations as are suitable for local economic development and public life, allowing public benefit and welfare civic organisations to play a greater role in rural and urban social service systems. We should actively foster the kind of social intermediary organisations required by the transformation of government functions that can co-ordinate with structural reforms of the administration and help promote the establishment and perfection of the socialist market economy…'.[18] Looked at another way, the large-scale crack-down campaigns are evidence of the flaws in the legal controls on social organisations that led to distortions in the functions of social organisations and had an impact on overall social stability and development. The campaigns also involved an

16 Thomas Silk, *Philanthropy and Law in Asia: A Comparative Study of the Non-profit Sector in Ten Asia Pacific Societies,* (San Francisco: Jossey Bass Publishers, 1999), translated by the China Sciences Foundation, in Chinese *Yazhou gongyi shiye jiqi fagui*, (Beijing: Zhongguo kexiu chubanshe, 2000), at p. 104.

17 Wang Ming *et al.*, *Reform of China's Social Organisations – From a Government Choice to a Social Choice (Zhongguo shetuan gaige – cong zhengfu xuanze dao shehui xuanze*), (Beijing: Shehui kexue wenxian chubanshe, 2001), at pp. 101-102.

18 Li Yong, *supra* note 10.

enormous operational cost for government and had a direct influence on changes in governmental function.

3 Approvals and *Laissez-faire* – A Comparative Analysis of the Relationship Between the State and Social Organisations

3.1 Social Organisations: Registration and Approval

In the strict sense, registration for social organisations refers to a formal legal process that a social organisation undergoes that places its establishment, existence, any changes to its status and its eventual winding-up with a supervisory agency as a matter of public record. It is the process whereby a social organisation assumes the status of an independent legal person and its attendant rights and powers. In theory registration should merely be the process whereby an organisation formalises its legal status and gains access to preferential tax policies and the right to fundraise. It should not have any fundamental influence on the organisation's right to exist and develop. The concept of freedom of association is at base the freedom of citizens to form groups and organisations without any need for official approval[19] so it follows that, in theory at least, registration should just be an option available to social organisations if they so choose, a precondition only if they want to enjoy some officially mandated privileges or engage in some special type of activity such as trade unions representing members in collective bargaining, or political organisations hoping to lobby for some policy or to participate in elections. This is because a social

19 Article 2 of the ILO's Freedom of Association and Protection of the Right to Organize Convention provides that right to organise is to be granted to 'workers and employers, without distinction whatsoever' or any need for official approval. At numerous conferences and in repeated statements down the years the ILO has emphasised that a system of approvals and the investigations of status that form part of some registration systems are a violation of the right to freedom of association. See *Freedom of Association: Digest of Decision and Principle of the Freedom of Association Committee of the Governing Body of the ILO*, (ILO: Geneva, 1996). If we also consider the confirmation given this stance of the ILO by the Covenant on Civil and Political Rights we have good reason to believe that prior approval and registration are not a basic constituent part of the exercise of freedom of association. Article 22, Clause 3 of the latter Convention states that 'Nothing in this article shall authorise States Parties to the International Labour Organization Convention of 1948 concerning Freedom of Association and Protection of the Right to Organize to take legislative measures which would prejudice, or to apply the law in such a manner as to prejudice, the guarantees provided for in that Convention'.

organisation is required to have the requisite status of an independent legal person to participate in this kind of public activity. Registration is beneficial to the state's exercise of administration but more importantly it is a way in which organisations can establish their public credibility. Transparency and openness, a stable organisational structure, sound financial practice and vigorous leadership are all important resources for social organisations.

For some organisations based on a common interest of their membership such as readers' groups or alumni associations, a simple organisational structure is perfectly adequate as they have little interaction on the public stage and any costs or debts they incur will be met through members' contributions, obviating the need for limited liability. They have little need for formal external oversight. In such cases registration is a costly waste of individuals' and society's time and a source of great real-life inconvenience. For example, there are often time limits on the reasons for establishing or maintaining a group. Some find that the process of registration takes longer than the actual realisation of their original objectives (in some countries, such as Japan, the registration process can drag on for well over a year).[20]

If, at the same time, the registration system is part of an approval mechanism or a requirement of some status for social organisations before they are allowed to engage in certain social spheres, then it has become a likely source of actual violations of the right to freedom of association. Another fundamental of freedom of association is the right of an individual to found or join organisations to protect or attain some personal interest. If the state uses a registration system to set the threshold for the exercise of this right too high, then individuals are prevented from satisfying such a need. If the state enforces its concepts and values in a process of checks and permissions before allowing an organisation to exist, then it is impossible to guarantee the independence of civil society. In the long term, linking civil society to state values and concepts not only sacrifices the former's independence and its ability to meet the need for protection of individual freedoms and satisfaction of individual desires, it also deprives the state of an external source of renewal, pressure and motivation for reform. This can lead to stagnation in the political system. A totalitarian state that has this kind of replication in the forms of state and society is not only the enemy of individual freedom, it is also likely to be the source of corruption, paralysis and stagnation in that society.

20 Thomas Silk, *supra* note 16, at p. 23.

3.2 Comparative Analysis of Methods of Social Organisation Administration

Domestic Chinese commentators often speak of two types of system for managing social organisations – a 'preventive system' and a 'punitive system'. The former refers to the state's use of a system of approval to control social organisations at source and exclude those it does not want from achieving legal status, as they are unable to register and indeed because of this are *de facto* illegal organisations. Such a registration system gives the state complete administrative control over social organisations' legal right to exist and hence provides a means to prevent the emergence and activities of illegal organisations. Asian nations, especially the countries of East and South-East Asia are usually regarded as exemplars of this 'preventive system'. A 'punitive system' is one where the state does not interfere in the establishment or activities of a social organisation unless it does something illegal, in which case the state will pursue redress. This is usually how the system prevalent in Western Europe is characterised.[21]

The preceding characterisation appears adequate as a basic description of the situation, but on closer inspection we find it is in fact somewhat wide of the mark. Sanctions against illegal organisations or illegal activities are something governments must apply whether they adopt a preventive or a punitive system. A democratic society does not permit citizens to live outside the law and of course the same applies to social organisations. Moreover, in terms of illegality of organisations, a preventive system can only guarantee the prior exclusion from legal status of organisations whose charters are illegal, not those whose illegality is only apparent in their later behaviour. The most likely outcome of a preventive system is the imposition by the government of its values and preferences on society. The organisations that are restricted are not only those which present an immediate and apparent threat to society, but any in which the government perceives such a potential threat and often organisations that in fact the government merely does not like or want. This means that the preventive system merely enforces government values but fails to actually prevent the establishment of genuinely illegal organisations. Registra-

21 This characterisation can be seen in numerous Chinese works, for example in Wang Shijie and Qian Duansheng, *supra* note 2. Some people regard any requirement for prior formalities before a social organisation can be formed as a 'preventive system'. See Kang Xiaoguang, *Shifts in Power – Changes to the Distribution in Power in a China in Transition (Quanli de zhuanyi – zhuanxing shiqi Zhongguo quanli geju de bianqian)*, (Hangzhou: Zhejiang renmin chubanshe, 1999), at p. 200.

tion is also a feature of the system for administrating social organisations in almost all countries; the difference lies in whether it is used as a way of enforcing prior approval. Do all organisations have to register or only those which want to enjoy some special status? Are unregistered organisations legal or illegal? Different countries take different approaches and attitudes to these questions which cannot be encompassed in the distinction between preventive or punitive systems. For example, in the case of checking registration applications, some checks are merely formalities, some involve actual investigation of the applicant. Some countries such as the Philippines have fast-track application systems that take only 24 hours. Regardless of the reasoning behind such a system, it is by nature largely a formality. For countries like Japan where the registration process can take a year or more, although such checks may still be formalistic the end outcome can be similar to a more substantive process.[22] This means we need to look at registration systems and the effect they have on freedom of association from a different perspective.

The truth is that the key question in either a preventive or a punitive system is the state's attitude towards and effect on the establishment of social organisations. Does the state take a permissive or a restrictive approach to social organisations? Does it treat them in the same way or make distinctions? Is prior approval required to establish a social organisation? In terms of the attitude of the state in pre-reform China and in the former Eastern Bloc nations, restriction was the basic order of the day for social organisations. Although in those times and places there were a small number of social organisations, they could only be described as another form of state power and not some means of citizens achieving an independent goal or protecting some personal interest. Citizens' interests could only be realised within the formal confines of the official system. Outside the officially-sanctioned 'mass organisations', citizens' organisations were regarded as illegal and were suppressed.[23] This state of affairs has changed greatly in the post-reform era in China and in the countries of Eastern Europe after the collapse of the Soviet Union. The great majority of Western nations take a relaxed or *laissez-faire* approach to the establishment of social organisations. More accurately, they adopt an attitude that moves from restriction and tacit approval to a permissive and supportive

22 Thomas Silk, *supra* note 16, at p. 23.

23 Report of Helsinki Watch Committee, *supra* note 1.

approach.[24] Government regulations act as a systemic guarantee of the healthy development of social organisations and official financial and tax policy support creates conditions that encourage the existence and activities of civic organisations.

The restrictive practices of pre-reform China and the old Eastern Bloc existed against a complex ideological and systemic background. In conceptual terms the hostility of Rousseau to civic organisations and the ideals of the kind of direct democracy practised under the Paris Commune were influential. Rousseau held that the emergence of civic organisations was harmful to a complete and indivisible sovereignty and prevented the formation of the general will, ending ultimately in division and the failure of the state.[25] Rousseau's theory of a general will provided the basis for the pursuit by socialist states of a unified and undisputed public consciousness and the restrictions on social organisations followed inevitably from it. At the same time, in the early years of the socialist nations they came under foreign pressure and the influence of wars leading them to choose a policy strategy based on nationalist principles. State control of the allocation of resources and social opportunity allowed social resources to be maximised but restricted the available social space for the existence of civic organisations. The habits and practices formed by the way in which socialist states used collective mobilisation and social participation in their conquest of political power also influenced their attitude to social organisations. Ultimately they found collectivist notions much better than social organisations as a way to realise the goal of a nation highly unified in ideological and spiritual terms. Of course, the realisation of such a collective goal exacted a price in the suppression of independent individual personalities and infringements of individual rights. The restrictive policies adopted by the socialist nations were also directly related to the low level of social productivity they faced at the time and the divided state of their societies and the as yet underdeveloped division of labour. As that division of labour reached a certain level, they were forced to adopt a more relaxed and permissive approach to a more pluralistic and multi-polar society. They also sought to foster an inter-

24 Christian Thomsett, *Freedom of Association: An Account of Article 11 of the European Convention on Human Rights.* Chinese translation by Jiang Xiaohong, in 'Collection of Materials on Freedom of Association' (*Jieshi ziyou ziliao Ji*), (Beijing: Institute of Law of the Chinese Academy of Social Sciences, 2002), at pp. 41-53.

25 Jean-Jacques Rousseau, The Social Contract and Discourses, translated by G.D.H. Cole (London: J.M Dent., 1913). The Chinese edition is translated by He Zhaowu, *Shehui qiyuelun*, (Beijing: Shangwu yinshuguan, 1980), at pp. 135-136.

mediate level of society to avoid stagnation of the social system and to compensate for the vacuum of power resulting from the process of transition. The rapid development of social organisations in China in the post-reform era is an expression of the demands of social development.

The permissive and supportive attitude of Western nations towards social organisations is not something they have always had. The recent history of the establishment of nation states has often seen them take a hostile attitude to social organisations as they sought to consolidate a unitary state and establish unitary markets. The prevailing attitude was that social organisations could have a negative impact on national unity and competition in a free market. The example usually cited at that time was the perceived role of the mediaeval guilds in holding back the development and technical progress of production and the formation of a unified market. Western nations, especially France, were also influenced by Rousseau's ideas and took a restrictive attitude to social organisations. It was only in later social developments, the rise of the public arena for the capitalist classes and the growth of workers' movements, that social organisations became an undeniable factor in society and began to play a role that was positive in overall terms, and the attitude of Western states towards them began to change to a more permissive and then even a supportive model.[26] This development followed a similar path to that of rights concepts and the guarantee of human rights. It could be said that how tolerant a state is of social organisations is a measure of its overall social development and also indicative of how well it safeguards its citizens' human rights.

3.3 A Comparative Analysis of Some Different Administrative Models

In terms of the interaction between the establishment of social organisations and state power we can divide administrative models into three types: an approval system, a partial approval system and a *laissez-faire* system. By approval system I mean that the state only allows organisations that have met approval requirements to be established; social organisations must receive permission from a state agency and register with them. Organisations that do not do this are *de facto* illegal. The overall attitude of the state is one of restricting the establishment of unregistered social organisations, and persons who

26 Lex Heerma van Voss, 'A History of Progress Towards Freedom of Association', paper presented at the conference on Legal Aspects of Social Organisations, organised by the Institute of Law of the Chinese Academy of Social Sciences in Beijing, May 2002.

set them up or take part in them can expect sanctions of some kind and the confiscation of group assets. This is the system adopted in many Asian countries. The approval system can be further sub-divided into single-agency and double-agency approval systems, and even multi-agency approval systems. Single-agency systems require that social organisations be set up having gained the approval of and registered with a single state agency. Japanese practice is an example of such a system. There is no one overall agency whose approval is sufficient to allow an organisation to be established. Various religious, charitable, educational, artistic and other public welfare organisations with non-profit objectives must gain the approval of a relevant government agency or regional governor or the education board etc. of their local government; community organisations need approval from their local mayor or township leader; medical groups from their regional governor. South Korea and Australia also operate single-agency systems in a similar way to Japan with the actual agency from which permission must be sought usually being decided by the specific nature of the proposed organisation. Dual-agency systems mean that as well as approval from the above kinds of government agency, organisations must also apply to a special registration agency to be checked and approved and to register before they can be set up. Taiwan, the Philippines, Thailand and Singapore operate such systems. Here organisations must usually first gain the approval of a government agency and only then can they apply for registration. These countries differ only in the specific nature of the registration agency. For example, in Taiwan it is the district court, in Thailand the local police; in Singapore charities register with a charities' commission. Mainland China operates a system of this type as well. Here the registration agency is the Ministry of Civil Affairs. The outcome of most Asian approval systems (except in Singapore) is a combination of requiring registration but otherwise interfering very little in social organisations; that is, although unregistered organisations do not have legal status, they are broadly tolerated by the authorities, who turn a blind eye to them as long as they are not doing anything patently illegal. Indeed, the government is often happy for them to exist. In South Korea, registered organisations account for 80% of the total number of social organisations. Figures from 1996 show that Japan had 250,000 registered non-profit organisations and 85,000 unregistered organisations.[27]

Western countries, however, mostly employ partial approval or partial registration systems. Ordinary groups are treated with a *laissez-faire* attitude,

27 Thomas Silk, *supra* note 16, at pp. 143, 204.

with states regarding the activities of social organisations as falling within the private sphere of citizen activity in which it would be inappropriate for legislation or the judiciary to interfere. The overall framework of national law provides legal guarantees for social organisations, protecting the activities of civic organisations from excessive interference by state power. The concept of freedom of association is thoroughly embedded in overall social administration: 'freedom of association includes individual freedoms and more generally the freedom of society towards the state, freely formed social organisations may be expected to play a positive overall role in society.'[28] As well as leaving ordinary social organisations to their own devices, the state may also impose certain restrictions on some special types of organisation. If an organisation wants to have the status of a legal person over and above the civil liability of its individual members, then it must register and meet certain legal conditions. Charitable agencies wishing to benefit from preferential tax policies must be granted the appropriate status by the tax authorities. Social organisations that wish to engage in some kinds of political activity may be required to register as a political party. There is also a difference between the basic nature of registration in Europe and in Asia. In the strictest sense registration is the system whereby types of legal status are granted, such as limited liability, tax-exempt status or the right to contest elections. It has no bearing on the social organisation's legal right to exist. In approval systems registration is the basis of and precondition for legality and without the former one cannot have the latter. In the sense of this distinction whilst Asian nations indeed operate an approval system, what is called a partial approval system in Europe turns out in fact to be merely a system of registration not of approval.

In theoretical terms the third kind of state administration of social organisations is complete *laissez-faire*; that is, the state makes no particular laws with regard to social organisations, seeing their activities in the same way as those of individuals and handling matters pertaining to them under the general body of law. In a certain sense the attitude taken by the governments of some European countries such as Germany and the Netherlands is close to such a *laissez-faire* approach although the laws on paper resemble a partial approval system. The registration of social organisations is formalized under civil law with special laws drafted for special types of organisation such as political parties. The historical development of the relationship between the state and social organisations in Europe is from restriction to non-interference and then a return to some

28 Report of Helsinki Watch Committee, *supra* note 1.

restrictions. However the early restrictions were on the very existence and activities of organisations. In the late 20th century, restrictions were mainly concerned with preventing social organisations from abusing their special status, banning prejudicial behaviour in membership policies and other questions of members' status. The new restrictions came from judicial practice rather than specific legislation, as can be seen from the body of case law of the ECHR.[29]

3.4 Possible Choices of Administration System

If we make an overall evaluation of the outlined models above for a system of administering social organisations, we may perhaps find that a partial approval system or partial registration system is a model that the state could adopt, maintaining a balance between a certain level of state control and allowing freedom of association. The reason for drawing such a conclusion is that the approval system and *laissez-faire* both have their limitations in theory and in practice.

If we consider the approval system, the first thing to be said is that it has major faults on a theoretical level: it is extremely likely that the exercise of the power of approval by the state will lead to the state enforcing its will to mould social organisations, granting legal status to organisations that accord with its ideas but excluding those that do not from social life. If this practice is maintained over the long term the outcome will be that the state moulds society to suits its own values and behaviour, leading to a complete interlinking of state and society and the extension of state power into all levels of social life, which will effect the complete restriction of society by the state. This is likely to lead to totalitarianism, the dangerous consequences for society of which are apparent from the history of German fascism and Stalinism in the former Soviet Union. In a totalitarian state there is no space for individual freedom or social democracy. Another likely danger of totalitarianism is the hostility it exhibits to those parts of human civilisation that are at odds with its goals of ever greater unity and conformity and which it will attempt to eradicate. Thus the all-pervasive control exercised by an extreme state is not just anti-society, it is likely to be anti-civilisation and anti-human as well. Totalitarian power also has other problems that have a broad impact on society. Totalitarian states

29 See cases of the European Court of Human Rights, http://www.echr.coe.int/Eng/Judgments.htm.

are unable to sustain their rule over the long term and their collapse leads to a power vacuum. The lack of civil society organisations means that the dismantling of totalitarian state power is often accompanied by complete social collapse and disintegration. Society and the state are obliged to pay an enormous price to re-establish social order and the lack of the restraining influence of civic organisations can mean that reconstruction can see the emergence of a new totalitarian regime or a corruption of political power.[30]

The second problem with the approval system is that it directly contradicts the principle of freedom of association. A basic part of that freedom is that it is a means whereby an individual can actualise some personal goal or defend some personal interest. A freedom to become oneself and to live life in the way that best pleases him or her.[31] Such a freedom naturally includes being able to live in a way which is not exactly the one your government would like you to choose. The approval system not only limits individual choice; by application of the filter of approval the government forces its values on its individual citizens, allowing the government's world to trespass into the citizen's world. Ultimately this can deprive an individual of their happiness, as this is something closely connected with the freedom to choose.

The approval system is also unworkable in practice. In those countries where it is used it is accompanied by a *de facto* system of *laissez–faire,* as the approval and registration of all social organisations is in fact far beyond the actual capacity of the state to effect and in fact is merely a kind of fable the state tells itself. The state is unable to restrict all social organisations under the aegis of its political power. To do so would require a totalitarian model. The success of such in a small country like Singapore does not mean it is widely applicable. Even for Singapore herself, total control of social organisations by the state has not been a successful paradigm for balancing individual freedom and state control. Individual freedom is restricted there.

Lastly, the requirement of approval for every proposed social organisation is a waste of resources. There really is no need for people to expend so much energy on a mere registration and approval process. Sometimes people form social organisations in pursuit of long-term goals which require broad participation if they are to be achieved. If they seek to register strictly according to state

30 Alexis de Tocqueville, *Democracy in America,* (Garden City, New York: Anchor Books, 1969), Chinese edition translated by Dong Guoliang, *Lun Meiguo de* minzhu, (Beijing: Shangwu yinshuguan, 1996), at p. 289.

31 George Kateb, 'The Value of Association', in Amy Gutmann (ed.), *Freedom of Association* (Princeton: Princeton University Press, 1998), at p. 40.

regulations on process and membership they are likely to damage their own organisational integrity.

Compared to the approval system, *laissez-faire* gives great freedom for the exercise of individual choice. There are no procedural limitations to an individual wanting to establish a social organisation or any required approval, which to an extent avoids peremptory interference by state power. Yet *laissez-faire* brings its own limitations. First, registration as a legal person is the necessary legal process whereby a social organisation achieves the status of an independent social actor, it provides a degree of credibility for the organisation and protects the interests of the organisation and any related third parties. These are all essential. A stable legal status and a healthy internal structure are preconditions for social organisations playing the fullest possible role; without that registration process social organisations lack the necessary external manifestation of these factors, which will impact on the organisation's ability to act and play its part in society.

Secondly, modern social organisations are complex and diverse both in form and substance. At the same time as they increase the ability of individuals to express themselves and achieve the things they want, they may well also present a threat to individual freedom. The abuse of the power of the group may give rise not only to social prejudice, affecting individuals' access to resources, it may also deprive some people of their opportunity to earn a living. This is of course an exceptional burden to place on an individual. As social organisations increase in size, differences in values they may have with the prevailing political order can also grow from a potential danger into an actual and present one, threatening the existence of democratic society. Furthermore, the scope of modern social organisations' activities transcends the boundaries of the sovereign state and we can see the impact of the activities of international social organisations in almost every country in the world. The Ford Foundation and Asia Foundation by funding scientific research, Amnesty International through advocacy for human rights and Greenpeace in its campaigns for the environment have all played active roles. Such internationalisation is a necessary corollary of globalisation and the internationalisation of human rights standards. But the activities of international organisations are also likely to have an impact on sovereign nations' management of their own internal affairs. If common international values are accepted, this will affect how a state judges its domestic priorities in its given environment and circumstances and thus influence a country's development and changes to its political system. Such influence is not always positive. The adoption by a state of a system of approval for the activities of social organisations, especially international organisations, is significant for safeguarding national sovereignty and allowing a country to maintain its independence in both international and domestic affairs.

The limitations of an approval system or *laissez-faire* do not in themselves provide proof of the rationality of a partial approval system. It may merely be the only option available in the face of the tensions between state power and individual rights and national regulation and individual freedoms, since it can to an extent achieve both the required degree of national regulation and the necessary protection of individual freedom. But if this is the system adopted it must be applied within proper limits, or the scope of approval may extend to become indistinguishable from an approval system, or it may be so minor as to end up being *laissez-faire*. Adopting a partial approval system requires firstly that it operates through a detailed list of requirements for registration, not by vague general principles, otherwise the government could exploit the imprecise nature of the latter to increase its restrictive powers. Specifically, in the normal course of affairs requirements for approval should be limited to such things as tax matters, the activities of foreign organisations and those of political organisations. It is an undeniable fact that the high threshold set by governments for legitimate status as a social organisation is a contributory factor in the emergence of illegal and secret organisations. The registration process should be transparent and its functions should include guiding and restricting. If a process is not transparent, it cannot play a role in guiding public behaviour and restricting arbitrary government. Such a lack also increases the operational cost for those involved in the registration process. A transparent process can create a mechanism for mutual trust between government and civil society and help to create an open and orderly social environment. Specific requirements for a transparent registration process include firstly, clear and specific conditions for registration that leave nothing unclear that would allow arbitrary interpretation by the registering agency, and also a process that is as short and simple as possible to avoid the registration agency deliberately dragging it out and adding requirements as a way of stopping a social organisation being set up.

Registration and approval should be clearly separated. Registration is the way in which an organisation achieves independent legal status and the condition for it becoming a legal person; that is, it may own and pass on property, pursue court cases and have legal liability in its own right as an organisation. Whether or not an organisation is registered does not determine whether it is legal or illegal. It is approval that is the precondition for the legal existence of a social organization. Having made the distinction between registration and approval clear, the distinction between the functions of the registration and approval agencies can also be clarified. Normal social organisations that do not require approval can apply directly for registration, which should be granted automatically if they meet basic registration requirements. Organisations that require approval should also be automatically registered once they have approval from the appropriate agency. The aim of such a distinction is to lessen the friction between the processes of approval and registration and avoid a replication of both functions, which increases the burden of registering a social organisation. Lastly, there should be mechanisms for complaints and legal redress. Where an organisation is denied registration or approval the persons involved should have a channel through which to seek judicial redress, allowing judicial agencies to restrict any illegal behaviour by government through judicial investigation. It must be emphasised that the right to freedom of association is a basic civil right and should be treated as such both in legislative and judicial terms. A basic right to administrative review of rejected applications is not adequate to provide effective redress.

4 Transitional and Replacement Measures and Their Limitations

4.1 The Dilemmas of the Transitional Period

Let us return to a discussion of the issue in China. Looked at from the point of view of long-term development, recognising and protecting the right to freedom of association and allowing the fullest exercise of it by our citizens is an unavoidable choice. For the registration of social organisations, the rational choice for a proper ordering of the relationship between state and society, and a realignment of state functions, is a partial registration system based on standard requirements combined with an overall attitude of *laissez-faire*. But in the currently prevailing circumstances, certain transitional measures are necessary for reasons I set out below.

First, as things stand both social organisations and their sponsoring agencies have taken on some functions that they ought not to have. Until these functions are removed, whilst the attendant social relationships are as yet not well ordered, and whilst there remain unresolved social problems, the complete separation of social organisations from the oversight of sponsoring agencies will be likely to lead to a number of unexpected difficulties. In China, the sponsoring agency is not only charged with approving the establishment of a social organisation, managing major affairs related to it and guiding its day-to-day operations – it is often also the provider of the resources that the social organisation uses, both material and in terms of social relationships. Social organisations rely on these to perform their function as social intermediaries. Without these resources the organisation would be likely to be unable to conduct activities, or at least not fully. The present state of affairs bears witness to this point. Although the Ministry of Civil Affairs has issued repeated instructions that senior cadres should not serve as officers of social organisations, this in fact happens in many cases, either openly or in a disguised form; furthermore, it is often organisations with this kind of leadership that have the greatest social impact. A questionnaire survey revealed that many social organisations rarely object to their sponsoring agencies' oversight, and indeed some even expressed the desire to be allowed more than one such agency to provide access to even more resources. As social organisations become increasingly civic in character they will pay a definite price in terms of access to resources. The complaint that sponsoring agencies interfered too much, and restricted the independent operation of social organisations came from the registration agency. This reminds us that administration is also a process whereby resources are claimed and allocated, and different agencies will have different views on how this should happen. Perhaps these complaints were motivated not just by the demands of a standardised administrative practice but also by a desire to control a bigger slice of social resources.

Social organisations themselves are not always simply social intermediaries, protectors of citizens' interests or promoters of public welfare. They may in fact provide a way for their sponsor agency to juggle its organisational finances, or to hang on to its powers in a disguised form in a period of governmental reform. Even more commonly they serve as a staging post to which sponsor agencies can send retired or elderly staff. Such practice does not conform to a strict interpretation of the relevant laws and social organisations should not undertake such roles. But in terms of the implicit rules of social action, such functions are seen as necessary or quite normal. In the shift from an all-powerful to a limited state, such buffer and transitional measures may not be entirely necessary, but they cannot be said to be entirely superfluous either. They probably act as a necessary smoothing factor in overall structural reform. The approval and management exercised by sponsor agencies are necessary procedural guarantees if social organisations are to continue to perform these 'extra-curricular' functions.

Second, where the government lacks both tolerance and also lacks belief in its own ability to control society and popular society does not have the appropriate intellectual climate, the dual system of permissions and registrations governing social organisations is to some extent a necessity. This is especially true where after a long period of an all-encompassing state, popular society lacks the capacity for participation and there are no rational mechanisms for popular participation and mobilisation. Management of social organisations in such conditions can easily mean either stifling civil society if you exercise management, or chaos if you don't. Thus a precondition for better management and increased social participation is the formation of mechanisms for popular participation, and mobilisation and a move away from the old mass campaign model.

Lastly, the function of the registration agency is defined as managing, fostering and developing civic organisations, placing an emphasis on management. There are two implicit choices in such definition. First, to control the development of civic organisations as far as possible, preventing them from becoming an independent social force and a threat to social stability. Government functions and administration are still guided by a mode of thinking that places officials and the populace in opposition. This can be seen from the continued restrictions on social organisations from establishing branch or subsidiary organisations, operating across administrative boundaries or setting up networks; and in the restrictions on certain types of popular organisations, such as the unemployed or migrant workers[32] – groups who are among the most marginalised in society and most in need of organisations to represent their interests. Second, social administration is still to a great extent controlled by the modalities of the planned economic era and the state still aspires to controlling the scale, geographic distribution and nature of social organisation development to keep it in line with overall social development, especially with the state's capacity for control and accommodation. In terms of the present definition of their task, both the sponsor agencies and the Ministry of Civil Affairs are fulfilling their obligations very well. Operating within the range of what policy allows and facilitates, they even make certain adjustments, and experiment with changes to the administrative system. So reform of the system for managing social organisations depends on the state making a rational definition of civic organisations' role and redefining that of the administrative agencies within the overall political framework. Without such systemic arrange-

32 Due to the inadequacies of the social security system in China, unemployed and laid-off workers often end up in poverty. Migrant workers are farmers who come to work in the cities but retain their rural registration status. The household registration system means that although migrants do the same or harder work than urban residents they are paid much less and enjoy worse working conditions and guarantees. Their rights are not properly protected.

ments, the administration of social organisations can be reformed, or alternatively innovations may be attempted within the limits of the prevailing model.

4.2 Possible alternative measures

It is an undeniable fact that the current system of administration severely restricts the emergence of civil society, and prevents it playing a full role in social life. The system of dual administration has become, in many ways a system of dual control and the conditional requirements for establishing a social organisation have been used to prevent organisations from setting up, and are an obstacle to their achieving legal status. Regular crack-downs have interfered with organisations' long-term planning, and encouraged them to adopt short-term strategies. The requirements in terms of membership, assets, and finding a sponsor are conditions that most grassroots organisations find impossible to meet, meaning that many potentially beneficial and useful social organisations are unable to achieve legal status and find themselves rendered illegal organisations. There are conflicts between organisations' lack of legal status and their other legitimate assets, which affect not just popular opinion of government policy but also how it judges and defines illegal organisations, because the government and public have different ideas about what constitutes legitimacy.

As things stand, there seem to be two ways of resolving this problem. One solution would be to reform the laws to lower the threshold for civic organisations, and to allow more of them to achieve legal status, with the Ministry of Civil Affairs acting as sponsor for those organisations who cannot find another agency to fill this role. The other possibility, acting within the current legal framework, would be to allow the various local civil affairs agencies to experiment with administrative practice by employing a simultaneous registration and recording system. Organisations which meet the requirements can be registered, those which do not but which present no political problems and are deemed to be socially beneficial can be recorded in agency files, giving them a level of legality, and making it easier for them to conduct activities. This would also change the way that administration currently only reaches down to county level, as the civil affairs network reaches further into the grassroots and would aid the establishment of a contact network for social organisations at township and urban community level, that could concentrate on solving the problems of continued existence many organisations face.

Implementing the first of these two suggestions would help standardise administrative practice, but it does present certain difficulties. There are cycles in legal reform, and changes to the way in which social organisations are regulated would influence the whole way the system works. Whilst we have yet to achieve a rational allocation of public powers, making such reforms would not sit well with the overall system for social administration. This means that the second option is probably the better choice. In recent years, similar experiments have been made in some localities to some success, such as the community registration and recording system tried out in Qingdao.[33]

In early 2002, the Qingdao Municipal Bureau of Civil Affairs – with the approval of the Ministry of Civil Affairs, their own Party Committee and the government – decided, after conducting appropriate research and theoretical discussion, to record on file as sub-groups those community civic organisations that did not meet the requirements for registration, but that were active in districts of the city. They chose four community divisions of the city to experiment with this system. The specific measures included reducing the administrative level at which checking and approval took place, allowing street committees to carry out this work, and registration to take place in local subsidiaries of the civil affairs network. They also lowered the requirements, combining and reorganising cultural and sporting groups to create a registered social organisation with a unified membership. For organisations where this was not possible they were required to have funds of CNY 3,000 to be recorded on file as separate organisations. 323 of the 452 community organisations in the city were checked and recorded in this way, 12 of which were social organisations in nature, with the other 311 more in the nature of popular non-enterprise work units. They were mostly engaged in cultural, sports or welfare activities. A thorough survey of 220 community organisations in one district was carried out, and after careful consideration, 100 of them were placed on file. These organisations were active in various urban resident committee administrations, giving them a set area for recruiting members and conducting activities and helping define what kind of activities they undertook. They were supported by sponsoring agencies and their local street committees, which disbursed some CNY 40,000 to them every year. In September 2002, the trial communities and the street and residents committees allowed a bottom-up recording process based on the survey work they had previously done. The municipal registration agency provided a standardised certificate for this and

33 The information about Qingdao is based on material provided by the Qinghua NGO Research Centre from research they conducted in Qingdao, in which I also participated.

public ceremonies were held in the four districts to issue them to the relevant organisations. At the same time the street committees in each trial district arranged for public posting of details of the recorded organisations' names, responsible officers, scope of activity and geographical area of work to allow the community to exercise oversight.

At the same time Qingdao Municipality set up a four tier monitoring network at the levels of city, district, street committee and residents' committee. Women from residents' committees undertook regular inspection rounds under this network, strengthening oversight and control over the civic organisations. As the trial period was coming to a close the different districts organised concerted crackdowns that led to the closure of 20 illegal organisations that had neither registered, nor filed as sub-groups. In the trial areas, both local community groups and formally registered organisations active in the district were included in the same administrative system. Street committees were expected to improve their organisation and work in concert with residents' committees to exercise guidance and management of these civic organisations.

There have been experiments in other parts of the country as well. In Ji Nan in Shandong and Nanjing in Jiangsu a system was developed based on the fact that many groups depend on higher level social organisations for their legal status. Social organisation liaison centres of one sort or another were set up in towns and street committees and given a legal registered status. Next the various local community organisations were allowed to place themselves under this centre as a means of achieving legal status as a sub-organisation. This method was popular with the organisations concerned as they gained a measure of legal or official recognition. In a country where official approval is still deemed to be very important this helped improve the organisations' credibility and protected them to an extent from inappropriate interference. It also provided them with access to social resources. Their new official status also made it possible for the organisations to participate in public life in their communities.

In Fujian, a policy was adopted to address the difficulty of establishing civic organisations in rural communities. They were treated as if they were internal organisations set up inside a work unit. They were able to set up and begin activities, and then register once they had developed enough to meet the required conditions.[34] This work has however only just begun and we must wait to see what specific social outcomes it brings.

34 This information comes from visits I made to the region.

4.3 Limitations of Alternative Measures and Objections to Them

Against a background of overall social reform in China, local governments are working hard to adopt what measures they can to reform their overly rigid administrative systems so as to meet the requirements of social development. We should be supportive of these efforts. China is a country of vast differences in cultures and regions, and local experiments where a standardised system of administration can be modified as appropriate to specific local conditions are beneficial to the overall efficiency of the system. The various modified measures tried out in different localities also show that there is room for flexibility under the system prevailing at present. How best to use this room is a question civic society and the government must answer. On the whole, we should affirm such positive trends in Chinese social change.

Keeping local community groups on file is indeed a feasible transitional measure and it provides an intermediary stage for both government and civic organisations. For the government it is a means of lowering the overly high threshold to legal status, expanding the scope for public participation, and increasing their public approval; for civic organisations it is a means of achieving legal status and it makes it somewhat easier for them to conduct activities. In a society like China where status is very important, it goes without saying that an officially approved status is very important in terms of access to resources and the ability to undertake public activity.

However, we must recognise that not all civic organisations are able to achieve this transitional recorded status and the process by which it is carried out is still one in which the government filters civic organisations, giving a measure of legal status to those it approves of. Yet there is still some distance between 'organisations that the government approves of' and 'organisations that meet citizens' needs' in terms of the development of a genuine civil society. Even as it relaxes registration requirements the government is considering ways of restricting illegal organisations, since if we accept the standards of the two regulations nominally governing them there are an enormous number and range of illegal organisations that the government is incapable of exercising full administration over. An important measure of government administrative capacity and vigour is its ability to integrate society. For a government to force an illegal status onto a vast number of civic organisations that have popular approval and could be beneficial to social development is extremely dangerous.

We should also be clear that regardless of what registration system is adopted the key reform lies in a change in the functioning of government. Otherwise any attempts at change will come to nothing. The system of recording on file makes setting up a civic organisation that bit easier, but we must not ignore the way in which it further strengthens the government's pre-existing management goals. If a policy which is in fact aimed at drawing out illegal organisations so they can be dealt with is presented in the guise of a service to civil society it will not only harm the latter but also the government itself. The establishment of community liaison centres and the community monitoring networks represents a downward extension of administrative control and is reminiscent of the old tactics of mass mobilisation. Such practices fail to meet the requirements for development into a modern society of civic autonomy, a professional management system and the formalisation of processes for social participation. Whilst welcoming such transitional measures we must be careful to consider clearsightedly their basic intent and advantages and disadvantages.

5 Conclusion

China is in a time of social transition and while former rules are probably no longer appropriate, new ones have yet to be established. Nor do we have examples of successful practice to serve as a guide. Thus learning from the experience of other countries is very important for us. From the above analysis we can see that a partial approval system is one sensible choice that can maintain a balance between citizens' freedom of association, with the state's need for social control, and have a positive significance in the development of civil society and the preservation of social stability.

At the same time we can see that in a country as large as China, with all its difference in levels of economic and social development there are difficulties in adopting one single administrative model. For this reason it is right that central government lays down overall guiding regulations but allows localities room for innovation and flexibility. A competition in such innovation between regions can create new opportunities for overall social development. In the present situation, where the definition of civic organisations given in the Constitution cannot be brought into the workings of the existing overall system, using regional experiments to invigorate civil society represents a very good way forward.

5

RESEARCH ON CHINA'S CIVIC ENVIRONMENTAL PROTECTION ORGANISATIONS

Chen Xinxin

1 INTRODUCTION

Freedom of association is one of the rights enjoyed by Chinese citizens. It is clearly set out in the Constitution and is also one of the basic human rights provided for in the International Covenant on Civil and Political Rights. Due to the special national and political circumstances of China, administrative regulations governing social organisations are quite restrictive. Of all the various types of social organisations, civic environmental organisations have comparatively greatest freedom of action and they coordinate and interact most effectively with government. Their influence is also the fastest-growing. There are already more than 2,000 civic environmental protection organisations registered with government agencies at various levels.[1] In the light of this prominent role, I have conducted a survey of 87 civic environmental organisations, communicating both directly and indirectly with the subject group, conducting telephone interviews, e-mail dialogues, and interviews in person and checking relevant websites. My aim was to take a narrowly focussed look at the present state and future development prospects of social organisations in China by means of analytical research on civic environmental organisations.

We speak of 'civic environmental protection organisations' as a conceptual contrast to 'governmental environmental protection organisations'. The dis-

1 According to figures made public at the second 'Sino-US Cooperative Forum for Environmental NGOs'.

Yuwen Li (Ed.), *Freedom of Association in China and Europe: Comparative Perspectives in Law and Practice*, Printed in The Netherlands, pp. 189-217.

tinction between 'civic' and 'governmental' reflects the difference between their internal management, staffing and financial arrangements. The management basis for governmental organisations is that they are run or set up by state agencies, state owned enterprises (SOE) or state institutions; they are subject to an administrative agency and their internal management arrangements closely follow those of government agencies. Civic organisations, in contrast, are voluntarily established by members of the public and not by official bodies, do not report to a higher-level agency and their internal management is based on a self-governing model run on democratic principles rather than having state-appointed officials. In terms of their personnel, governmental environmental organisations are composed mostly of full-time staff who enjoy the status of civil servants; their numbers are determined by official staffing limits and hiring and firing is carried out in accord with state rules and regulations; key staff are appointed in accordance with the official administrative level the organisation is treated as being equivalent to, and the choice of persons to fill these posts is heavily influenced by their superior supervisory official agency. Civic environmental organisations are staffed by part-timers and volunteers; the small number of full time staff are employed after a competitive application process; they have no official personnel complement; staff are appointed in accordance with the provisions of the Labour Law and associated regulations; key staff are chosen by a democratic electoral process with no question of their being appointed by superior supervisory agencies. In financial terms official organisations rely either totally or for the most part on official budgetary allocations and thus are influenced by state budgetary policy and their financial affairs are overseen by budgetary, auditing and tax agencies. A significant proportion of staff wages and benefits are funded by official budgetary allocations. Civic organisations raise and spend their own money and stand or fall financially on their own viability – they enjoy no official financial support.[2] Staff wages are paid entirely from their own funds. Their budgets, income and expenditures and management practices are overseen by fiscal and tax agencies but not by official state auditors.

Civic environmental protection organisations can be divided into two main types – student organisations and those formed by the wider general public. Student organisations can again be sub-divided into organisations established

2 Student environmental organisations do receive some indirect official financial support in so far as they receive funds from college budgets. Their personnel are subject to the supervision of the campus Communist Youth League or similar agencies. However, in their day to day activities they display the characteristics of other civic organisations.

in higher educational institutions and those run by primary and secondary school students. The organisations in the higher educational institutions are the main force among these. The earliest post-1949 forms of these student organisations were first seen on campuses in the 1950s.[3] Over the following decades they increased in both total number of organisations and in strength. Prior to 1994 this development happened slowly, with only a minority of university campuses having environmental organisations, but they grew steadily from that year and between 1998 and 2001 there was a noticeable upward trend in their development. The number of university student environmental organisations established in 1999 led to a doubling of the national total that had existed in 1998. This rate of growth continued in 2000 so that the national total of organisations reached almost a hundred. Today student environmental organisations can be found in every province of China and in the Hong Kong, Macao and Taiwan regions. In mainland China alone, more than two hundred student environmental organisations have been established in higher education campuses. However, there is an obvious imbalance in the distribution of these organisations – in the big cities with many higher educational institutions such as Beijing, Shanghai, Tianjin, Wuhan, Xi'an, Chengdu and Guangzhou we find many organisations; but only a few are to be found in provinces such as Hainan, Tibet or Guizhou. When conducting our survey we also found that in the big cities there were College Environmental Organisation Alliances bringing together senior figures from all the student organisations in the city in regular meetings where they could coordinate plans and activities for all the student environmental organisations in their area and represent their interests and concerns to government agencies in a more formal fashion. This is a very positive development.

2 The Social Background to the Emergence and Development of Civic Environmental Protection Organisations

In the years since reform and opening China's economy has developed at so rapid a pace that it has astonished the world. At the same time problems of environmental degradation have become ever more prominent: the over-exploita-

3 In the 1950s, some of China's agriculture and forestry colleges had organisations voluntarily organised by students who worked on anti-desertification and desalination projects and biological surveys. These were overseen by college authorities, who would appoint teachers to supervisory roles. They can be regarded as forerunners of campus environmental organisations.

tion of natural resources and their use in uneconomic and wasteful ways; the worsening of the greenhouse effect; unsettled global climate patterns; depletion of the ozone layer; acid rain; shortcomings in resource recycling and loss of species threatening biodiversity. This has not only presented barriers to sustainable development, it has introduced threats to the very well-being and existence of humankind. Although the Chinese central government has repeatedly stressed the need to avoid the tragedy of 'first polluting, then cleaning up' that has marked development in so many other nations, reliance on government intervention alone cannot offer fundamental solutions to the serious environmental problems China faces. Ordinary people, who are both victims of environmental pollution and probably also contributors to it, naturally wish to take action to protect the environment, motivated both by self-interest to ameliorate potential harmful consequences and by reflection on the impact of their own past behaviour. Thus we saw the appearance of civic environmental protection organisations.

The government has taken a relatively relaxed and supportive attitude to the emergence of civic environmental protection organisations and dealt with them in a much more permissive way than they treated 'interest groups'.[4] The main reasons for this are, firstly, that environmental protection is in the fundamental interests of all sections of Chinese society – a healthy living environment and sustainable development are not merely the demands of a special interest group. Thus the government's objectives and those of the civic environmental organisations were broadly in accord. The government was less concerned about any possible conflicts like those often seen when the interests of different special interest groups clash. Secondly, in a large country as populous as China, which has so many obvious differences between various sections of society and is still developing its economic strength, raising the public's environmental consciousness and enacting environmental protection are not tasks the government is able to accomplish on its own. There is an understanding among government at all levels that without widespread public support and participation, relying solely on government manpower, material and financial resources or conducting piecemeal environmental protection will not be adequate to provide fundamental solutions to the severe environmental challenges China faces both now and over

4 The term 'interest groups' refers to social organisations whose mission is to protect or obtain some sectoral or limited set of interests such as trades unions, farmers' associations, trade associations and political groups. This contrasts with public interest groups – that is those who do not seek to advance the interests of just one particular social organisation but those of society as a whole.

the long term. A combination of shortfalls in state capacity and numerous pressing problems has made the mobilisation of social forces for environmental protection a necessity. Government toleration and support of civic environmental organisations reflects this necessity. Thirdly, right from the start, China's civic environmental organisations defined themselves as inspirers and promoters of environmental awareness; they sought to offer specialist insights and avoided politicising issues, concentrating only on purely environmental problems. Their activities were limited to practical environmental initiatives, not political campaigns like those of environmental organisations in the West, some of them even developed into political parties.[5] China's civic environmental organisations emphasise joint interests and understanding in their dealings with government, displaying strong 'cooperative tendencies' and for the most part offering 'well-intentioned advice' and 'aid and assistance' to government. They do not adopt the strategy of Western green organisations which seek to advance their cause through protest, opposing government action and inaction that harms the environment or fails to protect it, to the point that they become opposition parties opposed to any ruling party. They conflict and clash with government far more often than they cooperate with them. Thus, not only will the activities of China's green organisations not have an impact on overall political stability, they in fact assist in the implementation of government, especially central government, environmental policy. This is another tangible reason for the more permissive environment in which China's green organisations operate compared to other social organisations. Fourthly, civic environmental organisations are independent; in the balancing of interests that is involved in environmental protection their closeness to the general public allows them to play a role and have an impact that the government cannot. Although there is a general desire to see the environment protected, conflicts of interest are unavoidable in the actual implementation of measures to achieve it. There is a general clash between the demands of short-term regional economic development and long-term environmental protection goals. Civic environmental organisations can take advantage of their status as disinterested parties to contribute specialist knowledge and assist the government in resolving conflicts by rational persuasion.

The development of civic environmental organisations in China is affected by a whole range of factors. In the years since reform and opening, progressive

5 The German Green Party is the classic example of this. Its forerunner was the German branch of Greenpeace, a civic environmental organisation, which gradually developed into a political organisation. In 1998 the Green Party achieved 8% of the vote in national elections and became part of the 'Red-Green' governing coalition.

international ideas on environmental protection have come to China where they have combined with a cultural tradition of love and respect for nature to grow ever more influential. Intellectuals played a vital role as progenitors in this process. Many of the current crop of civic green organisations were founded and are led by such individuals. The role of international movements was also important. Since environmental problems now present a global challenge, environmental organisations all around the world, especially in developed nations, are very concerned about China's environment and have given financial assistance to China's green organisations. Considering the funding difficulties the latter faced, this has been very important. The level of development of civic environmental organisations also affects China's international image. When in 1993 Beijing first applied to stage the Olympic Games the officials on the application committee had no way of answering questions from the IOC concerning civic environmental organisations in China. The rapid growth in these organisations since 1994 was certainly helped by Beijing's ongoing quest to stage the Games or, at least, the bid was one of the reasons for the tolerance shown to environmental organisations. In their turn, by actively participating in the bidding process, civic environmental organisations played a part in the successful application made in 2001.

3 The Composition of Civic Environmental Organisations

An analysis of the composition of China's civic environmental organisations must approach the question from two angles. First is the composition of their memberships by age. For China's green organisations this can be said to display peaks at both ends of the scale and a trough in the middle; that is a majority of members are young people or elderly with fewer middle-aged participants. Young people, especially university students, are the backbone of China's civic environmental organisations, both in campus organisations and as volunteers in organisations that draw membership from the wider public. University students are well-educated and have the advantages of good personal qualities, a sense of social responsibility and plenty of energy. They are active and creative. Both now and in the future, the actions and attitudes of university students will have a major impact on policy decisions in China. They are a group who will play an important role in the development and promotion of civic environmental organisations. If we can say that the emergence of green organisations is a response to the demands of the times, China's social and economic development and the growth of public awareness of environmental issues, then students and campus green organisations are at the vanguard of the movement. Of course, since students are not yet financially independent and are not yet income earners they cannot provide major funding support for environmental initiatives, only offering their intellectual and physical contributions, so campus organisations rely heavily on outside funding.

Also of note is the rising participation of junior and high school students in environmental protection as such ideas gain a wider public audience; a most welcome development. Young people adapt easily and are open to new ideas, eager for new concepts and aspirations. Participation in environmental protection can by a process of osmosis impart a love of life, an appreciation of nature's beauty and good environmental habits that will stay with young people for the rest of their lives and have a positive impact on their personal development. Not only are these younger children the university students of the future, they also motivate their parents (the middle-aged) to take an interest in environmental causes in a way nobody else can. The middle-aged are the biggest untapped section of Chinese society in terms of environmental awareness. The elderly (persons over sixty years of age) have a wealth of working and life experience and a long-term perspective. They have personal experiences of the changes wrought by environmental degradation and pollution and a profound understanding of the importance and seriousness of environmental problems. This often combines with reflection on and regret for their own past behaviour that may have contributed to the problem to produce a high level of enthusiasm for environmental protection. Those retired persons still in good health and financially independent are especially active and they have rich personal and social resources and the advantages of patience and persistence. Often all that restrains them from even more active roles is the inevitable loss of ability that accompanies aging, but in this they have a beneficial mutually compensatory relationship with their younger fellow activists. The middle-aged (those between forty and sixty years of age) are by comparison less involved in environmental organisations. This is largely a result of the general pressures of life and work this age group is burdened with. They are the generation that was born and grew up in modern China's most turbulent and politicised times, they have often not had a systematic education and for the most part know little about environmental issues and ideas. Also they tend to be practical rather than idealistic and consider that in the present Chinese social climate the as yet weak civic environmental movement will find it hard to achieve much in the way of concrete outcomes and are more dependent on government and state agencies to act on their behalf and more willing to support the latter. Of course, this group is at the core of society and controls most of its resources. In developed countries the support of the middle-aged played an important role in the growth of environmental movements, especially their rise in social prominence and politicisation. Many of the founders and core activists in China's currently influential civic environmental organisations come from this age group. The future growth of China's environmental movement should seek to draw on the potential of the middle-aged.

We may also consider the knowledge composition of environmental organisations. In the early days the membership of these organisations was largely drawn from those educated at university, and even as environmental consciousness has grown and spread, in rural areas founders of environmental organisations still tend to be farmers who are more knowledgeable, keen researchers and eager learners. By acquiring environmental knowledge, members of green organisations become further aware of the importance of environmental protection for both their own lives and indeed for the future sustainable development of humankind, which helps them avoid behaving in short-sighted ways. Thus regardless of the professional background of the membership, it is the understanding and desire for environmental knowledge that provides the basis for the existence and growth of the strong sense of purpose that civic green organisations display. Even in those ethnic minority areas where the emergence of some environmental organisations has been associated with religious belief[6] we can say that knowledge of environmental issues has played a decisive role. Because environmental knowledge was not given much importance in the national education system for a long time, the possession of environmental knowledge has no obvious direct relationship with a person's level of educational attainment. Except for graduates of institutes teaching environment-related subjects, the majority of people lack knowledge about environmental issues. This has been a factor in the generally weak social basis for environmental causes in China. It has made the knowledge composition of civic environmental organisations especially important. In the end an enthusiasm for the environment and a sense of responsibility are not in themselves sufficient to effect a real impact or achieve protection goals. In terms of professional background, we see many people from education and research or who have themselves worked in polluting industries, which reflects their knowledge of the issues. Volunteers far outnumber full-time staff in civic environmental organisations, indeed we may say that the organisations rely on volunteers for their existence and opera-

6 For example the religious reverence some ethnic groups hold for sacred mountains or particular animals has been a factor in local people forming organisations for their protection, including participation from local religious organisations.

tion. Here too a person's knowledge is a determinant of the likelihood of their being involved, with a high proportion of volunteers having received higher education.[7] This is a further demonstration of the influence of knowledge on the composition of civic environmental organisations.

4 Systems for Self-governance

A charter acts as the constitution of a self-governing organisation. Most civic environmental organisations have been autonomously established and continue to develop under the guidance of a charter. Our survey found this to be the case with more than 90% of organisations in our study, with a further 7% student organisations set up by their college authorities. 85% of the autonomously organised groups had an individual founder who was not only the principal drafter of their charter but also exercised a strong influence on the way the group developed. Even where the founder had since left the group the majority still maintain frequent contact with him or her. Of course most organisations' charters are drafted on the basis of collective discussions and decided upon by an appropriate democratic decision-making process. The charters contain clauses outlining an organisation's nature and mission; the type of activities it plans to undertake; its organisational model; procedures for choosing its decision-making bodies and their powers; conditions for membership and what rights and duties this confers; sources of funding and so forth. Most organisations' charters do not include provisions for the revision of the charter or procedures for winding up the organisation and disposing of any assets when that happens. The 'Regulations for Registration and Management of Social Organisations'[8] require an organisation's charter to include the organisation's name and address; mission, scope of activities and location where they will be conducted; conditions for membership and associated rights and duties; democratic organisational structure and procedure for choosing an executive body; winding up procedures and disposal of remaining assets, and other matters that should be stipulated in the charter. As we can see, the majority of civic environmental organisations' charters fall short of the legal requirement.

7 The term 'higher education' is used here to denote undergraduate level, as participation by masters and doctoral graduates is actually proportionately slightly lower due in large part to their applying their energies elsewhere and also related to the different age composition of these latter two groups.

8 See the Appendix I of this book.

The nature and mission of the organisation is a matter of great importance for civic environmental organisations and is usually set out in the early part of their charters. Clauses dealing with the nature of an organisation will usually clearly state the organisation's status as a legal organisation and how they achieved that, who their official sponsoring agency is, and their not-for-profit status. Mission statements for organisations not focussing on one particular geographical area may read 'to promote public environmental education, raise public environmental awareness, advocate a green civilisation and advance the cause of China's environment so that the Chinese people can enjoy the full benefits of sustainable development'.[9] Locally focussed organisations will place emphasis on the protection of their particular locale and the encouragement of sustainable economic development.[10] Here we should point out that although the regulations as currently formulated say that the registration agency need not recognise a new organisation applying to establish in an area where a similar organisation already exists,[11] this does not mean that organisations do not operate across administrative boundaries. In fact many local civil affairs departments do not seek to impose strict limits on the establishment of environmental organisations, only requiring that they have an official sponsoring agency. In order to better coordinate their external relationships, particularly those with government, many organisations include a clause in their charters stating: support for policies, measures and activities taken by the Chinese government, social organisations and individuals that are beneficial to environmental protection and sustainable social development and a willingness to cooperate in such; at the same time, where conditions allow, to monitor, criticise and call for redress from the relevant agencies in matters which are contradictory to these goals.

9 Excerpt from the Charter of Friends of Nature, see www.fon.org.cn/english/ (last visited March, 2005).

10 For example, the Charter of the 'Green River' organisation in Sichuan states their mission as 'promoting and organising for the protection of the natural environment of the upper reaches of the Yangtze River and striving to realise the sustainable social and economic development of this important watershed'. It emphasises its main tasks to be 'organising studies and visits to the upper Yangtze River and other rivers in Sichuan by scientific researchers, journalists and domestic and international environmental organisations; establishing a model ecological protection area'. For the Charter see www.green-river.org (last visited March 2005).

11 Art. 13 of the Regulations for Registration and Management of Social Organisations; Art. 11 of the Temporary Regulations for the Registration and Management of Popular Non-Enterprise Work Units. See Appendix II of this book.

It is worth noting that most civic environmental organisations set very broad goals in their mission statements, such as promoting public environmental awareness and education and reducing or ameliorating damage to the environment. There is a clear disparity between these lofty aims and the reality of the small scale and limited resources of most organisations; indeed this can lead to disillusionment and a sense of ineffectiveness for their members and may not be helpful in sustaining and advancing their cause under difficult circumstances. Organisations who set out clear and practicable goals in their mission statements will find it easier to focus members' energies and provide them with a sense of achievement. In the long term this is actually of more benefit to the achievement of those larger goals mentioned above.

The provisions in organisations' charters concerning the way in which they will conduct environmental education and activities to promote green culture are more varied. They include after-school clubs in schools and colleges, various types of adult education, publications, arts and media presentations, public campaigns and mass participation activities. The emphasis is on raising environmental awareness, especially among the young. They also encourage scientific research, information gathering and public opinion surveys to provide support for the environmental protection campaigns and raise the quality of their own work. They also use all available means to encourage friendly interaction and exchanges amongst their members.

The conditions for membership of an organisation are an important indicator of the inclusiveness and affinities of a civic environmental organisation. Most organisations' charters do not set strict requirements for prospective members, usually merely asking that they be willing to work for the protection of the environment. For example, Friends of Nature's charter says that 'all individuals willing to earnestly work for the protection of the environment, who agree with the mission and charter of Friends of Nature and are willing to contribute to the realisation of its goals may become members of the organisation having completed an application process and been approved by the Board; all enterprises, institutions or organisations who support or work in environmental protection, agree with the mission and charter of Friends of Nature, are able to comply with the mission of Friends of Nature in their day-to-day activities and who support and can regularly participate in our activities may become corporate members of Friends of Nature having been introduced by a member of the Board, having themselves completed an application and once that application is approved by the Board'.[12] The charter of Green River in Sichuan contains similarly worded provisions.[13] The charter of the student environmental organisation at Xiamen University requires that members should love nature, uphold the organisation's charter and be willing to accept organisational discipline.[14] These charters embody a spirit of voluntary membership and democratic self-management.

The rights and duties of members are an indicator of the nature of a self-governing organisation. Usually, civic environmental protection organisations' charters will provide for such members' rights as: the right to take part in or stand for elections and to vote; the right to take part in organisation activities; the right to organise activities in the organisations' name, subject to the Board's approval and their being consistent with the organisation's mission, and the right to receive assistance from the organisation in doing this; to share the organisation's information resources and take part in its external exchanges; the right to comment on, criticise and monitor the organisation's work; and the right to recommend new members. Members' duties and obligations usually include: to work earnestly to promote the organisation's mission; to respect the charter; to pay membership fees as stipulated; to uphold the rights and good name of the organisation, and to provide voluntary service to the organisation. Some organisations' charters stipulate the type of voluntary work members must do for the organisation and that it will be unpaid though out-of-pocket expenses may be reimbursed. For board members who give up more time there may be separate rules dealing with how they are to be compensated. In line with the principles of voluntarism most charters also make provisions for members wishing to leave the organisation – those wishing to leave will have their membership revoked once the request is filed. Many also lay down rules for expulsion of members as a means of protecting the organisation's security, interests and reputation. Anyone who violates the charter, harms the organisation's mission or reputation or breaks national laws and regulations may be expelled if the board so decides. Most charters also state that unless they have written approval from the board, members may not organise public activities, raise funds or establish contacts with other organisations or individuals be they foreign or domestic in the name of this organisation. Should any of the above occur the organisation will take no responsibility for the said actions and will ask the relevant authorities to prosecute offenders as the law provides.

12 Art. 9, Friends of Nature Charter, see *supra* note 9.

13 Art. 9, Green River Charter, see *supra* note 10.

14 Art. 7, Charter of Student Environment Organisation at Xiamen University.

Due to the international nature of environmental protection and its significance for the whole of humanity and thus the importance of international contacts between environmental organisations, charters will often provide for international and inter-regional cooperation and the organisation's participation in appropriate global campaigns. However, political and economic considerations show a need to set limits on such exchanges in a organisation's charter in order to protect its interests: hence the clause noted above forbidding exchanges in the organisation's name without written permission from the board and the disavowal of any responsibility for such contacts. Many organisations also provide for non-PRC citizens to take part in their activities as 'associate members'. Due to the sensitive nature of this issue, whilst charters will accord similar rights and obligations as those of full members to such associates, they also stress that their participation in activities is subject to specific circumstances and the provisions of any relevant national regulations.

Some civic environmental organisations establish a board of directors, in accordance with the provisions of their charters, which acts as the organ of highest authority within the organisation. The board will consist of a number of members usually elected by the wider membership of the organisation. They often have relevant specialist knowledge, management experience or social contacts or are core activists of the organisation. The main duties of the board are deciding the overall direction of the organisation's development, overseeing financial affairs and expanding the organisation's role in the community. The chair of the board, executive director and general secretary are chosen from among board members and form the actual core executive of the organisation. The board's powers usually include: drafting, revising and interpreting the organisation's charter; selecting and dismissing senior organisation officials; hearing and approving the organisation's annual work and financial reports; overseeing the implementation of work plans; deciding other important matters affecting the organisation; and selecting or appointing an honorary chair or consultants. Since the mechanisms used by international environmental organisations regarding the operation of their board of directors are already well established and effective it has become more common for Chinese organisations to adopt a similar model. However considering the relatively loose nature of many Chinese environmental organisations and a lesser familiarity with the procedures and characteristics of democratic decision-making, there may well be room for further improvements to these mechanisms to be made in the light of practical experience.

The status of key actors in environmental organisations and how they are chosen is an important standard by which their nature may be determined and judged. Often organisations that have an official background will have leaders who are senior government officials, whilst the actual direction of work will be left to a deputy (also with appropriate official status). They are usually appointed after the personnel department suggests names and the sponsoring agency confirms them, with any election usually a merely procedural affair. In civic organisations the leaders are often the actual chairpersons themselves though some organisations will appoint a well-known figure to act as chair whilst a deputy chair or secretary general with appropriate specialist knowledge and dedication to environmental causes will oversee day-to-day running. The leaders of civic organisations may be appointed, selected or elected. According to our own survey, 63% of research-oriented organisations chose their leadership by selection from members' recommendations, 22% chose them via a competitive election process and 6% had them appointed by their sponsoring agency. The other 9% used various methods, including a mix of selection and election.[15] Most civic organisations held open, free and fair elections. Candidates emerged either by grassroots recommendations or by putting themselves forward voluntarily. Although many organisation founders and core activists will be re-elected to senior posts on successive occasions this is usually a genuine reflection of the esteem in which they are held rather than the result of any forced choice or administrative interference. Formal elections follow basic democratic procedures with open competition, secret ballots, a public count of votes, monitoring of voting procedures, majority decisions and fixed terms of office. Senior figures in civic organisations will exercise collective leadership although founders or key actors may be more influential in this regard due to their personal authority. This does not, however, imply any kind of autocracy. It clearly demonstrates the harmonious relationship between civic organisations' non-monopoly, not-for-profit, free and voluntary nature and their democratic politics. The development of such organisations will not only be of benefit to environmental protection, it will also help to improve Chinese citizens' democratic and self-governing capabilities.

With an eye to preserving the stability and continuity of organisations, most charters allow leaders to serve consecutive terms in office. Terms of office and length of service tend to be quite long. This is different in student organisations due to the nature of the education system – most students take four years to

15 Organisations appointing leaders were usually campus environmental organisations since they came under the aegis of their school authorities, though such supervision differed from official administrative relationships, usually manifesting itself mainly in controlling the appointment of organisation leaders and overseeing activities.

complete a degree and hence the core leadership of campus environmental organisations is of necessity less stable and more fluid. The scale, administration, type of activities and information resources of campus organisations are also affected by this instability and it takes capable leadership from key actors to avoid excessive problems of this nature. Moreover, this instability increases the opportunity cost of government agencies and other environmental organisations cooperating with student organisations. Our survey found that terms of office of student organisation leaderships were never very long: 50% had served for between six and twelve months, and a further 40% for between a year and eighteen months, from which we can see how unstable campus environment organisations' leaderships are. This high rate of turnover in leadership and a low sense of belonging felt by members are difficult problems facing China's campus environmental organisations.

The internal organisational structures of different civic organisations vary quite a lot, influenced by the size of the organisation in question and the preferences of the founder. Most organisations are small or medium-sized (usually fifty to one hundred members). Of the organisations we surveyed 33% had fifty to one hundred members, 29% twenty to fifty members, 16% between a hundred and one hundred and fifty members and a few organisations with fewer than twenty members. There were seven organisations with between one hundred and fifty and two hundred members and only six with over two hundred members. This prevalence of small and medium-sized organisations means that most have fairly simple internal organisational structures. Our survey found this to be the case, with most only establishing such internal structures as were necessary to facilitate normal running. In this they did not differ greatly from other types of social organisations.[16] It would behove environmentalists to reflect on how the internal structure of their organisations could play a part in emphasising the unique features and advantages of environmental ideas. Some organisations, inspired by green political ideals, keep their internal structures very simple and do not set up any branch organisations, choosing instead to set up specialist organisations to oversee particular projects, such as 'water resource teams', 'battery recycling teams' and so forth. The emphasis is on

16 Chinese social organisations in many ways copy their internal structures from those of official institutions and can tend towards the bureaucratic. This is true of civic environmental organisations to an extent, especially in campus and semi-official organisations. In more developed countries green political movements' egalitarian and libertarian ideals and opposition to bureaucracy find embodiment in their organisations' internal structures and decision-making mechanisms.

project autonomy or the guiding role that actual activities have in overall organisation policy. The advantage of such a system is not just in the emphasis it places on practical activity; it also greatly reduces the waste associated with stratified bureaucracies, helps make specific projects sustainable over the longer term and keeps the organisation's activities focussed, ongoing and long-term.

5 Finances

Civic environmental organisations raise their own funds and are financially independent. Very few receive any direct government financial support. Their main sources of funding are membership fees and commercial sponsorship. Some better known organisations receive funding from overseas foundations or NGOs; for some this is their main source of money. Student organisations usually have their running costs met from the administrative budget of their college. To broaden potential sources of funding most environmental organisations' charters permit them to accept sponsorship and donations from agencies, social organisations, enterprises and individuals, be they in the form of money, services, equipment or printed materials, and allow an appropriate expression of thanks to be made to the donor. As a result of their environmental principles some organisations stipulate in their charters that they will not accept donations from tobacco companies or businesses which trade mainly in products derived from wild animals.[17] The majority of civic environmental organisations are short of money or lack a guaranteed source of income and find fundraising difficult. This is one of the major difficulties they face. A fairly large number of organisations succeed in roughly balancing their annual expenditure with their income, with shortfalls or surpluses less than CNY 3,000. Our survey found that over 90% of responding organisations listed funding difficulties as one of their most pressing problems, and of these 60% said it was *the* most pressing problem, another 20% called it their second largest headache, and the 10% ranked it third.

Different organisations get their funds from widely varying sources in varying proportions. Membership fees are collected by some 85% of organisations – 60% say it is their main source of funds, the other 25% rely on these fees to fund most of their activities (membership fees account for over 95% of all income). In relative terms larger and better known organisations rely less

17 Art. 20 of Green River's Charter is an example of such a clause, *supra* note 10.

on membership fees and the trend here is for them to be less and less important – some organisations only ask for nominal subscriptions from their members. Smaller organisations find membership fees much more important.

Sponsorship from commercial organisations is another important source of funding for many organisations, but the reality falls far short of what many would hope. Our survey found that only 40% of organisations are able to attract such sponsorship although for some of these organisations it may account for over 30% of their money. This proportion is also rising. Large sums of sponsorship money tend to come from foreign companies, domestic companies give less. Companies' interest in sponsoring environmental protection is related to the perceived benefits for their own commercial activities, a perception lacking in many domestic companies and not helped by the lack of incentives provided by current tax regulations and laws. This will have an impact on the development of civic environmental organisations.

Our definition of what constitutes government sponsorship affects our perception of the proportion of environmental organisations' funding that it provides. If we take it to be direct government sponsorship then it is very low. But if we include the support given to student organisations by the institutions they are active in then for them it represents a relatively high proportion of funds. In our survey 64% of student organisations were found to be in receipt of funding from their college authorities. For 20% of student organisations this was their main source of funds. For some it accounted for up to 80% of their money. Government sponsorship of student organisations cannot be called significant in overall national terms but is vital for certain individual campus organisations. At any rate such government funding accounts for 30% of all monies available to student environmental organisations.

All civic environmental organisations are permitted by their charters to accept international donations. The two main types of such donations are those from foundations and those from multinational corporations. The importance of such international funding has steadily increased as China continues to open to the outside world. Several of the domestic green organisations which are currently most influential rely largely on international funding for support. International foundations were the first to take part in popular environmentalism in China and they had an enormous impact on the early development of civic organisations. Currently, those organisations founded by prominent environmentalists draw most of their funding from foundations' project grants. Sponsorship from multinationals has become more important in recent years. Some organisations' mass participation volunteer activities have been funded in this way.[18] Some campus organisations also rely heavily on international funding – in some cases it accounts for 85% of their funds.

Faced with financial difficulties civic environmental organisations have adopted various strategies to expand their sources of funding. One major strand of thinking has been to use their accumulated knowledge and skills to earn money by accepting payment for environmental services. Some organisations have collaborated with companies to market environmental products, earning money from this to fund general running costs and their other activities. We can see that environmental organisations are adapting to circumstances and seeking new ways to fund their activities, finding money and partners by designing and implementing quality projects.

Organisations spend most of their money in the following ways: running various activities; developing new ways to spread their environmental message; the purchase of books, journals and multimedia resources; purchasing equipment (including items to be used in project activities, computers and communications equipment); and also in defraying the costs of field trips, lectures and other specific environmental programmes.

Most organisations' charters demand that they be transparent about their finances and that they provide regular accounts to both members and donors. All money should be used in supporting environmental activities. To make sure that actually happens many organisations have established reporting systems that require their board to conduct regular audits and issue such reports and also proposed budgets. Some also require that annual accounts be published in national newspapers to allow for public scrutiny.[19]

6 Monitoring

The monitoring of civic environmental organisations occurs in two ways, by administrative agencies and by responsible work units. Administrative monitoring is further divided into the monitoring of social organisations and the monitoring of professional leading work units. For social organisations monitor-

18 One well-known organisation announced on its website that it was unable to pay in full volunteer costs associated with a campaign to protect the Tibetan antelope because it had not yet received the money promised by the Ford Motor Company. This shows the impact such funding can have. See Green River website, *supra* note 10.

19 Art. 21 of Green River's Charter, *supra* note 10.

ing is carried out by the civil affairs department of the government which is responsible for overseeing the following matters:

- registration and record keeping with respect to establishment, modification and closure of social organisations;
- conducting an annual review of the social organisation;
- supervision and review in cases where social organisations fail to comply with the 'Regulations for Registration and Management of Social Organisations', and for applying disciplinary sanctions in such cases.[20]

Professional monitoring is carried out by official environmental agencies which are responsible for overseeing the following matters:

- investigating the social organisation's preliminary application, establishment, modification or cancellation of registration;
- supervising and guiding the social organisation in observance of the constitution, laws, statutory regulations, national policy, and in developing activities in accordance with their charter;
- conducting a preliminary appraisal of the annual review;
- assisting the registration and management agency and other relevant departments to investigate and deal with illegal activities of social organisations;
- together with other relevant departments, guiding the process of winding up social organisations.[21]

In practice it is professional monitoring that is most important. Only after the agreement of official environmental agencies is secured can an application be submitted to the social organisation registration agency to set up an organisation. Often the official environmental agencies will also monitor an organisation's environmental protection activities. If an organisation violates any relevant law in the course of its activities it will usually be the official environmental agencies that are the first to intervene. If problems that involve other jurisdictions are discovered they will invite the relevant agencies to resolve them. The social organisation supervision agencies are less involved, dealing mainly with registration matters and not getting involved in oversight of an organisation's activities.

20 Art. 27 of the Regulations for Registration and Management of Social Organisations.
21 Art. 28 of the Regulations for Registration and Management of Social Organisations.

Monitoring by work units denotes the oversight and management exercised by the work unit to which an environmental organisation is accountable or which set up the organisation. This is most often the case for student campus organisations. In the normal course of affairs a campus environmental organisation comes under the supervision of the campus Communist Youth League committee, the student work department or the Student Association. Our survey found that this was the case for 80% of student organisations. In 17% of cases they were overseen by departmental branches of the same bodies. Most student organisations have teachers appointed to act in a guiding role, responsible for overseeing the propagation of environmental knowledge and the conduct of organisation activities. Our survey found such to be the case for 60% of organisations. In half of these cases the teacher oversaw environmental knowledge and in 40% they guided activities, including their planning and management, and also helped with coordination and communication with college authorities and the protection of the campus environment.

7 The Role of Civic Environmental Organisations

Civic environmental organisations can play an extremely important role in carrying forward the development of environmental causes in China. There are five key aspects of this.

First, they can inspire public awareness. Of the organisations we surveyed, 8% listed 'raising public environmental awareness' as their primary goal. A further 36% placed this second on their list of priorities, and 30% put it third. It was a goal for 90% of all organisations. Student organisations survey all placed raising students' environmental awareness as an objective; for 70% it was their primary goal; 23% placed it second on their list of priorities and 7% third.

Second, they can develop capacity. Green organisations have carried out various activities to make the public aware of the environmental crisis and to promote the taking of personal responsibility for environmental protection. They can foster the development of a group of specialists and decision-makers with strong environmental knowledge, thereby providing a rich human resource to serve in the resolution of environmental problems. Of our survey organisations 80% listed fostering such talent as a primary or secondary goal. In geographical terms, since volunteers come from all over the country they can help spread environmental activism to new areas as individual catalysts in their home towns. In terms of time, we know that the young people who today form the core of the environmental movement will be among the key social actors of the future, and they will carry their environmental awareness with them into the various fields in which they pursue their careers and into their wider social lives. Some campaigns are targeted on the younger still – primary and junior school students – which are an even longer-term contribution with enormous potential and truly sows the seeds for a greener future.

Third, they can resolve real-world problems. Most organisations aim in their activities to contribute to the resolution of actual real-world environmental issues and have made especially strong contributions in a number of areas. 595 of surveyed organisations listed solving local environmental problems as an important goal. They started with small projects first, mobilising local environmentalism by their own example of action. Our survey found that 53% of organisations had engaged in these kinds of activities to address local problems (such as combating pollution from improper disposal of polythene bags; encouraging separation of waste and the recycling of discarded batteries; or preventing unsustainable logging). In terms of advocacy, organisations like Friends of Nature campaigned against inappropriate mountain sports that were threatening the ecology of Meili Mountain; Global Village of Beijing worked to promote 'green communities' that encouraged urban residents to make environmental responsibility a part of their everyday lives. The Xiamen University student organisation helped stop developers building on land in an egret sanctuary and students from Guangxi Normal University were instrumental in drawing attention to the need to protect rare forest resources in Wanyanhai.

Fourth, they can express popular sentiment and provide information and assistance to government. Civic environmental organisations can use various means to make government agencies and officials aware of public opinion on environmental questions, and use their own knowledge and understanding to provide policy suggestions to address such issues. For example, one organisation worried about the threat of extinction facing the Tibetan antelope wrote to a Deputy Premier of the State Council of China and also the Prime Minister of a foreign country that provided the largest illegal market for products made for this animal, these actions elicited positive responses. Prior to these they had suggested to the Forestry Department that coordinated anti-poaching campaigns be carried out in Qinghai, Tibet and Xinjiang, a proposal that ultimately led to the well-known 'First Kekexili Campaign' of April 1999.[22] Interaction with government agencies like State Environmental Protection Agency (SEPA)

22 More information on this can be found at the Friends of Nature Website, *supra* note 9.

or the Ministry of Forestry can provide mutual support, encouragement, supplementation of skills and where necessary restraint, all of which help to create a more widespread coordinated environmental response across society. Government agencies at various levels supporting and in turn relying on civic organisations in environmental protection work not only helps the official bodies concentrate on the most important issues and lessens the burden on their resources, it also helps mobilise public participation in protecting and improving the environment and advances the overall cause of sustainability.

Fifth, they help improve China's international image. As we noted above, the lack of local green NGOs adversely affected Beijing's 1993 application to host the Olympic Games. The bid for the 2008 games invited organisations such as Friends of Nature and Global Village of Beijing to take part as consultants. When the IOC inspection team visited the city in 2001, they visited a green community established by the Global Village of Beijing and heard Liao Xiaoyi describe the significance of this civic initiative. This made a strong impression on the IOC evaluators. As citizens celebrate the success of Beijing's bid, they should remember the part green organisations played in making it a success although of course it was not for such plaudits that they worked so hard.

Of course, China's green organisations have only just begun to make their presence felt in the five areas outlined above and much work still lies ahead. Environmental organisations should pay particular attention to solving local environmental problems and preventing the worst environmental degradation. The most effective way to carry out actions aimed at these goals is to learn from one another and share experiences, developing human resources and spreading green consciousness. This will also be the best way to promote environmental organisations' own development.

8 Ways for Environmental Organisations to Have Influence

(1) Make specific proposals to government and leaders

To affect specific environmental protection issues civic environmental organisations should first acquaint themselves with the situation through communication and interaction with local green organisations, government, media and enterprises and then make specific proposals to the relevant government agencies or leaders. For example, one organisation concerned about air pollution and the falling water table in Beijing made constructive proposals on these matters to the municipal government, specifically concerning proposals to increase the capacity of the Zhangfang reservoir. They said that although Beijing is the nation's capital it is not right that the city should expect surrounding districts to pay the price in restricted development for improvements to Beijing's environment. This view was accepted and relevant policies adopted.[23] Improved external relationships are not only good for civic organisations' own growth and development; they also help their interlocutors. Exchanges and communication bring mutual assistance and joint progress.

(2) Improve influence by implementing environmental protection initiatives

Practical activities include both educational campaigns and environmental protection actions. Educational campaigns can include promotion of reduced energy use and the use of renewables; biodiversity and the relationship between ecological balance, geology and human environments and so forth. Methods used can be lectures by environmentalists, book signings by prominent figures, forums, cultural events and days of action and working to inspire public enthusiasm for environmental causes. Actions can include safe disposal of used batteries, tree planting, waste separation and recycling and other practical initiatives. These can have a marked impact in a given area and help give organisation members and volunteers a sense of achievement. However, since such activities often require the cooperation and support of official agencies or specialists, if they are not carefully planned they may well not be easy to keep up over the longer term.

(3) Influence media opinions

Media opinion is an important factor in a democratic society hence it is sometimes known as the 'Fourth Power'. In all nations, the role of the media is important for both environmental education and protection activities. In some countries there are television channels exclusively dedicated to ecological and geographical issues, like the National Geographic and Discovery channels, which play an important role in environmental education. Civic environmental protection organisations in China have learned the advantage of cooperating with the media and in some cases have done this to good effect. For example campaigners seeking to protect the Tibetan antelope were concerned about the imminent disbanding of an anti-poaching team in Zhiduo County, Qinghai. By cooperating with a national television station and 12 regional stations to together contact senior officials at the State Council they were able to draw attention

23 *Id.*

to this issue.[24] After this the television station involved continued to pay attention to environmental issues and report on the activities of this organisation. Mobilising media attention is especially important in smaller towns and less developed parts of the country and is sometimes the only way to have an impact. In such areas the demands of economic development often lead to the crudest methods of natural resource exploitation and heavy-polluting industries may well be the backbone of the local economy. Local authorities, motivated by sectional interests will often be slow to punish such environmental destruction or will even be openly tolerant of it. Activities by civic environmentalists will meet the opposition of local vested interests and even bring them into confrontation with local government. In such circumstances a direct approach to the government will not work but concerns may be aired and solutions suggested through the media, reaching both the general public and higher level state authorities and appealing for their support. There are numerous examples of the successful employment of such a strategy. We may expect that as public consciousness of their right to information increases and as reforms of the systems controlling the news media are carried out, use of the media to influence public opinion will become an even more effective strategy for environmentalists and relationships between media agencies and green organisations will continue to grow closer.

9 Difficulties Faced by Environmental Organizations

Fundraising is the most important problem facing the great majority of environmental organisations. Our survey found that 90% of them said this was so. The main strategies for resolving this problem are to use social resources to fund activities and public fund-raising. Because members can only provide so much funding and there is little likelihood of increased financial support from government, grants and sponsorship from foundations and enterprises are increasingly seen as a major potential source of new funding. Experience in other countries proves that this is the case. However, companies in China lack any incentive to sponsor green organisations and as yet care little about environmental issues. Problems with both structural and human causes prevent foundations from playing the kind of funding role for China's environmental organisations that they do overseas and sometimes they simply fail to provide the support they

24 *Id.*

should. Financial difficulties have had a severe impact on the enthusiasm of volunteers for participating in environmental causes. If reforms to the overall system are not forthcoming many organisations will be forced to cease activities, with organisations in underdeveloped regions most at risk. The consequences in that case will be most unfortunate.

The majority of environmental organisations are extremely short of the necessary equipment. Of the organisations we surveyed only 30% had they own fixed place of business and just 35% have a fixed telephone contact number, 60% had an e-mail address and 40% had their own web-page, three quarters of whom were able to update their sites regularly. However, only 4% of organisations had well-known and frequently visited websites. We found that only half the surveyed organisations had such organisational essentials as banners, promotional materials or access to office space. 38% said they had no equipment of any kind at all. Only 25% owned books or journals suitable for use in environmental education while fewer still had more specialist equipment such as multimedia materials, recycling equipment or scientific survey instruments. At the present time the rise in the number of civic environmental organisations in China is not matched by a rise in their overall capacity. Most campus organisations have neither telephone, nor office due to severe lack of funds. In such circumstances it is hard for them to carry out effective campaigns. A student organisation in the early stages of existence that cannot have a significant impact on their campus will find it hard to attract support from government, their college or commercial sponsors. Core activists need large reserves of patience, the ability to grow in adversity and turn difficulties into opportunities.

The dissemination of information is extremely patchy. Environmental organisations, especially student organisations, have numerous ways of keeping up to date with international and domestic environmental news. In our survey 94% of them agreed this was so. Information came from the press, the internet, broadcast media, other domestic environmental organisations and by attending lectures and forums.

The mass media play an important role in the dissemination of information about environmental issues. But apart from a few of the better known organisations, few civic environmental organisations maintain contacts with the media, particularly not organisations in underdeveloped areas, and they fail to use this means of spreading their message. Many organisations exist in a state of semi-isolation from the outside world – they may take information from external sources but they send nothing back. Naturally the outside world thus takes little interest in what they are doing. Another common shortfall is in opportunities for interaction and exchange – networking among organisations and with other interested parties is still in its early stages. Organisations need to work on improving the two-way flow of information. This current imbalance means environmental organisations fail to make the best use of the media outlets that they get their information from as they do not disseminate information about their own activities through them. 80% of surveyed organisations said that newspapers were one of their primary sources for environmental information and 60% cited television. Although these seems to show television as of less importance for green organisations, for the public at large it is the main source of news and information and would be an effective means of spreading the environmental message. However the strict controls on content and the monopoly control exercised over broadcasting prevent environmental organisations from exploiting this medium. Of course, the growth of the internet has provided a significant outlet for environmental information with vast potential. 78% of surveyed organisations used it to provide environmental information and promote awareness and many thought it was their most important means of reaching a wider audience. The internet is already being used by organisations to both gather and disseminate information and will doubtless only become more important in this respect in the future, even if economic circumstances hold back the full development of this new medium in the short term.

There is a lack of coordination and a failure to get the most out of limited resources. The semi-isolation of so many green organisations prevents them interacting with one another, sharing resources and coordinating actions. A combination of this and the limited resources available to civic environmental organisations severely restricts their ability to play a fuller role in society. Pressing real world demands require that environmental organisations begin to pool their resources and coordinate better as soon as practicable so as to make the most of the little they have. Happily, there are signs that this is beginning to happen amongst student organisations, who have long been the pioneers of China's environmental movement. They have set up a website called 'Green SOS'[25] where resources and information can be pooled for sharing and the collective public impact of the participating organisations can be greater than the sum of its parts. It avoids the waste of resources if every organisation sets up a website of its own and attracts a greater number of visitors than scattered individual efforts would. The site is a collaboration between three environmental alliances that seek to provide a database of best project practice and provide

25 www.greensos.org (last visited June, 2005).

a forum for online interaction and the sharing of knowledge and experiences where all participants are valued.

10 CONCLUSION

The future development of China's civic environmental organisations is closely connected to whether or not an effective legal framework is established there. In the 1990s the growth of green organisations occurred alongside efforts to reform the legal system. The problems environmental organisations now face are due in large part to the fact that they have continued to develop but the law has not. In the light of this and considering both domestic practise and international experience I would like to suggest the following reforms.

Firstly, a system of tax incentives should be drawn up, and foreign and domestic enterprises encouraged to support civic environmental organisations. Tax advantages for charitable donations are a feature seen in many countries. Companies are by and large motivated by a desire to make money and it is unrealistic to expect them to support environmental causes for reasons of principle alone. Current Chinese tax regulations make no provisions for tax incentives or exemptions on corporate charitable giving. This means that if a company wants to sponsor an environmental organisation it must do so from its after-tax earnings, the only motivation for which would be a conscious support for environmental causes. In China, where neither the economy, nor environmental awareness are as yet fully developed, this is an unlikely scenario and is reflected in the present financial difficulties most environmental organisations find themselves in. Even in countries where environmental awareness is more widespread, reliance on principled support alone without accompanying economic incentives would not be a sustainable model. China should draft laws as soon as possible that exclude charitable donations from calculations of commercial and income tax; a progressive tax system could offer increased rewards for greater giving. Of course this would need to be accompanied with appropriate monitoring mechanisms to avoid abuse. As well as economic incentives, a system of honorary awards could be established to encourage mutual benefits for both donor and recipient.

Secondly, there should be a relaxation of administrative controls to provide greater space for the development of civic environmental organisations. Although existing controls are more relaxed for green organisations than for other social organisations, they are still too restrictive. This is detrimental to social, economic and cultural development and the fostering of citizens' capacity for self-governance. It is also detrimental to effective government and encourages wasteful bureaucracy in official agencies with the concomitant increased burden on the public purse. It indirectly encourages abuses such as illicit taxation and can even lead to conflicts of interest between the state and its citizenry. To speak specifically of the environmental sector, excessive administrative controls make it difficult for civic organisations to register; it leaves them little space for their activities and it reduces the diversity of available funding sources. This is detrimental to the development of environmental organisations and the overall cause of environmental protection. The government should seek to further relax controls. For environmental organisations there is no need to apply the general principle of not allowing similar organisations to register at the same administrative level[26] and organisations should be encouraged to set up and register. Also to address the particular circumstances prevailing in China, environmental organisations should be allowed to adopt various 'self-help' strategies to resolve their financial dilemmas. Under a general principle of remaining as not-for-profit organisations, environmental organisations should be allowed to earn money by providing environmentally friendly products and services, money that can be used to fund organisational develop-

26 Art. 13 of the Regulations for Registration and Management of Social Organisations stipulates that 'if in the same administrative area there is already a social organisation active in the same or similar area of work, there is no need for a new organisation to be established' and the registering agency should turn down an application to set up a new organisation. There is a similar clause in the regulations governing popular non-enterprise work units. In practice this is usually understood to mean that legislators intended to limit the number of civic organisations to make the task of management easier. This is not the appropriate interpretation. Given that freedom of association is a right enshrined in the Constitution, where an administrative regulation restricts the exercise of such a right for reasons of expediency without the backing of relevant legislation there is a suspicion that those administrative rules are in violation of the Constitution. In legal discourse the basis for a judgment of whether or not there is a need for legislation should be centred on persons applying to set up civic organisations who have explicit rights, not government officials who are merely public servants. Administrative controls should be a means of balancing the rights of different actors by regulating the actions of one organisation that is exercising its rights with an overall goal of better protecting the rights of all. The aim should certainly not be to restrict rights for administrative convenience. The precedence of the exercise of rights over administrative control is the basis for government reforms in many countries. If the formerly prevailing attitude common among government officials that administration takes precedence does not change, then they will be unable to adapt to the demands of social development and the exercise of the people's rights.

ment and environmental protection activities. They should be further supported in this with other preferential policies.

Thirdly, an incentive system for environmentally friendly businesses and enterprises should be established, thus indirectly helping civic organisations as well. China's current compulsory national environmental standards are few and set at low levels. Their enforcement is also very difficult for a variety of practical reasons. This means that environmentally friendly businesses do not enjoy the competitive edge that they deserve nor have they developed as quickly as they might have, had the system been more conducive. International experience shows that this sector will develop when the state drafts strict environmental laws and enforces them rigorously. In the present economic and social circumstances in China it is not enough to rely on spontaneous popular demand for environmentally friendly products or the fact that businesses will voluntarily respect environmental standards, and such a strategy would fail to protect our natural heritage and the health of our population. Thus the only possible solution is to enact strict environmental legislation and enforce it properly. Although such legislation could not yet demand standards like those in the developed world, they should be set as high as practicably possible. This is the only way to encourage the market to favour environmentally friendly products and services and to provide a competitive edge to businesses that meet environmental standards. The costs will be repaid in great economic benefits. The wider application of environmental technologies will also be beneficial to a general raising of environmental awareness and hence provide still greater opportunities for civic environmental organisations to play a role, utilising their advantages in knowledge and drawing on wider and more various sources of funding. Their development will be indirectly supported by the normal operation of the economy.

6

LEGISLATING FOR FOUNDATIONS IN CHINA: HISTORICAL DEVELOPMENT, PRESENT STATE AND MAIN CHARACTERISTICS

Mo Jihong

1 INTRODUCTION

China's system for governing foundations has been gradually put in place as the process of 'reform and opening' has consolidated over time. In the 1980s the State Council brought forward a 'Method for Managing Foundations' (*Jijinhui guanli banfa)* to serve as a legal basis for regulating the activities of foundations. However, the lack of a mature civil society in China has meant that the general public have only a limited understanding of the nature, status and function of foundations and hence the development of foundations has proceeded only with difficulty. Combined with a legal environment which is still less than ideal in which Chinese social organisations have to operate, the process of running a foundation unavoidably encounters problems of one kind or another. This has meant that for some time now the activities of foundations have shown various irregularities. Over the course of twenty years of practical application, China has accumulated some experience in regards to managing foundations and has gained a clearer understanding of what they are and what they do. There have also been improvements in the legal environment within which foundations carry out activities for the public welfare. It was against this background that, on the 11th February 2004, the State Council approved the 'Regulations for the Management of Foundations' (*Jijinhui guanli tiaoli*). They came into effect on 1st June of that year.

The enactment of these Regulations established a sound administrative basis for the continued development of foundations in China. The Regulations were

Yuwen Li (Ed.), *Freedom of Association in China and Europe: Comparative Perspectives in Law and Practice*, © 2005 Koninklijke Brill NV, Leiden. Printed in The Netherlands, pp. 219-248.

drafted in the light of successful examples of similar legislation in other countries, but were also firmly rooted in the realities of the current state of foundations in China. They make detailed stipulations regarding the general principles governing the management and registration of foundations; the processes by which they are established, altered or disbanded; appropriate organisational structures; the use and management of their assets; the role of government and wider society in oversight and also what legal liabilities foundations should be subject to. The Regulations provide an essential legal basis upon which the system of administering foundations can be further improved, and the foundations themselves can play a still fuller role in supporting public welfare activities. It would be right to say that as the rule of law continues to develop in China and as social organisations continue to proliferate, the system for administering foundations will become more standardised and more appropriate for meeting the demands of civil society for foundations to fulfil their role as service providers for public welfare organisations.

2 A BRIEF OUTLINE OF THE EMERGENCE AND DEVELOPMENT OF FOUNDATIONS IN CHINA[1]

In the present legislative environment in China there are many types of social organisations that are related to a fund in some way, but only a few that can actually be considered foundations in the full legal sense.

There are at present a few different types of fund organisations in China, such as those established with funds allocated by the government, social security funds and fund management companies. But these organisations' funds are completely different in nature from the funds of legally recognised foundations. Government funds are established under their own set of laws and regulations, or by some other government document, and their money is levied from a particular set source. The levy has clearly set boundaries and standards. Examples of such funds include the Three Gorges Project Construction Fund, the Civil Aviation Infrastructure Construction Fund and the Agricultural Devel-

1 The description of the historical development and current state of China's foundations given in this paper is drawn mainly from the speech on the Regulations for the Management of Foundations made by Sun Weilin, Director of the Bureau of Civic Organisations Management of the Ministry of Civil Affairs, to the training forum held in Guangxi. The text of the speech is available on the Ministry's website: http://www.mca.gov.cn/artical/content/200422514006/20046892746.html (Last visited March 2005).

opment Fund. There are also funds established through budgetary allocations. Government funds have a stable funding source. The money they spend comes from their principal. The Social Security Fund is the result of using legal measures to allocate and reallocate a portion of national income, such as the national insurance deductions from individuals' incomes, or funds recovered from reducing holdings of shares in State enterprises. The securities and investment funds managed by fund management companies are one type of financial instrument, a kind of trust and investment based on securities; the investor receives dividends and undertakes risk in proportion to their investment. The investment is usually in stocks or bonds. A foundation, on the other hand usually receives its funds through donations from individuals or organisations, and they are to be used for some public welfare enterprise; they are expended in welfare activities without seeking financial recompense. This is why the former types of fund organisations are not usually called foundations in China. Some are known as fund management committees (*jijin guanli weyuanhui*), some as special funds (*zhuanxiang jijin*), and some as fund management companies. Only organisations managing funds used for public welfare ends are called foundations. According to the provisions of the 'Regulations for the Management of Foundations', under the present Chinese legal system a foundation is a non-profit legal person that uses the assets donated by natural persons, legal persons or other organisations for public welfare ends. As organisations that are non-profit legal persons, foundations have the following characteristics: they are not agencies of the state or government and do not rely on state funding for their work, rather collecting funds from domestic and overseas donations; they are not subsidiary bodies of state agencies or private enterprises, but are independent legal agencies with the power to allocate their own monies and carry out their activities independently as the law provides; the basic difference between them and corporations or private enterprises is their not-for-profit nature, relying on donations from various sectors of society as a source for their funding and also disbursing those funds as freely given grants.

Foundations have only existed in China for a short time, appearing only in the post-reform era, a history of some twenty years to date.[2] The China Children and Teenagers' Foundation founded in July 1981 was the first foundation established as a civic body. After this a whole host of public welfare foundations were established working in sectors such as education, health,

2 The earliest foundations in the world appeared in the 10th century A.D. See the Chapter by Rupert Graf Strachwitz, 'Associations and Foundations in Germany: Service Providers or Agents of Civil Society?' in this volume.

poverty alleviation and disaster relief. In the 1980s there were just six national-level foundations. The growth in the total number of foundations has accelerated steadily since the 1990s. After the State Council promulgated the 'Method for Managing Foundations' in 1988 the Ministry of Civil Affairs began registering foundations. At that time there were two different administrative levels for registration: with the national Ministry, or with one of its line agencies at provincial level. To date there are some 1,200 registered foundations, of which just over 80 are registered with the Ministry at national level. The activities of these foundations touch upon almost all areas of social life. Grouped by the main theme of their work we find: charitable foundations represent 31.68% of all registered organisations, educational 19.14%, cultural 18.27%, science and technology 10.1% and others 20.5%.[3]

As to the size of these foundations, the 80 or so national-level foundations have total assets of almost CNY 3 billion (USD 364 million). The largest of them, the Tsinghua University Educational Foundation has assets of CNY 520 million (USD 63 million). Ten of the national-level foundations have individual assets in excess of CNY 100 million (USD 12 million). Among the local foundations, except in the coastal provinces, a general lack of funds is quite evident. According to 1999 statistics from the People's Bank of China, the funds of some 40% of local foundations fail to meet the standard originally required – that they have assets of at least CNY 2.1 million (USD 255,000) or the equivalent in foreign currency. That situation has remained largely unchanged up the present day.

The majority of foundations succeed in carrying out public benefit activities in accordance with the law, and in compliance with their own constitutions. The vast majority of national-level foundations are quite active in this respect. For example, an evaluation of their 'Project Hope' carried out by the China Youth Development Foundation in 1998 claimed that, at year end 1996, 1,601 county-level administrative divisions had students in receipt of assistance from Project Hope – that is 75% of all counties in China. In nationally designated poor counties Project Hope's coverage was even more complete. 96.3% of townships, 63.3% of schools and 41.3% of villages had students in receipt of assistance from the Project, which was playing a significant role in promoting education in impoverished parts of rural China. At the same time the Project was having a positive social impact for China as a whole. More than 90% of

3 Figures published by the Ministry of Civil Affairs on 3rd March, 2004 list 83 nationally registered foundations, published in full in the *People's Daily Overseas Edition*, 20th April, 2004, at p. 7.

urban residents knew at least something about Project Hope, and it had succeeded in arousing benevolence and an appreciation for education throughout society. This helped carry forward the construction of Spiritual Civilisation. In 2000 the China Foundation for Women's Development began a project called 'Love the Land: Water Cellars for Mothers'. They solicited charitable donations from the public to fund the construction of cement water cellars in arid parts of Western China. To date the project has raised almost CNY 111 million (USD 13.5 million) of which CNY 101 million has already been disbursed as aid. The Spring Bud programme run by the China Foundation for Children and Teenagers which supports girls who have dropped out of school was able to raise CNY 285 million (USD 34.5 million) between 2001 and 2002. CNY 232 million has already been spent building schools in poor areas and in direct grants to girl students. The All-China Sports Foundation has spent over CNY 2 million (USD 242, 000) buying injury insurance for China's outstanding athletes, helping allay their fears for their post-sport careers and encouraging them in their endeavours to win glory for the nation. Many foundations have achieved notable results and made major contributions to public welfare. However some 20% of foundations have not spent money on public welfare initiatives for quite a lengthy period of time, or are riven by internal difficulties, to the point that they appear to exist in name only. Take, for example, the Friends of China Foundation (FCF), set up in October 1989. In its early years its numerous activities, such as publishing a journal, called Friends of China, organising study trips abroad and facilitating trips to China from overseas' visitors, earned it a positive reputation with the general public. But after 1998 the journal ceased publication and the internal affairs of the foundation fell into disarray that in turn caused chaos with their various projects. In July of 2002 the FCF's sponsoring agency, the National Tourism Administration, was forced to send a management team to take over management of the Foundation's affairs. The FCF remains in difficulties to this day and has yet to resume normal working.[4] Differences between the levels of activities of local foundations are

4 FCF's legal representative Dong Sheng has written numerous letters to the Ministry of Civil Affairs and the National Tourism Administration asking that the foundation's problems be solved and that it may return to normal working as soon as possible. I have also made contact with the relevant agencies concerning this on several occasions in my role as legal consultant to the FCF, but the difficulties remain numerous. The most prominent issue is that those agencies have not genuinely regarded the Foundation as an independent legal person. The problems of the FCF are a reflection of the structural problems besetting the currently prevailing system for administering foundations in China. The types and nature of these problems are set out in the petition written by

even greater. Foundations in the wealthy coastal regions are well funded and are able to play quite an active social role; those in the inland provinces tend to be less active and thus have less of an impact.

As to the relationship between foundations and the government, the government exercises quite a tight control over foundations. This is especially noticeable in terms of members of the boards of foundations and appointed legal representatives, who are often senior government officials serving in a joint capacity. This naturally leads to a situation where foundations' activities are heavily coloured by the influence of government. According to the provisions of the 1988 'Method for Managing Foundations,' 'leading members of foundations may not be currently serving employees of government agencies'. However, there are foundations where this does happen. Some foundations are run as if they are public institutions, with official staff allocations and operating costs paid out of government budgets. Many government agencies are active participants in foundations' fundraising and grant-making activities. For example, a certain foundation will have the government come forward to help it raise funds, funds which although ostensibly now come under the control of the foundation are in fact disbursed according to government decisions. The foundation is independent in name but in reality is merely an agency of the government.

Issues concerning foundations preserving and increasing the value of their assets have led to all sorts of complications in practice. An investigation of national-level foundations conducted by the People's Bank of China in the mid 1990s found many of them were actively investing or otherwise utilising their principal funds, with some even making loans or acting as guarantors. The 1988 'Method' stipulates that 'foundations may not run or manage enterprises'. The 'Notice concerning Further Improving the Management of Foundations' issued by the People's Bank also clearly states that 'preserving and increasing the value of a foundations assets must be entrusted to a financial organisation to carry out'. The People's Bank has conducted a number of rectification campaigns amongst foundations in order to enforce this principle. These led to a measure of improvement in the overall situation. However the majority of foundations complained that they were not making good returns either from investments in the stock market or through running enterprises. For example, one foundation chose an inappropriate investment project and has yet to recover either the interest or the principal of that investment. At year end 2001 this foundation

Dong Sheng entitled 'The Final Struggle: The FCF is already at the Crisis Point between Life and Death' (Internal document).

had CNY 179.36 million (USD 21.74 million) circulating in external investment, of which CNY 153.14 million (USD 18.56 million) is unlikely to be recouped. The majority – 85.3% – of external investments are five or more years overdue, which is 72.5% of the foundation's total assets. It is to avoid situations such as this, especially considering the current state of the market, that foundations are in any case themselves unwilling to risk external investments. Their main methods for preserving or increasing the value of their assets are either by keeping it in the bank or by buying treasury bonds. Currently, around 50% of foundations also seek to increase their assets in other ways as well, mainly through buying stocks, commercial bonds, equity investments or by running commercial ventures. Of course, they only use a part of their funds for such activities, hoping to invest in a way that reaps rich returns but involves little risk. In practice though, there have been numerous legal disputes arising from inappropriate investment activity by foundations. The most notable of these was the China Youth Development Foundation. A series of poor investment decisions led to a number of celebrated lawsuits that had a negative impact on the Foundation's public image.

In sum, China's foundations are still at a very early stage of their development, especially if compared with their peers in developed nations. We are still a long way from those countries that have a thriving foundations sector, rich in funds, well-run, operating to set standards and enjoying an enabling policy environment. The main problem we face is an inadequate understanding of what foundations actually are; we have been unadventurous in our thinking about them and progress in the sector has been made only in small steps, with many problems still existing in the overall administrative framework. Not only does the government lack a systematic set of measures to foster and support foundations, largely leaving them to their own devices, they are themselves falling short of proper standards and plagued in varying degrees by all sorts of problems. The vast majority of foundations have only a small amount of funds and are run very much as if they were government agencies. The Li Jia Cheng Foundation in Hong Kong has over CNY 5 billion in assets and the largest foundations in the world are richer still. Yet the combined assets of all of China's national-level foundations total only just over CNY 3 billion, less than one private foundation. Moreover, many of China's foundations actually do very little, content to hang up their name-plate, raise a little money and pay a few people's wages without ever getting round to actual public welfare work. Some are hard to distinguish from their government sponsors, failing to manage their funds properly and ending up as little more than a reserve fund for their sponsoring agency, or, worse still, having their assets misappropriated by individuals. On top of this there are also so-called 'project funds' set up without any legal or registration process whatsoever. Their money comes from public donations but it is managed without any proper legal process. Hence strengthening the development of foundations in China is an onerous task. A key to achieving this will be the various registration agencies properly exercising their legal duties of supervision and management so as to ensure that foundations can truly be of service to public welfare.

3 THE DEVELOPMENT OF CHINA'S FOUNDATIONS LEGISLATION AND ITS CHARACTERISTICS

In the early years of New China, although administrative regulations were drafted concerning the registration of social organisations, such as the 'Temporary Measures for the Registration of Social Organisations' passed by the State Council *(zhengwuyuan)* in 1950, or the 'Detailed Regulations for the Implementation of the Temporary Measures for the Registration of Social Organisations' promulgated by the Ministry of Internal Affairs *(neiwubu)* in March 1951, neither these, nor any other regulations touched upon matters concerning foundations. The 'Method for Managing Foundations' passed at the 21st meeting of the Standing Committee of the State Council in September 1988, and promulgated by State Council Order No. 18 later that same month, was the first piece of legislation concerning foundations seen in the People's Republic of China (hereafter the 1988 Method).[5] Article 2 of the 1988 Method stipulates that, 'this method when referring to a foundation means a civic non-profit organisation that is a legal person and carries out the management of monies voluntarily donated by domestic and overseas social organisations or other organisations or individuals'. Thus the 1988 Method gave the first clear legislative definition of the legal nature and status of foundations. This legal status and nature was further clearly confirmed in the 'Regulations for Registration and Management of Social Organisations' passed in October 1989 (hereafter the 1989 Regulations).[6] The General Principles of these Regulations state that all 'social organisations organised within the territory of the People's Republic

5 Available at: http://www.sdxintai.gov.cn/xinyongzhongxin/zcfg/p31.htm (Last visited March 2005).

6 Available at: http://www.nbu.edu.cn/allwebs/xbbjb/zcfg/shttdj.htm (Last visited March 2005).

of China such as associations, academic associations, federations, research associations, foundations, friendly societies, promotional bodies and chambers of commerce' should apply for registration under their provisions. Prior to 1999, the registration and management of foundations was handled according to the 1988 Method and the 1989 Regulations, implementing a tripartite system of administrative responsibility involving a sponsoring agency, the People's Bank of China and the Ministry of Civil Affairs: the sponsor gave initial approval, the Bank further checked and approved and the Ministry carried out registration. This in effect treated foundations as financial institutions or quasi-financial institutions. For a decade or more the 1988 Method served to provide an important guarantee that regularised the activities and promoted the healthy development of China's foundations. However, the Method was not a perfect solution and contained no provisions concerning how foundations should be organised, their internal decision-making processes, accounting systems, asset management or mechanisms for their oversight by society. Other provisions in the 1988 Method bore the imprint of the then prevailing planned economy thinking. It was not an entirely appropriate piece of legislation for foundations' proper legal status as independent legal persons. As reform progressed and the market economy grew, it became ever more apparent that it was necessary to redress faults in the legal system governing foundations and provide a better all-round systemic foundation for their further development. The 1988 Method no longer met foundations' actual needs, either for administrative oversight, or for sectoral development. At the same time changes were occurring within the administration of foundations. After 1999, by order of the State Council the People's Bank no longer took part in the administration of foundations, all functions being assumed by the Ministry of Civil Affairs alone. The administrative system set out in the 1988 Method was no longer used and could not be used by the Ministry as the basis for its registration work. Because of this, beginning in 2000, according to the State Council's legislative plan, the Ministry of Civil Affairs began a complete revision of the Method. They held numerous consultation forums and specialist research conferences, and after much debate, and in the light of experiences in other countries in this field, produced a draft 'Regulations for the Management of Foundations' which was submitted to the State Council in March 2001. After this the Ministry collaborated with the Legislative Affairs Office of the State Council in further consultative research, conducting meetings and surveys in Heilongjiang, Shanghai, Fujian, Guangdong and Jiangsu and holding forums with relevant government agencies, academic specialists and foundations themselves. During numerous redraftings, detailed discussions were held and individual reports written on some of the specific issues that the Regulations were to address: preferential tax policies; appropriate levels of expenditure as a proportion of assets; standards for the establishment of special funds by a foundation; procedures for registering and overseeing larger public fund-raising foundations; and questions concerning preserving and increasing the value of foundations' assets. After this thoroughgoing preparatory work was completed, the 'Regulations for the Management of Foundations' were debated and passed in principle at a meeting of the Standing Committee of the State Council in February 2004 (hereafter the '2004 Regulations'.) On the 8th March, Premier Wen Jiabao signed them into law, and they came into effect on the 1st June, later that same year.[7]

The 2004 Regulations have 48 Articles in 7 Chapters, containing provision for, respectively, the general principles governing the registration and management of foundations; their establishment, modification and cancellation; organisational structure; management and use of assets; monitoring and oversight by government and society; and their legal liability. Compared with the 1988 Method there is not just more content overall, the Regulations are also more systematically arranged and represent a complete redrawing of foundation legislation. All through the 2004 Regulations, the guiding principles of both fostering the development of foundations and promoting their growth by regulated management are apparent. With these as the guiding principles we may also perceive eight other characteristics apparent in the Regulations which will be examined below.

3.1 Public Welfare

The 2004 Regulations emphasise the public welfare nature of foundations, and stress the importance of public welfare as their goal. A public welfare orientation is a distinguishing characteristic of foundations and they should only be established to work towards such a goal. This is the main legal characteristic that distinguishes them from an ordinary business enterprise legal person. Guaranteeing the public welfare nature of foundations is the fundamental purpose of the Regulations. The beneficiaries of public welfare organisations are commonly certain unspecified individuals or groups; so long as a person or group falls within the parameters laid out in that organisation's guiding principles they are eligible for financial assistance. Foundations raise their

7 The Regulations for the Management of Foundations is contained in Appendix III of this book.

money from society and offers services to society. The 2004 Regulations contain numerous clear rulings to allow foundations to achieve these aims. For example, by defining a foundation as a 'a non-profit legal person established in accordance with these regulations that employs assets donated by natural persons, legal persons or other organisations for the purpose of engaging in some public welfare enterprise' (Article 2), they emphasis foundations' public welfare nature and draw a distinction between them and trust investment funds, profit-oriented fund management organisations and other civic mutual benefit organisations. Foundation's public welfare nature implies that their funds must be used for public welfare ends and also that they must be protected. Item 1 of Article 27 of the Regulations stipulates that 'the assets of a foundation and its other sources of income are protected under the law. No work unit or individual may take a portion or the whole thereof or misuse them in any way.' Article 33 states that 'monies left over when a foundation is wound up should be used for public welfare ends as stipulated in the foundation's charter; funds which cannot be used in this way will be donated by the organ in charge of registration to another public welfare organisation with similar aims and objectives to the original foundation. Any such action will be made public.'

Furthermore, the 2004 Regulations also stipulate a series of other specific provisions to ensure that public welfare ends are served, such as a requirement for the foundation's charter to specify the organisation's public welfare nature; the prohibition on naming a specific individual, legal person or organisation as beneficiary; requirements about internal administrative systems and external oversight, especially public oversight; a requirement for transparency, especially making accounts public, and so forth. We may say that, by making clear the public welfare nature intrinsic to foundations, the 2004 Regulations share the same fundamental principles that guide similar legislation in developed nations.

3.2 Management by Type

The 2004 Regulations establish the principle of 'Management by Type' and encourage all sectors of society to take part in public welfare activities. The majority of the foundations currently registered in China raise money by seeking donations from wider society, known as public fundraising foundations. Since incomes are still not particularly high in China at the moment, most businesses and other organisations still have limited resources to donate.[8] The government had a number of reasons for wanting to adopt a set of appropriate polices that could satisfy the aspirations of potential donors: to avoid making charitable giving unnecessarily burdensome for businesses or individuals, to rationalise how public fundraising foundations operate and to effectively control this aspect of their activity, and to encourage those newly wealthy businesses and individuals who do want to give, but wish to ensure that their donations are properly used. This is why the regulations distinguish between foundations that are oriented towards fundraising from the general public, referred to as 'public fundraising foundations' and those that are not referred to as 'non-public fundraising foundations'.[9] 'Non-public fundraising foundations' can be named after a foundation or individual. If they are established with money from a private individual, relatives of that person may serve in positions on the foundation's board of directors within certain limitations. The international experience is that foundations of this type are a way of putting private wealth to social ends, and an effective way of encouraging its use in assisting disadvantaged

8 It is interesting to note that although private wealth has grown considerably in recent years, there has not been a corresponding rise in charitable donations. The newly rich have not been conspicuous for their charitable instincts, preferring rather to squander their wealth on conspicuous consumption.
The *International Herald Tribune* reported: a spokesperson for the Whole China Foundation on Charities complained, 'we have received a total of CNY 7,747,533 in donations. Of that there was only one major donation by wealthy individual, who gave CNY 2 million'. The spokesperson for another recipient of donations, the Ministry of Civil Affairs, said 'We don't get any donation from wealthy individuals; they are almost all from businesses donating as an organisation'. The reporter learned however that those businesses did include many owned by prominent members of China's most wealthy. Also, many of the charitable activities businesses have been keen to publicise have ultimately come to nothing. They advertise these schemes heavily but never actually pay over money to partner foundations. One dairy producer set a number of conditions concerning its promotional rights when discussing a donation to a foundation, including arranging public audiences with senior state leaders, but even after all these were satisfied they only handed over CNY 200,000, of a promised donation of CNY 1 million. The foundation found that getting the rest of the money was a long and drawn out process. The reporter also found that although there are over 10 million registered businesses in China, fewer than 100,000 have ever made charitable donations, less than 1% of all businesses. Source: http://news.163.com (30th March, 2004). (Last visited March 2005).

9 During the drafting process, there was a time when the text of the Regulations referred to 'public fundraising foundations' and 'private foundations'. However, since the latter term was deemed too narrow to encompass all 'non-public fundraising foundations', the final draft settled on the latter term as the logical counterpart that according with the method was settled upon for distinguishing types of foundation.

groups. It is a way of redistributing wealth, encouraging businesses and individuals to be enthusiastic givers, promoting general charitable giving and opening up more sources of funding for public welfare initiatives. When a private individual or business establishes a non-public fundraising foundation not only are they supporting public welfare goals they are also helping their own economic success by improving their public image. The 2004 Regulations stipulate that the state will give policy encouragement and support to non-public fundraising foundations. They enjoy less stringent requirements in terms of the names they can use, their conditions for registration and in how they can use their money. The requirements for public fundraising foundations are much stricter, in order to regulate public fundraising activities, preserve available charitable resources, avoid over-burdening the general public and preserve social stability. The 2004 Regulations make different provisions in regards to such matters as the conditions under which the two types of foundations may be established, what officers they may have and how much money they spend on public welfare as a proportion of their total assets, embodying the policy of treating the two types of foundations differently.

3.3 Supervising International Foundations

In recent years, especially since China's accession to the WTO, there has been a marked rise in the formation of organisations in China by foreign nationals, and activities by overseas non-governmental organisations (NGOs), yet there are no administrative or registration regulations covering such bodies. The policy has been to neither recognise nor have dealings with them, but also not to suppress such organisations. This has not stopped unregistered organisations carrying out activities; overseas organisations working in China are becoming more numerous and more active by the day. Figures show that around 40 foreign or non-mainland Chinese NGOs are active in Yunnan province alone, including many foundations. That such active organisations escape government supervision is good neither for their objective of supporting public welfare work in China nor for the proper regulation of their activities and the protection of national security and stability. Improving the administration and registration of overseas organisations is a pressing requirement for allowing further opening up to the outside world, fuller realisation of the principle of the rule of law, and appropriate protection of social stability and there is an urgent requirement for legislation on the matter. The 2004 Regulations are well adapted to this new situation, bringing overseas organisations within the ambit of the framework of laws governing domestic Chinese civil society organisations, and registering and administering them accordingly. They make no distinction as to the nationality of the founder of a foundation. They permit overseas nationals and residents of Hong Kong, Taiwan and Macao to establish foundations in China, and also allow overseas foundations to establish representative organisations here, encouraging foreign funding of public welfare initiatives. Not only do the 2004 Regulations solve many of the problems of administering and registering overseas foundations, they also represent a useful practical experiment that will be of benefit in future revisions of the regulations covering social organisations and popular non-enterprise work units, so that they too clearly provide for overseas groups.

That the Regulations permit overseas foundations to engage in appropriate public welfare activities in China fits with international practice in the administration of foundations and will be beneficial in promoting international exchanges and cooperation, in increasing potential sources of funding, and also in learning from the more mature experience and practices of international civil society organisations. This will improve the capacity of domestic groups. The Regulations bring the administration of the activities of overseas foundations into the framework of domestic civil society organisations (CSO) laws and stipulate that international agencies should undertake public welfare activities that appropriate for public welfare in China. International foundations are now civilly liable for the activities of the representative organisations in China. Since China is still a developing nation and resources are limited, the Regulations do not permit overseas foundations to fund-raise or receive donations here.

3.4 Broad Provisions for Preserving and Increasing the Value of Assets

Preserving and increasing the value of assets is one of the most important parts of the operation of a foundation. If this is regulated too strictly, foundations lack vitality; if too lax the risks associated with preserving and increasing assets are heightened, making this a very hard policy to balance correctly. To reduce risks to their assets and ensure that they remained oriented to public welfare, the 1988 Measures set strict limits on how foundations could use their money. For example, Article 6 stated that 'foundations may not run or administer businesses', Article 70 that 'foundations may place funds with financial organisations in order to earn interest and may also buy bonds, stocks and similar equities, but they may not take a holding of more than 20% of any individual enterprise. The 'Notice concerning Further Improving the Management of Foundations' issued by the People's Bank further stipulated that 'the preservation and increase of the value of a foundation's assets must be entrusted to a financial organisation'.[10] However, in practice these regulations failed to achieve their desired effect. There is no basic contradiction between a foundation running a business or holding a controlling stake in an enterprise and their basic nature as public welfare organisations, nor is it a reflection of their overall exposure to risk. Foundations differ greatly from one another and over-specific regulation on financial strategies can hardly suit each and every one of them. This is why the 2004 Regulations follow international practice and set no specific requirements as to how foundations should approach this issue, laying down only general principles and broad guidelines. The emphasis is on public scrutiny and internal monitoring to set limits on how foundations manage their money. At the same time regulations were made for 'compensation for errors'. This requires board members who are party to decisions that lead to a loss of a foundation's assets to assume responsibility for making financial restitution, ensuring that such activities will be conducted carefully.

3.5 Encouraging Fund-raising and Public Welfare Activities – Creating a Virtuous Mechanism for the Flow of Funds

Foundations, as non-profit organisations that engage in public welfare activities, need adequate and sustainable financial support if they are to enrich society. Their ability to raise and employ funds is the deciding factor in whether or not they can survive and grow. Only if they can raise sufficient money can they work towards the goals they set themselves in their charters. At present many foundations are unable to raise money and carry out few activities with any real impact. This lack of vitality leads to their gradual decline. Yet those foundations that have healthy funding cycles have achieved this by establishing good public reputations by virtue of their activities. Towards this latter mode of operation the Regulations provide systemic guarantees, setting a major criterion for judging a foundation's public welfare status as how much they annually expend on such activity. Public fundraising foundations must spend a sum equivalent to at least 70% of their previous year's income on public welfare activities; non-public fundraising foundations must spend not less than 8% of their previous year's surplus on the welfare goals set out in their charter.

10 See: http://www.mca.gov.cn/artical/content/200422514006/200442394652.html (Last visited March 2005).

If they fail to do this they will be penalised and perhaps even closed down. This means that if foundations fail to raise enough money for their required annual expenditures, both for activities and to cover fixed running costs such as wages and benefits, they will see a steady decrease in their principal. If this falls below a given amount, they will be wound up. Hence in future bodies which are foundations in name only but which do little welfare work will find themselves with little legal protection.

3.6 Principles of Openness and Transparency

As public welfare organisations, to a certain extent foundations are undertaking some of the public services functions that were formerly the preserve of the state, and thus they enjoy certain preferential treatment and policies. They control access to some public welfare resources and their activities are a matter of proper public concern. Thus foundations have a heavy burden of social responsibility and with the extent to which their activities conform to appropriate norms has an impact on the preservation of charitable resources and the allocation and usage of public welfare assets. It also affects how they are perceived and thus the overall development of the public welfare sector. Hence foundations must be both well-managed and willing to accept a high level of public scrutiny to maintain a high level of public trust. Thus the laws must provide good mechanisms for both government and public scrutiny of foundations' affairs. The Regulations do make many provisions in this respect, fully meeting those above requirements. Article 5 makes clear that: 'Foundations carry out public benefit activities in line with their charters. They should abide by principles of openness and transparency'. Moreover the Regulations outline how government and public supervision should be carried out. They stipulate the respective responsibilities of both the registering agency and the sponsoring agency during registration, in everyday work, and during annual reporting procedures, and also make detailed provisions regarding a range of illegal activities and how they should be penalised.[11] The Regulations also require foundations to submit to annual inspection and audits by tax and financial regulatory authorities. After their annual inspection foundations must make their annual report public in a media outlet decided by the registering agency, allowing public scrutiny.

11 Tymen van der Ploeg believes that scrutiny of foundations is better carried out by the courts than by a government agency, since the former will be based on legal standards of proof and the latter on policy standards. See his paper in this volume.

Public fund-raising foundations must make public detailed plans for how they intend to spend the money they raise. How surplus funds are disposed of is also to be made public.

3.7 Standardised Internal Regulatory Mechanisms

The Regulations also emphasise the need for foundations to set up standardised internal regulatory mechanisms. Good internal regulatory mechanisms provide impetus for the preservation and growth of a foundation. Aware of the failings in this respect of many foundations, the Regulations require that they establish a variety of internal regulatory mechanisms based on charter, and the section on 'organisational structure' provides what are appropriate to foundations' status as public welfare legal person. This makes clear that the board of directors is the decision making body in a foundation, sets standards for how such a board is constituted, and processes by which decisions are to be made, and how monitoring and supervisory mechanism should be put in place. It sets up systems to avoid a clash of interests between officers of a foundation and its overall public welfare goals, including limiting the number of directors who may be paid and banning a foundation's legal representative from simultaneously holding a similar position in any other organisation. This serves to encourage self-discipline in foundations' activities.

3.8 The Principles for Tax Incentives and Oversight of Tax Affairs

The Regulations make clear the principles for tax incentives, and strengthen oversight of tax affairs. Using tax instruments to support and oversee foundations and offering tax incentives to charitable donations reflect widely used international practice. Indeed if we consider how money and materials are gathered for public welfare initiatives and how they operate in other countries we can see that the use of tax incentives to promote foundations and other non-profit bodies is the major way in which governments support their efforts. There are two main aspects to such government tax policies: allowing cash and in-kind charitable donations to be written off against a donor's tax assessment; and lowering taxes on the commercial activities carried out by funds. For example, the tax laws in Japan calculate a sum of money that a company or individual can donate each year to charity for which they will be exempted from income tax. In the US companies are allowed to donate up to 5% of their pre-tax income to charity in line with tax regulations passed in 1954. In 1962 it was further allowed that donations over 5% of income in a given year could be carried over and written off against the following year's tax bill, a provision which was extended to five years in 1965. The earliest US policies towards public welfare activities exempted them from tax, seeing as they were performing certain of the state's functions. After the Second World War, since the number of non-profits had risen exponentially largely due to this tax exemption policy the situation got a little out of hand. In 1952 Congress initiated an investigation into the non-profit sector. This revealed that over USD 7 billion in tax revenue had been lost to evasion between 1951 and 1960 of which a great deal was due to tax-exempt bodies. With widespread criticism from many sectors of society into the behaviour of foundations, in 1969 tax reform was implemented. This stipulated that foundations had to pay income tax at 4% per annum and that also a foundation was obliged to spend a set proportion of its assets on social welfare initiatives every year. Moreover foundations had to make public details of their income, expenditure and overall assets holdings. After 1973, through the efforts of many foundations, investigations were conducted on foundations' activities. The results of this survey led in turn to further tax reforms.[12]

From this we can see that tax incentives and tax exemptions are important components of an enabling policy environment for foundations and other CSOs. China is still at an exploratory stage in this regard. A series of tax incentives have been introduced to encourage public welfare initiatives and they have had a definite impact, but the policies have not been introduced systematically and are scattered across a plethora of official documents and instructions. Their implementation has also been plagued with numerous problems. Article 26 of the Regulations states that, 'foundations, their donors and beneficiaries enjoy tax benefits as stipulated by law and administrative regulations', which establishes the principle that all three parties – donors, foundations and beneficiaries – are entitled to tax breaks. Specific tax policies are still being researched by the Ministry of Finance and the State Tax Administration. As well as benefiting from incentives, foundations are obliged to register for tax in compliance with the relevant laws and to submit themselves to the oversight of the tax authorities. Foundations which break the law may find that their tax incentives are revoked for the period of their offence. By confirming the validity of tax

12 Lester M. Salamon and Helmut K. Anheier, *In Search of the Non-profit Sector: The Question of Definition*, (Baltomore: John Hopkins University Institute for Policy Studies, 1992), at pp. 1-22.

incentives, the Regulations encourage the development of foundations and also strengthen their oversight.

In sum, the 'Regulations for the Management of Foundations', as the most important law governing foundations in China, clarify the nature and status of foundations, confirm their rights and obligations, establish the principles by which they are to be registered and administered, and make provision for almost every aspect of that latter work. They will be the most important legal document affecting the development of foundations in China for quite some time. The promulgation of the Regulations provides a vital legal framework not just for foundations themselves, but also for the agencies charged with their supervision, and guarantees the legitimacy of both parties' actions.

4 A Legal Framework for Foundations

As well as clarifying the nature and status of foundations, the 2004 'Regulations for the Management of Foundations' also establish an important legal framework for major aspects of their existence and activities. Compared to that of the 1988 Method, this framework is both more rational and more practicable. The major aspects of the framework established by the 2004 Regulations are described below.

4.1 Non-profit Legal Person Status

The 1988 Method regarded foundations as a type of 'social organisation'. This was obviously not conducive to getting the most from the special nature of foundations. Hence the 2004 Regulations define foundations as 'non-profit legal persons', both a more accurate description and also helpful to foundations more effectively conducting public welfare activities.

Article 2 of the 2004 Regulations states: 'These regulations, when referring to a foundation mean a non-profit legal entity established in accordance with these regulations that employs assets donated by natural persons, legal persons or other organisations for the purpose of engaging in some public benefit enterprise.' This says in effect that foundations are not profit-seeking bodies, that they are independent with full civil capacity and capable of accepting full civil liability. The term 'non-profit legal person' is not unique to Chinese law. The 'General Principles of the Civil Law of the People's Republic of China' define four types of legal person: official organ legal persons, institutional legal persons, enterprise legal persons and social organisations legal persons.[13] The 1988 Method placed foundations in the latter category. However, since foundations are largely concerned with the movement and employment of money and lack the characteristics of a membership-based social organisation, such a categorisation is not appropriate. For example, in Japan foundations are regarded as financial institutions. This problem has been considered in the drafting of the Civil Code that is currently underway. In order to avoid clashing with the intentions of that legislation once it is brought forward, the 2004 Regulations no longer sought to define foundations as social organisations but rather chose to emphasise their non-profit nature.

4.2 Foundations' Non-profit Status and their Operating Practices

One of the defining characteristics of foundations is their non-profit nature. This means that seeking profit is not one of their objectives, not that they cannot earn profits from their operating practices. This clearly distinguishes their activities from those of commercial legal persons. The latter are conducted with the aim of making a profit that will eventually be allocated to investors, managers, operatives and employees. In the course of conducting public welfare activities (for example a charity concert), foundations will often also engage in money-earning operations in order to preserve or increase the value of their fund, but these are only undertaken so that the public welfare work can continue and thus do not affect the foundation's non-profit status. A foundation's assets cannot be allocated to its officers or employees, they may only draw such wages as national law allows.

4.3 The 'Dual Responsibility System' for Administering Foundations

The 1988 Method established a tripartite system of administration for foundations which included a sponsoring agency, the registration agency and the People's Bank. The 2004 Regulations set out a 'dual responsibility' system. This is an important principle of the Party and the central government for civil society organisations. The detailed provisions for this dual system outlined in the 2004 Regulations sets out the responsibilities of both the sponsoring and

13 See Sections 2 and 3 of the General Principles of the Civil Law of the People's Republic of China.

registering agencies and how they should share the work of administering foundations. During registration, the registering agency is responsible for the final approval of an application to register a foundation, their branch or representative organisations, or a representative of an overseas foundation; the sponsor takes responsibility for initial checking of these organisations. Article 34 stipulates that in day-to-day administration:

> The organ in charge of registration of foundations has the following responsibilities in regards of monitoring and management:
> 1. Conduct annual inspections of foundations and representative bodies of overseas foundations;
> 2. Conduct day-to-day monitoring and supervision of how foundations and representative bodies of overseas foundations carry out activities in line with these regulations and their own charters; and
> 3. Penalise those foundations and representative bodies of overseas foundations whose actions violate the regulations.

Article 35 provides that:

> Sponsors have the following responsibilities in regards of monitoring and management:
> 1. Give guidance and monitor foundations and representative bodies of overseas foundations on carrying out public benefit activities in accordance with the law and their own charters;
> 2. Give preliminary approval to the annual inspections of foundations and representative bodies of overseas foundations; and
> 3. Coordinate with the organ in charge of registration and other law enforcement agencies in the investigation and punishment of any illegal activities by foundations and representative bodies of overseas foundations.

4.4 Foundations' Internal Organisational Structure

The 2004 Regulations make detailed provisions concerning foundations' internal organisational structures, especially concerning their board of directors, legal representative, supervisory officials and general staff. Article 21 states:

> The board of directors is the decision making body of a foundation and should carry out their responsibilities as laid down in the charter in accordance with the law. The board of directors should meet at least twice a year, with two thirds of directors

> in attendance as quorum. Decisions must obtain a simple majority of those attending a meeting to be valid.

Section 4 of Article 20 makes detailed provision concerning members of a foundation and its legal representative, that the 'board of directors will appoint a chair, deputy chair and secretary general elected from amongst their membership. The chair of the board is the legal representative of the foundation'. Article 21 also sets out the main parameters of the board's powers:

> Decisions concerning the following major items require a two thirds majority of directors attending a meeting to be effective:
> 1. Revisions to the charter;
> 2. Election or dismissal of the chair, deputy chair or secretary general;
> 3. Major fundraising or investment activities as stipulated in the charter;
> 4. The division or amalgamation of the foundation.
>
> The board of directors should have minutes kept of their meetings which should be read, approved and signed by members in attendance.

Article 22 stipulates that:

> A foundation should appoint a supervisory official, whose term of service will be the same as a member of the board...The supervisory official will keep check of the financial records and accounts of the foundation in accordance with a process laid down in the charter and monitor the board's compliance with the charter and with the law. When attending a board meeting the supervisory official has the right to question and make suggestions to the board, and should also report on relevant matters to the organ in charge of registration, the sponsoring agency and also the tax and auditing authorities.

In order to ensure that the Board of Directors can and will fulfil its duties, and that it will not seek private benefits, the Regulations set limits on who may be eligible, and under what conditions, to serve on it. Section 2 of Article 20 states that, 'for non-public fundraising foundations established using the assets of a private individual, no more than a third of board members may be close family relations of that individual; for other foundations, close relations may not serve simultaneously as directors'. Section 1 of Article 22 states that, 'members of the board, their close relatives or financial staff of the foundation may not serve as supervisory officials'. Also, Articles 23 and 24 set limits on board members' and officers' terms of office. Article 23 states that:

> The posts of Chair and Deputy Chair of the Board of Directors or Secretary General should not be taken by persons currently employed by state bodies. The legal representative of the foundation may not at the same time be the legal representative of any other organisation. The legal representative of public fundraising foundations and non-public fundraising foundations whose original funds are of domestic Chinese origin should be a person who is a legal resident of mainland China. The posts of Chair and Deputy chair of the Board of Directors or Secretary General should not be taken by persons who because of committing a crime have been put under public surveillance, detained or imprisoned within 5 years of the end of that sentence; nor by those who are currently or have formerly been under sentence of having their political rights removed; nor by those who have served in such posts and had legal culpability at other foundations that were closed down for illegal activities within 5 years of the closure of the said foundation. Should a board member find there is a connection between their personal interests and the interests of the foundation, they should not take part in decision making related to the matter; nor should a board member, the supervisory official or their close relations have any kind of business dealings with the foundation. The supervisory official and board members not serving in a full time post at the foundation may not be paid.

Article 24 further provides that 'residents of Hong Kong, Macau or Taiwan, or foreign nationals serving as chair, deputy chair or secretary general of the board of a foundation or as legal representative of the representative organisation of an overseas foundation must be resident in mainland China for at least three months every year'.

Also, section 2 of Article 29 states that, 'a foundation may not allocate more than 10% of its total expenditure to cover staff wages and benefits and overheads'. The above listed provisions provide an effective guarantee that foundations maintain their public welfare nature by setting stringent demands and standards concerning who may be their officers and staff and how they operate. They prevent foundations being used in the service of some person or persons' private gain.

4.5 Regulations Regarding Foundations' Original Funds

The Regulations manage foundations by type, distinguishing between 'public fundraising foundations' and 'non-public fundraising foundations'. The distinction between these two lies in their source of funding, the former raises money form public donations, the latter is funded from the donations of certain individuals or organisations, and may not engage in public fund-raising.

This typology makes clear that it is permissible to establish non-public fundraising foundations. This achieves two objectives: strict control can be exercised over charitable giving; and a policy environment is created conducive to encouraging the wealthy to set up foundations.

The Regulations also make distinctions in the requirements for original funds. National-level public fundraising foundations must have at least CNY 8 million (USD 941,000), local public fundraising foundations, at least CNY 4 million, and non-public fundraising foundations, CNY 2 million. Public fundraising foundations are required to have larger original funds than non-public fundraising foundations and national-level foundations more than local. This standard is derived from three considerations. First, this limits the proliferation of too many public fundraising foundations, and encourages more non-public fundraising foundations. Second, it guarantees that foundations have sufficient resources to conduct activities and maintain operations. International experience and the situation in China show that CNY 8 million will allow national-level different public fundraising foundations to both cover their operating expense, such as wages, and carry out public welfare activities. Public fundraising foundations with less than 4 million are often unable to do this, as are non-public fundraising foundations with less than 2 million. If they cannot do this there is no point to their existence. Third, in light of the present state of development of foundations in China, the requirement for original funds must not be set too high. Figures gathered by the People's Bank in 1999 showed that only half of national-level foundations had more than CNY 8 million in funds. Apart from a few wealthier areas the situation was even worse for local foundations. Close to 40% of them did not even have the CNY 2.1 million then required. This shows that it would be wrong to ask national-level foundations to have more than CNY 8 million, and since local foundations have a smaller base from which to seek donations they should naturally require less original funds.

4.6 Stipulating the Level of Expenditure on Public Welfare

Section 1 of Article 29 of the 2004 Regulations stipulates that:

> The amount of money spent annually by public fundraising foundations on the public welfare activities stipulated in their charter must not be less than 70% of the previous year's income; non-public fundraising foundations annual expenditure on the

> public benefit welfare stipulated in their charter must not be less than 8% of the surplus from the previous year.

This stipulates what proportion of funds should be spent on public welfare to encourage foundations to fulfil their charter obligations by investing in public welfare, and puts a stop to those foundations that are currently unwilling or unable to do this.

The proportion of expenditure to income is a good measure of the effectiveness of public fundraising foundations who seek donations from the public. Figures show that the average such proportion for national-level foundations is 50%. The Regulations, with the aim of encouraging greater investment in welfare activities, require that expenditure must be of a level at least 70% of the previous year's income.

Non-public fundraising foundations do not fundraise, usually relying on interest or regular investment from their principal donor to cover the cost of their activities. Hence setting the standard for expenditure based on income would not be appropriate. It is more rational to base this calculation on a calculation of their total funds. This standard is set at a lower level that encourages both expenditure and the overall development of non-public fundraising foundations. The Regulations require that an amount not less than 8% of the previous years' surplus be spent on public welfare.

4.7 Oversight of Foundations' Financial Operations

The 2004 Regulations place limits on eight aspects of foundations' financial operations. Firstly, the source of funding should be legal. Secondly, in preserving and increasing the value of their fund they should uphold principles of legality, safety and effectiveness. Thirdly, major fundraising or investment activities should be approved by the board of directors under special procedures and a supervisory official should be appointed to oversee financial operations. Fourthly, policy decisions should be unconnected with the personal interests of board members or the supervisory official. Fifthly, neither the supervisory official, nor members of the board not serving as officers of the foundation, may accept remuneration for their work, nor may those receiving such remuneration be more than a third of the board. Sixthly, annual expenditure on welfare activities must meet the standards set. Seventhly, foundations that are unable to carry out activities should be wound up; and finally, once a foundation has been wound up, any remaining funds must be allocated to public welfare initiatives.

4.8 Foreign Citizens Establishing Foundations, and Overseas Foundations setting up Representative Organisations in China

The Regulations do not distinguish between the nationalities of the founders of foundations. They allow foreigners in China to establish foundations and overseas foundations to establish representative organisations.

5 Issues Requiring Further Research

Overall, the clarification given in the 2004 Regulations concerning foundations' legal nature and status has removed the vestiges of the influence of the old planned economic system. It has changed the management model established under the 1988 Method, granted foundations a status as independent non-profit legal persons, and emphasised the public welfare role of both their existence and their activities. It has introduced the concept of 'purposed assets' into Chinese law. It has drawn on overseas experience in laws for both non-profit and financial bodies to lay a solid legislative foundation for the healthy development of foundations in China and their increased role in public welfare. By establishing rules and processes to govern foundations' activities, the Regulations have provided a clear legal basis for them to operate under and have largely sorted out the ways in which foundations are different from other legal persons. However, due to the present limitation of the overall legislative situation in China, there remain problems that foundation run into in the course of their operations that the Regulations have not been able to fully resolve. The Regulations are contradictory in places. The following are issues that require further exploration and perhaps, at the appropriate juncture, resolution either by revising the present Regulations, revising other relevant legislation or by drafting a 'Foundations Law'.

5.1 Problems of Taxation[14]

Article 26 of the Regulations states that, 'foundations, their donors and their beneficiaries enjoy tax benefits as stipulated by the law and administrative regulations.' To date, the major preferential tax policies aimed at foundations have been: they are exempt from enterprise income tax on the interest from their investments; business can offset public welfare and relief donations against the income tax on 3% of their annual tax liability; foreign-invested companies donations to things other than public welfare and relief are exempt from corporate income tax; individuals who donate a sum equivalent to 30% of their tax liability are exempt from personal income tax; materials donated for welfare or relief initiatives may be exempted or charged reduced customs duties; and social organisations (including foundations) are exempt from stamp duty when contracting for land or buildings to be used to provide office, educational, medical, research or military facilities.

We can see that foundations do enjoy some guarantee of preferential taxation. However, remaining shortcomings in such policies in China mean that they have little impact in encouraging corporations or individuals to make donations. Donations tend to affect income tax liability, but China's tax system relies largely on indirect taxation, so these preferential policies have less impact on charitable giving. Donations may only be offset against 3% of the total tax liability to reduce corporate income tax – such a low level that making donations will not be of much help in reducing a businesses' tax bill. Worse, the enterprise must pay tax on donations above this set amount, which is a disincentive to giving. Also, corporate income tax operates on fixed rates which do not help to encourage giving. Similar is true of personal income tax. Here the proportion of tax affected by charitable giving is also low.[15] Nor has China yet introduced an estate tax as another means for encouraging donations to foundations.

14 For detailed information see: People's Daily Overseas Edition, 20th April, 2004, at p. 6.

15 A few years ago an actor earned a large some of money from appearing in a commercial, which he donated to a foundation, something that was widely reported at the time. However he soon found the tax authorities intended to levy tax on this money, much to the actor's bafflement. He had done a good thing and he was taxed for it! See Jin Dongsheng, 'The Current Situation of Preferential Tax Polices for China's NPOs and Some Problems', a paper presented at the Conference on Tax Reform Concerning NPOs, organised by the Research Centre on NPO Law Studies at the Law School of Peking University, 6th March, 2004.

5.2 Inherent Biases in Government Policy

At present there are great difference between foundations in China in terms of organisation and how they were set up, in how much money they receive in donations and other factors. For example, some of the registered national-level foundations are entirely the creation of government and tend to exercise a monopoly over their given field. Others are entirely the work of private individuals. These radically different backgrounds can have an impact on foundations' ability to fundraise, and some even get what almost amounts to policy support. For example, during the SARS crisis of 2003, government agencies issued orders that donations could only be given to the All China Federation on Charities and the Chinese Red Cross and official donations could only go to the Ministries of Civil Affairs and Health. This kind of policy limits foundations' capacity to develop their fundraising abilities and creates distinctions in how different foundations are treated by the law. Similarly, some sponsoring agencies treat the foundations they oversee as if they were subordinate parts of their own organisations, not only requiring that they reward the sponsors financially, but also assigning people to directly manage how the foundation is run. This seriously impedes their ability to act independently. So how best to clearly divide foundations from government is a question that must be further explored and resolved.

5.3 Distinguishing between the Reasons for Foundations and Other Kinds of Social Fund Organisations

Foundations exist to carry out public welfare activities, and these activities should not be just for particular groups within the population. However, in China at present we still see various types of fund management organisations that have some public welfare characteristics, but only seek to benefit some special group, such as equities investment fund companies. A distinction in law must be made between foundations and these other kinds of organisation, allowing the public to more effectively donate money to foundations. The government and other social actors should sponsor promotional campaigns to make sure that the public have a clear understanding of this issue.

Although foundations and equity investment funds are both fund management organisations they differ in their basic natures. Firstly, they are organised differently: foundations are non-profits, equity investment funds are profit-seeking organisations. Secondly, their ownership relations are different. Foundations are founded on the basis of donations where ownership of funds is transferred, while equity investment funds take investments and ownership of funds remains with the investor. Thirdly, foundations are established for a different end: they seek to increase public welfare and extend social benefits as widely as possible. Equity investment funds, on the other hand, seek to benefit their investors and their only goal is to turn a profit. Fourthly, they are managed differently. Equity investment funds are entrusted by investors to operate on their behalf and invest in the stock market and are influenced by investors in the way they operate their business with an emphasis on earnings, foundations are a type of collective social assets and are managed with an emphasis on security, with earnings of secondary importance.

5.4 The Management and Oversight of Foundations' Assets

Over the long period of time since foundations first appeared in China and in which they have developed, the system for managing and overseeing their assets has been very poor. Not only have foundation funds sometimes been used to engage in commercial activities forbidden by law, there have also been numerous example of board members or employees allocating funds in the most irregular of fashions. This is especially marked when foundations have been wound up, with former board or staff members misappropriating remaining funds. Although the Regulations have given detailed provisions concerning the management and oversight of foundations' assets there is still a need for a system requiring strict internal management mechanisms, proper external auditing and public oversight. Foundations operations and use of funds should be open to media scrutiny and the role of specialists such as lawyers and accountants in such work is particularly vital. The most pressing need at present is for improved oversight and management of non-public fundraising foundations, especially private foundations. Many other countries have very strict systems for administering and monitoring private foundations. For example, in Austria, permission was granted to establish private foundations in 1993, and few government limits were set on their creation, but the government did not grant them any preferential financial policy concession in order to avoid their misuse for improper private ends.[16]

16 See Tymen van der Ploeg's paper in this volume.

6 Conclusion

All in all, the Regulations for the Management of Foundations that came into effect in June 2004 have provided a fairly comprehensive and systematic set of standards concerning foundations' legal nature and status, and for the various legal questions that arise in the course of their activities, that meet the needs of the rule of law and allow foundations to play a full part in the promotion of public welfare. They are the legal basis for the healthy development of foundations in China. They have learned from the experience of previous domestic legislation, and best international practice, and represent an advance in step with the times.

PART II

EUROPEAN PERSPECTIVES

7

CIVIL SOCIETY AND THE NON-PROFIT SECTOR IN THE NETHERLANDS

Paul Dekker

1 INTRODUCTION

'Social organisations' are an important phenomenon in the Netherlands. Compared to other European countries, the country shows high levels of membership and volunteering in voluntary associations, an extremely large number of (operational) foundations, and the largest private non-profit sector, in terms of percentage of total paid employment. The camaraderie of club life and the community spirit of common interest organisations are seen as part of the national identity, although this may now be under threat. Non-profit service providers, such as schools and hospitals, are important not only economically but also culturally: they are still perceived to be the result of what are considered typical Dutch traditions of private responsibility for common interests, of religious pluralism and of a non-authoritarian state.

This chapter is meant to offer information about the associational and economic side of Dutch social organisations, to show differentiations and trends, and to discuss the functions and potential benefits of non-state and non-commercial membership organisations and service providers. I will not try to compare Chinese and Dutch figures or administrative and legal aspects of organisations, and neither will I enter into general discussions about Confucian and Protestant civil societies or the broader framework of different political systems, Eastern and Western values, and so on. I hope that the presentation and discussion of the very different situation of a small country with a huge sector of social organisations, such as the Netherlands, will prove valuable for

Yuwen Li (Ed.), *Freedom of Association in China and Europe: Comparative Perspectives in Law and Practice*, © 2005 Koninklijke Brill NV, Leiden. Printed in The Netherlands, pp. 251-282.

discussions in a huge country with a small sector of social organisations, such as China.

The chapter begins, in the following section, with an explanation of the two international concepts that are used to describe and discuss Dutch organisations: civil society and non-profit sector. Section 3 offers some international, mainly European comparisons and Section 4 examines in greater detail the patterns and trends that characterise the Netherlands. Regarding the social and political impact of activity in social organisations, Section 5 deals with some international literature and empirical research and Section 6 with findings in the Netherlands. The final Section concludes by discussing the findings and offering some reasons to stimulate voluntary associations and private non-profits.

2 Civil Society and Non-profit Sector

Typical Dutch terms used to refer to organisations which are non-commercial and which do not belong to the state, are 'private initiative' (*particulier initiatief*) and 'societal midfield' (*maatschappelijk middenveld*). The first term focuses on the origins of many organisations: groups of citizens organized in voluntary associations to pursue issues that outweight individual interests. Until the 1990s the term was often abbreviated to 'PI' to indicate the field of non-profit service providers that were the offspring of the private initiatives (but had turned into vested interests). Nowadays the abbreviation is seldom used, and the term 'private initiative' itself has become somewhat ambiguous since it can now mean private commercial initiatives as well. The term 'societal midfield' was introduced in the 1970s and focuses on the intermediary functions of organisations, mainly between the individual citizen and the state, but also between different groups in society.

On the one hand, the organisations in the 'societal midfield' represent the interests of their specific groups at government level and try to influence public policymaking. On the other hand, many of these organisations provide a service to the government, for instance by implementing and monitoring policies. The term primarily depicts interest, advocacy and political organisations, but the societal midfield discourse normally includes other voluntary associations and all non-profit service-delivering organisations as well, and even public service providers as regards their role as intermediary organisations, i.e. the role they may play to express values and voice the interests of their clients, integrate these groups in society, link them to politics, etc. The English term 'civil society' was welcomed in the 1990s as a modern and international alternative to 'societal midfield'.

Nowadays societal midfield and civil society appear to be used more or less interchangeably, but upon further consideration they often stress different aspects of the same organisations, respectively their vertical (citizen-state) and horizontal (citizen-citizen) intermediary role. Rather than reflect further on the Dutch terminology and the history in which it was developed,[1] in this section I will introduce two international concepts to analyse the present state of 'social organisations' in the Netherlands: 'civil society' and 'non-profit sector.'

2.1 Civil Society

Civil Society has many conflicting definitions. In the Western world the concept is sometimes used to refer to the whole of society – a society characterized by some sort of 'civility' in the relationships between individuals and groups, or by the existence of some autonomy of social, economic and political domains. More often, it is used to refer to a sphere of society. This sphere is traditionally regarded as opposing the state (although parliaments are sometimes mentioned as part of civil society) and most Western authors also consider that it opposes the market economy and is located outside the intimate sphere of family and close friendship ties. In positive terms it is described as the societal domain within which voluntary associations or associative relations are dominant.[2]

1 See Ary Burger and Paul Dekker, *The Non-profit Sector in the Netherlands,* (The Hague: Social and Cultural Planning Office, 2000).

2 See Paul Dekker and Andries van den Broek, 'Civil society in comparative perspective', (1998) 8 (1) *Voluntas*, at pp. 11-38, and Mark E. Warren, *Democracy and Association,* (Princeton: Princeton University Press, 2001). Well-known theorists of civil society might, however, explicitly include the market or family life in their definition of civil society. Compare Victor Pérez-Díaz, *The Return of Civil Society,* (Cambridge: Harvard University Press, 1993) at p. 57: '... social institutions such as markets and voluntary associations and a public sphere which are outside the direct control, in a full or in a mitigated sense, of the state'; Michael Walzer, 'Equality and civil society', in Simone Chambers and Will Kymlicka (eds.), *Alternative Conceptions of Civil Society,* (Princeton: Princeton University Press, 2002) at p. 35: '... all social groups that are or can be understood as voluntary and non-coercive, thus excepting only the family, whose members are not volunteers, and the state, which, even if its legitimacy rests on the consent of its members, wields coercive power over them'; Jean L. Cohen and Andrew Arato, *Civil Society and Political Theory,* (Cambridge: MIT Press, 1992) at p. ix: '... a sphere of social interaction between economy and state, composed above all of the

Evident in some definitions, and more often in the selection of phenomena to be discussed or empirically investigated, there is a focus on political relevance in the sense of being active in the 'public sphere', being involved in interest representation or directed towards the public interest.[3] While this is definitely an interesting perspective from which to analyse civil society, I favour a definition of civil society that refers to the non-state, non-market and non-private societal domain where 'voluntary associations' are dominant. In the conceptual map by Mark Warren (figure 1), 'pure associative relations' are at the heart of civil society: 'pure' because elements of voluntary associating can be found everywhere in society, and 'relations' because the frame or result of associating is not necessarily an association in the sense of an organisation.

Figure 1: 'Locating civil society' by Mark Warren[4]

	Means of social coordination				
Closeness of social relations	Power (legal coercion)		Social norms & communication		Money
Distant	States				Markets
		Mediating associations: 'political	Mediating spaces: publics	Mediating associations: 'economic	
Intermediate		society'		society'	
			Civil society (pure associative relations)		
Intimate			Families, friendships		

In this chapter I will nevertheless focus on voluntary associations in the sense of organisations. There are no clear-cut criteria for deciding which associations

intimate sphere (especially the family), the sphere of association (especially voluntary associations), social movements, and forms of public communication.'

3 Compare Dietrich Rueschemeyer for whom civil society means '... the ensemble of organized social activities, formal and informal, that are not directly grounded in family and kinship, economic production and exchange, or the state but are politically relevant.' Dietrich Rueschemeyer, 'The Self-organisation of Society and Democratic Rule', in Dietrich Rueschemeyer, Marilyn Rueschemeyer and Björn Wittrock (eds.), *Participation and Democracy in East and West,* (Armonk: M.E. Sharpe, 1998) at p. 18.

4 Warren, *supra* note 2, at p. 57.

to include that currently reside in the grey area somewhere between civil society and the other realms. Due to the importance of voluntariness in our conception of civil society, associations which one 'grows up in', or from which one can only extract oneself at considerable cost, are not part of civil society. As voluntariness implies a certain plurality on the supply side, institutions that hold a monopoly in a given domain, such as state churches or monopolistic trade unions, also fail to qualify. Organisations do not need to have their origins in altruistic motives, neither are they required to focus on the general public or on public debate. However, one might perhaps reasonably exclude inwardly directed organisations that have no impact on society at all and organisations that reject any public reflection on their pursuits.[5]

2.2 Non-profit sector

The term, 'non-profit sector' is less philosophical or ideological and more descriptive, and for that reason is easier to define in an operational way. In what has been one of the biggest international comparative social science projects in recent years, the Johns Hopkins Comparative Non-profit Sector Project, entities are defined as non-profits if they meet five criteria.[6] They must be:

- Organisations, i.e. they have an institutional presence and structure.
- Private, i.e. they are institutionally separate from the state.
- Not profit distributing, i.e. they do not return profits to their managers or to a set of 'owners'. The organisations can be 'profit seeking' as long as the profit is reinvested or used for the purpose of the organisation.
- Self-governing, i.e. they are fundamentally in control of their own affairs.
- Voluntary, i.e. membership of them is not legally required and they attract some level of voluntary contribution of time or money.

Of course, in practice these criteria are sometimes difficult to apply and many disputable decisions must be made in order to arrive at a consistent selection

5 Consequently one would exclude certain religious sects and terrorist groups, but not all religious organisations as such, nor undemocratic or unpleasant organisations (such as the Ku Klux Klan).

6 Lester M. Salamon, Helmut K. Anheier *et al.*, *Global Civil Society,* (Baltimore: The Johns Hopkins Center for Civil Society Studies, 1999), at pp. 3-4.

of organisations. The last two criteria are particularly difficult as they raise questions regarding the definition of relative concepts such as when is an organisation 'fundamentally' in control, and what is 'some level' of voluntary contribution? In the Netherlands, large numbers of vested non-profits that deliver welfare state services appear to be borderline cases in these respects.

The association (*vereniging*), the foundation (*stichting*) and the church (*kerkgenootschap*) are the three basic types of non-profit organisation in the Netherlands. Churches have no specific legal regulations, though they might be organised as associations or foundations. Foundations and associations are regulated in the Civil Code as regards their general characteristics, rules for establishment and dissolution, internal governance, accounting and legal representation. The main difference between foundations and associations is that associations have members and foundations do not.[7]

Civil society and the non-profit sector are both located between market and state as a social (and political) sphere and an economic sphere, respectively. The central criterion for civil society is voluntariness. For non-profit sector, besides autonomy from the state, the central criterion is the use of economic surplus, with voluntariness as a secondary, but often disputable and hard to use criterion.

3 The Netherlands in comparative perspective

Table 1 provides some insights based on data from recent surveys into the level of participation in a large number of organisations. The Netherlands and the Scandinavian countries are characterised by a high level of organisation of the 'societal midfield'. In these countries the percentage of the population who are members of social organisations is high, and a relatively large number are

7 Another difference is that foundations can only be formal, whereas associations may be informal. Informal associations are established without any formal action and no statutes are laid down in a notarial deed; registration at the Trade Register of the Chambers of Commerce is voluntary. In 1999, this register included 131,395 foundations and 92,955 'formal' associations. The foundation is a very simple legal form in the Netherlands and many foundations only serve private goals (such as preserving family property, administering stocks, promotion of goods or common interests, and delivering services). Most 'public purpose' foundations are operational foundations; there may be less then 10,000 foundations or funds (*fondsen*) that are involved in transferring money for public purposes. See the chapter of Tymen van der Ploeg in this book for further legal information.

members of more than one organisation. At the other end of the scale are France and the Southern European countries, where there is a low level of organisation; and the other Western European countries lie somewhere in between. The Scandinavian countries are characterised by the strong position of the trade unions. Compared to other European countries, the most striking features for the Netherlands are the high percentages of membership organisations concerned with nature and the environment, and the wide support for organisations concerned with the promotion of consumer interests.

Table 1: Organisational membership, 1998 (%)[8]

	NL	BE	DE	FR	IE	LU	AT	UK	DK	FN	SE	EL	IT	PT	ES
Sports clubs	37	20	29	19	29	25	20	20	38	21	36	8	11	10	10
Organisations for the protection of nature, animals and the environment	25	5	7	4	1	11	10	8	14	7	15	2	2	1	1
Trade unions or political parties	18	8	8	4	6	11	11	11	51	37	51	3	4	3	3
Social organisations or religious organisations involved in charity	16	5	8	4	8	11	8	10	9	13	13	3	8	4	3
Churches or other religious organisations not involved in charity	16	4	6	3	8	5	10	11	5	8	5	2	7	4	3
Clubs or societies for hobbies or shared interests	16	4	11	2	11	4	9	11	18	16	19	1	1	1	0
Cultural or artistic clubs	11	9	4	10	4	10	6	5	16	7	10	7	5	5	6
Consumer organisations	11	1	1	1	0	9	1	1	5	1	19	0	1	1	1
Human rights organisations or movements	5	2	1	2	2	3	3	2	5	2	7	0	2	0	1
Youth organisations	3	6	2	2	5	9	5	5	5	6	4	1	1	2	2
Other societies or organisations	9	8	7	8	7	3	4	7	7	9	11	4	4	3	4
Not a member of any association	21	52	47	60	49	43	47	47	16	28	15	76	66	74	72
A member of a single association	32	32	33	28	31	29	29	30	29	38	26	19	25	21	22
A member of two or more	47	16	20	12	20	28	24	23	56	34	58	4	8	6	6

Figure 2 presents national combinations of data about the membership and levels of volunteering in voluntary associations.[9] We see that membership of civil society organisations is particularly widespread in Scandinavia and the Netherlands, but the percentage of members that are active as volunteers is modest

8 Population aged 15 years and over. Source: Eurobarometer 50.1 (autumn 1998), weighted results (see: http://europa.eu.int/comm/public_opinion/index_en.htm).

9 Compared to 1989/90 and findings in other research, the level of volunteering in West Germany is implausibly low, and that in Great Britain implausibly high. One reason for the peculiar extreme position of Great Britain is probably the strong underreporting of normal membership of sports clubs.

in these countries (though as a percentage of the entire population, the number of volunteers is higher than in other European countries).

Figure 2: Civil society, patterns of membership and volunteering in 20 European countries in 1999/2000[10]

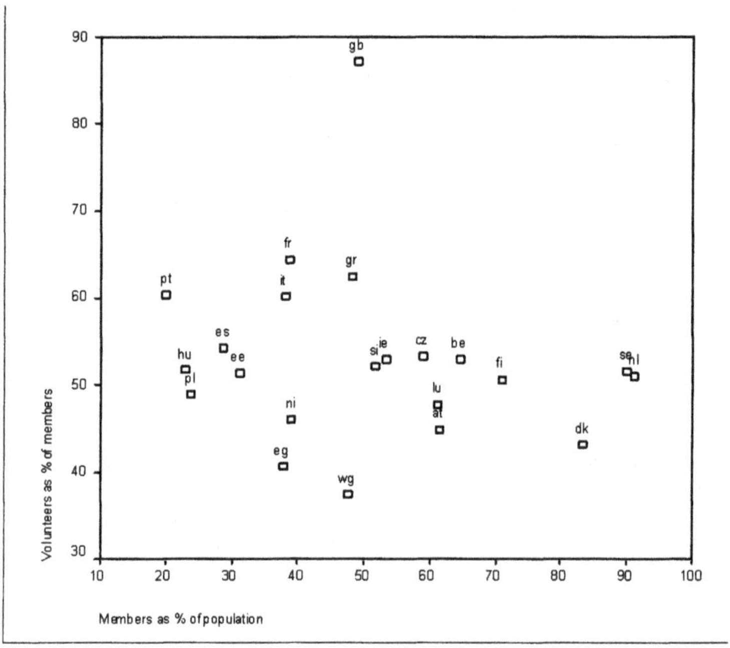

The opposite of this pattern is found in the Southern European countries, with smaller percentages of the population belonging to organisations, but larger

10 These measurements are based on the question: 'Please look carefully at the following list of voluntary organisations and activities and say a) which, if any, do you belong to?; and b) which, if any, are you currently doing unpaid voluntary work for?'
The list includes 14 specified categories, and a category for 'Other groups.' 'Religious and church organisations' have been excluded as a specific category for reasons of comparability. 'Members' are individuals that belong to at least one of the organisations. Volunteers are those doing voluntary work for at least one of these organisations (all volunteers are also supposed to be members). Country code: Austria (at), Belgium (be), Czech Republic (cz), East Germany (eg), West Germany (wg), Denmark (dk), Estonia (ee), Spain (es), Finland (fi), France (fr), Greece (gr), Hungary (hu), Ireland (ie), Italy (it), Luxembourg (lu), Netherlands (nl), Poland (pl), Portugal (pt), Sweden (se), Slovenia (si), Great Britain (gb), Northern Ireland (ni). Source: European Values Study 1999-2000 (see: http://www.europeanvalues.nl/index2.htm).

percentages of the members volunteering (however, because of the substantially lower membership rates, volunteers are a smaller percentage of the population than in Northern Europe). Compared to the 'broad civil societies' of the North and the 'elitist civil societies' of the South, most other European countries, including the new democracies of Central and Eastern Europe, combine modest membership rates with modest activity of the members. In 1989-90 there was a marked contrast between these countries and the 'active civil societies' of North America with both high levels of membership, and high levels of volunteering by the members.[11]

In the Netherlands a process of modernisation of civil society, in which old mass organisations are withering away and new types of organisations are on the rise, seems to be taking place more quickly than anywhere else. It has been shown elsewhere that the present-day recruitment power of political parties, trade unions and churches in the Netherlands is already weak in international terms, and dwindling further.[12] Compared to countries such as Austria and Finland, only a small proportion of Dutch voters are members of a political party; compared to the Scandinavian countries only a small percentage of Dutch workers are members of a trade union; and compared to all other European countries the Netherlands has a very high percentage of non-church members. For these three types of organisation the interest in membership in the Netherlands clearly lags behind the European average. This cannot be said of the affinity with other types of organisation. According to both survey measurements and absolute membership and support figures, the Dutch – together with the Danes and the Swedes – are the most massively organised nations in sectors concerned with nature and the environment, human rights, consumer interests and sports, hobbies and culture. In terms of the size of human rights and international aid organisations, as well as organisations concerned with nature and the environment, the Netherlands is among the world leaders.

As well as membership and levels of volunteering, a further topic of importance is the economy of associations and foundations. The Dutch non-profit sector is very large by international standards. Measured as a percentage of

11 See Dekker and Van den Broek, *supra* note 2. Comparable data from the World Values Study 1999-2000 are not available yet, but figures for volunteers as a percentage of the population again suggest high levels of activity for the USA (66%) and Canada (47%); Virginia A. Hodgkinson, 'Volunteering in Global Perspective', in Paul Dekker and Loek Halman (eds.), *The Values of Volunteering*, (New York: Plenum, 2003).

12 *The Netherlands in a European Perspective* (The Hague: Social and Cultural Planning Office, 2001), see: http: www.scp.nl (last visited March, 2005).

full-time equivalents (FTEs) in non-agricultural paid employment in 1995, the Netherlands has the largest non-profit sector of all 22 countries studied in the second phase of the 'Johns Hopkins comparative non-profit sector project'. Table 2 shows some international comparative data for the 13 countries of the Organization for Economic Cooperation and Development (OECD) included in this phase of the project. As the first column shows, in the Netherlands, Belgium and Ireland the employment share of the non-profit sector is over 10%, well above the other West-European countries (and far higher than the non-OECD countries in the project, which show figures ranging from 0.4% in Mexico to 3.7% in Argentina).

Table 2 also provides some information about the structure of the non-profit sector with regard to the three main fields of activity of non-profits for all twenty two countries in the project. It illustrates what the share of non-profits in these fields is in the total non-profit sector of a country, and how important non-profits are compared to public services and for-profits in each field of activity. In the Netherlands health, social services and education and research account for almost 90% of all non-profit employment; this is the highest share, but not an exceptional one. More marked is the UK's small share, largely due to the dominance of public institutions in its national health system. What is more surprising for the Netherlands, is the large share occupied by health – it is smaller than in the USA and Japan but far higher than the share of the non-profit sector in other European countries. It is surprising because from the history of the Dutch non-profit sector, and the constitutional protection of private schools, one would have expected education to occupy the leading position. The last columns of the table – the shares of non-profits in the total employment per field of activity – disclose that Dutch non-profits do have the biggest share in the educational field after Ireland. In the field of social services, Ireland and Spain pass the Netherlands, but overall, non-profits in the Netherlands appear to have a dominant position as regards the share of employment.

Table 2: Non-profit sector employment by country and in main fields of activity, 1995[13]

	Size of the non-profit sector[a]	Three fields in the non-profit sector[b]			Non-profits in the three fields[c]		
		Health	Social services	Education and research	Health	Social services	Education and research
Netherlands	12.9	42	19	27	70	71	65
Ireland	11.5	28	5	54	41	100	72
Belgium	10.5	30	14	39	.	.	.
Israel	9.2	27	11	50	44	29	37
US	7.8	46	14	21	47	54	22
Australia	7.2	19	20	23	17	61	21
UK	6.2	4	13	41	4	22	36
Germany	4.9	31	39	12	23	55	10
France	4.9	15	40	21	12	41	12
Spain	4.5	12	32	25	10	84	17
Austria	4.5	12	64	9	15	62	6
Japan	3.5	47	17	22	60	56	25
Finland	3.0	23	18	25	12	13	15

a: Non-profit (full-time equivalents paid) employment as% of total non-agricultural employment.
b: Non-profit employment as% of total non-profit employment.
c: Non-profit employment as% of total (public, non-profit and for-profit) employment per field of activity.

The figures in table 2 are about paid employment. But the non-profit sector also attracts unpaid or voluntary labour. Measurements of levels of volunteering are less reliable than measurements of paid work. However, the study found that in the Netherlands volunteering FTEs account for about 6.1% of total non-agricultural paid employment, a figure so much higher than that of other countries that we can be fairly certain that the Netherlands combines the highest levels of both paid and unpaid labour among the 22 countries in the second phase of the Johns Hopkins project. The volunteer input in other countries with a non-profit sector which is large in terms of paid employment, is much smaller: 2.6% in Ireland, 2.5% in Belgium and 1.8% in Israel.

13 Source: Johns Hopkins comparative non-profit sector project (see: http://www.jhu.edu/~cnp/).

Public revenues (including private health insurance) make up 59% of the income of the Dutch non-profit sector, fees and charges account for a further 38%, leaving only 3% for private giving. Private giving is a minor source of income everywhere in Europe, except in Spain where it accounts for 19% of the revenues of their relatively small non-profit sector. The next highest is 13%, in the USA. Compared to the other countries with a large non-profit sector, the Dutch sector is relatively highly dependent on fees and charges (38% compared to 19% in Belgium and 16% in Ireland). The greater dependency on public funding in Belgium and Ireland (both 77%) is interesting for the Dutch debates because in the Netherlands it is often supposed that the offspring of the private initiatives have become extremely dependent on subsidies.

In this comparative section, the Netherlands has been shown to be a country with a large and well established civil society and non-profit sector. Modernization of the civil society seems to be taking place more quickly in the Netherlands than anywhere else. Old mass organisations (churches, trade unions and political parties) are withering away and relatively new organisations in the areas of human rights, international solidarity, and the environment are enjoying massive support. The Dutch non-profit sector turned out to be the largest out of 22 national non-profit sectors compared in economic terms in 1995, mainly because of the many private organisations that deliver welfare state services. Its dependency on public funding is substantial but smaller than in some other countries with a large non-profit sector, and voluntary work is not pushed aside by paid professionals.

4 Patterns and Trends

As regards developments in membership of voluntary organisations, and volunteering in the Netherlands, table 3 first shows institutional data from and about large voluntary organisations. The data is drawn from information from organisations that had 50,000 or more members or donators in the period 1980-2000.[14]

In 2000, the total membership of all organisations together had increased by 9.5 million compared with 1980, from 26.1 million to 34.7 million members.

14 No distinction has been drawn between membership and donating money. Most people probably cannot tell the difference: they think they are a 'member' of Greenpeace because they regularly give money and receive a magazine for donators.

Since 1980, the number of Dutch members of one of the six large church communities had fallen by 16%; the number of members of women's organisations has fallen by a quarter and the membership of the three largest political parties has declined by no less than 44%.[15] Membership of organisations concerned with nature, conservation and the environment has grown enormously (by 524%), as had the membership of 'moral issue groups' (by 669%). International solidarity, health care, the elderly and consumer interests have also seen substantial growth.

Table 3: Members and supporters of large voluntary organisations, 1980 and 2000 (in 1,000)[16]

	1980	2000	% change 1980–2000
Political parties	342	192	– 44
Women	259	194	– 25
Churches and religion	9.511	8,004	– 16
Broadcasting	2,818	3,118	+ 11
Employees	1,616	1,877	+ 16
Sport and leisure	3,782	4,486	+ 19
Employers and self-employed	237	307	+ 30
Elderly	387	520	+ 34
Consumers	3,178	4,795	+ 51
Health	1,644	3,581	+ 118
International solidarity	1,852	4,386	+ 137
Environment and nature	484	3,021	+ 524
Abortion and euthanasia	26	200	+ 669
Total	25 136	34 681	+ 33
Population	14 091	15 864	+ 13

15 Including all other parties would not make a big difference. Actual membership is now about 2.5% of the electorate; in 1960 this figure was about 10% which was already low by European standards. These figures are lower than those from the surveys, but the latter include other political organisations and, probably more importantly, they are inflated because people consider party membership of another member of the household as a kind of family membership.

16 Source: Data provided by the organisations and gathered by the Social and Cultural Planning Office of the Netherlands (www.scp.nl). 'Large voluntary organisations' were those organisations with at least 50,000 members and supporters in any year between 1980 and 2000.

In contrast to what is often assumed, the increased degree of organisation of the Dutch population is not primarily the result of a rise in 'selfish' consumer and interest organisations, or a 'hedonistic' sports sector. As in other countries, a shift appears to be taking place in the Netherlands from 'secondary' face-to-face organisations to 'tertiary' mailing-list organisations. Robert Putnam has identified this shift in America, and argues that it has adverse consequences for the development of social networks, and the building of 'social trust' in society.[17] Ranged against these drawbacks are political benefits such as democratisation and the stimulation of large-scale public debate. Whatever the outcome of this balancing of the pros and cons of modern organisations may be, it is clear from the topics in table 3, that a shift from secondary to tertiary organisations is not a move from common good to personal interest organisations. It is, however, a shift to more passive and distant involvement of individuals in civil society.

A more active form of voluntary involvement is volunteering. There are several definitions of volunteering, but in almost all the definitions in the Netherlands, and in most definitions elsewhere, we find four elements: it is non-obligatory, it is unpaid, it is carried out for the benefit of other groups, society as a whole or a specific organisation, and lastly, it takes place in an 'organised context'. Survey-based estimates of the number of volunteers in the Netherlands vary between 20% and 50% of the population, depending on the phrasing of the questions,[18] the preceding topics in the questionnaire and the method used to conduct the surveys.

Until recently, identical survey instruments have not revealed any trend towards a decline in the number of volunteers, nor towards any decrease in the average time that they devote to voluntary work. However, findings for the year 2000 are contradictory. The 'time budget study' suggests a substantial decrease between 1995 and 2000. The results of the survey that asked participants whether they ever did anything in connection with volunteering (the question, 'Do you ever do...') showed that the percentage of volunteers from the population aged 18 years and over went down from 46% to 32% (40% in 1990), and according to the diary of this survey the percentage of volunteers

17 Robert D. Putnam, *Bowling Alone,* (New York: Simon & Schuster, 2000). Compare Theda Skocpol, 'Advocates without members', in Theda Skocpol and Morris P. Fiorino (eds.), *Civic Engagement in American Democracy,* (Washington, D.C.: Brookings Institution Press, 1999).

18 For example, the phrasing of questions varies from, 'How many hours a week do you devote to the following activities?' to 'Have you, during the past year, done anything...?'

in an October week went down from 32% to 26% (29% in 1990). But the 'Cultural changes in the Netherlands' opinion survey shows no decline: percentages of the population aged 18 years and over spending an average of one hour or more each week doing voluntary work fluctuate between 26% in 1994 and 31% in 2002. In view of these contradictory results and earlier fluctuations in the time budget studies, it is too early to conclude that there has been a significant decrease in the number of volunteers. Several data sources do suggest a shift between age groups – there are more older people becoming involved, and they seem to spend relatively more time on volunteering. However, we do not yet know whether this is evidence of a generational shift (which will result in an overall decrease in volunteering as an inescapable outcome in the long run) or whether it is merely evidence of a delayed start, due to the fact that nowadays, students and starters on the labour market are busier.

The non-profit sector and civil society overlap as the vast majority of voluntary work takes place in the non-profit sector.[19] However, the economically important non-profit service industries are not voluntary associations, and most volunteers and voluntary associations do not consider themselves as contributing economically to a non-profit sector. As regards the non-profit sector, a rough division can be made between private non-profit service providers (some of them being associations) on the one hand and voluntary associations and interest organisations on the other.

Table 4 offers more information about the structure of the non-profit sector in the Netherlands. Public funds constitute the largest share (59%) of non-profit revenues in the Netherlands; private earnings (such as payments by clients, membership fees) are the second most important source with 38%; while private giving covers only 3% of the non-profit sector revenue. The division between paid and unpaid labour and of the financial resources differs markedly between the different fields in the non-profit sector. In the Netherlands, as well as in other countries,[20] a distinction can be made between typical 'welfare state services' (the three main fields mentioned in table 2 – health, social services, education and research – and the capital-intensive field of social housing) and

19 According to a survey in the mid-1990s, 83% of Dutch volunteers said they worked in non-profits, 10% in public agencies and 0% in commercial organisations (7% did not know).

20 Helmut K. Anheier and Jeremy Kendall (eds.), *Third Sector Policy at the Crossroads,* (London: Routledge, 2001); Jon Van Til, *Growing Civil Society,* (Bloomington & Indianapolis: Indiana University Press, 2001).

'the rest', with more membership and advocacy organisations that are normally associated with the idea of civil society.

The 'welfare state' non-profit services dominate the non-profit sector in the Netherlands; they account for 84% of total expenditures and 90% of total paid employment. Since these groups are so dominant, their sources of income largely determine the revenue structure of the entire non-profit sector. Private giving is insignificant for these services, as its share of just 1% indicates. For the other 'Hopkins-groups' combined, the share of private giving is 17%.

Table 4: Structure of the Dutch non-profit sector, 1995 (%)[21]

	Employment (FTE's)			Revenues		
	Paid	Unpaid	Expenditures	Public	Fees	Giving
Health	42	7	28	96	3	1
Education and research	27	14	20	91	8	1
Social services	19	21	13	66	31	3
Housing and development	2	0	23	7	93	0
Subtotal 'welfare state services'	90	42	84	66	33	1
Culture and recreation	4	36	6	27	65	8
Economic interest organisations	2	1	2	0	100	0
International	1	2	2	45	20	35
Environment	1	4	2	23	60	16
Law, advocacy and politics	1	6	1	4	85	11
Philanthropy and voluntarism	0	0	1	0	94	3
Religion	1	8	1	0	18	82
Subtotal 'other areas'	10	58	16	19	65	16
Total non-profit sector	100	100	100	59	38	3

Many of the present non-profit service providers once started as private initiatives of citizens. Over many decades they have become an integral part of the Dutch welfare state, as non-profits with often only a small amount of voluntary input (donations, volunteers or board members) and autonomy. Nowadays, even the non-profit status of many organisations can be disputed. Boundaries between non-profits and for-profits have become blurred, and hybrids of public and private, and non-commercial and commercial service

21 The term 'revenues' denotes percentages of total revenues; 'public' denotes tax revenues and social insurance premiums (including private health insurance); 'fees' denotes fees, charges, membership dues; 'giving' denotes private giving. Source: Data gathered by the Social and Cultural Planning Office of the Netherlands (www.scp.nl) for the Johns Hopkins comparative non-profit sector project (http://www.jhu.edu/~cnp/).

delivery are developing in various fields. Examples include the mergers of state/municipal schools and private non-profit schools to form collaborative structures; the combination of commercial and social tasks in housing associations and insurance companies; the incorporation of new commercial activities in hospitals; home care organisations that run temporary job agencies; and social welfare agencies that are entering competitive markets for coaching and consultancy, quite apart from the consequences of the introduction of similar concepts and tools of management, planning and control across all issues. The hybridization of non-profits is giving rise to discussions about the identity of the sector, the need for new forms and strategies, and calls for organisations to become more business-like as well as calls for a revival of the spirit of citizens' initiatives and the roots in the ethos of civil society.[22]

To summarize, the successful development of Dutch social organisations has led to a civil society with huge numbers of members and supporters but limited associational life, and to an economically significant non-profit service sector, with limited private initiative left.

5 Strongly Claimed but Weakly Supported Benefits

> In the recent literature, the revival of civic associations and the civic sphere is offered as a panacea for all the main illnesses of modern society – alienation, isolation, excessive anarchic and individualistic capitalism, social disintegration, and political indifference.[23]

> Within democratic theory a remarkable consensus is emerging around Tocqueville's view that the virtues and viability of a democracy depend on the robustness of its associational life.[24]

In many pleas for the revival of voluntary associations and civil society, we find combinations of arguments drawn from different political and theoretical

22 Anheier and Kendall, *supra* note 21; Paul Dekker, 'The Netherlands: From private initiatives to non-profits and back?', in Adalbert Evers and Jean-Louis Laville (eds.) *The Third Sector in Europe,* (Cheltenham (UK): Edward Elgar, 2004).

23 Yael Tamir, 'Revisiting the Civic Sphere', in Amy Gutman (ed.), *Freedom of Association,* (Princeton: Princeton University Press, 1998), at p. 214.

24 Warren, *supra* note 2, at p. 3.

traditions.[25] Communitarian arguments of mutual support, solidarity, group identity and moral development easily lead to liberal and pluralist arguments about the importance of freedoms of expression and association and the value of competing associations, and both of these arguments may be complemented by participatory arguments for a strong deliberative democracy, or corporatist arguments for strong intermediaries around the state.

Social capital and *public discourse* can be considered as the two basic benefits of voluntary associations and civil society.[26] The term 'social capital' refers to 'features of social organisation, such as trust, norms, and networks that can improve the efficiency of society by facilitating coordinated actions'[27] or '... connections among individuals – social networks and the norms of reciprocity and trustworthiness that arise from them.'[28] The term 'public discourse' refers to reflection on social problems, the articulation of collective values, and the development of political goals in a society. 'Social capital' and 'public discourse' both offer a good focus for analysing and discussing the contribution of volunteering from a civil society perspective. We use the term 'social capital' in a less comprehensive way than is usual in current discussions about the civil society. By placing public opinion formation next to social capital, and on an equal footing, we draw attention to the political side of civil society. Thus, we can highlight the fact that what is beneficial for the formation of public opinion is not necessarily so for the formation of social capital (for example pressure groups with little membership participation), and we avoid exaggerating the advantageous characteristics of the concept of 'social capital'.

Expectations of the benefits of the civil society and non-profit sector can be formulated on at least three levels:

1) Countries with a large civil society or non-profit sector do things better than countries without;
2) Voluntary associations and non-profit organisations do things better than public organisations and commercial enterprises (and individuals/private households/informal networks); and

25 Evidently, civil society is a more popular concept than non-profit, and advocates of the non-profit organisations often present these as parts of civil society to advance their case.

26 Dekker and Van den Broek, *supra* note 2.

27 Robert D. Putnam, Robert Leonardi and Raffaella Y. Nanetti, *Making Democracy Work,* (Princeton: Princeton University Press, 1993), at p. 167.

28 Putnam, *supra* note 17, at p. 19.

3) Individuals involved in voluntary associations and non-profit organisations do things better than individuals who are not involved.

While, I will concentrate on the micro-level of individual differences, I will first make some remarks about the other levels.

At the *macro-level*, there is a strong pluralist tradition in political science that views voluntary associations, in particular non-overlapping, 'cross-cutting' interest groups, as beneficial for democracy. Various publications have shown positive statistical 'effects' of the density of voluntary associations on national levels of social trust and political involvement, and on prosperity and the quality of political democracy.[29] Putnam's comparative analysis of twenty Italian regions revealed that the performance of regional government was strongly correlated to the 'degree of civic community'.[30] Civic community refers not only to individual characteristics such as reading newspapers, voting and organisational membership, but also to collective characteristics such as the presence of a tight network of social organisations, including a broad spectrum of organisations, ranging from trade unions through sports clubs to choirs.

On the other hand there are doubts on the part of some economists due to rent-seeking interest groups that disturb competition and slow down growth.[31] Furthermore, there are some very worrying political manifestations of vibrant associational life:

> The Weimar Republic had a vibrant and well-organised civil society that gave birth to and nurtured the Nazi movement. High levels of associational participation in pre-war Italy correlated very nicely with votes for Mussolini. The new civil societies of Russia and Eastern Europe are home to groups like the Russian National Union and the Romanian National Union, which organize large numbers of citizens around fascist ideologies. The former Yugoslavia arguably had one of the most developed

29 Putnam, *supra* note 17; Sjoerd Beugelsdijk, *Culture and Economic Development in Europe,* (Tilburg: Tilburg University Center Dissertation Series, 2003); Paul Dekker, Peter Ester and Henk Vinken, 'Civil Society, Social Trust and Democratic Involvement', in Wil Arts *et al.* (eds.) *The Cultural Diversity of European Unity,* (Leiden/Boston: Brill, 2003).

30 Putnam *supra* note 17.

31 Mancur Olson, *The Rise and Decline of Nations,* (New Haven: Yale University Press, 1982).

civil societies of any Eastern European country, and yet this did little to prevent the war and the 'worst massacre in Europe since WW II'.[32]

At the *meso-level* there are various ideas about the potential benefits of non-profits compared to for-profits and public organisations. In the Johns Hopkins Comparative Sector Project the following 'contributions' were gathered in the literature:[33]

- The service function: The service that is provided by non-profit organisations would be higher in quality, greater in equity and lower in cost.
- The innovation function: Non-profit organisations can be expected to be pioneers in their respective fields of operation.
- The advocacy and social change function: Non-profit organisations are involved in producing major policy innovations and are involved in active advocacy.
- The expressive function: Non-profit organisations are able to perform a broader function as vehicles of individual and group self-expression.
- The community building function: By encouraging social interaction, non-profit organisations help to create habits of trust and reciprocity that in turn contribute to a sense of community.

A cross-national comparative publication about the findings of the Johns Hopkins Comparative Sector Project as regards these benefits is underway; the Dutch researchers often found only limited evidence of the benefits in their case studies.[34]

Expectations at the *micro-level* are similar to expectations at the macro-level, although there is no logical need for this correspondence. A high level of civil

32 Simone Chambers, 'A Critical Theory of Civil Society', in Simone Chambers and Will Kymlicka (eds.), *Alternative Conceptions of Civil Society*, (Princeton: Princeton University Press, 2002), at p. 101.

33 Peter L. Hupe and Lucas C.P.M. Meijs (with Marianne H. Vorthoren) *Hybrid Governance – The Impact of the Non-profit Sector in the Netherlands,* (The Hague: Social and Cultural Planning Office, 2002) at p. 132. Possible 'drawbacks' were surveyed too, for instance 'particularism' (by being responsive to special groups, non-profits can be discriminatory in their operations), 'paternalism' – (the liberty of individuals can be constrained because of the patronising rules on non-profit organisations) and 'amateurism' – (because of their reliance on volunteers, non-profits may not be able to take advantage of latest techniques, or they may relay on the unique skills of a particularly effective individual that cannot easily be replicated).

34 Hupe and Meijs, *supra* note 33, at p. 138.

society activity can stimulate a culture of trust among all citizens, without marked differences between those who are active and those who are not.

The relationship between social and political participation has been an important issue in the study of political behaviour for decades. Much research in this field has supported the conclusion of Almond and Verba:

> [A]ny membership – passive membership or membership in a nonpolitical organisation – has an impact on political competence. Membership in some association, even if the individual does not consider the membership politically relevant and even if it does not involve his active participation, does lead to a more competent citizenry.[35]

Almond and Verba observed an impact of organisational membership on politics, but a greater impact among 'officers', defined as those who hold any form of official position within their organisation or who actively participate in the decision-making of voluntary associations. Almond and Verba argued that active participation trains people politically. Apart from active membership, multiple memberships and the perception of one's organisation as a political entity also strengthen the political impact of social participation.[36]

Many researchers after Almond and Verba have found that organisation members are more likely to be active in political life than are non-members. However, the causality is still a matter of discussion, many of the statistical relationships posited have been weak, exceptions have been recorded, and certain caveats have been entered.[37] Different sorts of association can have different effects on the political behaviour of their members, and the effects may also vary between different social groups. Membership may be a collective resource for political involvement which is particularly relevant for people who lack individual resources. Some research suggests that lower status groups need

35 Gabriel A. Almond and Sidney Verba, *The Civic Culture*, (Newbury Park: Sage, 1989 [the first edition was 1963]) at p. 265.

36 Almond and Verba, *supra* note 35, at pp. 256-265.

37 Compare Marvin E. Olsen, *Participatory Pluralism,* (Chicago: Nelson-Hall.Olsen, 1982); Geraint Parry, George Moyser and Neil Day, *Political Participation and Democracy in Britain,* (Cambridge: Cambridge University Press, 1992), at pp. 85-119; Sidney Verba, Kay Lehman Schlozman and Henry E. Brady, *Voice and Equality,* (Cambridge: Harvard University Press, 1995); Jan W. van Deth, 'Introduction', in Jan W. van Deth, (ed.) *Private Groups and Public Life,* (London: Routledge, 1997); Jaak B. Billiet and Bart Cambré, 'Social capital, Active Membership in Voluntary Associations and some Aspects of Political Participation', in Jan W. van Deth *et al.* (eds.) *Social Capital and European Democracy,* (London: Routledge, 1999); Putnam *supra* note 17, at pp. 336-344.

group-based processes of political mobilization if they are to catch up with the higher status groups in terms of political activity.[38]

In the literature, several reasons are discussed for why social participation breeds political involvement.[39] Verba, Schlozman, and Brady mention three aspects of the 'politicizing experience' of participation in non-political institutions:

> For one thing, undertaking activities that themselves have nothing to do with politics ... can develop organisational and communication skills that are transferable to politics. In addition, these non-political institutions can act as the locus of attempts of political recruitment: church and organisation members make social contacts and, thus, become part of networks through which requests for participation in politics are mediated. Moreover, those who take part in religious or organisational activity are exposed to political cues and messages – as when a minister gives a sermon on a political topic or when organisation members chat informally about politics in a meeting.[40]

Besides 'civic skills' (such as learning to participate in meetings, to chair meetings, to write letters and so on) and formal and informal political information and mobilization, voluntary association may also function as 'schools for democracy' in a broader sense: people learn to tolerate and to deal with diverging opinions, they become informed about what is happening in their neighbourhood and in the wider community; the organisation provides social contact, it may broaden the sphere of interest, and engender norms of co-operation and trust among its members.

In comparative European research with data from the European Values Studies, we have found, at the individual level, positive statistical effects of participation in voluntary associations on social trust and the political involvement indicators in most countries.[41] Across the board the effects were strongest for political action – suggesting that participation-to-participation mechanisms might be more important than the socializing impact of associational life – and education appears to be a more important factor than leisure participation in encouraging people to get involved in democratic politics, and to trust their

38 Walter Korpi, *The Democratic Class Struggle,* (London: Routledge and Kegan Paul, 1983); Verba *et al., supra* note 37, at pp. 19, 328.

39 It is notable that the reverse causality, from political involvement to social participation has received very little attention.

40 Verba *et al., supra* note 37, at p. 40.

41 Dekker and Van den Broek, *supra* note 2; Dekker *et al., supra* note 29.

fellow citizens. This finding, also reported in other research, should temper high expectations of the social and political blessings of associational life. Policy-makers who care about the loss of social trust and political involvement might do better to keep focused on their efforts to improve education rather than simply joining the calls for community and the revival of associational life. Our findings confirm that associational life can play a positive role in the development of, what Almond and Verba term, 'competent citizenry', but it is *not* a compensation for a lack of individual resources. In the next section, I will examine in more detail some Dutch findings.

6 A closer look at individual differences in the Netherlands

Table 5 offers an overview of different distributions of passive and active membership in various sorts of organisations in the Netherlands in 2002, and differences in what has become the core indicator of social capital in population surveys: (generalized) social trust. The survey question was: 'Generally speaking, would you say that people can be trusted, or that you can't be too careful in dealing with people?' Possible answers are 'Most people can be trusted', 'Can't be too careful' and 'Don't know', and the first answer is supposed to indicate social trust.

Table 5 demonstrates clearly that there is no simple general relationship between involvement and social trust. As far as differences in trust are a consequence of involvement, they call for more in-depth analyses of associational life and the members' experiences.[42]

As regards the political effects of associational involvement, we first analyse data from the Dutch 'Civil society and volunteering' survey held in the winter of 1996/97. Respondents received a list with ten 'kinds of organisation', eight of which are summarized in the five groups listed in table 6.[43] Are people

42 Compare Dietlind Stolle, 'Getting to Trust', in Paul Dekker and Eric M. Uslaner (eds.) *Social Capital and Participation in Everyday Life,* (London: Routledge, 2001).

43 Nine sectors are identified either by the organisations as such ('trade unions, professional organisations, employee organisations') or by their interests or target groups (organisations for the environment and animal welfare; organisations for children and young people) and 'any other organisation or group'. One question is 'Are you a member of or a contributor to an organisation of this kind?', another question is 'Do you ever do any voluntary work for an organisation of this kind?' As regards 'membership', the question does not distinguish 'horizontal' face-to-face from 'vertical' mailing-list organisations. Respondents are even explicitly invited to include non-membership

who are members of voluntary organisations and who volunteer in different fields more involved in politics?

Table 5: Membership categories and social trust in these categories: categories in the population (%) and those with trust in the category (% trust).[44]

	Does not belong to this group		Does belong but never participates		Has participated once or twice		Has participated more than twice	
	%	% trust	%	% trust	%	% trust	%	% trust
A political party, club or association	85	54	10	61	2	62	3	62
A trade union or professional association	77	54	15	62	4	65	4	54
A church or other religious organisation	66	54	14	51	4	52	16	65
A sport group, hobby or leisure club	39	52	8	55	8	45	45	60
A charitable organisation or group	68	53	14	61	8	52	10	67
A neighbourhood association or group	76	55	10	60	8	51	6	55

As expected, positive relationships between social participation and political involvement predominate over cases of statistical insignificance and one negative relationship (members of churches show less political participation, even when adjusted for the effects of gender, age and education. To give an impression of the extent of the differences: membership vs. non-membership of a leisure organisation makes a difference of 87% vs. 77% for the intention to vote, 11%

organisations by the formulation 'a member of or a contributor to'. One of the nine sectors combines political parties with 'other organisations with a general social or idealistic goal (such as Amnesty International, a fair trade shop, etc.); because we are interested in the relationship between social and political involvement, this sector is left out. The same applies to 'any other group'.

44 The survey was taken in 2002, from a population aged 18 and over. Participants were asked the following question to determine membership categories: 'People sometimes belong to different kinds of groups or associations. The list below contains different types of groups. For each of type of group, please ... say whether you have participated in the activities of this group in the past 12 months.' Source: International Social Survey Project (Social network II module).

vs. 8% for involvement in party politics, and 56% vs. 46% for feelings of political efficacy. Volunteering vs. non-volunteering in the field of interest organisations makes a difference of 90% vs. 79% for the intention to vote, 21% vs. 7% for involvement in party politics, and 61% vs. 49% for feelings of political efficacy.

Table 6: Political involvement[a] as a statistical effect of social participation, 1997,[45] (unadjusted odds ratios (or) and adjusted odds ratios (aor).[b])

		Vote		Party		Efficacy	
(% of population)		or	aor	or	aor	or	aor
Membership:							
Leisure (sports, hobby, cultural or women's association)	(43)	1.4*	1.4*	1.4*	1.0	1.5*	1.2
Service (children, school, health care, social welfare)	(22)	2.1*	1.6*	1.7*	1.5*	1.5*	1.3*
Interest (union, neighbourhood council, action committee, etc.)	(39)	2.3*	1.6*	1.9*	1.3*	1.8*	1.4*
Environment (animal welfare, environment, conservation)	(31)	1.9*	1.2	1.9*	1.4*	1.9*	1.4*
Religion (church, philosophical organisation)	(43)	1.4*	1.4*	1.4*	1.6*	0.9	1.0
Volunteering:							
Leisure	(24)	2.0*	1.4*	1.5*	1.0	1.5*	1.1
Service	(21)	1.8*	1.4*	1.4*	1.0	1.5*	1.2
Interest	(16)	2.2*	1.6*	3.4*	2.7*	1.7*	1.4*
Environment	(3)	1.4	0.9	4.4*	3.0*	2.3*	1.8*
Religion	(16)	1.8*	1.5*	1.8*	1.6*	1.2	1.1

a: The intention to vote (81% yes), involvement in party politics (9% yes) and one item for political efficacy (50% disagreeing with the statement 'People like me have no influence on what the government does.')

b: Odds ratios are adjusted for the effects of the other membership or the other volunteering categories, and for sex, age and education the other indicators in the column. A coefficient above 1 means a positive effect of the indicator on trust, a coefficient below 1 means a negative effect. Significance: * p<.05 (two-tailed).

45 Population aged 18 years and over. Source: Civil Society and Volunteering Survey 1997, conducted by the Social and Cultural Planning Office of the Netherlands (www.scp.nl).

How important is volunteering compared to passive membership, and how important are these two indicators for social participation, compared to the level of education, traditionally the best single simple factor to explain variations in political participation? To keep the analysis manageable, the sectors in table 7 are combined: 82% of the population are members of an organisation in at least one of sectors mentioned in table 5, 48% have done voluntary work in at least one of sectors. Combined, 16% are neither a member nor a volunteer, 35% are only a member, 47% are both a member and a volunteer, and 2% are only a volunteer. If we merge the latter two groups, we get three categories of social participation: none (no membership and no volunteering), passive membership only and volunteering.

Table 7: Political involvement in social participation and educational categories (%)[46]

		Education			
	Social participation	Low	Middle	High	Total
Vote	None	53	72	88	68
	passive membership	70	84	88	80
	volunteering	80	84	96	86
	Total	70	83	92	81
Party	None	1	2	10	3
	passive membership	3	8	14	8
	Volunteering	10	10	21	13
	Total	5	8	17	9
Efficacy	None	20	49	57	39
	passive membership	31	47	70	47
	Volunteering	38	59	72	57
	Total	32	53	70	51

Table 7 shows the positive political involvement effects of social participation in general and for each educational level. However, activity as a volunteer does not always have an additional effect to passive membership. The table further suggests that education is still at least as important a factor as membership or volunteering in explaining differences in political behaviour. Once again, this

46 Survey taken in 1997, from a population aged 18 and over. Source: Civil Society and Volunteering Survey 1997 (see note 45).

cautions against overstating the importance of associational factors compared to individual resources.[47]

Table 8 displays the effects of two sorts of civil society involvement on two sorts of trust: social trust, measured with the illustrative trust question used in table 5, and political trust, measured as disagreement with the statement that ministers and state secretaries mainly pursue their own interest.

Table 8: Social and political trust as statistical effects of memberships,[48] (%) and adjusted odds ratios (aor)[a].

	Social trust		Political trust	
	%	Aor	%	Aor
Member of probably a 'face-to-face'- organisation:[b]				
- No	48		53	
- Yes (59%)	64	1,6***	64	1,3**
Member of probably a 'mailing list'- organisation:[c]				
- No	47		52	
- Yes (46%)	69	2,0***	68	1,6***
Sex:				
- Male	57		61	
- Female (50%)	58	1,1	58	0,9
Age:				
- 18-39	60		62	
- 40-59 (41%)	61	1,0	65	1,1
- 60 and over (30%)	50	0,8*	50	0,7*
Educational level:				
- Low	41		42	
- Middle (46%)	56	1,4*	62	1,8***
- High (31%)	71	2,4***	70	2,3***

a: Odds ratios are adjusted for the effects of the other indicators in the column. A coefficient above 1 means a positive effect of the indicator on trust, a coefficient below 1 means a negative effect. Significance: *** p<.001, ** p<0.01 and * p<.05 (two-tailed).
b: Is a member or contributor of a sports club or an association for culture, arts , hobby or a common interest.
c: Is a member or contributor of an organisation for the environment, nature conservation, third world, human rights or peace.

47 Ken Newton, 'Social Capital and Democracy', in Bob Edwards, Michel W. Foley and Mario Diani (eds.), *Beyond Tocqueville,* (Hanover: Tufts University Press, 2001); Dekker and Van den Broek, *supra* note 2.

48 Survey taken in 2002, from a population aged 18 and over. Source: Parliamentary Election Study 2002; weighted results (see: http://www.bsk.utwente.nl/skon/).

This table again shows some statistical support for the benefits of associational involvement and for the equally important impact of education. Interestingly, the 'mailing list' organisations do not show smaller effects than the 'face-to-face' organisations, although they offer hardly any possibility to develop trust by interaction. This absence of differences raises serious doubts about whether the data is evidences for genuine effects of associating, rather than the result of self-selection.[49]

7 Conclusions: From Claims to Aims

The reason for the lack of strong effects of participation in voluntary associations at an individual level could be that the formation of social capital and public opinion is increasingly taking place in different settings, such as the informal sphere, via the media, in relationships of paid employment and in the sphere of collective provisions. Voluntary association is distributed across the whole of society and characteristics of non-profits are being copied by public organisations.

In addition, the organisations of the existing civil society are not the voluntary associations of the stereotypical civil society, and the actual participation in them is not what it is theoretically assumed to be. In this connection we can refer to three trends:

- Private initiatives that were once undertaken by volunteers are developing into non-profits and hybrid 'service industries'.[50] On average, they probably still play a bigger role than public and commercial organisations in fulfilling the intermediary, social-integrative and political-expressive functions which are the extensions of the ideals of civil society, even though they can no longer be regarded as forming part of that civil society.
- Associations and interest organisations are developing from 'face-to-face' to 'mailing list' organisations (compare Table 3). This is not necessarily unhelpful for the formation of public opinion in a modern 'media democracy', however, the internal democracy of the organisations is problematic

49 Compare Marc Hooghe, 'Voluntary associations and democratic attitudes', in Marc Hooghe and Dietlind Stolle (eds.), *Generating Social Capital* (New York: Palgrave, 2003); Per Selle and Kristin Strømsnes, 'Membership and democracy', in Dekker and Uslaner, *supra* note 43.

50 Dekker, *supra* note 22.

and the formation of genuine social capital (stored in social networks and not just in social attitudes) is virtually impossible.

- Voluntary work is shifting away from 'active membership' towards 'unpaid work'.[51] The extra activity within and from associations is being replaced by genuine (albeit unpaid) work in which the mutual relationships are determined not by the volunteers themselves but by officers of the organisation. Although this is not an entirely negative trend – precisely because of the increased professionalism, and lower group involvement, new people can be recruited and new social relationships can arise – voluntary associations are nevertheless losing their force.

Developments such as these reduce the capacity of (former) organisations and activities of civil society to form social capital and shape public opinion. But does this necessarily undermine the idea of the civil society, and is it a reason to discount the political and public interest in civil society as so much useless nostalgia? No, just as Gandhi felt that it was not the West but rather the Western ideals which were worth striving for, so we should not focus too much on the practice of civil society, but should rather translate the idea of civil society into a perspective for change.

An interesting starting point for this shift from claims to aims is found in the work of the American organisational theorist Charles Perrow. He presents 'in roughly declining level of importance' the following criteria to determine whether a non-profit contributes to civil society: that a 'public, collective good is produced, using volunteer labour in substantial amount, with room for social interaction that is not on organisational terms, and below market wages are paid.'[52] In this perspective, a 'public, collective good', which is designed for all relevant groups outside the organisation, is better than a collective good that is merely for the members of the organisation, or a specific subgroup of society. The substantial volunteer labour criterion implies that goals and operations of the organisations have to be changed if around half of the volunteers have stopped their contribution, thus the threat of exit can change goals and operations. Free social interaction means that members of the organisation socialize as persons and not as employees who are restricted by the interests

51 Paul Dekker, 'On the Prospects of Volunteering in Civil Society', (2002) 4 (3) *Voluntary Action,* at pp. 31-48.

52 Charles Perrow, 'The Rise of Non-profits and the Decline of Civil Society', in Helmut K. Anheier, (ed.) *Organisational Theory and the Non-profit Form,* (London: Centre for Civil Society, London School of Economics, 2001), at p. 34.

of the organisation. Paying employees less than market wages must be possible because of compensatory gratification such as the enjoyment of contributing to a common good, or the higher quality of social interactions. According to the fulfilment of these criteria, Perrow talks about 'good', 'intermediate' and 'bad' non-profits. While his specific criteria may be disputable, normative criteria are clearly essential in discussing claims by non-profits to be part of civil society, or their aims to become so.

Aside from civil society discourse, there are arguments for private non-profits as providers of public services. I will briefly consider four arguments.

(1) Compared to public service providers, private ones are still better able to deal with cultural diversity in the population. Services that are highly salient in this respect, such as educating children, homes for the elderly and other long-term full-time care and assistance with moral and psychological questions, are the traditional fields of private initiatives. Old religious and ideological divisions have lost much of their significance, but the argument may apply to new groups in a multicultural society.[53] However, in the Netherlands at present, 'multicultural society' is often seen as a threat to the tradition of allowing and supporting denominational organisations in delivering public goods with public money to particular groups. The tradition is challenged by new organisations that might hamper the integration of immigrants. An example in Dutch society is the development of Islamic schools. The benefits of these new non-profits are controversial because of possible negative effects on learning the Dutch language and the integration of immigrants, but in general, non-profits can positively buffer the tension between the equality of citizens and their particularities as people with problems and needs, such as pupils and patients and so on.

(2) A second argument in favour of non-profits is that they are still better able to attract voluntary resources. They can appeal to religious obligations, group loyalties and a sense of community; they might be more easily trusted because of their smaller scale or the status and more immediate accountability of their leaders; or they can meet a more diffuse demand for identity and exclusiveness among potential volunteers and philanthropists. The availability of additional financial means, unpaid labour and resources for self-regulation are attractive assets of private non-profits for policymakers who want to develop models of 'new public management'.

53 Compare Will Kymlicka, 'Ethnic Associations and Democratic Citizenship', in Amy Gutman, (ed.) *Freedom of Association,* (Princeton: Princeton University Press, 1998).

The main challenge will be to organise relations between governments and non-profits in a way that both autonomy and interdependencies are recognised, and opportunistic behaviour is discouraged.

(3) Thirdly, private non-profits might offer the best setting for the development of professional organisations. In various areas of public services a reassessment of professionalism seems underway. After many years of disciplining professionals to organisation-oriented and cost-conscious employees, it is felt now that in many organisations a caring professional ethos has suffered too much from the bureaucratic and economic logics. The calls for more professional autonomy and more respect for the street-level professionals are directed against politicians and government officials, as well as market-oriented managers. They apply to schools, hospitals, nursery homes and social work organisations, irrespective of their public or private status. However, because of their legal autonomy, private non-profits might be in a better position to experiment with new forms of professional self-government.

(4) 'Surpluses of purchasing power' form the basis of a fourth argument. Citizens sometimes want to spend more money on collective services than they are supposed to, or than they are allowed to. For reasons of equality it is difficult to allow people to spend extra money on the state school of their children, or the state nursing home of their parents. This leads to the absurd situation that people can spend whatever they can afford on private goods, but not on public goods. Or they have to choose between poor public services or purely private commercial services. Non-profits can organize group solidarity between the large-scale solidarity of the welfare state and the individual escape to the market. Again, non-profits can buffer the tension between the equality of citizens, and their specificity in terms of wealth and willingness to spend extra money for the benefit of a smaller group of citizens. Politically, this is a very controversial argument in the Netherlands: what level of parental contribution is acceptable for primary schools whose basic expenses are paid by (or should principally be covered by) public funds? How much inequality is acceptable between primary schools as basic facilities for all citizens? The question of equality and minimum standards of collective provisions will probably be an important topic in the years ahead. Will we stick to the 'social-democratic' model of generally accessible, high-quality general public services, or accept that public services are minimal services and that the better-off look for better facilities in the market, in line with a more liberal ideology, or can we find a 'communitarian' way of using group solidarities for the benefit of all?

These are arguments concerning private non-profits that are basically financed with public money. Recently, 'civil society' has been introduced in a policy paper of the Dutch government more or less as an alternative to services paid with collective means. As part of a process to 'modernize' the government wants to 'give responsibilities back to civil society'.[54] The purpose is to make people less 'dependent' on the government and it is completely irrelevant whether they find alternatives in informal arrangements, commercial services or voluntary initiatives. This use of civil society for everything except the state is somewhat unusual, but it demonstrates the popularity of the term. Civil society might however be relevant for Dutch politics in a more authentic sense as a sphere of voluntary associations and self-government. In that sense it can be seen as an alternative sphere of social and political involvement:

> Within national states, both government and the private sector can be humbled a little by a growing civil society that absorbs some of the public aspirations to self-government, without casting off its liberal character as a non-coercive association of equals. Because they tend to their own affairs and take more responsibility on themselves, citizens inhabiting a vibrant civil society worry less about elections and leaders and term limits and scandals; and they simultaneously free themselves from the 'free' markets that otherwise imprison them in a commercial mentality that leaves no room for community or for spirit.[55]

This is a highly topical suggestion in view of the political uproar in the Netherlands in 2002.[56] There is still discussion about whether the social unrest and electoral turbulences of that year were the result of deeper disaffection, primarily an expression of boredom with or irritation at the politicians in power, or just a hype created by politicians and the media. Whatever it was, a higher level of involvement in politics has not been the outcome. Political democracy continues to be basically a 'spectators' democracy' with citizens who oscillate between excessive expectations of their own influence and indifference, but lack democratic experience. Activities such as board membership in the associations of civil society, voluntary participation in the administration of non-profits and so on, offer opportunities for practical democratic involvement, and for developing a more realistic approach to politics and government.

54 See website: www.andereoverheid.nl. (Last visited February 2005.)

55 Benjamin R. Barber, *Jihad vs. McWorld,* (New York: Random House, 1995) at p.285.

56 Paul Dekker, Martijn Lampert and Frits Spangenberg, 'Political disaffection: The Netherlands in 2002', Paper presented at the annual Wapor Conference, Prague, September 2003 (available from the author, p.dekker@scp.nl).

8

LAW AND ASSOCIATIONAL LIFE IN BRITAIN

Richard Fries

1 INTRODUCTION

There is a long history of 'associational life' in Britain. Much of this has consisted of informal local activity, whether in pursuit of private objectives of a social or recreational nature, or serving a more public interest. Linked to, and growing out of, informal action are a wide range of organised associations and other citizen bodies. It has become fashionable, especially in academic circles, to refer to all of this activity, both informal and organised, as civil society. The British experience is characterised by the fact that historically the state accepted only a minimal responsibility for social provision, looking to individual citizens and communities to undertake much of that which is regarded as the function of the public sector in modern states.

The 20th Century was marked by the growth of state involvement, culminating in the creation of the Welfare State in the mid-century, under which government, central and local, took lead responsibility for welfare and other social provision, for education, health and other services necessary to the public well-being in the modern world. In recent years however the contribution of the citizen, individually and in the community, has become increasingly important. The development of the legal and institutional framework – and its continuing reform, a matter very much on the current political agenda – is determined by

Yuwen Li (Ed.), *Freedom of Association in China and Europe: Comparative Perspectives in Law and Practice*, © 2005 Koninklijke Brill NV, Leiden. Printed in The Netherlands, pp. 283-308.

this experience. This paper aims to trace this influence in describing the situation in Britain now.[1]

In Britain the most widely used term covering the sphere of organised citizen activity is 'voluntary sector', at least among those involved in it. The wider public and the media most often refer to 'charity', which is in many respects a narrower term, both in law and colloquial usage. There is no agreed definition of what the voluntary sector covers; nor, except for statistical purposes, is one needed, since it is neither an administrative nor governmental term nor is it a legal concept. It may be helpful at the outset to set out the main terms used in Britain, with an indication of their commonly accepted meanings.

1.1 Main Terminology

Voluntary sector itself refers to organisations which are voluntary in one or more respect. The main components of voluntary bodies are voluntary governance, either by trustees or members; the use of volunteers, either entirely or alongside paid staff; and reliance on voluntary funding, either from public fundraising or other forms of independent funding, regardless of whether public or governmental funds are used as well.

Voluntary action is linked to the notion of voluntary bodies, and refers to activities and programmes started on independent 'citizen' initiative. 'Civic engagement' and 'community action' are other ways of expressing similar ideas. The reforms planned by the present Government place much emphasis on this dimension, and seek to encourage 'active citizenship'. The department of government with lead responsibility is the Active Communities Directorate in the Home Office.

Charity, and the related notion of philanthropy, refer, in ordinary usage, to 'doing good', in particular to helping to relieve poverty, sickness and other ills of life. Charitable activity has a long history and has been through many forms. Its reputation, and its role in British life, has likewise fluctuated, particularly in relation to the role of the State. Charity is underpinned by an old and complex legal code. The legal meaning of charity is however significantly different from the popular meaning, being much broader in important respects.

1 At the time of writing, a Charities Bill is before Parliament. It will give effect to proposals for fundamental legal and institutional reforms.

Mutuality covers a parallel, and to some extent overlapping, tradition of self-help. This refers to a range of organisations in which the members cooperate together to achieve common ends – hence the alternative name of cooperatives. Such bodies may also be called friendly societies or benevolent societies.

The terms *not-for-profit* (or *non profit*) organisations and *non-governmental organisations* (NGOs) are used. Not-for-profits is, however, more commonly used in the USA which, though having the same common law legal system, does not retain the charity law system to the same degree as Britain. NGO tends to be used to refer to charities and other voluntary bodies operating overseas.

To avoid making the distinctions set out above the term *third sector* is sometimes used, as a distinction from the public and market sectors.

2 The Extent of the British Voluntary Sector

It is impossible to give a precise figure for the size of the voluntary sector in Britain. Most obviously this is due to the fact that there are no registration or administrative requirements which have to be undertaken in order to set up a voluntary body as such. Less obviously it is impossible to establish a precise figure because, in the absence of any legal or administrative requirements for establishing a voluntary body, the point at which an informal grouping of citizens constitutes a voluntary body is an arbitrary judgment.

It is estimated that there are over half a million voluntary bodies in the United Kingdom. The largest group, discussed at length below, are registered charities – there are nearly 190,000 based in England and Wales. The restriction to England and Wales is due to the fact that registration is the responsibility of the Charity Commission, whose responsibilities are confined to England and Wales. When allowance is made for charities based in Scotland and Northern Ireland, and charities which for various reasons are exempt from registration, the total number of charities (which can only be an estimate) in the whole of the United Kingdom is about a quarter of a million.

There are a great many local community bodies in Britain. For the reasons given above no precise figure can be given for such bodies, but it is estimated that they amount to around a quarter of a million in total.

Many voluntary bodies do not have charitable status since they do not meet the public benefit requirements described below. The largest category are sports clubs, which are not regarded as charitable because they are for their members' benefit, rather than that of the wider public. They are estimated to amount to some 150,000. Other categories of non-charitable voluntary organisations include some 30,000 cultural and arts organisations and 20,000 social clubs.[2] Thus altogether there are over 200,000 non-charitable voluntary organisations, and a grand total of up to three quarters of a million voluntary organisations in the United Kingdom.[3]

3 Civil Society

The term civil society has old historical and philosophical origins. It has been revived and promoted by students of the voluntary sector, including some practitioners, to refer to the whole of the 'third sector'. There is no agreed definition of 'civil society'. It does however exclude government, the public sector and profitable commercial organisations (the market sector). The term is used to cover a variable range of institutions. At its widest, it refers to the sphere of life which is not determined by government or the market. It often means the extension of family and neighbourhood, as the sphere which individuals determine among themselves. In Britain political parties are normally regarded as part of the political process, distinct from civil society.[4] Trade unions are also not normally regarded as part of civil society. They are given legal rights and status under special legislation.[5]

'Civil Society' often refers to organisations within it. In that usage it is comparable to such terms in the voluntary sector and third sector (though, as discussed in the next paragraph, with an added nuance of virtue). A convenient definition of civil society is provided by the social philosopher Ernest Gellner:

2 An authoritative survey of the 'charitable and wider not-for-profit sector' in the United Kingdom is contained in chapter 2 of the UK Government's Strategy Unit Report, *Private Action, Public Benefit*, (Cabinet Office, September 2002) at pp 13 – 28. Available at: http://www.number-10.gov.uk/su/voluntary/report/downloads/strat-data.pdf (Last visited February 2005.)

3 The Charities Bill, referred to in footnote 1, may alter this, especially in respect of sports clubs.

4 Political parties are subject to separate electoral law, though participation in the political process is open to any lawful organisation and indeed to individuals not backed by any organisation.

5 This is a relatively recent development – securing employment rights was an important part of the history of associational life in Britain during and beyond the Industrial Revolution.

'that set of diverse non-governmental institutions which is strong enough to counterbalance the State'.[6]

Civil society is part of political debate. It is regarded as a necessary component of a healthy and diverse society, counterbalancing the power of the State and of profit making organisations. Exaggerated claims have been made for the superior values of civil society organisations and it is increasingly becoming recognised that the mere fact of being non-governmental and non-profit-making does not of itself give civil society organisations a higher virtue than public or market bodies. That there should continue to be freedom to pursue private ends, provided they are compatible with the wider public well-being is however a fundamental principle of the British constitution. It has now become an established part of public policy that 'civil society' organisations in the community should play an important role in providing services. How civil society should be underpinned and encouraged through the legal and regulatory framework is the basic issue. As noted in the introduction, present government policy widely reflects this concern.

4 Principles of Law and Regulation for Civil Society

The fundamental principle of civil society as it has developed in Britain is freedom of association. People can come together to pursue legitimate ends freely. The role of the law is seen as underpinning and encouraging the responsible exercise of that right. Processes of registration and accountability should reflect that principle and facilitate, not inhibit and control, the creation and operation of civil society organisations.

The qualification, that ends pursued by civil society organisations must be legitimate, highlights the fact that the right to create associations is not absolute. Organisations which promote purposes which run contrary to the public interest, for example because they are criminal or create civil disharmony, cannot claim the right to freedom of association. How the balance is struck between the right to pursue private purposes and the wider public interest is one of the most sensitive issues in the law and regulation of civil society. It is especially topical in the post 9/11 world in relation to terrorism.

The right of free expression is another fundamental principle of civil society. Again it cannot be absolute. Constraints on, for example, inflammatory language

6 Ernest Gellner, *Conditions of Liberty: Civil Society and its Rivals*, (2nd Edition, London: Penguin, 1996), at p. 5.

that threatens communal harmony counterbalance freedom of expression. But limitations on the involvement of civil society organisations in the political process must be balanced against the principle of free expression.

The need for integrity and good practice in civil society organisations, and the legal and regulatory arrangements to secure it, must reflect the principles of freedom of association. The starting point is the need for self-regulation, whereby the civil society sphere promotes its own standards. Constitutional arrangements that secure independent accountability, thus maintaining public confidence, are complementary to the development of good standards within the sector.

In recent decades the European Convention on Human Rights and Fundamental Freedoms (ECHR) has come to play a fundamental role in safeguarding the responsible exercise of the basic human freedoms. The ECHR gives legal backing to the exercise of freedom of association[7] and the other freedoms. States like the United Kingdom, which are signatories to the ECHR, are bound by it and alleged breaches may be challenged in the European Court of Human Rights. At the same time the ECHR recognises that the exercise of the freedoms cannot be absolute. It contains qualifications which permit action which overrides freedom of association and the other freedoms in the interests of public safety and similar public considerations. However, the standard of proof required by the Court before it will allow the exercise of the basic freedoms to be set aside is high. In the United Kingdom, the Human Rights Act 1998 was enacted recently to give effect in domestic law to the rights and freedoms expressed in the ECHR.

5 Charity

Charity is the 'dominant form' for civil society organisations in Britain. That is to say, charity is both the most common legal form for voluntary organisations to take, and it is also the most highly developed in legal and regulatory terms. Colloquially, the word 'charity' means helping the poor and needy. In law, the essence of charity is public benefit. Thus voluntary organisations which serve the public benefit may be charities.

The British legal system is based on common law. That is to say, the legal tradition developed by the courts over centuries determines the law as it is in

7 See ECHR, Art. 11.

the present and how it develops with changing circumstances. Britain no longer has a pure common law system, in so far as statutes passed by Parliament set the framework within which the courts apply common law principles. In the case of charity law, however, the role of Acts of Parliament is less than it is, for example, in the criminal law. A description of charity law must therefore describe its historical origins and growth.

The principles of common law are important in understanding charity law. It does not operate on the basis of a definition of charity, even in legal terms. Rather, it is based on a set of principles applied and adapted by the courts, and by the Charity Commission, which in this respect has the powers of a court. This makes charity law a complex area to describe.[8] The advantage, in the view of common law practitioners at any rate, is that the underlying principles of charity law can be adapted to changing circumstances as the needs of society, and indeed the role of charities, change. This capacity of charity law to grow and change 'organically' is an important feature of the common law system. In the view of charity lawyers this virtue outweighs the disadvantages of complexity and obscurity – complaints levelled at the system by reform-minded critics. The proposals for reform currently under consideration in the Charities Bill introduced into Parliament at the end of 2004 envisage giving charity law a statutory basis, but stop short of replacing charity law entirely by a statutory system.

The law on charity as currently applied is conventionally dated to the Preamble to the Charitable Uses Act 1601. Charity and charity law did not of course start in 1601. Many charitable foundations go back much further than 1601. The Sheffield Town Trust, for example, celebrated its 700th anniversary in 1998. This is a good example of a civic foundation with a continuous, if varied, history of philanthropy going back over centuries. Its role has essentially been to help the poor of the city of Sheffield. Many foundations in the housing, health and educational field long predate 1601: many schools, hospitals and almshouses (providing accommodation for the poor) all have a history going back many centuries.

The history is important in understanding the 1601 Act and its relationship to present day law. Throughout Europe, charitable foundations were an important part of that which we would now call social provision, reflecting then

8 Being based on common law, charity law is set out in textbooks rather than statute law. There are a number of authoritative textbooks, in particular Hubert Picarda, *The Law and Practice Relating to Charities*, (3rd Edition, London: Butterworths, 1999), and Peter Luxton, *The Law of Charities*, (Oxford: Oxford University Press, 2001).

as now the wish of rich benefactors to contribute to the well being of society by helping the needy – and their wish to preserve their names as benefactors. What is distinctive in British history was the consequence of the Reformation and the dissolution of the monasteries marking the end of the Middle Ages, and the distinctively religious based social provision of that era. 1601 was a period of social and economic change and upheaval. The 1601 Act was part of a set of measures, of which the Poor Law was the most prominent, by which Elizabeth I sought to secure good order in Tudor England.

The 1601 Act itself, long ago repealed, was designed to strengthen the law against the abuse of charitable resources, to ensure that they were used for the intended charitable purpose in the public interest. The Preamble to the 1601 Act is a list of charitable purposes. It is neither a definition of charity, nor a comprehensive enumeration of all that was regarded as charitable then. What the Act did was restate what were regarded as purposes which served the public interest in post medieval society. It covered such issues as maintaining highways and bridges, as well as more obviously charitable purposes like tending for the sick and needy. The Preamble was thus a distinctive initiative of the monarch to harness to public policy ends the commitment and wealth of public spirited citizens.

It is worth examining the origins of charity law, not merely because they have a bearing on the present content of charity law, but also because they highlight a feature of the common law tradition which remains distinctive. This is that charity is the natural partner of the State. Indeed the legal concept of charity, embracing what is in the public interest, encompasses the purposes of the State. The relationship of charity to government in British history, and in Britain today, is a dialogue between what the State itself seeks to secure directly by government action and what it leaves to be delivered by the charitable endeavour of citizens individually or collectively. The dialogue has always involved advocacy of new policies and criticism of government, alongside service provision; however the partnership differs in principle from the Continental European civil law tradition of foundations as private bodies, and indeed the notion that public purposes are secured by the State. Thus the notion of charity, as a public sphere, is at contrast with the current notion of civil society, as a sphere of activity that counterbalances the State. This contrast has an important bearing on the role of and policy towards charity in the modern world.

There has been much change during the 400 years of common law development of charity law since 1601. A key date is 1891, the *Pemsel* judgement of the great judge, Lord MacNaghten.[9] This shows the common law at work, in drawing together what by then were nearly three centuries of charitable law under the Preamble, and in particular a century and more of engagement of charity, and philanthropy, with the economic and social consequences of the Industrial Revolution. In what, significantly, was a tax judgment, Lord MacNaghten categorised charity, as it had developed over the centuries, as comprising four 'heads': relief of poverty; advancement of education; advancement of religion; and other purposes beneficial to the community.

As the last, open-ended head makes clear, Lord MacNaghten was not providing a definition of charity. Under the common law there is no definition. Some common law jurisdictions, notably Barbados,[10] have sought to provide a definition of charity in legislation, but most still regard the lack of a definition as an essential virtue of charity law on account of the flexibility that its open-endedness affords. Nevertheless the lack of a clear and up-to-date legal concept of charity set out in legislation, together with other technical considerations, has led most common law jurisdictions to contemplate introducing legislation to modernise the basis for charity law. How this is being approached in Britain is discussed in more detail below.

6 The Distinctive Characteristics of Charity

That an organisation, be it a foundation, trust, association or limited company, has a public benefit purpose is only one of the fundamental characteristics required for charitable status. Three other essential features of charities, which make them appropriately regarded as a core part of civil society, are that they are independent, non-profit-making and non-political bodies.

Independence, in particular independence from government and the State, is characterised, and given legal underpinning, by the role and duty of the charity's trustees. Every charity, whatever its legal form, has trustees. They have absolute legal responsibility for the activities their charity undertakes in pursuit of their purposes. Their overall duty is to use their powers and resources in the best interests of their charity and its purposes. Practical issues arise of course, particularly in the modern world, where charities often contract with

9 *Income Tax Special Purposes Commissioners v Pemsel* [1891] AC 531.

10 Charities Act 1978, *The Laws of Barbados*, Volume VIII, Title XVIII, Chapter 243, LRO 1989.

public authorities to deliver public services using public resources. But the principle that it is the trustees, and they alone, who are legally responsible is legal guarantee of the independence of charities.

The non-profit requirement, strictly speaking non-profit distribution, is the legal requirement that ultimately all a charity's resources must be devoted, directly or indirectly, to the charity's purposes. Charities may incur administrative costs, and they may devote resources to activities such as fundraising, campaigning and publicity; but the ultimate justification for expenditure must be the contribution it makes to the charity's charitable purposes. Furthermore, the trustees must be able to justify their expenditure on that basis, as being reasonable expenditure towards fulfilling their purposes. Commercial activity such as trading is permissible within this framework, though again it must meet the test that it helps to achieve the charitable purpose.

The non-political requirement is more complicated, with technical and indeed reform issues in charity law. But in essence the law requires charities and their trustees to avoid activity which is inappropriately political; and no charity may have a political purpose. The contention that charities should not be party political, in the sense of being associated with or supporting a political party, is uncontroversial. Charity law goes further, in interpreting the concept of 'political' as including seeking to change the law or government policy. The law does, however, allow charities to campaign and contribute to public debate on issues of political concern provided they are relevant to the achievement of their charitable purposes. This is important as charities play a significant part in public debate and the formation of public policy.

The basis for this principle of charity law reflects its origins in trust law. The courts have a historic role of ensuring that the purposes of a charity are fulfilled. Traditionally in Britain the courts have regarded issues concerning changes in the law or government policy as matters for Parliament over which the courts are not competent to pass judgment. Thus an organisation whose purpose is specifically to bring about changes in the law or government policy has been regarded as political and not charitable. But charity law, as now interpreted, does give charities extensive rights to engage in political action including advocacy, lobbying and campaigning, providing such action is intended to further the charitable objects of the organisation. Thus children's charities can and do campaign on the government policies and laws that affect children and their interests.

Charity law affects organisations active in the field of human rights in particular. Provided they are not operating outside the law there is no restraint on the establishment of voluntary bodies to pursue the protection of human rights. But while Amnesty International, for example, is active in campaigning in support of the human rights of individuals in Britain, a court judgment in 1982 determined that it is not a charity, on the basis that its purpose is political.[11] Recently, however, following the passing of the Human Rights Act in 1998, voluntary organisations with human rights objectives can now be more freely regarded as charities, the legal reasoning being that human rights is now enshrined in British law.

To summarise, one may characterise charities as bodies with a public benefit purpose, governed by independent trustees, whose resources are devoted to that purpose on a non-profit distribution basis and which are non-political.

7 Institutional Forms of Charities

Charities take many forms, ranging from unincorporated associations to bodies established by statute or Royal Charter. The three standard 'models' are association, trust and charitable company. It is a striking characteristic of charity in Britain that the institutional forms that charity takes are not specific to charity. There is no separate area of law that regulates charitable form or indeed that is specific to voluntary action or civil society. Thus the nature and form which associations, trusts and companies may take covers a wide range of activities and extends into both the public and market sectors as well as the not-for-profit sector. This is not a satisfactory situation and one of the reforms will create a new form, the charitable incorporated organisation (CIO).

While it is the purpose which defines charities, the basic forms that charities take are association and trust. Historically, they were the basic legal forms which private individuals could adopt under the common law system to undertake voluntary action (association), or devote wealth to a purpose of their choosing (trust). Naturally the state has, over the centuries, been concerned to regulate private sources of power. The growth of the legal framework for charity reflects the privileged status and legal protection which Government, Parliament and the courts have given to citizen action in the public interest. That is the essence of the concept of charity. Association reflects the principle of freedom of association which is at the heart of modern concept of civil society, and trust is the traditional form for philanthropic benefaction. Associations and trusts have continued to provide a secure legal basis for charitable activity; however,

11 *McGovern v Attorney General* [1982] Ch 321.

the need for incorporation, to limit the liability of board members, has become an increasingly important issue, hence the growth of 'charitable company' status alongside association and trust.

In English law associations are the loosest legal form. An association consists simply of a group of individuals who come together to pursue a common purpose. It may have a written constitution, and in spheres where associational activity is well developed, such as sports and leisure, there are often model constitutions, provided by umbrella bodies for their member organisations. But associations as such have no legal personality in their own right. Legal form is provided by the governing rules of the association, which set out the purpose, powers and membership of the body. Legal liability, however, rests with the members, individually and collectively. Thus any transactions, such as property purchases, are the responsibility of all the members. For the pursuit of common private interests, such as sports, the association form is ideally simple and uncomplicated. Under the common law no legal process, such as court or government registration, is involved. Association, for philanthropic as well as other purposes such as cultural and political, became common in the 18th and 19th centuries.

Association form was, and remains, ideally simple for informal groups without complicated structures and resources. But even for small bodies the lack of legal personality becomes a difficulty once property ownership becomes involved. For charitable associations, that was long ago remedied by enabling them to incorporate for such purposes as property title, thereby enabling the association, as distinct from its members, to own property. This does not however provide the association trustees with protection from personal liability for the debts and losses that their associations may incur. For this reason, limited company form has become a common form for charities to adopt. Thus many charities are formed as companies and accordingly registered with and subject to the requirements of Companies House, the public body responsible for the oversight of companies. This gives the trustees the protection of limited liability, but at the expense of legal complexity. The trustees are the directors and therefore subject to dual forms of legal obligation, under both companies and charity legislation. The Charities Bill provisions for the CIO, referred to above, will simplify this situation by creating a new institutional form of charitable incorporated organisation, giving trustees all the protection of incorporated status but overseen only under charity legislation, outside company legislation.

The trust is the original legal form of charity, long predating the 1601 Act. It derives from early English Law, particularly ecclesiastical law forming a branch of law known as equity law. The basic concept is the simple notion of enforceable promise – money or property given (or 'entrusted') to one person to hold on behalf of a third person rather than as a personal possession. This form lent itself to charitable benefaction, whereby a donor established a trust to be applied for a specified purpose by its trustees according to the donor's stated intentions. In principle the legal form is flexible and informal. The normal way of establishing a trust is through a will or deed – the document setting out the intended purpose of the donation. This should of course be a carefully drawn up legal document but this need not, in law, be so. Many trusts have been established by informally drafted deeds in wills and indeed much difficulty and subsequent litigation has arisen through imprecise drafting.

The will of Sir Henry Wellcome, establishing the Wellcome Trust, now by far the largest charity in Britain, is an example of an idiosyncratic founding document – now rewritten to meet its modern needs. The Wellcome Trust's charitable purpose, reflecting Sir Henry Wellcome's intentions, is medical research. Distributing over £400m a year, it is the largest source of funding for medical research in Britain, exceeding that spent by the Government.

A trust may be formed without any written document at all. All that is necessary is money or property to be given for a particular purpose. Thus it has been said that trust defines a relationship – between donor, trustee and beneficiary – rather than an organisational structure. This is important in establishing control and regulation over collections made, for example, in response to disasters or emergencies. Such monies are 'impressed with charity' on the basis that the purpose of the donation is to give money to a charitable purpose. It thus constitutes a charitable trust, subject to the requirements of charity law. Naturally it is normal practice to establish a charitable trust by means of a properly drawn up legal deed or will; but the protection of the law from the outset can be important. For example, the deed drawn up for the Diana Princess of Wales Memorial Trust was made in response to the spontaneous giving which arose after her death.

8 The Registration of Charities

It is a principle of association under the common law that there is no legal process or registration requirement. For many years the same held true for charities as well. The Charities Act 1960, which restructured the Charity Commission (see below), created a registration requirement for charities. The Act set up a register of charities under legislation for the first time. Though the Act strengthened the regulation of charities the register was designed not merely as a mechanism of control or supervision, it was equally for public information and to benefit charities themselves. Indeed registration is a right as well as an obligation. Maintaining the register remains one of the prime functions of the Charity Commission.

With certain exceptions charities established in England and Wales are required to register with the Charity Commission. The Commission is obliged to register any organisation which meets the requirements of charity law, in particular having exclusively charitable objects. The consequence of registration is an authoritative confirmation of charitable status, which is binding in law. One of the reasons why sponsors are keen to obtain charitable status is the fiscal relief which charities are automatically accorded through that status. The Inland Revenue are legally required to accept, and benefit accordingly, all bodies registered as charities by the Commission. The Commission's determination is final, and subject only to legal appeal, though in novel or unusual cases the Commission does give the Inland Revenue the opportunity to comment before it makes a decision.

The Register of Charities has nearly 190,000 charities registered. Most are small – local voluntary or community bodies with low financial turnover. The largest are multi-million pound enterprises. Charities range from national institutions like the National Trust, responsible for the maintenance of heritage buildings, Oxfam and the Royal Society for the Prevention of Cruelty to Animals (RSPCA), through specialist bodies, such as the Samaritans, providing a helpline for potential suicides, Arthritis Care, one of many charities dealing with particular medical conditions, and Help the Aged, providing help and assisting the elderly. The largest 200 have an annual turnover of over £10m with another 2,500 or so in the £1-£10m bracket. At the other extreme well over 100,000 registered charities fall below the Charity Commission's monitoring threshold of £10,000 turnover a year.

The requirement for charities to register reflects the fact that they are both civil society and public bodies. As part of civil society charities are independent; but they have charitable status because they are dedicated to a purpose which is in the public interest. They are not, therefore, the concern only of their members and supporters. There is no legal or administrative requirement for the generality of voluntary bodies, such as social clubs, to register either with the courts or a government department or agency.

The main benefits of charitable status are security of legal status, tax relief and access to funding. Additionally, many foundations make grants only (or preferentially) to registered charities; and public confidence in charities makes charitable status desirable for fundraising. Registration is the basis for accountability in return for the benefits of charitable status.

In deciding whether an application for registration meets the legal requirements the Commission applies the tests developed under common law principles since the 1601 Preamble. The *Pemsel* judgment still provides the current framework within which the Commission operates. Applications which fall within the poverty, education and religious headings are presumed to fulfil a public benefit purpose, though that can be rebutted in the particular cases. For other issues, under the so called '4th head,' the public benefit requirement has to be satisfied case by case.

Under the proposals in the Charities Bill for the reform of charity law the scope of charity will be defined in legislation; and all charities, regardless of their purpose, will have to satisfy a public benefit test, set out in Charity Commission guidelines. The Bill sets out a list of purposes which are charitable. These are derived from the decisions of the courts and the Charity Commission, rather than being a new list; and, as under present law, the list will not be an exhaustive definition of charity in any comprehensive sense.

The list proposed by the Government is as follows:

- Prevention or relief of poverty;
- Advancement of education;
- Advancement of religion;
- Advancement of health or the saving of lives;
- Advancement of citizenship or community development;
- Advancement of the arts, culture, heritage or science;
- Advancement of amateur sport;
- Advancement of human rights, conflict resolution or reconciliation, or promotion of religious or racial harmony or equality and diversity;
- Advancement of environmental protection or improvement;
- Promotion of animal welfare;
- Relief of those in need by reason of youth, age, ill-health, disability, financial hardship, or other disadvantage;
- Other purposes beneficial to the community.

The legislation involves complex technical provisions to cover the relationship between the new statutory list and the common law processes of determination which the Bill preserves. The final open-ended category is essential. An important function fulfilled by the Charity Commission is to determine novel applications. In the words of a distinguished Law Lord, Lord Wilberforce, the courts and the Commission 'have to keep the law moving as new ideas arise or old ones become obsolete or satisfied'.[12] In this way the common law basis for charity allows for the changing needs and circumstances of society. The Charities Bill retains this power by giving a statutory basis for the Charity Commission's approach of relating novel purposes to ones already accepted by analogy. Examples of novel decisions made under the existing law by the Charity Commission reflecting this principle include: the promotion of good community relations; the promotion of ethical standards in business; fair trade for third world producers; and the removal of charitable status from gun clubs.

The fact that tax relief is an automatic consequence of charitable status is an important, and much prized, privilege (though, as noted above, by no means the only benefit of charitable status). The rationale is that charitable status is, by definition, in the public interest and should be given encouragement by the Government. It is for the charities themselves to decide how to fulfil their public benefit purpose, whether or not that accords with government policy or priorities. While Government naturally chafes against this from time to time it is an important part of the diversity of civil society.

9 THE CHARITY COMMISSION

The Charity Commission was established as a public body in 1853. Since then its role has been redefined a number of times. It is now both the registrar and regulator of charities and exercises a number of functions in fulfilment of a number of purposes. The Register of Charities is now a more accessible source of public information about charities, and is displayed on the Commission's website. The Register's principal purpose however is as the basis for the Commission's core responsibility, the regulation of charities. Registration with the Commission is, in effect, entry to a support and supervisory relationship with the Commission. The rationale for this relationship requires separate discussion.

The distinctive regulatory role of the Charity Commission has grown up in parallel with the development of charity law and has common origins in the 1601 Act. The Charity Commission as an organisation was established in 1853. At that time its functions were those of the courts: to modify charities' trust deeds where changing circumstances required modernisation, and to redress abuse or mismanagement of charitable trusts. The need for the Commission

12 *Scottish Burial Reform and Cremation Society v Glasgow Corporation* [1968] AC 138.

arose from the fact that the Chancery Court, as well described by Charles Dickens, the specialist court for charity issues, was hopelessly clogged up by archaic rules and procedures.[13] The Commission was simply an agency set up to free up the charity legal process.

The concept of charity regulation was already established under the 1601 Act – itself an Act passed to provide correction for the abuse of charitable trusts. In effect, the premise for the regulation of charities was the need to ensure that the purposes of the charitable benefaction were complied with. Under English law the Attorney General, as *parens patriae*, had responsibility for protecting the public interest in compliance with the charitable purpose of trusts. From time to time Parliament appointed roving Charity Commissioners to survey charitable trust and report on abuse. Extensive reports in the early 19th century, which revealed widespread abuse and neglect of charity led to the creation of the standing Commission. Thus, the fundamental principle underpinning charity regulation, translated to modern circumstances, is that charitable resources are devoted to the public interest and must be safeguarded for that public purpose.

The Charity Commission, as constituted at present, is a public body of some six hundred staff with an annual budget approaching £30m. At present it is a non-ministerial government department that exercises statutory powers under the Charities Act 1993. It is under the direction of five Commissioners, the Chief Commissioner who is full-time head of department (an administrator rather than a lawyer), two legal Commissioners, one full-time and one part-time, a part-time accounting Commissioner and a part-time Commissioner from the voluntary sector. The Commissioners are appointed by the Home Secretary, by open competition in accordance with the requirements for public appointment. They are answerable to Parliament through the Home Secretary. The Commission's budget is met out of public funds, and the Commissioners are accountable to the Home Secretary for the efficient running of the department. The Commission is independent of the political process in the exercise of its statutory powers, being answerable to the courts for the actions it takes over charities.

The Government's reform proposals envisage retaining this constitutional basis for the Commission, though this is controversial since it rejects the recommendation of the Parliamentary Committee which scrutinised the Bill on publication – that the Commission should be statutorily independent of government. At the time of writing the outcome is uncertain. The Commission's

13 See Charles Dickens, *Bleak House,* (London: Penguin Classics, 2003).

governance is modernised, with a board of nine members, more of whom will be drawn from the charitable sector (but appointed by the Home Secretary under the same process as at present) overseeing a staff lead by a chief executive.

The Commission has five broad functions: registration, accountability, monitoring, support, and enforcement. The distinctive nature of the Commission, in contrast to jurisdictions where regulation is tax led, is that its overriding objective, to be strengthened by the new Bill, is to increase public trust and confidence in charity. It is thus an independent partner of the charitable sector, using its powers to maintain trust in the concept and law of charity, and promoting integrity and good standards in charities. As described below the focus of the Commission's work – and the bulk of it in terms of activities – is devoted to encouraging good standards of governance, administration and financial management in charities. Thus while it is properly regarded as a regulatory authority, its interpretation of its regulatory responsibilities is broad, with much emphasis on preventative work rather than investigation and enforcement.

The Commission's registration function, as described above, is both legal and administrative. The role of the Commission in determining what organisations have charitable status makes it the first and principal determinant of the law of charity. Relatively few charity status cases are the subject of appeals to the courts so the Commission's role is crucial. This is important since the common law concept of charity is that it develops in response to changing needs and circumstances. As described above the Commission has instituted a long running review of charitable status as embodied in the register. Important issues of legal and public policy arise over the role and authority of the Commission in developing the law. This is a central concern in the reform of charity law.

The legal determination of status is the essence of the Commission's registration decision – once it is satisfied registration is required. However, following the strengthening of the Commission's powers the registration process also involves establishing that a charity is properly formed, with a viable constitution and governance arrangements. While the right to registration cannot be made dependent on satisfying this check, it is the necessary first step to the on-going supervision required by the new legislation.

A key part of the strengthening of the Commission has been to improve the accountability of charities. The law now requires charities to prepare an annual report of activities and accounts, in a prescribed form. This is graduated according to the size of the charity, small charities having to produce a simple statement of what they have done in the year, supported by a simple statement of payments and receipts. These must be available for inspection by the Commission or any *bona fide* enquirer, but do not have to be sent to the Commission on a matter of routine. The report and accounting requirements, together with audit requirements, increase in complexity with the scale of a charity's activities. For charities with a turnover of £10,000 or more a year (some 60,000) the reports must be sent in to the Commission. They are thus available automatically for public inspection and for Commission monitoring.

The rationale for charity accountability is that charities owe their status and privileges to their commitment to the public interest. The public at large is therefore entitled to know what use charities are making of the resources they have and how they are seeking to fulfil their charitable purposes. The framework of accountability which the Commission has established is based on the Statement of Recommended Accounting Practice for Charities (SORP). It is designed to meet a number of objectives. The graded sophistication of the requirements is designed to reflect the governance and management needs of the charity, so that the reporting requirements encourage good management. As mentioned, the requirements are also designed to encourage transparency by charities. This is reflected in the detailed reporting requirements, for example for openness in reporting grants made by grant-making foundations. Finally the requirements are designed to enable the Charity Commission to fulfil its supervisory responsibilities over charities.

The Charities Bill builds on the recent strengthening of the Commission's supervisory role. Reflecting the measures undertaken by the Commission under the powers conferred by the 1993 Act, the new legislation puts responsibilities on charities and the Commission designed to make the contribution of charities to the public interest more subject to public accountability. This reflects the rationale for the regulation of charities, namely that their special status and privileges are based on the fact that they serve the public interest.

The core of the Charity Commission's supervisory role, as now constituted, is the monitoring of the annual returns from the 60,000 or so registered charities above the monitoring threshold of £10,000 turnover. There are two parts to this: examining the returns to make sure they comply with the SORP requirement ('compliance'), and following up issues which, on the face of the returns, appear to give rise to questions ('monitoring'). The compliance stage is part of the process of ensuring that registered charities meet the accountability and transparency requirements of reporting. It is, in effect, part of ensuring that, in recognition of their public status, charities are appropriately open about their circumstances and activities. Progressively the register on the Commission's website will contain information about the activities and finances of charities, thereby enabling people to see instantly what charities are doing with the money they receive. Monitoring is part of the on-going active relationship the Commission maintains with registered charities. It focuses on identifying issues on which the Commission's powers or experience can be brought to bear. These may concern the legal framework or the powers of the charity, or its governance, management or financial arrangements. The essence of supervision is to ensure that charities operate within the law – and have a constitution which best enables them to meet their objectives; and adopt good practice in the way they conduct their affairs. The Commission does not – and cannot – directly supervise the effectiveness of how charities seek to achieve their goals. Indeed the principle of independence of charities means that it is for the trustees, not the Commission, to determine how they are going to fulfil the purposes which make them charities.

Most of the Commission's day-to-day work with charities comes under the broad heading of regulatory work. This however covers a wide range of constructive activities working in cooperation with and support of charities. It includes using legal powers, which avoid costly and time-consuming hearings in court, and giving advice on matters of law and good practice. A particularly important legal role of the Commission is to make what are called 'schemes' to amend a charity's constitution. This may involve giving it new powers, modernising its procedures or even amending its purposes. Under charity law the original purposes of a charity, as set out in its founding document, may only be changed on strictly limited conditions. The extent to which changes can be made depends on the precise form of constitution, it being easiest in the case of charitable companies and most restrictive in the case of charitable trusts. The mechanism is the long established doctrine of *cy pres*, under which purposes which can no longer be fulfilled can be adapted to enable a charitable trust to continue to function. It is a fundamental principle of the concept of trust, like foundation, that the intentions of the benefactor should be protected. Indeed that is the heart of the regulation of trusts and foundations, both historically and conceptually. Balancing respect for a founder's wishes with changing needs and values is a delicate issue of law and policy, as relevant and difficult today, as we try to attract the 'new rich' to set up philanthropic initiatives, as in the past. English law allows a measure of flexibility, enabling trusts to be modified wherever the original intention has become obsolete or ineffective. The Charity Commission has the power to devise schemes for this purpose. A striking example of how far this can go is the scheme which amended the foundation document which established the Bridge House Estate Trust to maintain the bridges, like Tower Bridge, over the Thames at the City of London.

Its powers have been modified to enable it to give charitable grants throughout the whole of the Greater London area, making it, thanks to the valuable property the Trust owns in London, one of the major grant-giving trusts in the country.

The Commission's advisory support function is multifarious. As can be seen from the Commission's website, it provides a wide range of guidance material on matters of charity law and practice, written in plain, non-technical English, to make it accessible to voluntary trustees with neither professional legal nor accountancy skills. This supports the role of the Commission in giving advice on request to individual charities. But the Commission is developing a systematic programme of visits to charities, based on monitoring and risk assessment factors, in order to identify issues in which the Commission's powers and expertise can help. The support function thus incorporates a preventative role, seeking to identify, in the light of Commission experience, potential problems.

The Commission's regulatory support role thus links in with its enforcement role – a combination which has been questioned. From its origins the Commission has had the powers of the courts to intervene in charities where there is mismanagement, or risk to resources. These have been strengthened, enabling the Commission to investigate suspected abuse or mismanagement and take remedial measures, such as the removal of trustees and the freezing of assets. The use of such powers of intervention is however a last resort, and the Commission seeks to identify problems early and seek corrective action before enforcement is necessary. To avoid the confusion of 'friend' and 'policing' roles feared by critics the Commission maintains a separation of support and investigation functions, with an evaluation process before cases are assigned.

The Charity Commission's remit and competence are concentrated on legal, governance and financial matters. It is not responsible for – nor, given the breadth of issues covered by charitable status, could it have the expertise to – pass judgment on the effectiveness and efficiency of charities (though the Charities Bill envisages it playing a more active role in requiring charities themselves to account for the impact they make).

The Commission's fundamental aim is to maintain public confidence in the integrity of charities. This means providing a framework within which a charity's compliance with the legal and accounting requirements of charity law and regulation can be monitored. The reporting requirements are thus directed at ensuring that a charity gives sufficient account of its activities and finances so that the Commission – and other interested parties – can check that it is operating prudently within its legal framework.

The Commission's first objective is thus to ensure that charities are able to maximise their potential within an effective legal, accounting and governance framework. This is supported by two additional objectives, namely 'to promote sound governance, better working and accountability' and 'to secure compliance with charity law and deal with abuse and poor practice'.[14]

What a charity achieves in its field is not a matter which the Charity Commission can or should assess. This has to be left to those concerned and knowledgeable in the field concerned. Since trustees are not accountable for the performance of their charity in this respect, there are concerns about holding charities to account for efficiency and effectiveness. The new reforms will address this to some extent by making charities report on what they achieve. But it is an important principle that charities should be independent and that diversity and innovation should be encouraged within the charitable sector, even at the expense of dubious outcomes (which is in any case a subjective judgement).

Those bodies that provide funding, both government and private, play an important role in testing the effectiveness of charities. The accountability of the recipients of grants, or the parties receiving contracts, for achieving results that meet the expectations of their financers is a tangible way in which the substantive performance of charities is assessed.

10 MUTUALITY

Running parallel to charity, there is, in Britain, a well established tradition of 'self-help' organisations. In contrast to the tradition of charity, which emphasises the altruistic principle of 'doing good' for *others*, the principle of *self-help* focuses on the needs of the members of the organisation. In the 19th century the working class response to the challenges of the industrial revolution was to establish member groups in which people clubbed together to make provision jointly for the community collectively. Retail provision, especially of food, through cooperative shops is one important example which continues. This tradition of cooperatives, mutuals, housing associations, building societies and friendly societies, is of growing interest in Britain as the principle of self-help has attracted more emphasis in the voluntary sector. One example is the development of the credit union movement, in which banking services are provided

14 See *Charity Commission Corporate Plan 2003-06*, available at Charity Commission website: http://www.charitycommission.gov.uk/spr/pdfs/corpplan03.pdf (Last visited March 2005).

on a member, community basis in deprived areas in which commercial banking facilities are inadequate.

The need for separate legal forms for self-help organisations alongside charities has diminished in recent years as the strict interpretation of charity law as excluding beneficiaries from being trustees of charities has been relaxed. The old interpretation held that any benefit, whether remuneration in the form of money or receiving the services of the charity, was forbidden to trustees. It has become increasingly accepted that it is good practice that users should play a part in the governance of voluntary organisations. Following this principle the Charity Commission now allows users to be trustees of a charity provided there are adequate arrangements to prevent conflict of interest. Thus self-help organisations can qualify for charitable status – an example of the role of the Commission in modernising charity law under its own powers. A good example of this development is the standard principle that housing associations, providing social housing, include tenants on their management boards.

Nevertheless there is scope to encourage mutuals as an alternative to charities and the Government's reform proposals envisage the creation of a new form of cooperative to be called Community Benefit Societies.

11 Voluntary Sector and the State

The relationship between voluntary bodies, especially charities, and the State has always been close. This reflects the origins of modern charity – as a partnership between the public spirited citizen (especially the well-to-do) and the State both pursuing the public interest. It also reflects the fact that, until the creation of the Welfare State in the mid 20th century, most social provision was left to voluntary action. The tradition that voluntary bodies met social needs in co-operation with the public authorities, and at the same time took a public position on policy issues continued over a long period, a key example being the Charity Organising Society (COS) which oversaw relief of the poor in cooperation with the local parish relief. The reforms of the Welfare State switched the balance, so that for most social policy provision became the responsibility of public authorities. But the partnership continued, and, with changing circumstances, has developed and changed – the COS, for example continues to be active in supporting poor families, under the name of the Family Welfare Association. The role of voluntary bodies in promoting and campaigning for policy initiatives and charges has always been an important function. Examples include disability, housing and homelessness, and criminal justice. The restrictions of charity law which prevent political bodies from being charities do not apply to activities in pursuit of charitable ends. In fact, one of the roles of the Charity Commission is to give guidance on political campaigning by charities, and their right to engage vigorously in such activity provided that it does contribute to their charitable aims.

The essence of charitable status combines commitment to the public interest with independence. It thus provides a suitable legal and institutional form for many bodies which might be regarded as part of the public sector (rather than civil society or the 'third' sector). For example the British Council, promoting interest in and understanding of British culture and society, and the Arts Council, responsible for allocating public (and national lottery) money to arts bodies, are both charities. Although much of their funding comes from government, and government plays a role in their governance, charitable status reflects the fact that their responsibility is for the public interest as they interpret it, rather than as determined by the government of the day.

Many charities have been set up at the request of or with the encouragement of government. Examples are the Women's Royal Voluntary Service (WRVS), set up originally to harness women's voluntary movement for men as well as women (still with government funding); the Citizens Advice Bureaux (CAB), set up with government support to provide an advice service on provision and entitlements available for social and economic need; and the Immigrants' Advisory Service (IAS), providing independent advice to would be immigrants on immigration rules and procedures.

It has become common in recent years for government, at local level in particular, to establish charitable bodies to fulfil statutory responsibilities, in particular for housing and recreation. These charitable bodies operate at 'arms length' from the Government, and on an independent basis, but with public funding. In parallel, contractual partnerships have become increasingly common between public authorities and voluntary bodies, under which services are provided independently by the voluntary body at the expense of the public authority. A framework of principles, setting out the basis on which this partnership should be developed, has been established as a result of negotiations between Government and representatives of the voluntary and community sector. This is known as the 'compact', which is established at national level (separately for England, Wales, Scotland and Northern Ireland) with local compacts developed at local authority level.

This is an important development which the Government is encouraging with a number of initiatives designed to strengthen the voluntary sector and its capacity to work with public authorities. This does however raise issues of striking a balance, between the independence of voluntary bodies and the spirit of voluntary action on the one hand, and the danger of being co-opted as an agency of the State, determined by the policies (and politics) of government, and controlled by financial considerations on the other. In order to underpin the legal independence of charities the Charity Commission has issued guidance on good practice by charities in entering into contracts with public authorities designed to safeguard their independence.

12 ENTERPRISE AND COMMERCIAL ACTIVITY

Voluntary bodies, including charities, have always been able to engage in commercial activity in Britain. Schools, for example, have always been able to charge well-to-do parents of pupils, while also providing free or subsidised education. In recent years the role of entrepreneurial activity on a public interest, non-profit basis has become increasingly emphasised. Many charities reflect this. One well established example is the Jorvik (Viking) Centre, a highly successful visitor attraction maintained by the York Archaeological Trust. More recently the Wildfowl and Wetlands Trust (WWT) has redeveloped redundant reservoirs in West London in collaboration with the Thames Water Board and local property developers to form an environmental resource in West London.

To facilitate this development, and in particular to encourage a public interest contribution to the economic regeneration of deprived areas, the Charity Commission has published guidance on charitable status for regeneration bodies, using the flexibility of charity law to widen the scope for charities engaging in 'profit-making' activity in pursuit of the public interest. The essential test is that surpluses ('profit') made through commercial activity must be devoted to the public purpose.

Some commentators, while welcoming the development of charity law in this way, argue that a new form of non-profit organisation is needed. Proposals for a 'public interest company' were put forward in the Strategy Unit Report. The concept is to create a new legal and institutional form of company with all the financial, commercial and governance freedom of company form, but with the overriding principle that its activities are dedicated to a public interest purpose. Examples are provision of public utilities (such as water) and broadcasting. This has been given effect by the creation of a new form of company under the name of 'Community Interest Company' in the Companies (Audit, Investigations and Community Enterprise) Act 2004.[15]

13 CONCLUSION

This is an exciting moment of development for voluntary, charitable and community activity in Britain. After a period in which core public services were financed and provided more or less exclusively by public authorities, with voluntary action largely confined to supplementary provision and innovation, government is now looking to community organisation at all levels to engage in partnership to meet public needs. This has opened many opportunities for voluntary bodies but also raised many issues both of principle and practice. Reform debate, both within government and in the voluntary sector, is live now.

15 'An Introduction to Community Interest Companies', Department of Trade and Industry Document, (December 2004). Available at: http://www.dti.gov.uk/cics/pdfs/cicfactsheet1.pdf (Last visited March, 2005).

9

ASSOCIATIONS AND FOUNDATIONS IN GERMANY: SERVICE PROVIDERS OR AGENTS OF CIVIL SOCIETY?

Rupert Graf Strachwitz

1 INTRODUCTION

Providing a legal definition of the not for profit sector in Germany requires an understanding of Germany's political, legal, and cultural traditions. Germany is a Roman law country, but also has strong common law traditions. It has a culture dominated by Christianity, even though practising Christians no longer form a majority. It has a long tradition of fighting for freedom and civil liberties, sometimes with success, though very often without. On the other hand, Germany is the country of Kant and Hegel: philosophers both rooted in the thoughts of the enlightenment, but also, particularly Hegel, firmly positioned in the French tradition of supremacy of the state. As a general rule, the law has, more often than not, been more important to many Germans than the notion of freedom, though due to the history of Nazi oppression, they are also rightly sensitive towards issues concerning citizens' rights.

Moreover, Germany is a federal country and some aspects of the legal framework for not for profit organisations are governed by state law rather than federal law. Also, increasingly, European law – the set of intergovernmental agreements on the European Union – is influencing and indeed superseding national law. Furthermore, a very large portion of what is generally described as charitable service provision, is organised and managed by one or other of

Yuwen Li (Ed.), *Freedom of Association in China and Europe: Comparative Perspectives in Law and Practice*, Printed in The Netherlands, pp. 309-325.

the established Churches,[1] all of which enjoy a high degree of autonomy under the German Constitution.[2] And finally, charity in Germany, indeed as in most other cultures, is deeply rooted in history, so charity law has developed over centuries and certainly lacks the systematic approach that some new areas of legal regulation tend to provide.

For all these reasons, a short overview can be no more than an attempt to paint a general picture and point to some key elements; it will certainly have to miss out on many details. The endeavour is, however, of particular interest at this moment in history, since as elsewhere, academics, practitioners, and policy makers have begun to see the need for reforming the overall framework of charitable activities, and indeed, in 1999 a Commission of the Federal Parliament on the Future of Civic Engagement was formed (*Enquete-Kommission des Deutschen Bundestages zur Zukunft des buergerschaftlichen Engagements*). It presented its report in June, 2002. Among the many recommendations to Parliament, particularly noteworthy was the suggestion that the fiscal laws governing tax exempt organisations should be thoroughly revised, while admitting that the details and indeed the basic system of new legislation would still have to be established. This suggestion implicitly acknowledged that the present system encompassed some serious deficiencies. This paper therefore will not only present the legal framework currently in existence, but, developing the ideas in the aforementioned report, will also comment on the weaknesses of the present system and offer some thoughts on possible changes.

2 The Nature of a Not-for-Profit Organisation (Charity)

In the course of history, there has been a constant change in public opinion on what actually constitutes a charity. The notion of a *pia causa,* as used in the Middle Ages, included any deed pleasing to God, be it helping the needy, the embellishing of a church, educating the young, or even defending Christendom against the infidels. While the generality of the approach has remained unchanged, the rise of the state to its present importance all over Europe narrowed the scope of any personal voluntary action for society until, towards the end of the 20th century, the welfare state and socialist society were both perceived as failing to provide all necessary services, let alone embrace all the

1 In particular, the Roman Catholic Church, the Protestant Christian Churches of Lutheran, Calvinist and Unionist denominations, and the Jewish community.

2 The Constitution *(Grundgesetz)* of 1949; for church autonomy see Article 4, 140.

citizens' needs and wishes. Germany has a strong tradition of a welfare state, and indeed East Germany was one of the most rigid socialist societies. But Germany also invented the principle of subsidiarity as an historical compromise between government supremacy and non-governmental provision – basically church-based service provision in the areas of health and social services. However, this principle never extended to other areas such as education, research, or the arts. In these areas, voluntary action was always very much restricted to what was either deemed irrelevant or useful to the government. Even sports clubs gained tax exemption in the 1910s on the grounds that they were aiding the war effort.

The fact that many tax exempt organisations do not provide services at all, but constitute self help or advocacy groups, has never been systematically addressed in German charity law. The European Commission lists service provision, self-help, advocacy, and resource and coordination (intermediary activities) as the four valid forms that associations and foundations can express themselves in, and particularly welcomes the contribution and involvement of advocacy groups.[3] Nevertheless, German lawmakers and government administrators to this day are not at all sure whether anything beyond service provision is ultimately legitimate. Robert Putnam[4] and others have developed an even more modern concept of charity, as a contribution to a democratic society, regardless of the actual activity. Such a concept is clearly still a long way from becoming a theoretical basis for legislation. Charity is widely perceived as a servant to the government and the extraordinarily high level of government funding is taken as proof for this.[5]

Under these circumstances, it is hardly surprising that in attempting to define the legal nature of a charity, the first point of reference is fiscal law. This is more so, since fiscal engineering has become one of the prime instruments of government policy. Fiscal law in Germany limits charity in the sense that it is tax exempt to the activity of legal entities (as opposed to natural persons). These are defined in the law on corporate taxation.[6] They may apply for and

3 'Communication on Promoting the Role of Voluntary Organisations and Foundations in Europe', 1997, available at: http://europa.eu.int/comm/enterprise/library/lib-social_economy/orgfd_en.pdf (Last visited March, 2005).

4 Robert Putnam, *Making Democracy Work*, (Princeton: Princeton University Press, 1993).

5 See the findings of the Johns Hopkins Comparative Nonprofit Sector Project, in: Lester Salamon, Helmut K. Anheier, Regina List, Stefan Toepler, S. Wojciech Skolowski and Associates, *Global Civil Society, Dimensions of the Nonprofit Sector*, (Baltimore MD: The Johns Hopkins Center for Civil Society Studies, 1999), Chapter 5: Germany.

6 The Corporation Tax Law (*Koerperschaftssteuergesetz)*, s. 1.

be granted tax exemption by the tax authorities if by statute and actual activity they meet the detailed conditions for charitable activity laid down in the general tax law.[7] Natural persons and taxable corporations may deduct donations to recognised charities from their taxable income.

From this, it is clear that it is within the authority of the state to define what constitutes a charitable proposition as a public purpose and who may thus be entitled to tax exemption. Quite recently, there has been some discussion as to whether activities for the public good needed to gain exemption from taxation in the first place, or whether they were actually outside the state's authority to impose taxes upon its citizens. Obviously, this viewpoint is far removed from a traditional German notion of overall state authority, and it is interesting that the question should be raised at a moment when the government is having increasing difficulties in collecting enough taxes to fulfil its obligations. Also, it has been argued that the power to define what constitutes a public good rests with Parliament alone and should not be exercised, as is the case at the moment, by the government bureaucracy, let alone by the government agency charged with collecting taxes (which is naturally disinclined to exempt areas of activity from taxation). In this context, the model of a specialized agency like the Charity Commission for England and Wales has been viewed with some sympathy by reform orientated practitioners.

In any case, it has become very clear that tax law alone will not suffice to describe a legal framework for charitable organisations. Since they are legal bodies, civil law will apply first.

3 Charities in Civil Law

Since in the tradition of Roman law there has to be a principle of definition, and since fiscal law and civil law are closely intertwined, albeit not always perfectly concurrent, it is necessary to discuss the status of charities under civil law before entering into a full discussion of the fiscal implications. This is a complicated task, as the status of a legal entity under fiscal law is not restricted to legal persons under civil and public law. Civil law, as laid down in the Civil Code of 1896 (*Buergerliches Gesetzbuch*),[8] basically recognises four forms of legal persons, the corporation (*Handelsgesellschaft*), the registered association (*eingetragener Verein*), the civil law foundation (*Stiftung buergerlichen Rechts*),

7 See the Tax Code (*Abgabenordnung*), ss. 51-68.

8 In force since 1st January, 1900.

and the cooperative society (*eingetragene Genossenschaft*). Tax law lists a further two forms, the non-registered association (*nicht eingetragener Verein*), and the non-autonomous foundation (*nicht rechtsfaehige Stiftung*), as relevant legal entities, both of which are highly important as legal forms for charitable activities. It is therefore important to point out that legal personality under civil law is not the only way for a charity to meet the requirements of fiscal law.

One rule is notable by its absence. While tax exempt bodies are required to file annual statements with the tax authorities, these are not made public. Nor are these bodies in any way compelled to publish any information whatsoever on their statutes, activities, finances, officers or any other matter. While those who are active in fundraising usually find it serves their interest to provide at least some information to the general public, those who are not, for example endowed foundations, are, more often than not, decidedly secretive.[9] When the latest very minor reform of foundation law was enacted in 2002,[10] it was suggested that a publication clause be introduced. The foundation lobby was successful in suppressing this suggestion.

3.1 Associations[11]

Of these forms, the association (*Verein*) is by far the most numerous one. The right to associate is a constitutional right.[12] The legal form of association is, with a few exceptions, restricted to not-for-profit, though not necessarily tax exempt, activities. Associations are membership organisations; they are governed by their members. Over 500,000 registered associations exist in Germany; the

9 Less than 10% of all German foundations publish an annual report, less than 30% will provide figures on their endowment or budget on request. See Rainer Sprengel, Statistics on the Nature of German Foundations, A Research Report (*Statistiken zum deutschen Stiftungswesen, ein Forschungsbericht*), (Berlin: Maecenata, 2001).

10 Law on the Modernisation of Foundation Law (Official Journal I, S. 2634) (*Gesetz zur Modernisierung des Stiftungsrechts 2002) (Bundesgesetzblatt I, S. 2634).*

11 The predominant legal bases for an association (Verein) are ss. 21-79 of the Civil Code, and the specific law on associations, *Gesetz zur Regelung des oeffentlichen Vereinsrechts (Vereinsgesetz)*, dated 5th August 1964. For more information see: Bernhard Reichert, *Manual of Association and Organization Law (Handbuch des Vereins- und Verbandsrechts)*, (Neuwied: Luchterhand, 1999); Kurt Stoeber, *Manual of Associations Law (Handbuch zum Vereinsrecht)*, (Koln: Schmidt, 1997); Eugen Sauter, Gerhard Schweyer, *The Registered Association (Der eingetragene Verein)*, (14th Edition, Munchen: Beck, 1990).

12 Article 9 of the Constitution (*Grundgesetz).*

number of non-registered associations is estimated at an additional 500,000. Registration is with the courts and involves filing the statutes and the names of legal representatives, but not of annual reports. Registration results in the association becoming a fully operational legal personality and regulates issues of liability and contractual obligations. Members of non-registered associations remain personally fully liable.

The form of registered association has become the standard form of organising a charity and has superseded all previous forms like Royal Charters, Privileged Societies and so on, which did exist up to the 19th century. Our largest nonprofits, the social welfare umbrella organisations,[13] are organised in this fashion, but there is an increasing feeling that a legal form that serves a local membership organisation perfectly well may perhaps not be appropriate for a multi-million turnover service provider with a paid staff of 400,000.[14]

To form an association, a minimum of seven natural or legal persons must agree on the statutes. If they wish to register the association as a legal person, the minutes of the meeting in which the statutes are voted on and the first officers of the association are elected, must be confirmed by public deed, i.e. by a public notary. The notary will also confirm the signatures of the officers who apply for registration. It is worth noting that although the right to associate is virtually unrestricted, and conferring legal personality is a registration process, not a government concession, the procedure is very much one of application, and it bears considerable resemblance to applying for a favour at the dispensation of the government. The application is made to the civil court, where registers of associations and limited companies are kept.[15] Notwithstanding the constitutional right to associate, and notwithstanding the fact that the notary, and in many cases the members and their counsel, have given legal advice as to the wording of the statutes, it is an unfortunate practice of the court officials to introduce their own legal opinion and refuse registration if this is not adhered to. And since any amendment to the original wording needs to go through the same procedure of confirmation by a notary, registration can sometimes take

13 For example, The German Red Cross, German Caritas (*Spitzenverbaende der freien Wohlfahrtspflege).*

14 German Caritas, including all its branches and affiliated organizations, is the largest non governmental employer in the country, larger than even the biggest corporations.

15 *Vereinsregister*, kept with the County Court (*Amtsgericht).* A new regulation on the register was enacted by the federal Ministry of Justice in 1999: Regulation concerning the Associations Register and Other Questions of Register Law, 10 February 1999 (*Verordnung ueber das Vereinsregister und andere Fragen des Registerrechts vom 10. Februar 1999).*

an inordinately long time. As long as the registration process has not been completed, the association is of course a non-registered one, which implies full personal liability on the part of its officers.

The Civil Code contains some very specific regulations on internal governance. For example, a registered association has to adhere to democratic principles: the general assembly of members must be the highest authority within the association and be able to take up and decide upon any issue relevant to the life of the association. In practice, however, ways in which associations go about their business differ widely. Whereas some are truly exciting fields of democracy in action, others tend to leave everything to their boards, the annual general meeting agreeing to every proposal the board puts before them. Within wide limits, this is the autonomous decision of each association, as is the recruitment policy for new members. Unlike in other countries such as the United States, in Germany, any association may refuse membership on whatever grounds it sees fit – gender, nationality, religion and so on.

3.2 Foundations[16]

While they are not nearly as numerous, foundations *(Stiftungen)* are the other notable legal form charities may take. While not expressly mentioned in the Constitution, the right to set up a foundation can be derived from the general personality rights that are laid down in Article 2. Unlike common law countries, Germany has accorded foundations a distinct legal personality since the 19th century. However, foundations may be created under other legal forms as well, and may serve other than charitable purposes as well, with the exception of purely commercial purposes. In practice, 98% of all autonomous and non-autonomous foundations are tax exempt.

16 The predominant legal base for autonomous foundations is ss. 80-89 of the federal Civil Code (Buergerliches *Gesetzbuch*). There is no specific legal base for non-autonomous foundations which are considered to be dealt with in general trust law. In fact, the only authoritative mention of non-autonomous foundations is in tax law where they are listed with the other legal entities that can attain tax exemption (s. 1, 1 *Koerperschaftsteuergesetz* – the law on the taxation of legal entities). Foundations that are incorporated as limited companies (*Stiftung GmbH*) or as associations find no mention in the law. See: Rupert Graf Strachwitz, *Stiftungen nutzen, führen und verwalten – ein Handbuch*, (Frankfurt/Main: Campus, 1994); Werner Seifart and Axel von Campenhausen, *Handbuch des Stiftungsrechts*, (2nd Edition, Muenchen: Beck, 1999).

By their nature, foundations are the oldest charities still in existence. The oldest ones still on record are said to go back to the 10th century A.D. Contrary to the assertion of some social scientists, it is perfectly clear today that foundations are predominantly a bourgeois urban phenomenon, not a feudal one, though rulers and aristocrats have been known to set up foundations too. It is therefore not surprising that the rise of urban communities saw the number of new foundations growing. The original form of foundation is probably the non-autonomous one (known in common law as the trust), which is based on the principle of a handover of assets to a trustee with a clear mandate on its usage. Townships, universities, and religious communities were the most frequently sought trustees, and thus accumulated large conglomerates of trusts over the centuries. Around the 18th century, however, a new custom was introduced – boards of trustees were created specifically for one particular trusteeship, thus paving the way for what is known today as the autonomous foundation. In the post-Napoleonic reorganisation of the law this specific form of foundation gained a special legal status, the definitive difference being that autonomous foundations do not have outside owners or members – they are self-owned.

To compensate for this, they are subject to government supervision under civil law, as well as to the fiscal supervision that covers all legal and indeed natural persons. Supervision is regulated by state law and differs from state to state in some details, though not in principle. The intrusiveness of state supervision is restricted by law to ensuring the observance of the law and of the founder's will as laid down in the statutes – it may not include interference with the actual activities. The underlying logic is perfectly sound – the government, acting in the interest of the public, takes on the long-term task of ensuring the fulfilment of the founder's will in the absence of owners or members. But the original thinking went beyond that. For one, the French position of hostility to any form of intermediaries between the citizen and the state, though it had not actually influenced the concept of society in 19th century Germany, had not gone totally unnoticed. More importantly, the supremacy of the state resulted in nearly any form of activity beyond the immediate personal sphere being subjected to a government concession. Originally, this would have applied to associations and business companies as well as foundations. It is therefore hardly surprising that the right to associate freely, and without the requirement of governmental permission, was a prime battleground in the 19th century battle for civil rights. The 1919 Republican Constitution that elevated this right to constitutional rank did not include foundations, and while government concessions for business activities had gone out long before that, the theory of law until the beginning of the 21st century clung to the principle that permission to set up a foundation was a government concession that could be legitimately refused.

Under these circumstances it is not surprising that instances of government agencies overstepping their authority were relatively common. Since supervision included the approval of the statutes, founders were obliged to clear the wording with the relevant authority before the actual act of founding. In nearly every case, the founder being a newcomer to the foundation community, government officials, while often tendering sorely needed advice and suggesting amendments that would ensure the foundation's functioning, saw fit to influence founders as to the purpose and the governance of the foundation. Political directives and personal preferences thus easily found their way into the statutes. The implications of this practice were considerable, especially since, under the general theory of foundations, they are set up to enact the founder's will as expressed in the statutes at the time of their creation.[17]

This was one of the reasons why, in 2002, the civil code was reformed. It had long been argued that potential founders were deterred from creating autonomous foundations and even any type of foundation by their suspicion that they would be subject to excessive government interference in doing so and in conducting the foundation's business. Indeed, some resorted to the form of non-autonomous foundation despite its limitations, or incorporated as a limited company in order to keep the government out. On the other hand, it was felt that more private wealth should be channelled into pursuing purposes of public welfare. As a result, the new wording of the law[18] determines that any citizen has the right to create a foundation and to have this foundation recognised as an autonomous legal person, provided certain formal conditions are met. These conditions include a binding commitment to endow the foundation on a scale sufficient to enable it to pursue its statutory goals,[19] a precise wording for these goals, the determination of a name and a legal seat, and provisions for the governance of the foundation.

Following this reform, the states are now obliged to amend their own laws (which to date only 6 out of 16 have accomplished), since federal law supersedes state law and a number of provisions in existing state laws no longer

17 Compare the position with associative bodies which, in principle, represent the ever developing will of their members and therefore regularly revise their statutes.

18 *Gesetz zur Modernisierung des Stiftungsrechts 2002 (Bundesgesetzblatt I, S. 2634).*

19 Contrary to popular belief, the endowment does not necessarily have to yield a revenue and can be of any type that may serve its purpose. Thus, for example, an arts foundation may be endowed with works of art only, a hospital building may be sufficient to create a hospital foundation and so on.

conform to the reformed federal law. The purpose of the reform is to reduce government intervention, strengthen foundation autonomy and thus make foundations more popular. It is fairly clear that this will be accomplished, albeit to a varying degree in different states.

Two important developments in the state of the art of charities in general have found their way into foundation reform. First, and this is entirely a state matter, foundations are increasingly required to produce financial reports according to the system that has long been common in business companies. Though by law, any system will still suffice, the legal requirement of presenting audited reports will produce this result, since the auditors have no option but to follow the rules established within their own professional organisation. Secondly, the door has at last been opened to more transparency. Whereas there is still no legal obligation for any charity to publicise any information on its activities and financial situation, the fact that public foundation registers will now have to be introduced will certainly result in at least these organisations being more open to the interested public.

Non-autonomous foundations are legally owned by their trustees. Since trust law in Germany is far less developed than in the U.K. or the U.S. the range of possible activities and the legal potential of such a trust are severely limited. Also, trusteeship is commonly vested in a sole legal person, rarely in a sole natural person, and more rarely still in more than one person. Still, for a grant making charity of small or medium size and endowed with liquid assets, the non-autonomous form is perfectly sufficient, and, since these trusts are not subject to civil law supervision, do not have the often quite cumbersome procedures of annual general meetings to deal with, and only require a very modest endowment, they are considered the easiest possible way of organising a German charity.

One further aspect of foundations needs to be mentioned. While the number of autonomous and non-autonomous foundations in Germany can be estimated at about 18,000, there exist about 100,000 foundations under church law that are commonly not included among the foundations at all. A foundation of this type is the legal owner of virtually every parish church in Germany, and a plethora of others are centuries-old tithes that in former times provided for the living of the local clergy. We know very little about all these, since they come under the constitutional autonomy of the churches and are neither regulated, nor supervised by government authorities. It is only when these foundations enter into activities beyond the mere promulgation of the faith that they come under the aegis of the government. Indeed, some of our largest charitable institutions are foundations of this type. In this context, it is interesting to note that the churches do not usually consider themselves as civil society organisations at all.

3.3 Mixed Charities and Charitable Companies

As mentioned above, since the 1950s, there have been cases of mixed charities which carry the name *Stiftung,* while in fact being incorporated as associations or as (charitable) limited companies. The reasons, besides sidestepping government supervision, more often than not have to do with perceived benefits that attach to the word *Stiftung*; this is especially the case if the new charity is planning to enter into fundraising. It seems unfortunate that a group of German foundations that is particularly well known abroad belongs to this type: the so-called political party foundations are all, with one exception, registered associations *(eingetragener Verein)* in law with no significant endowment, and are highly dependent on government funding.[20] In the recent practice of the courts associations are no longer registered bearing the name *Stiftung*, as this is rightly deemed confusing.

While the forms discussed so far are predominantly designed for and used by not-for-profits, others, corporate forms in particular, can attain tax exempt status if they conform to the same rules. In recent years, the not-for-profit limited company *(Gemeinnuetzige GmbH)*, often not using the word *Stiftung*, has become a serious option when organising related businesses of foundations and associations and in setting up new charities. Tax exempt public companies *(Gemeinnuetzige AG)* are rare, but do exist. These companies are naturally subject to corporate law as well as charity law. While cooperative societies do not exist as tax exempt by their own will, expressed by their lobbying organisations, there is an undercurrent of opinion in favour of revising this rigid position.

All this may seem exceedingly complicated, and would be all the more so if all the minor details and historical remnants were to be included. Public bodies that perform basically the same services have also gone unmentioned although the large number of irregularities and borderline cases would merit dealing with them at some length. It serves i.a. to underpin the argument put

20 For example, *Konrad-Adenauer-Stiftung e.V., Friedrich-Ebert-Stiftung e.V., Hanns-Seidel-Stiftung e.V., Heinrich-Boell-Stiftung e.V., Rosa-Luxemburg-Stiftung e.V.*. The exception is the *Friedrich-Naumann-Stiftung*, a regular autonomous foundation.

forward earlier that German charity law, going back a long time in history, is necessarily not as clear cut as a systematic new approach would render it.

4 Charities under Fiscal Law

It has already been stated that German law grants tax exemption to legal entities in view of their charitable disposition and activity. Tax exemption (*Steuerbeguenstigung)* entails exemption from income tax (*Einkommensteuer*), potentially from estate tax (*Vermoegenssteuer),*[21] and inheritance tax (*Erbschaftssteuer*). It does not entail exemption from VAT, and the exemption from income tax is restricted to income from an endowment, from donations, and from certain related businesses, such as the operation of a hospital or a museum. The clause concerning related business has, in recent years, come under severe criticism from the European Union which sees it as an impediment to fair competition, and the enforcement of substantial changes is to be expected.

Exemption is granted, provided the legal entity meets very specific requirements in two very distinct fields. Primarily, the entity has to serve one or several purposes specified in the law. Firstly, the law classifies charities under three headings:

1. Charities serving the public good (*Gemeinnuetzige Zwecke*)
2. Charities serving individuals in need (*Mildtaetige Zwecke*)
3. Charities serving church purposes (*Kirchliche Zwecke*)

While 'church purposes' remain unspecified, specification being left to the Churches themselves, and 'individuals in need' are defined as being in need on the grounds of illness, age or financial deprivation, 'serving the public good' presents the biggest problem in terms of definition. It is specifically in this area that a complete revision is called for. The existing list of purposes has been added to so often, and for so many different reasons, that a common definition is hardly apparent, and indeed does not appear in the law at all. For no obvious reason, the purposes are grouped under three headings, each of which comprises very diverse activities. A more detailed list of activities is only partly to be found in the law and has been modified by government without the direct involvement of Parliament. While obviously unofficial comprehensive lists exist

21 Estate tax exists, but currently only in theory, as the rate is 0%.

for practical purposes, the legal sources are scattered over the most surprising legal documents.[22] The list includes classical charitable purposes such as health, social services, the arts, youth care, education, and nature conservation, as well as some new ideals like ecology, and some more unconventional purposes such as amateur radio transmitting, flying model airplanes, breeding dogs or playing chess within a membership organisation. Interestingly, goals such as building democracy, furthering voluntary or community action and similar general purposes find no mention at all.

Under the general principle that any of these purposes has to be furthered by a legal entity, there exists a whole range more specific rules to be observed. Again, some are obvious, such as that the public good has indeed to be furthered, and exclusively so. Thus, for example, operating a museum is a charitable purpose only if the museum is open to the public. Also, the statutes have to contain a strict non-distribution clause, and there are restrictions on the percentage of management costs. Here again, there have been changes in recent years. A significant one is that professional fundraising involving much higher costs is now permissible.

Furthermore, an exempt entity must, on principle, carry out its charitable purposes itself. The collection and redistribution of funds to other exempt institutions is regarded as a legitimate exception. This indeed applies to all grant making foundations, but it is one of the reasons why grant making has never been seen as the prime purpose, let alone as the definitive element, of a foundation in Germany. Moreover, an exempt entity is compelled to spend its income within a year after the end of the year in which it has been received. This is one of the rare instances where rules for foundations differ from those that apply to other exempt bodies. They are not expected to spend their endowment; indeed there is no rule as to the percentage of it that has to be spent. Nor are there rules governing the nature of the investments. Generally speaking, however, there is no distinction in tax law between public charities and private founda-

22 While the basic legal source is the general Tax Law (*Abgabenordnung*), s. 52, most of the recognized charitable purposes are listed more comprehensively in an annex to a government regulation on income tax as they concern tax deduction for donors: Annex 1 to s. 48 (2) of the Income Tax Implementation Regulation: list of the purposes which are generally recognised as especially eligible for promotion in the meaning of s. 10 b (1) of the Income Tax Law (from 1st January, 2000) (*Anlage 1 zu § 48 Abs. 2 der Einkommensteuer-Durchführungsverordnung: Verzeichnis der Zwecke, die allgemein als besonders foerderungswuerdig im Sinne des § 10b Abs. 1 des Einkommensteuergesetzes anerkannt sind (ab 01.01.2000).*

tions. Private foundations become public charities following their recognition as tax exempt bodies.

Finally, the effect of tax exemption on donations should be mentioned. For the majority of listed purposes, tax exemption entails deductibility of donations on the part of the donor. Following the principle of utility to the state, different purposes carry differing quotas of deductibility. Donations to research and the arts, as well as to help to individuals in need, may be deducted from up to 10% of the donor's taxable income, while 5% is permitted for all other purposes. Donating an endowment to a foundation since 2000 carries a much higher, and not income-related, deductibility.[23]

Relatively recently, a discussion has begun in Germany on whether the system of tax exemption is in fact appropriate. For one, a whole range of smaller not-for-profit organisations (estimates say 2/3 of all charities) have to claim and periodically reclaim tax exemption, although they would not qualify for tax anyway, due either to their small size or the fact that they do not make a surplus on their turnover. Tax exemption for them is no more than a means to gain reputation, to be included in certain government grant programmes, to be accepted as an advocacy group and so on. A huge amount of bureaucratic procedure could be saved if a simpler system was introduced.

Moreover, it seems increasingly doubtful whether the tax authorities are best equipped to judge whether a certain activity is, in a more general sense, charitable. Tax offices are primarily responsible for collecting taxes, and as many of them as possible, and will thus necessarily look at tax exemption from a negative viewpoint. An application from a nongovernmental service provider, which would perform the same service as a government agency at a cheaper cost, might be looked upon more favourably than one from an advocacy group that will only cause the government trouble by asking uncomfortable questions and clamouring for citizens' rights. More importantly, there is no focus point within the revenue service where the appropriateness of exempting or not exempting certain activities can be fairly established, preferably with the assist-

23 *Gesetz zur weiteren steuerlichen Foerderung von Stiftungen 2000 (Bundesgesetzblatt I, S. 1034.)* It is worth noting that there are six different systems of treating voluntary donations to charitable organisations in Europe. While Germany allows a deduction from the donor's taxable income, in other countries (e.g. France) the deduction is made from the tax burden. Austria and Finland have no deduction; Italy and most central and eastern European countries have a system of earmarking a small percentage of one's tax burden in favour of recognized charities; United Kingdom charities claim a percentage of donations received from the internal revenue, while the donor gets no deduction; and Greece actually taxes the charities on the donations they have received.

ance of non-partisan experts. In short, tax officials frequently lack the expertise needed to adequately evaluate an activity hitherto unknown, and rely overly on their preconceived notions that are more often than not drawn from the popular press. And while, of course, applicants need not accept a first ruling, they will probably not be strong enough to carry their case through the administrative hierarchy and the courts, a procedure that may very well take ten or more years. The idea of a charity commission, based on the British model, has therefore recently been introduced into the discussion.

5 Conclusions

A charity, in the German sense, is a legal entity, though not necessarily a legal person, that is destined to become active in the interest of society at large, which, in theory at least, disregards private interests. The activity may extend to numerous fields, and distinctions as to the legal treatment of different activities are made only in regard to their utility to the state. Unlike other countries, including some particularly strong democracies like France, the right to be charitable in an organised fashion has never seriously been contested. It is part of Germany's culture, and encompassed in the constitutional rights of German citizens. But precisely because this is so, the legal framework for this area of society is exceedingly traditional and no longer corresponds to a systematic approach to the definition of the role of government, the business community, and civil society within a modern political order.

The legal entities involved can be of very diverse nature, and preference to particular forms is accorded for reasons of public interest, as defined by the state. Civil law and tax law are intertwined, while differing somewhat in defining the nature of a legal entity. Over the past 25 years, charity legislation has undergone numerous amendments. Many of these have been introduced for political reasons, though none have changed the principle of recognition as developed in the 19th century. In the light of recent societal development, and the emergence of civil society as a separate agent of public affairs and a driving force of social change, a thorough revision has been suggested, though not yet accomplished.

In its report, presented to Parliament in 2002, the Parliamentary Commission on Civic Engagement pointed out these deficiencies. In suggesting a whole range of amendments to existing legal regulations, it also called for a new outlook. Since government in modern societies is neither able, nor indeed supposed, to manage and control all aspects of public welfare and public activity, the commission argued that there was a real danger of matters being traded in the market place, that for a variety of reasons did not belong there. It would therefore be necessary to enhance the importance of the third realm of public action, often termed the third sector, and now more commonly civil society. Also, it would be important to make the distinction between market and non-market nongovernmental action quite clear, to avoid creating a pseudo-market, i.e. a market that competes with other markets while enjoying special privileges, while at the same time liberating the not-for-profit sector from the traditional overdose of government interference, and limiting government action to law making and law enforcement.

This train of thought necessarily implies a fundamental reorganisation of tasks. What needs to be done by government, business, and civil society respectively, is a matter of principle, as well as one of expedience. In any case, scope and limitations of civil society need to be scrutinised from a view point of human and civil rights as much as from one of popular will and aspirations.

It seems clear from the foregoing that a drastic revision of the legal framework, as yet rooted in 19th century political beliefs, is unavoidable. When Parliament began to discuss the revision of the laws for foundations, many believed this popular theme to be the gateway for the far more difficult tax, or rather tax exemption, issues.

Other European countries, faced with a similar analysis, have in recent years done more. The United Kingdom, the Netherlands, France, and Italy, to name just a few, have introduced sweeping changes. Whether a different systematic approach will be introduced in Germany as regards deductibility of donations; whether tax exemption will in future be granted for reasons of approach, motive, and contribution to civil society rather than merely for those of usefulness to the state; whether consequently the not-for-profit, non-distribution aspect will gain supremacy over the charitable purpose aspect; whether new civil law forms will be developed, and whether judgement on eligibility will pass from the tax authorities to an independent government agency, remains to be seen.

10

THE LEGAL IMPLEMENTATION OF FREEDOM OF ASSOCIATION IN THE NETHERLANDS AND OTHER WESTERN EUROPEAN COUNTRIES

Tymen J. van der Ploeg

1 INTRODUCTION

The term 'freedom of association' has a number of dimensions. It implies, firstly, the freedom to *establish* associations – voluntary organisations, including foundations – in order to pursue any purpose that is not contrary to public order. It also implies the freedom of individuals to decide to *join* such an association, and also in due course to resign their membership. Furthermore, it implies the freedom of the organisation to determine the criteria for membership, and to refuse membership to individuals.

In Article 11 of the European Convention on Human Rights and Fundamental Freedoms,[1] this right is recognized as a universal human right and state parties to the Convention are bound to ensure its protection. The Convention restricts the ability of states to pass legislation, or otherwise act in a way which would unnecessarily curtail this freedom.[2] Restrictions are only allowed as far as they 'are necessary in a democratic society in the interest of national safety or public safety, for the prevention of disorder or crime, for the protection of health or morals or for the protection of the rights and freedoms of others.'

1 Convention for the Protection of Human Rights and Fundamental Freedoms (European Convention on Human Rights, as amended) (ECHR), Art. 11.

2 Compare also International Covenant on Economic, Social and Cultural Rights (adopted 16 December 1966, entered into force 3 January 1976) 993 UNTS 3 (ICESCR), Art.8, and International Covenant on Civil and Political Rights (adopted 16 December 1966, entered into force 23 March 1976) 999 UNTS 171 (ICCPR), Art. 22.

Yuwen Li (Ed.), *Freedom of Association in China and Europe: Comparative Perspectives in Law and Practice*, © 2005 Koninklijke Brill NV, Leiden. Printed in The Netherlands, pp. 325-352.

This makes it rather difficult for legislators, policymakers, governmental authorities and judges to limit freedom of association. Firstly, restrictions have to be discussed in democratic debate, and any restriction must be laid down in formal law. Secondly, the restriction must be made in pursuance of a legitimate aim, and must be limited to what is adequate and necessary for that purpose. The authorities cannot merely present policy reasons; they must show that the restriction is necessary. The citizens of the state parties to the European Convention have a direct right to complain about any infringement of their rights to the European Court of Human Rights at Strasbourg.[3] There is not a great deal of case-law regarding Article 11 of the European Convention that involves Western European countries.[4] The judgments concerned do not allude to the requirements for the establishment of associations, or the supervision of them.

Sections 2-4 of this paper discuss the legal regulation of freedom of association. This analysis takes place on three levels: firstly, tracing the historical development of the law on associations in both the Netherlands and other countries in Western Europe. The following section describes the rules that apply to registration, and how they relate to accountability and transparency. Finally, section 4 considers the legal means for protecting public order and the general interest.

Section 5 of the paper outlines more broadly the position of voluntary organisations, and their relationship with the State, focusing mainly on The Netherlands, but referring in places to comparative perspectives from Western Europe. It starts by reviewing the basic theory and practice of civil society, before examining the role of non-governmental organisations (NGOs) in functioning as agents for collective action. It continues to explore the theme of the realisation of civil society by considering various means for fostering the activity of non-governmental organisations: these include tax advantages, subsidies, and finally the regulation of fundraising activities.

3 ECHR, Art. 34.

4 See Clare Ovey and Robin White, *Jacobs and White, The European Convention on Human Rights,* (Oxford: Oxford University Press, 2003), p. 290 ff.

2 The Freedom of Association and Law of Associations and Foundations

2.1 The Netherlands

2.1.1 Historical Development of the Law on Associations

The right to freedom of association first gained legal recognition in the Netherlands in the Constitution of 1848, Article 10: 'The right of inhabitants to associate and gather is recognized. The law regulates and restricts the execution of that right in the interest of public order.' The law that regulated this was the Law on Associations and Public Meetings of 1855.[5]

The Law of 1855 contained four paragraphs on associations. The first paragraph concerned establishment: it stated that for the establishment of an association, no governmental approval was required. The second paragraph concerned prohibited associations, setting forth the circumstances under which associations were considered to be contrary to public order, and outlining the procedure whereby an association could be declared forbidden by a civil judge. The third paragraph concerned the legal personality of associations. It stated, in Article 5, that to receive legal personality an association required governmental approval.[6] This approval was given for a period of less than thirty years.[7] When an association wanted to receive legal personality for a period longer than 30 years, or for an unlimited duration, it needed recognition by a formal law, though this never occurred in the history of this law. Recognition was granted on the basis of the statutes of the association. They should, among other things, contain the purpose of the association (Article 6). Recognition could be refused on the grounds of the general public interest (Article 7). Amendments of the statutes should also be approved by the government (Article 8). Statutes and amendments that had been approved were published in the Netherlands Government Gazette (Article 9). Associations without legal personality could function as such in society. They were generally considered to be contracts comparable with a partnership. The fourth paragraph laid down some rules about the applicability of the foregoing provisions. They included

5 Law of 22 April 1855, Staat Blad 32.

6 Formally it was recognition by the Crown, but in practice the Ministry of Justice was involved.

7 In practice all associations with legal personality were established for 29 years and 11 months.

the rule that the paragraph on forbidden associations was also applicable to foundations[8] and other legal persons.[9]

In this way freedom of association has led to a new legal form: the association with legal personality.[10] The purpose of the association could be anything, as long as it was not contrary to public order or public morality. The only remaining limitation after 1874 was and is that an association may not have a cooperative purpose.[11] The association form may be used for enterprises, but the profit may not be distributed to the founders, the members of internal bodies, or to the members. The general association form can also be used by trade unions and political parties.[12] Religious organisations can choose to use the association form, though they have more freedom regarding their organisational structure when they choose the form of a church.[13]

During the processes of establishment and amendment of statutes, the government controlled the content of the statutes, especially the purpose of the association. Over the course of time there have been a number of cases where the Ministry of Justice refused to approve of the statutes. These refusals concerned associations that were considered to be against public morality[14] or associations that were directed towards social revolution, often through violent means.[15] It is clear that the use of these criteria is closely connected with the public policy of the time. The organisations that were refused legal personality as associations were not, however, completely banned from society – the legal

8 The foundation was regulated for the first time by the Law on foundations of 31 May 1956, Staat Blad 327.

9 This follows from Art. 14, Sections. 1-2. All corporations were called associations then.

10 The idea of the association as legal person was already present in a Civil Code concept of 1820.

11 The royal approval of the statutes of the *Amerongse kredietvereniging* (a cooperative society) was refused. In 1876 the first law on cooperative societies came into force (Law of 17 November 1876, Staat Blad 227).

12 In Germany, political parties are ruled by the Law of Parties (*Parteigesetz)* of 24 July 1976, BGB l. I, 1967, 773. It contains detailed rules on internal organisation, state financing and financial disclosure. Political parties and trade unions in Belgium choose not to ask for legal personality; they can however execute their societal functions without it.

13 The Dutch Civil Code, Book 2, Art. 2, states that churches are legal persons and are regulated by their own statutes.

14 Associations to promote Neo-Malthusianism and atheism were refused recognition in the period between 1920 and 1930. An association of homosexuals was refused in the 1970s. They have since been recognized.

15 For this reason, over a long period before World War II, social democrat and communist organisations that did not reject violent revolution were refused recognition.

form of foundation was available for them, for which no governmental recognition was required.[16]

The rules about the organisational structure of associations formulated during the period from 1855 to 1976 were rather limited.[17] The Ministry of Justice made a list of elements that should be part of the statutes. These uncodified rules and policy standards in fact formed the structure of the associations during that period. Informal associations were also accepted in practice; for instance they were able to open a bank account. Most associations, however, preferred the position of an association 'with royal approval,' as it conferred greater societal status.

The law of 1855 remained in force for a long time without many amendments. This situation could have continued until now, had the regulation of legal persons not been included in the far-reaching reform of civil law. After the Second World War it was felt necessary to modernize, more specifically to systematize, the entire civil code. The second book that was planned dealt with legal persons. The association was included in this book.

The old law of 1855 was replaced by Title 2 of Book 2 of the Civil Code. In the first drafts of the new Title 2 some sort of governmental approval was still incorporated, but in a later and definite proposal the element of governmental interference was removed. Instead of governmental approval as a requirement for legal personality, the requirement for associations with full legal capacity became a notarial deed of establishment, including the statute of the association. The reason behind this change of system lay in the international standards to which The Netherlands adhered,[18] that dictated that trade unions should have the right to be established without governmental interference. The easiest way to fulfill this requirement was to remove the governmental interference in the establishment of all associations.[19]

16 See below section 2.1.3. For legal means against organisations contrary to public order, see below section 4.

17 Apart from the law on association and public meetings, there were some general rules for corporations ('moral bodies') in the Civil Code of 1838 that were applied to them. These rules stated that there has to be a management board and that the members form the general assembly.

18 See European Social Charter, Art. 5, and the ICESCR 1966, Art. 8.

19 While the Law of 1855 was in force, Art. 7 of this law provided that trade union freedom was recognized; this was added by law of 10 December 1964, Staat Blad 492.

2.1.2 The Requirements for the Establishment of Associations

According to Book 2 of the Civil Code, since 1976 the conferment of legal personality on associations is a private matter, and there is no requirement of governmental approval either at the time of establishment or at any later stage. 'Freedom of association' is not mentioned explicitly in the Civil Code. It is laid down in the Constitution, which retains the same provision from the Constitution of 1848.[20]

According to Book 2, Title 2 of the Civil Code there are two types of associations: formal and informal associations. Formal associations have full legal capacity, whereas informal associations have only limited legal capacity. When the establishers of an association want to have full legal capacity they have to go to the public notary, who will record the establishment, including the statutes of the association, in a notarial deed. Associations which choose to remain informal have limited legal capacities: they cannot buy or sell estate, they cannot inherit property, and the members of the management board are personally liable for the debts and obligations of the association. However, informal associations do have legal personality. Thus the changes ushered in by Book 2 of the Civil Code of 1976 can be summarized as follows: the formal procedure to establish an association with full legal personality has changed from a requirement of governmental approval in the law of 1855 to the notarial deed, and the virtually unregulated informal association has been remodeled as an informal association with legal personality, albeit with limited legal capacity. The rules on associations in Book 2 of the Civil Code of 1976 are, with the foregoing exceptions, also applicable to informal associations.

Title 2 of Book 2 of the Civil Code contains an extensive set of rules regulating the organisational side of the association.[21] Compared to other jurisdictions, this law contains a large number of mandatory rules. There are specific rules governing a number of areas, including: the admission of members and the termination of membership; the appointment and dismissal of the board members; the general meetings of members and of delegates; the annual report and balance sheet and the control over them; the association's competence to impose obligations on members; and the procedures for amendment of the statutes, and for dissolution of the association. The rules in Book 2 of the Civil Code are meant to safeguard the essentially democratic character of associations, and to protect their members. When organisers do not want such a type of

20 In the Constitution itself it is found in Art. 8.

21 See Art. 26 ff.

organisational structure, they can opt for the foundation form, which is discussed below.

2.1.3 Foundations

In The Netherlands the foundation has had legal personality since before the French occupation (beginning 19th century). After the re-establishment of Dutch sovereignty in 1813 it lasted until 1882 when a judgment of the Dutch Supreme Court[22] held that a foundation recorded in a notarial deed (in this case a testament) is recognized as a legal person. There was no legislation about the foundation as such but in several laws the establishment of foundations by private legal act was presupposed. The foundation became a vehicle for all sorts of purposes. In the 1920s and 30s the government used the foundation form for many agencies that were essentially privatized in this way.

The Law on Foundations of 1956 was the first legislation to regulate the establishment and other aspects of foundations in modern times. This law and the provisions on foundations in the Dutch Civil Code of 1976 stipulated that the establishment of a foundation had to take place by a notarial deed. This could be a testament. The process of establishing foundations involves no governmental interference.

A characteristic of foundations is that they may not have members. This element distinguishes the foundation from the association. Furthermore, foundations may not distribute their profits to the members of the board or others, but they may make payments which have a social or charitable character. Like the association, the foundation is not limited in its purposes.

The foundation is often an attractive alternative to the association form, as Book 2 of the Civil Code contains virtually no rules regulating its organisational structure. Particularly when establishers of an organisation are fearful of losing control of the organisation, they will opt for the foundation. There is no general assembly which may dismiss the members of the management board. It is up to the statute to regulate the processes of appointment and dismissal of the members of the management board of a foundation. The amendment of statutes is also regulated in a different way. In an association this is the competence of the general assembly of members. In a foundation the amendment of statutes is only possible if the statutes provide for amendment, and it must be carried out in accordance with any conditions that are stipulated

22 Supreme Court, 30 June 1882, W. 4800 (*M.van Wessem c.s.- Weldadige Stichting van Heutz te Venlo*).

(Book 2, Article 293 of the Civil Code). While, in law, a foundation only has one internal body, the management board,[23] the legislator made some special rules to exercise external control on foundations. This control is not in the hands of the executive branch of government, but of the courts. Upon the request of the public prosecutor, or of interested persons, the court may dismiss members of the management board in the case of mismanagement; the court may also appoint board members where they are lacking, and, under certain circumstances, amend the statutes of the foundation.[24] While there are very few examples where the public prosecutor has taken such action, interested persons have proved to be more active.

2.2 Other Western European countries

Other Western European countries also recognized freedom of association in their constitutions during the 19th century. However, the regulation of the association *as a legal person* took longer in most countries. In Germany this is regulated in the German Civil Code of 1896 (*Bürgerliches Gesetzbuch*). In Switzerland this is regulated in the Swiss Civil Code of 1907 (*Zivilgezetzbuch*). In France, while freedom of association was, on the one hand proclaimed by the constitution of 1848, it was, on the other hand, undermined by the prohibition of associations and meetings of more than twenty persons.[25] Only in 1901 did a special law about the association, and its legal personality, come into being.[26] In Belgium the constitution of 1831 already recognised freedom of association, but the regulation of the regular association with legal personality occurred only in 1921.[27] The situation in Austria is different. In 1951 a law on associations came into force, which mainly laid down rules of criminal law, but the civil law aspects remain barely regulated. In the Austrian system associations are as such legal persons. Austria is thus the only country out of those mentioned in which the freedom to establish an association without legal personality does not exist.

23 The statutes may however provide for other internal bodies.

24 See the Civil Code, Book 2, Arts. 298, 299 and 294.

25 French Penal Code, Arts. 414-416.

26 Law of 1 July 1901.

27 Law of 27 June 1921 regarding non-profit making associations (*vereniging zonder winstoogmerk*).

The way in which legal personality is obtained varies from country to country. In Germany, legal personality is obtained by the registration of the association at the District Court of its seat. The application for registration is laid down in a notarial deed (compare Article 58, German Civil Code). The court will register the association as a legal person, unless the public administration that is informed states that the association is prohibited (see Article 61, German Civil Code).

In Switzerland, the statutes must make apparent the will of the establishers for the association to become a legal person (Article 60, Swiss Civil Code). Belgium requires only the publication of the statutes in the annexes of the Official Journal (Articles 2 and 3, Law of 1921).

France has a system in which associations can have different levels of legal personality. When the association has submitted its statutes, and the names and addresses of the members of the management board to the head of the regional government, and consequently the public prosecutor has given his consent, and the statutes are published in the Official Journal, it obtains limited legal capacity. For most associations this status of '*association déclarée*' is sufficient. An association with limited capacity may request full capacity. To obtain this status the association has to obtain a declaration of public utility from the Ministry of Interior. An association with public utility (*association d'utilité publique*) receives this declaration of public utility for a period of at least three years. The government monitors during this period with discretionary power whether the association meets the standard for public utitlity.

When we look to the requirements for the establishment of *foundations* in these countries, it appears that government is generally more involved than with the establishment of associations.[28] That has to do with the fact that in these countries the purpose of the foundation according to the law generally has to be 'charitable' or for the public good. Thus, the involvement of the State is motivated by the fact that the State is the protector and promoter of the public good and the general interest.

According to the law in Germany, the state authorities have to approve of the establishment of foundations. State authorities also exercise a supervisory power over the foundations that are active in their state. The power the state exercises is not a discretionary power; it is a control over the legitimacy of the acts of the internal bodies of the foundations.

28 For more information about foundations in comparative perspective: Frits W. Hondius and Tymen J van der Ploeg, 'Foundations', (2000) (Volume XIII) (9) *International Encyclopedia of Comparative Law*; and J.C.B. Mohr (Paul Siebeck), Tübingen, 2001.

In Austria the state is also heavily involved in both the establishment and the supervision of general foundations. As in Germany, the Austrian authorities exercise a control on legitimacy. In 1993, a new type of foundation was introduced – the private foundation. Government is not involved in the establishment of this type of foundations, and they have no fiscal privileges.

In France the government, more precisely the State Council (*Conseil d'état*), is heavily involved in the establishment of foundations, and in the supervision of them. The State Council has discretionary power, which means that its judgments may be based on legal and policy grounds.

Until 2003, Belgium also had a system in which government had to approve the statutes before the foundation could be established as a legal person. However, the new Belgian law on associations and foundations, of 16th January, 2003, introduces, next to the general foundation, a private foundation for which governmental approval is not necessary. The private foundation is a foundation that has not requested the recognition of public utility by the relevant Ministry; yet it should still have an altruistic purpose.

The United Kingdom along with the Irish Republic is a special case in Western Europe. It does not belong to the civil law family, but to the Anglo-American common law family. The United Kingdom has no codified constitution, but its legal system does recognize freedom of association. In the area of nongovernmental and nonprofit organisations it has legal forms different to those in the continental countries. It attributes importance to whether assets are used for a charitable purpose; a body with exclusively charitable purposes is a charity. The law on charities dates back to the 17th century. The Charities Act 1993 only applies to England and Wales. The other parts of the United Kingdom have their own legislation. The Charities Act stipulates that charities must be registered with the Charity Commission. This semi-governmental agency has supervisory powers over the administration of charities. Being a charity has no relation with being a legal person. Charities in England take a number of forms. These include trusts which are legally not comparable with associations and foundations. In this article I will only incidentally refer to the charity.[29]

29 For more information about English charity law see the article by Richard Fries in this book.

2.3 Observations

In general, the rules about the establishment and supervision of associations and foundations are codified in the countries of Western Europe on the basis of their own constitutions prior to the establishment of the European Convention on Human Rights. Up to now, the European Court of Human Rights has not heard applications from citizens of Western European countries that challenged the legislation of associations and foundations, or the application of such legislation, on the basis of its conformity with the right to freedom of association. The rare cases before the Court that did raise claims of infringement of the right of association concerned how membership of associations could lead to adverse consequences in other areas, such as in employment as a civil servant.[30]

However, the way in which organisations exercise their freedom of association may lead to infringement of other human rights. An interesting case is a political party in The Netherlands, the *Staatkundig Gereformeerde Partij* (SGP), which allows only men to become voting members of the party; women can only become non-voting members. There have been efforts to convince the public prosecutor to request the dissolution of the association because it is contrary to public order to discriminate against women. Until now the dominant opinion is that the association has this freedom, not only because of freedom of association but also of freedom of religion, as the specific place of women was based on religious dogmas.[31] There are however those who do not consider such cultural diversity acceptable. One may expect similar conflicts to arise concerning the way some Islamic groups choose to exercise their freedom of association and of religion. Up to now the limits have not been fixed.

Although there have been no major conflicts regarding the legislation and supervision of the establishment of associations and foundations, whether they are in conformity with freedom of association and more specifically if the restrictions are really necessary is contestable. Two issues deserve further

30 See ECHR *Vogt* vs *Germany*, Judgment of 26 September 1995, Series A, No. 323, (1996) 21 EHRR 205: A restriction preventing teachers from being members of the Communist Party was found to be not proportionate.

31 See H.-M. Th.D. ten Napel, 'A Dutch Taliban? (*Een Nederlandse Taliban*?)', in N.F. van Manen (ed.), *De multiculturele samenleving en het recht*, (Nijmegen: Ars Aequi 2002), at p. 151.

discussion: the informal association in The Netherlands, and secondly, the issue of governmental supervision or court supervision.

(1) Inadequacy of the Dutch law regarding informal associations
It is submitted that the Dutch law on formal associations is satisfactory. The extensive rules on the internal organisation are necessary to distinguish an association from a foundation, and to protect the participants and third parties. Organisers can opt for a foundation if they do not want this structure: they only need go to the public notary. Furthermore, formal associations can also be converted into a foundation.[32] The procedure requires a decision by the general meeting with a nine-tenths majority, a notarial deed and a court license.

The problem arises, from the perspective of freedom of association, when citizens want to organise *informally*. Dutch law stipulates that every association, whether formal or informal, falls under the same regulations concerning organisation. Thus they are not free to choose their own way of organising. They also have to conform to the rules on internal structure. I submit that this runs contrary to the principle of freedom of association. A decision of a court in the city of Utrecht illustrates the extent of the legal regulation. The case concerned the suit against a group of people that called themselves Fascism Research Collective (*Fascisme Onderzoeks Kollektief*). The group declared that it was an informal club, but not an association; it had no organisation and no budget. The court held that the group was an association and therefore legal person: it had already worked for some years, had acted externally under a name, and was well-known. The court deduced from this 'objectively' the intention to establish a legal person (*in casu* an association).[33]

The existence of an informal association with legal personality has already given rise to a number of problems in court procedures. Sometimes one party will bear the risk that the other party will prove that it is not a legal person, or that the other party will contend that the obligation or the property concerned belongs not to him personally, but to an association.[34] This stems from the unclear distinction between an informal association and other informal forms of voluntary cooperation. It is, therefore, desirable to require a formal act for

32 Civil Code, Book 2, Art. 18.

33 District Court Utrecht, 12 February 1998, NJ 1998, 935.

34 See: Dijk-Van der Ploeg, *Of Association and Foundation, Cooperative and Mutual Society* (*Van vereniging en stichting, cooperatie en onderlinge waarborgmaatschappij*), (4th edition, Deventer: Gouda Quint, 2002), at p. 35 ff.

the attainment of legal personality.[35] That also restores formally freedom of association because it provides the choice to make use of an informal association, which is not regulated by law. Members can organise in that form as they wish, knowing that they are not a legal person. In practice, this freedom of internal organisation already exists, because judges do not enforce the application of the rules of Title 2 of Book 2 of the Civil Code on informal associations, but that is in fact contrary to the law.

(2) Supervision by government or the courts?
An important issue is whether the supervision of associations and, more importantly, foundations, should be exercised by the government or by the courts upon request of the public prosecutor (or interested persons). There are a number of reasons for considering control by the Courts advantageous compared to governmental control. By court control, the acts of the private organisation and its participants are directly evaluated. The court evaluates the lawfulness and legitimacy of the acts of the foundation and its participants, but not the public utility or desirability. There must be sufficient means at the disposal of the public prosecutor to perform investigations regarding NGOs.

In case of government control, there is a considerable danger that the government will rely on policy arguments rather than legal arguments; that the control is not only on lawfulness, but also on usefulness. Such a form of control constitutes an illegitimate involvement in a private organisation by government. Even when the government takes measures because the board has acted contrary to the law or the statutes, this has a significant disadvantage compared to judicial control. The organisation or in some cases interested persons, may have the right to appeal against the governmental decision to the administrative court. However, in evaluating the governmental control this court only evaluates the actions of the governmental body to a limited extent, and only considers the actions of the organisation and its participants in an indirect way.[36] It would make a difference if the governmental supervising agency did not have the competence to take measures itself, but had to apply to the administrative court.

35 I advocate the same concerning the church, for the establishment of which Dutch law does not provide for formal rules.

36 Compare Tymen J. van der Ploeg, 'A Comparative Legal Analysis of Foundations: Aspects of Supervision and Transparency', in Helmut K. Anheier and Stefan Toepler (eds.), *Private Funds, Public Purpose*, (Dordrecht: Kluwer Academic, 1999), at p. 70 ff.

In that way the court would evaluate the acts of the board of the association directly.

3 REGISTRATION: ACCOUNTABILITY AND TRANSPARENCY

From the previous sections it is evident that in Europe, 'registration' is not the decisive moment in the establishment of an NGO[37] or in the attainment of their legal personality. Nevertheless often the registration of an NGO in a public register is required or takes place at some point. A public register can be helpful to participants and third parties, including governmental authorities.[38]

In The Netherlands, both associations and foundations have to be registered in the Commercial Register, which is held by the regional Chamber of Commerce. For their existence as legal persons the notarial deed suffices,[39] but as long as they are not registered, the members of the management are liable for the obligations of the legal person. Also, an informal association may be registered. A consequence of this is that creditors first have to go to the association, and only if the association refuses to pay, may they sue the members of the management board.

The registration process involves the notarial deed in which the statutes are included, and the members of the management board, with the information confirming their representative power. If members of the management board are competent, their competence to represent the legal person is always unconditional and unlimited.[40] Other important events are also registered, such as the dissolution of the legal person. When an event, such as the dissolution of the association, is not registered in the Commercial Register of the Chamber of Commerce, it cannot be objected against third parties who are ignorant of this event.

Associations and foundations with a commercial enterprise of some size have to apply the rules regarding the balance sheet and financial reporting for companies.[41] Therefore, they also have to register the balance sheet at the

37 The word 'non governmental organisation' includes associations and foundations and charitable organisations.

38 See Hondius and van der Ploeg, *supra* note 28, at p. 100.

39 The notarial deed is not necessary for informal associations.

40 This rule stems from the first European Directive on company law, that the Dutch legislator has expanded to all legal persons regulated in Book 2 of the Civil Code.

41 Civil Code, Book 2, Art. 360.

Commercial Register.[42] These rules do not apply to foundations and associations with a small commercial enterprise, or with a non-commercial enterprise, such as hospitals, schools and so on. In certain sectors, like housing corporations and hospitals, special laws regulate these matters, including requiring the publication of the balance sheet. In general, neither the annual reports, nor the minutes of the meetings of the management board or general meeting are registered, and there is no other requirement to make them public.

The legal persons that are registered have to pay annually a small fee to the Chamber of Commerce. When an association or a foundation does not pay its fee and has not revealed the information of the members of its management board, the Chamber of Commerce has, by law, the competence to dissolve the legal person. Case law has established that the Chamber of Commerce does not have the right to dissolve the legal person when this legal person is apparently still functioning, for instance because it responds to the Chamber of Commerce or engages in activities which are known to the Chamber of Commerce. The Commercial Register is open to the public. What is registered in the Commercial Register can be relied upon by other persons, like creditors; third parties may rely on the register even when, unbeknown to them what is recorded is incorrect.

In most of the other Western European countries mentioned, associations and foundations are registered, though in separate registers, and not at the Chamber of Commerce. In Germany, the District Courts have registers of the associations that are established in their district. In several states of Germany the state as supervising government keeps a public register of foundations established in their state. The foundations have to send their balance sheet annually to the supervisory governmental agency.

Since the new law of 2003, registration for associations and foundations also takes place at the district court in Belgium. Associations and foundations have to send their annual accounts to registries of these courts. The association register and the foundation register at the court are open to the public. Large associations and foundations also have to send their annual accounts to the National Bank of Belgium. In France the data of an associations can be found at the regional government of the place where it is established, while for foundations one has to submit a request the State Council. In Switzerland associations are in general free to register in the Commercial Register, but for commercial associations this is mandatory.[43] Charities in England and Wales have to be

42 Civil Code, Book 2, Art. 394.

43 Swiss Civil Code, Art. 61.

registered at the Charity Commission. Larger charities have to send their accounts to the Commission annually, which monitors them. The balance sheets of the registered charities are open to the public.

4 Legal means for the protection of public order or general interest

As legal persons, associations and foundations also enjoy human rights, as far as they are applicable to them. According to the formulation of freedom of association in the European Convention on Human Rights[44] the state may restrict freedom of association for the protection of public safety, public health and public morals, and for the protection of the rights and freedoms of others. In this way, the government has to define and control the boundaries of freedom of association. It can do this in a *preventive* and in a *repressive* way. In general, Western governments exercise responsive control. They do not require associations to obtain permission to operate. They only take measures when associations and other NGOs perform illegal activities.

In the Dutch criminal law, sanctions against NGOs and their board members are regulated in two ways: firstly, when legal persons contravene the criminal law, through the members of their management board or by other officers or employees, the legal persons themselves can be punished. The persons who authorised the criminal act are also liable to prosecution, either jointly with the legal person or separately.[45] Secondly, participating in an organisation whose purpose is to commit criminal offences is a criminal offence, punishable by up to 6 years imprisonment or a fine of € 45000. Founders, managers and board members of the organisation may receive punishment of one third more.[46]

Dissolution of a criminal organisation is not regulated in the Criminal Code, but is a sanction of civil law. When associations or foundations perform criminal activities they will be declared prohibited and dissolved by the district court.[47] In recent times political parties have been dissolved by judges because they

44 ECHR, Art. 11.

45 Criminal Code, Art. 51. In Arts. 342, 343 and 347, the members of the management board and of the supervisory board of a legal person are specifically punished if they have participated in or approved of fraudulent bankruptcy and fraud.

46 Criminal Code, Art. 140, ss. 1and 3.

47 Civil Code, Book 2, Art. 20.

incited discrimination against foreigners.[48] If only the purpose is criminal, the court allows the legal person to change its purpose into a purpose which is not against public order.[49] An effect of dissolution is the liquidation of the property of the organisation. The name of the dissolved organisation may not be used any more. It is not possible to prevent the former members from establishing another organisation, but they must ensure that they do not repeat the illegality. The Criminal Code, Article 140, section 2, rules that participation in the continuation of the activities of a legal person that is declared forbidden and dissolved is punishable by a maximum of a year's imprisonment or a fine of € 4500.

In general it can be said that the public prosecutor does not actively act as watchdog on activities of associations and foundations. He merely acts on information from the public, and the media, unless the organisation is openly active in the criminal sphere.

The European Court on Human Rights provides states with only a very limited margin of appreciation regarding the dissolution of associations, which are in practice often political parties.[50] It must be clear that dissolution of the organisation is the only solution. It would also be contrary to freedom of association, if associations were required to get permission from the state authorities for holding meetings, or if they were obliged to open their meetings to the public or to the authorities.[51]

Regarding foundations, in countries where foundations are characterized by a 'public good' purpose, governments generally supervise both their establishment and activities. The recognition of legal personality can then be refused on the grounds of public interest. The government has committed itself to protecting the use of the funds that are meant to be devoted to the public interest, and the State is seen as the sole or highest protector of the public interest. In Germany, the state government exercises this supervision on behalf of the founders, to make sure that the property is used according to their will.[52]

48 See HR 9 March 1976, NJ 1979, 363 (NVU), HR 30 September 1997, NJ 1998, 118 (Centrum Partij), District Court Amsterdam 18 November 1998, NJ 1999, 377 (NVU/Centrum Partij).

49 Civil Code, Book 2, Art. 20, Section 2.

50 Ovey and White, *supra* note 4, p. 292 ff.

51 The authorities may have this right when there is an apparent threat to the public order.

52 See: C.R.M. Versteegh, *De Goede Doelstichting (The foundation for public benefit)*, (diss. VU, Utrecht: Lemma, 2003).

5 Autonomy of Associations and Responsibility of the State: Theory and Practice of Civil Society

5.1 The Theoretical Background

The right to freedom of association presupposes that participants enjoy a degree of autonomy from State. How much space private organisations enjoy in society is predominantly dependent on the approach the government adopts towards them. The Netherlands is a parliamentary democracy where there have always been coalition cabinets. There has always been room for minorities, as these could in a future cabinet form a majority in coalition with others. From the beginning of the 20th century in many sectors of society private organisations (associations and foundations), were established to further a common or general interest, seen from the perspective of the ideological group.

There were four main ideologies with influence in society and politics. They all accepted the important place of NGOs, but from differing perspectives.

According to the Catholic 'subsidiarity principle', the 'higher' level (the government) has to give responsibility to the 'lower' level (private organisations), if this lower level is competent for this responsibility. This principle has become a basis for European policymaking and regulation.[53] This view presupposes a hierarchical relation between state and private organisations.

The Protestant (Calvinist) principle of 'sovereignty in its own sphere' has a less hierarchical view of society. In this view every community (institution) has its own sovereign sphere and principles. The state has the responsibility for integrating the different sovereign entities in the State on the basis of the general interest. It should minimize its interference in private organisations and should only interfere on the basis of this general interest.[54]

The 'principle of decentralisation' was adhered to by the socialists. For the socialists the well being of the citizens forms part of the tasks of the state. Because of their contribution it is good to have private organisations for common and general interests, but they have to be aware of the fact that they form a decentralised government. This view is commonly held by municipalities that

53 See the Treaty Establishing the European Community (Treaty of Rome, as amended), Art. 5. In areas where the Community according to the Treaty does not have exclusive competence, it acts only in case the states do not sufficiently realize the purposes according to the subsidiarity principle.

54 See Herman Dooyeweerd, *Roots of Western Culture*, (Toronto: Wedge Publishing Foundation, 1979), at p. 40 ff. The other social philosophies are also debated in this book.

subsidise NGOs, and among the staff members of the subsidised NGOs. However, this approach appears to be less helpful when central government withdraws itself from the area concerned.

The liberal view,[55] which was the view of the dominant elite in earlier times, is that in society Parliament should have the leading position. Parliamentary democracy is therefore most important, next to the market for the non-political area. The liberals accepted NGOs because of their adherence to the right to freedom of association. They fear NGOs wielding semi-political power because they are not always democratic or representative.

One can argue that there is also a relationship between the idea of the free market and freedom of association. The free market is based on the free will of the citizens to organise their own economic activities. When people have the opportunity to establish economic activities of their own choice, they enjoy freedom as an important part of their life. It seems inconsistent for this freedom to be limited only to economic life. The same freedom motivates people to establish private nonprofit organisations for purposes they think fit. In a way these nonprofit activitics arc made possible by the economic activities, because these have produced funds and time. As long as these voluntary organisations do not endanger the State or society, it seems from that perspective to be logical to allow this freedom to the citizens.

5.2 Practice in The Netherlands[56]

The above-mentioned theories have had their role in the course of time: they have fashioned the way in which the interaction between the State and NGOs is found acceptable by the different groups of society. Because a dominant ideology did not exist, the ideological views on society did not have a strong normative influence on law and practice. In fact NGOs and the State cooperated on a pragmatic basis. As long as the State and the NGOs could be of use to each other, they worked together. When for certain purposes the State or the NGOs thought they could work better alone, they did so. The State had power because of its financial reservoirs; the NGOs had power because of their knowl-

55 In The Netherlands the liberal party includes of old libertarians as well as the conservatives.

56 See Ary Burger and Paul Dekker, with Tymen van der Ploeg and Wino van Veen, The Nonprofit Sector in The Netherlands, Working document 70, (The Hague: Social and Culture Planning Office, 2001).

edge of the field, and their networks and contacts. This has led to a situation in many areas of Dutch society whereby public tasks are executed by NGOs. This is true for housing, health, health insurance, facilities for the elderly, educational institutions, social welfare,[57] broadcasting, development aid, and so on.[58] Subtle connections developed between government and NGOs in relation to planning, financing, formulation of requirements and supervision. In a way, the situation in the Netherlands could be described as corporatist, but that is only true for certain fields, and even there it is mostly a weak form of corporatism. By this I mean that the law does not give specific rights to certain groups, as in Germany where, concerning welfare, a fixed number of umbrella organisations are accorded the right, the finances and the responsibility to execute a specific public task within limits regulated by law.[59] Umbrella organisations in The Netherlands have very rarely occupied such a position. As representative organisations of a specific sector they generally have a right to participate in the discussion about the policy and planning of the government. This is sometimes laid down in the law, but even when not, governmental bodies are open to deliberation with NGOs. It is considered a matter of good governance that their wishes and ideas are taken into account. A lot of activities of NGOs are subsidized, especially if they are public tasks regulated by law.

Since the 1990s government has reduced its involvement in the operation of the social activities mentioned above. It has sought to change from the situation in which it bears the responsibility, pays for, and regulates these public activities, which are operated for the main part by NGOs, into a situation in which the NGOs have more responsibility and are asked to regulate the sector by way of self-regulation instead of governmental regulation. Government at the same time declared that many sectors of social services should be more market-oriented and less government-financed. In fact however, there is no real 'market' in many areas. It is submitted that the position of NGOs in the field is, in many areas, mostly the result of effective operation in the 'market of

57 See Tymen J. van der Ploeg, 'Changing Relationships between Private Nonprofit Organizations and Government in The Netherlands', in Kathleen McCarthy (ed.), *The Nonprofit Sector in the Global Community,* (San Francisco: Josey Bass, 1992), at p. 190 ff.

58 For sociological and financial facts regarding the Dutch nonprofit sector in comparison with other states see Lester M. Salamon and Helmut K. Anheier *et al.*, *Global Civil Society*, (Baltimore: The Johns Hopkins Center for Civil Society Studies, 1999), at p. 145 ff.

59 For more information on Germany see Helmut K. Anheier, in Benjamin Gidron, Ralph Kramer, Lester M. Salamon, *Government and the Third Sector: Emerging Relationships in Welfare States*, (San Fransisco: Josey Bass, 1992), at p. 31 ff.

influence' and not necessarily of good policy or representativeness. There is, on the other hand, no great danger that the NGOs will possess uncontrolled power in certain areas. The NGOs have no fixed positions, but are principally always dependent on political (democratic) decision-making, and they have no established rights.[60] When an organisation with a dominant position is not functioning well, the government can decide to stop the subsidies.[61] While this is true from a formal legal point of view, sociologically and politically the relations between government and nongovernmental organisations are less simple to describe. This way of organising the 'partnership' between state and society[62] has its advantages and disadvantages, seen from ideological and economical perspective.

5.3 Civil Society in Europe

The situation whereby NGOs play an important role in society alongside the state, and citizens enjoy not only political rights, but also the right to participate in private organisations, for their own, common or general interests, and in which they can manage things in their own way is often called 'civil society'. In the European Union[63] there is a clear call for the promotion of this civil society. Civil society is rooted, among other things, in freedom of association and the subsidiarity principle.

Governments and NGOs may have close links, but this does not mean that government can use NGOs as vehicles for its own purposes. When governments want to exercise more control on the producers of a certain product or on certain professionals, by using associations and foundations in which they have to participate or upon which they are dependent, there arises a serious risk that the government will act contrary to the right to freedom of association. The

60 In the area of public broadcasting, education and development aid the positions of the NGOs are more fixed.

61 In the General Law on Administration of 1992, Art. 4:51, the rule is provided that in the case of subsidies being received for the same activities for three years or more, the subsidy can only be stopped after a reasonable time.

62 About this partnership see also Herman J. Aquina, in Gidron, Kramer, Salamon, *supra* note 59, at p. 57 ff.

63 See the report of the European Commission, *The Strengthening of the Role of Associations and Foundations in Europe*, COM (97)0241-C4 0546/96 and the Note: *The Commission and Nongovernmental Organisations: Building a Strong Partnership*, COM (2000) 11 def. 128.1.00.

right to freedom of association may be infringed when citizens have to become members of an association of professionals involuntarily.[64] Government may request enforced membership of a professional organisation, but this has to be regulated by law. In The Netherlands it has been regulated in this way for lawyers and public notaries through the Dutch Bar Association and the Royal Notaries Professional Organisation respectively. These types of organisations are not considered private organisations and they do not belong to civil society. Thus they do not fall within the ambit of freedom of association. There are a number of ways the government can further the public interest by facilitating NGOs, which can be profitable both for the government and for the private organisation, in which freedom of association and the subsidiarity principle are recognized and by which civil society is promoted. Four such ways are: the regulation of collective litigation, taxation, subsidies, and the regulation of fundraising.

(1) Collective litigation[65]

A specific way in which both associations and foundations can play a role in society is via collective action. In Dutch case law it has been recognized since the 1970s that associations and foundations can under certain circumstances litigate, not only for their own interest, but also for the interests of their own group, or on behalf of the general interest. In 1994 a regulation about this subject was codified in the Civil Code, Article 3:305 a. According to this rule, associations with full capacity and foundations may litigate to protect the interests of other persons which are equal to their own interests, as long as the statutes confirm that the association or foundation is concerned with these interests. This makes it easier to serve common interests. The collective claim of the association or foundation may be dismissed if the organisation is not considered to be representative enough. The law also makes it possible to litigate for the protection of general interests. The phrase 'interest of other persons', mentioned in Article 3:305 a, has to be interpreted in an expansive way.

The collective litigation principle can be used by an organisation to get a judgment concerning the legality of actions and situations. The claim can be that the judgment has to be published in the way the court thinks fit and on

64 See ECHR *Sigurjónsson* vs *Iceland*, Judgment of 30 June 1993, Series A, No. 264, (1993) 16 EHRR 462.

65 See H.U. Jessurun d'Oliveira, 'Group Actions in Civil Procedure', in E.H. Hondius and G.J.W. Steenhoff (eds.), Netherlands Reports to the Thirteenth International Congress of Comparative Law in *Montreal 1990*, (The Hague: Asser Instituut, 1990), at p. 135 ff.

costs of the parties that the court thinks fit. Damages in money cannot be claimed.[66]

(2) Taxation

In The Netherlands, nonprofit organisations are not required to pay income tax, as this type of tax is only imposed on individuals. Legal persons are subject to company tax when they undertake commercial activities. As associations and foundations are not, by definition, commercial, they are normally not subject to company tax. Yet they are required to pay this tax when they carry out commercial activities that compete with regular commercial enterprises. So the choice of the legal form association or foundation for certain commercial activity will not help an entrepreneur to avoid paying company tax.

When the association or foundation with an enterprise is directed to a public benefit, it is generally exempt from company tax, either partially or completely. This is explicitly provided for in the case of hospitals, elderly homes, psychiatric hospitals, public libraries and housing corporations.

NGOs with a public benefit purpose have special tax benefits regarding gifts and death duties. For sums under a certain amount they are, as receiver, tax exempt, and when the gift or legacy is of a higher amount, the tax rate is only 11% (instead of the usual tax rate of around 50 %).

Gifts from citizens to public benefit organisations are tax deductible when the gifts amount to more than 1 and less than 10% of the gross personal income per year. Also such gifts are tax deductible for legal persons that have to pay company tax. Total tax deductibility can be arranged by making a covenant with an association to donate annually a certain amount for at least five years. Tax facilities in the area of VAT are rather rare.

The decisions about tax facilities are made by the relevant tax inspectors. There is, unlike in Germany, no general definition of what a public benefit organisation is. It is not necessary that the tax inspection has accepted the public benefit status of an organisation before it can enjoy the advantages. There is a list of recognized public benefit organisations at a central tax office (in the town 's-Hertogenbosch) for gift and death duties, but for tax deductibility it is not a requirement that the organisation is on this list. This is only required

66 Recently Book 3, Art. 305c of the Dutch Civil Code has been introduced on the basis of European rules regarding consumer interests, in which foreign organisations which are registered on a special list have the right to collective litigations for consumer protection.

in cases of a five year-covenant. When there is a dispute between the NGO, the donor or the tax authority, it falls to the court to resolve it.

Some years ago a government committee proposed a system in which recognition as a public benefit organisation would be required before tax privileges could be enjoyed and discussions are ongoing.

There is no restriction for public benefit organisations, or other NGOs, regarding political activities, as is the case in the United States of America and England and Wales.[67] They all may be engaged in political activities. The idea behind the restriction of political activities is that the State should not subsidize politics. The counter-argument is that not giving this tax incentive to private initiatives willing to promote their political views makes it nearly impossible for poor groups to make themselves heard, and that only rich groups will be able to afford to make themselves heard. It seems that the difference in thinking between the Western European and the Anglo-American countries is that in Western Europe tax benefits are given because the State recognizes voluntary organisations as important for society – the idea of civil society – while in Anglo-American thinking they receive tax facilities because they help the State in its tasks. In Continental European countries even gifts to political parties are tax deductible, illustrating the difference in viewpoint as compared to the Anglo-American countries.

(3) Subsidies

In Western European countries it is considered normal that local, regional or central government subsidize the activities of NGOs. The granting of subsidies is partly regulated by law and is partly a matter of the policy of the government authorities. In The Netherlands there are rules about subsidy relations per sector of society. Mostly these rules, which are combined with planning, are drafted by the NGOs and the government together.

The granting of a subsidy is a decision of an administrative body and appeal against it is possible to a higher administrative body. In The Netherlands, the recent General Law on Administration contains a special provision concerning subsidies by which the requesting organisations are protected. Also the requirements for NGOs regarding matters such as financial statements are regulated. It is evident that, while in civil law the legislation on associations and foundations is very lenient, the government directs the life of many associations and foundations through the requirements for subsidies.

67 See Richard Fries' article in this book.

As is described at section 5.2, government is dependent on the activities of NGOs in many areas of society, and the NGOs are dependent on governmental subsidy. Many public tasks are executed by private NGOs: primary education, health care, social care, youth help, addiction care, probation work and so on. It is in these circumstances not easy, or even impossible to distinguish between the public interest and the interest of the NGO. This has become very clear by the recent decision of the Cabinet to decrease the subsidies of many large organisations. Many umbrella-organisations in sport have had their subsidy-income drastically reduced. In particular, the costs for the organisations themselves will no longer be subsidized. Government says, with some justification, that it is not responsible for the existence of the organisations. It is however clear that when government has subsidized an NGO for a certain period it is not easy for this NGO to compensate for the loss of subsidy by private donations. In many societal areas the governmental planning and financing of the activities determine the life and death of the private organisations. The government not only supervises the private organisations on the basis of the subsidy relation or other service providing contract, but it has policy making power over them, for as long as they are strongly dependent on the subsidies. Thus, private organisations should always remain open to and provide for the possibility of continuing their activities without governmental finances.

In Germany in certain areas of social life private organisations have a preferential position, such as in welfare work. There are five top associations which undertake the planning of welfare work together with government. NGOs have to be associated with one of these top associations to gain access to the system. In this system the government has bound itself to subsidize the activities that are part of this planning. In Germany in this way formally the principle of subsidiarity is recognized.

In France the government designates organisations in certain sectors of society. Sectoral legislation fixes specific requirements about internal organisation, the transparency and the supervision of the NGO. With this classification the organisation has access to public finances.

(4) Fundraising

Fundraising is, for many associations, an important means of income apart from the contribution of the members. For foundations it is even more important as this is often the only way to receive money, unless the government provides subsidies. The traditional form of fundraising is the street collection. The collection in churches is not considered fundraising, as this is done inside the church and not in public. In The Netherlands there have been changing regulations concerning public collections. They vary from the requirement that the organizers of the collection have to provide notice to the local authorities 72 hours before, to the requirement of a permit to collect, issued by the local government. This last system has been used since 1929. From the start of this permit system an important role has been played by the Central Archives (CA), a private foundation to promote transparent fundraising and to combat the abuse of fundraising, which was established by the Association of Secretaries of Poor Relief Boards and some private foundations in 1925. When an association or foundation with a charitable purpose requested permission to conduct public fundraising the municipality asked for advice from the CA. On the advice of the CA the municipality took the decision. Negative advice was given when the organisation or the organizers had a criminal record, or when the organisation had the same purpose as an organisation already in existence, or when the organisation had a religious or political aim. In general the municipalities followed the advice of the CA.

Since 1991 there has been no national legislation on fundraising, but local communities may, under the General Police Bye-law, require a permit for collections if it is in the interest of public order. This change in legislation altered the name and position of the CA. The name of the foundation CA was changed to Central Office for Fundraising (*Centraal Bureau Fondsenwerving*, CBF). Together with the fundraising organisations, and with the municipalities, who are all linked to the CBF, a code for fundraising organisations has been drawn up containing rules for the composition of the board, for policy making, propaganda, the use of the funds, and the balance sheet and financial report. Organisations can apply for a hall mark (*keurmerk*) at the CBF. The office of the CBF extensively screens the organisation. The hall mark is issued for five years. The CBF itself has received the license to issue a hall mark from the Dutch Council for Accreditation, which is also a private council, recognized by the national government as the official council for accreditation. Instead of legislation, which was vague, or governmental policy, there is now self-regulation. The basis for the enforcement of the code is the contract by which the charitable organisation receives its hall mark. The way in which the CBF has regulated this issuing of hall marks has received widespread acceptance in the field of fundraising organisations. The CBF will not refuse to issue the hall mark merely because the fundraising organisation has the same purpose as an organisation which already has the hall mark. Neither will it refuse merely because the organisation has religious or political motives. The government has publicly declared that it has trust in this system in which the private CBF plays the dominant role. It has even started to structurally subsidize the CBF again. It also appears that within the circles of other organisations for the public good, which are not actively fundraising, the need is felt to receive such a hall mark. The hall mark is useful for organisations that undertake fundraising at national level. For organisations that operate at a local level this is not necessary, as they are known to the local authorities.

6 Conclusion

Freedom of association in The Netherlands and some surrounding Western European countries has a long history. Although the right to freedom of association as such was recognized in constitutions halfway through the 19th century, it took most countries quite some time to create the legal forms of private law for non governmental (and non profit) organisations. In addition to association form for this purpose, foundation form is also an alternative. There is a great deal of variation in the way associations and foundations are regulated in continental Europe. Some countries have rather heavy governmental involvement; others have less, or none. It is interesting to note that in some Western European countries government sees itself as the sole protector of the public interest, and therefore involves itself in the establishment and supervision of foundations. All of these countries are parties to the European Convention on Human Rights. Up to now the citizens have not challenged such legislation at the European Court of Human Rights.

Registration is not always the decisive moment for the attainment of legal personality for associations and foundations. Nevertheless, registration can have important functions, for instance to provide information to third parties about the organisation and their board members and representatives, as well as to publish financial statements, thus furthering the transparency of organisations. If an association or other NGO is involved in criminal activities, both criminal law and civil law provide measures to tackle the organisation and its managers. The organisation and its managers could face criminal prosecution, and the organisation can also be dissolved by the civil court.

In practice, the place of associations and foundations in society is founded partly on the legal basis as sketched above, and partly on the relations between the government and the existing voluntary organisations. In Dutch politics one can see that different ideologies have different views on this relationship. In practice, however, all agree that nongovernmental organisations should have an important role in society. This has had its effects in many fields. In the

European Union as a whole there is the clear view that NGOs should play an important role in society. Only in this way can we speak of 'civil society'. A special role associations and foundations can play in society is to represent groups through collective action. In this way NGOs can play the role of a private prosecutor. It is doubtful if that is always appropriate.

Government can ask NGOs to execute public tasks in many fields. Apart from regulations for specific fields in society, there are more general ways to foster these organisations. One such way is by tax benefits. If an organisation is focused on the public well-being, there is a reason to provide it with tax advantages, for instance regarding donations to the organisation.

Government can also stimulate specific NGOs by subsidising them. In The Netherlands this happens on an *ad hoc* basis each year, but when an organisation has been subsidized for a while, it will not be stopped abruptly. In Germany and France government establishes a more permanent relation with certain organisations.

In a free-market society, NGOs are heavily dependent on fundraising as a source of income. Government can regulate this by law, but it is also possible to leave it to self-regulation, as is the case in The Netherlands. For instance, a private foundation that always had close links with government, the Central Office for Fundraising (*Centraal Bureau Fondsenwerving,* CBF) has become a substitute-legislator and supervisor in the field of fundraising.

In short, NGOs can provide for more variety in society than when all tasks for non self-interest goals are accomplished by the state or other governmental agencies. In The Netherlands the situation is liberal, as the government is not involved in the establishment of associations and foundations as legal persons. This lack of governmental control has not led to anarchy or chaos in society. The public notaries apparently do their job in a satisfactory way. Of course, the state should maintain its supervision, and combat the abuse of NGOs and criminal activities. We have seen that sometimes organisations can function as private prosecutors and private legislators. Although these functions are not connected with governmental authority and are dependent on the free will of the participants involved, they seem to work in practice. Government does not feel threatened by the existence of NGOs. It promotes them by giving them tax facilities and subsidies. A democratic state functions optimally with lively NGOs, just as NGOs can operate optimally within a democratic and stable state.

CONCLUDING OBSERVATIONS

Yuwen Li

Understanding and exercising the right to freedom of association, in a modern sense, is a relatively new phenomenon in China. The reform of 'old' social organisations and the emergence of new, privately-initiated, non-profit organisations only began to occur in the 1980s, and such organisations continued to expand throughout the 1990s. Within a short period these new organisations have become a vibrant force in society. There now exists a plethora of different organisations, engaged in fulfilling a host of different societal functions such as improving the environment, working with women's rights, poverty alleviation, providing legal aid for disadvantaged groups, protection of orphans and disabled children, and providing services for those suffering from HIV/AIDS.

A defining feature of many of these newer organisations is the relative independence that they are able to enjoy, something that results from a number of their characteristics. Most of them are staffed by dedicated individuals; in the past predominantly retired government officials filled these roles, but the new movement has seen some younger activists and students coming to the fore, bringing with them their youthful enthusiasm and innovation. Their funding comes mainly from transnational companies, foreign donations and from membership contributions. The internal structure of these organisations reflects, to a certain degree, democratic decision-making processes and transparent management structures. They tend to organise activities that avoid conflict with the government or government policy, and to pursue their goals by adopting a non-confrontational strategy. As a result, they have been able to make independent decisions, free from government interference. Local government has kept its

Yuwen Li (Ed.), *Freedom of Association in China and Europe: Comparative Perspectives in Law and Practice*, © 2005 Koninklijke Brill NV, Leiden. Printed in The Netherlands, pp. 353-359.

distance through its policy of 'three nos'– non-recognition, non-interference, and no abolition.

The government's policy of 'small government, big society' also instigated change on several fronts. The adoption of the policy necessitated the devolution of some responsibilities from government to society, so the government decided to initiate the establishment of some social organisations so that it could devolve a degree of responsibility whilst retaining the ability to exercise some control via the organisation. The policy has also been responsible for catalysing the reform of the old social organisations. Initially these government-organised NGOs (GONGOs) tended to play a very limited role, functioning merely as part of the bureaucracy and in an inefficient manner. The significant change really came about in the 1990s, when central government decided on a new policy of separating government and social organisations, requesting that such organisations have their own finances, hire people by themselves, and decide on their own activities, marking the emergence of new social organisations.

In spite of this significant development, there remains a huge gulf between the present state of China's burgeoning civil society and the legal environment, which remains unfriendly towards associations. The attitude of government, central government in particular, is cautious, and it is preoccupied with maintaining social stability. The expanding civil society organisations are seen by some as a potential threat to this stability, hence the government follows its past practice by choosing to maintain excessive control over the establishment of such organisations. The reformists in post-Mao China period often said that 'to liberate thought' meant merely to depart from the rigid communist ideology. However, true liberalisation of thought in the relationship between state and society is a more profound concept and may not come as easily. The main hurdle lies at the door of the top decision-makers, who are yet to be convinced of the indispensable role civil society organisations can play in modern society. Associational life has not been a feature of China's contemporary history. In recent decades the government has prioritised economic reform, with initiatives such as the reform of state-owned enterprises, and encouraging foreign investment and private business. Such initiatives have brought about significant achievements in the economic sphere, but there has also been a downside: environmental degradation, the widening gap between rich and poor, increasing unemployment in both urban and rural areas, the ever-increasing level of corruption – these problems all pose enormous challenges to the government.

Many Chinese scholars have pointed out that the government is unable and/or unwilling to address all these problems on its own. It seems advisable to assume that dealing effectively with all these problems will require the mobilisation of social forces. In this regard, it is in its interests to acknowledge the potential utility of civil society organisations, rather than to view them as a threat, and to understand that in supporting them it may well be able bring about an outcome advantageous to all involved; in the long run it may well constitute a necessary factor for social stability. The progress that Chinese civil society has made so far is part of an irreversible trend, and the eventual emergence of a developed civil society is inevitable. The only remaining variable is the pace at which this process will take place. This will depend on the interplay between a number of actors. Central government and the legislature bear the responsibility for formulating reasonable policy and a functional law, while it is up to local government to implement them. Civil society organisations must of course continue to provide the driving force behind the movement, to prove that they have the capacity to make a positive contribution, to win wide social support, and to remain accountable to the public.

In addition to the role of government, and the civil society organisations themselves, the contribution of academics to the process of liberalisation must not be understated. The expansion of civil society so far has been matched by the advancing capacity of the Chinese academia, who have consistently shown overwhelming support for civil society organisations. They have reached a stage of maturity whereby they are able to provide constructive and incisive critiques of the prevailing current system of governmental administration of social organisations, and its legal framework. Thanks to their critical analysis it is easier to find an explanation for the present situation that prevails in China, in which the legal system lags behind the emerging civil society, restricting its healthy development. In many respects scholars have been successful in advocating their ideas. It was the academic community that forged the link between the status of social organisations and freedom of association, and articulated the shortcomings that exist in the present legal system. They have emphasised that the core significance of freedom of association is that it allows citizens to act on their own initiative, free from government intervention, and they have concluded that a balance must be struck between aims of social stability and the realisation of individual freedoms.

The interaction between academics and government features a number of positive developments in recent years. Academics have been invaluable in playing the role of intermediary between government officials and civil society organisations. They have undertaken this role through a number of initiatives. For instance, in 2002, 2003, and 2004, the Institute of Law of the Chinese Academy of Social Sciences and the Faculty of Law of Utrecht University jointly organised three international conferences on legal aspects of social organisations, sponsored by the Royal Dutch Embassy in Beijing. Officials from both the Ministry of Civil Affairs and provincial civil affairs department were invited to all these conferences. They listened to other speakers, gave comments, replied to questions, and, most importantly, willingly delivered insightful speeches. In the absence of other open channels for academics and the public at large to communicate with government officials about government policy, such conferences offer invaluable opportunities to exchange views, and have been beneficial for all involved. Academic institutions have also invited government officials to join their delegations on visits funded by foreign sources to observe NGOs in other countries. Such visits provide government officials the opportunity to liaise with, observe and understand the NGO sector in greater depth.

Furthermore, government institutions have also organised international conferences to which Chinese scholars were invited to as keynote speakers. For instance, in October 2004 the Legislative Affairs Office of the State Council co-organised with the EU-China Legal and Judicial Co-operation Programme the International Seminar on Rebuilding the Legal Framework of Chinese Social Organisations in China. At that seminar most Chinese speakers came from academic circles, while the European speakers were mainly from NGOs. A collection of papers presented at the seminar was published by the Legislative Affairs Office of the State Council. In the book Dorit Lehrack (International Senior Advisor to the China Association for NGO Cooperation) made several significant and critical recommendations to China. Among the suggestions were the introduction of the concept of 'public utility' in order to determine whether associations served the public interest; the replacement of the double registration procedure with a simpler one which encouraged the founding and functioning of public utility associations; the amendment of present practice to allow only one association of its type on each level of administration, exemplifying a demand-driven approach; the introduction of a set of incentives to encourage donations to public welfare causes; giving attention to building the capacity of associations when improving legislation; and the provision of an adequate budget. Such a publication can only inspire hope that the government is seriously contemplating a revision of the law and consolidating opinions. It remains to be seen whether a substantively improved legal framework can be established, and if so when. Moreover, the remaining question will be whether the laws can be implemented in practice.

Increasingly, academic institutions are inviting representatives of civil society organisations to the international conferences they organise. Taking the example of the conferences by the Institute of Law of the Chinese Academy of Social

Sciences and the Faculty of Law of Utrecht University mentioned above, there were no NGO participants at the 2002 conference. In 2003, after the conference attended by Chinese academics, government officials, and foreign experts, a separate seminar was organised for Chinese academics, foreign experts and NGO representatives. At that time the conference organisers were afraid that if government officials and NGO representatives sat in the same conference room, confrontation between them might occur. However, at the 2004 conference, academics, government officials and NGO representatives each accounted for about one third of Chinese participants respectively. The conference proceeded smoothly: the NGOs complained about the legal obstacles as well as administrative bureaucracy, while government officials presented their arguments but also displayed a commitment to improve. Consequently, the conference was very successful in bring different voices and experiences together and in stimulating a new way of thinking in approaching the expanding Chinese civil society organisations.

The foregoing demonstrates that through the combined effort of government, civil society and academia, it is possible to advance a constructive dialogue, and the outlook is promising. This confidence must be tempered with patience, and the process of evolution must be supported by a spirit of mutual cooperation between government and civil society organisations, not one of confrontation. This relationship will necessarily differ depending on the field in which the organisation works – for example, mutual cooperation will be easier to establish with organisations working in environmental protection, and against domestic violence. In other areas such as education and health, government needs the services provided by civil society organisations. At present, it can also be said that there will remain an unavoidable tension between the government and certain types of organisation, for instance human rights organisations and religious organisations. Nevertheless, the existence of such a tension is not necessarily a reason for alarm. Such a tension is to be found even in Western countries, and is, in a sense, an inevitable and unavoidable aspect of the nature of certain organisations. Government should not expect all organisations to speak with one voice with government, and should accept that though certain organisations exist to play the role of 'watchdog', this does not mean that they constitute a threat to social stability.

One official concern is that liberalisation in the law will lead to a proliferation and eventual surplus of civil society organisations in China. However, such a concern is unfounded – the existence of civil organisations should depend on their own capacity. If they enjoy public support, provide good services and receive sufficient funds, they will 'survive', win in competition and maintain sustainable development; if not, they will be forced to close down. The government cannot, and should not attempt to plan for a total number of civil society organisations and dictate the life and death of a particular organisation.

Creating a friendly legal environment for civil society organisations in China will require a multifaceted strategy. The citizen's right to freedom of association must be enshrined by law, enacted by the National People's Congress. The registration system must be entrusted to the relevant government organisation and updated in order that it may function effectively; it must realistically be capable of efficiently dealing with the registration requirements for social organisations, and most importantly it should be designed keeping in mind that its purpose is to provide a service for social organisations rather than to burden them for administrative reasons. Once an applicant meets the conditions required by law, the relevant registration authority should issue a certificate. The procedure should allow for flexibility, and for small-scale organisations to follow a simple registration procedure by filling in documents for the relevant authority to keep on the record. Consequently, such a reform should lead to the complete abolition of the sponsor system. The government must also design and outline a system of tax incentives to aid the financial viability of associations. In the long term, it will also be important to endow civil society organisations with the status of legal persons in the civil code, in order that they receive the same treatment as other legal persons, and at the same time to provide special tax incentives for those engaged in serving public interests.

The legal framework should depart from the position that prevails at present wherein successful registration may be contingent on being politically aligned with the government. Such governmental control should be loosened, and the existence of civil society organisations should depend on social legitimacy, recognition, support and participation from the public. This would in fact make the job of 'controlling' organisations of the government far easier, as they would subject to a more meaningful and transparent system of control by public opinion.

The contributions of the European experts in this book explore different systems of regulation that have developed over time, reflecting each country's unique political and social development; they are accommodated within the legal framework and traditions of each particular country. Despite the differences between the systems of regulation, they all share the fact that their outcome embodies a respect for freedom of association. The legal cultures of the different jurisdictions covered in this part of the book vary widely, but they all have in common their adherence to the European Convention on Human Rights, which is clearly exerting a pervasive influence on the legal systems of its State parties. While the European experience contrasts with that of China, this part of the book is far from self-congratulatory, and the authors grapple with the shortcomings of their respective jurisdictions and how to introduce reforms to meet the evolving and expanding role of associations. While the systems described may not, and perhaps should not, provide a model for China to attempt to replicate, they should inspire confidence in those that doubt the positive contribution that civil society can make when given the liberty to operate independently within a legal system that embodies respect for freedom of association.

APPENDICES

I

REGULATIONS FOR REGISTRATION AND MANAGEMENT OF SOCIAL ORGANISATIONS

People's Republic of China State Council Order No. 250
Published by the State Council at the 8th ordinary session on 25/9/98, to take effect from that date.

No. 1 – GENERAL PRINCIPLES

Article 1 These regulations are issued in order to guarantee citizens' freedom of association, to protect society's legal rights and interests, to promote the registration and management of social organisations, and promote socialist material and spiritual civilisation.

Article 2 In these regulations 'social organisation' means voluntary groups formed by Chinese citizens in order to realise a shared objective, according to their rules and to develop non profit making activities.

All groups other than state organs may join social organisations as institutional members.

Article 3 To become established, social organisations must be approved by the authorised department [*zhuguan danwei*] and follow the registration procedure set out in these regulations.

Social organisations must have the status of a legal entity [*faren tiaojian*].

Yuwen Li (Ed.), *Freedom of Association in China and Europe: Comparative Perspectives in Law and Practice*, © 2005 Koninklijke Brill NV, Leiden. Printed in The Netherlands, pp. 363-372.

These regulations do not apply to the following organisations:

I. Peoples organisations which participate in the Chinese Peoples Political Consultative Conference.
II. Organs under the administration of the authorised State Council departments.
III. State organs and groups, enterprises and institutional units [*shiye danwei*], and their internal bodies or groups.

Article 4 Social organisations must observe the constitution, state laws, regulations and state policy; must not oppose the basic principles of the constitution, harm the unity, security or ethnic harmony of the state, or interests of the state and society, or the lawful interests of other organisations or citizens, or offend social morality.

Social organisations may not undertake profit seeking activities.

Article 5 The state will protect social organisations and their activities conducted in accordance with the law, regulations and rules; other organisations or persons must not unlawfully interfere with them.

Article 6 The Ministry of Civil Affairs and local Civil Affairs departments at county level and above are the basic peoples government agencies for registration and management of social organisations. (Below, these are referred to as 'registration and management agencies' [*dengji guanli jiguan*]. State Council relevant departments and local government relevant departments at county level and above, or organs empowered by the State Council or local government at county level and above, serve as the relevant leading units of social organisations in related trade, scientific or other professional areas (These are below referred to as 'professional leading units' [*yewu zhuguan danwei*]).

Laws, administrative laws and regulations regarding the supervision and management of social organisations, will take effect in conjunction with other laws, administrative laws and regulations.

No 2. ADMINISTRATION

Article 7 National level social organisations must register with and be managed by State Council registration and management agencies; local social organisations must register with and be managed by the local People's Government registration and management agencies; inter-area social organisations must register with and be managed by common higher level peoples registration and management agencies.

Article 8 If the registration and management agency and the professional leading unit are not in the same place as a social organisation, then supervision and management can be deputed to local registration and management agencies and professional leading units.

No. 3 REGISTRATION

Article 9 Candidate social organisations must be investigated and approved [*shencha*] by a professional leading unit, and applying persons [*faqi ren*] must make preliminary application to the registration and management agency.

Article 10 To establish a social organisation the following conditions must be satisfied:

I. An organisation must have more than 50 individual members or more than 30 institutional members or, if it has both individual and institutional members, a total of at least fifty.
II. It must have a standard name, and organisational capacity.
III. It must have a fixed location.
IV. It must have staff with qualifications appropriate to the professional activities of the organisation.
V. It must have lawful assets and a source of funds. National level organisations must have a minimum of 100,000 *yuan* to cover their activities; local social organisations and inter-area social organisations must have a minimum of 30,000 *yuan*.
VI. It must be legally liable in its own right.

A social organisation's name must comply with the law and statutory regulations and must not offend public morality. A social organisation's name must reflect its activities, character and area of operations. Where national organisations use 'Chinese', 'All-China' *etc*, in their titles, they must be approved in accordance with the relevant state regulations. Local social organisations cannot use 'National', 'Chinese', 'All China' *etc* in their names.

Article 11 Persons applying to set up social organisations must supply the registration and management agency with the following documents:

I. Preliminary application.
II. A document of approval from the professional leading unit.
III. A record of assets and proof of right of use of premises.
IV. Verification of identity and basic situation of intended people in charge and persons applying.
V. A draft of the constitution.

Article 12 Within 60 days of receiving the documents stipulated in Article 11 of these regulations, the registration and management agency must decide whether or not to approve the registration of an organisation, and in the case of refusal must explain the reason to the persons making the application.

Article 13 The registration and management agency will not approve the registration preparation in any of the following cases:

I. If it can be shown that the objectives and area of work of a social organisation applying for the first stage of registration do not comply with Article 4 of these regulations.
II. If in the same administrative area there is already a social organisation active in the same [*xiang tong*] or similar [*xiang si*] area of work, there is no need for a new organisation to be established.
III. If the persons applying or the intended persons in charge have ever received criminal sanction of being deprived of their political rights, or do not possess complete civil liability [*bu juyou wanquan minshi xingwei nengli*].
IV. If deception is employed in the preliminary application.
V. Other cases prohibited by law or administrative rules and regulations.

Article 14 Within six months of the date of approval of the preliminary application by the registration and management agency, the social organisation must hold a general meeting of members, or a general meeting of members' representatives to pass a charter, establish an executive body, appoint office holders [*fuze ren*] and a legal representative [*fading daibiao ren*], and apply for final registration to the registration and management agency. During this preparation period the organisation must not undertake any activities other than preparing for registration.

A social organisation's legal representative must not at the same time act as legal representative person for another social organisation.

Article 15 A social organisation's charter must include the following items:

I. Name and address
II. Objectives, professional area and the geographical area of activity
III. Membership qualifications, rights and duties
IV. Democratic organisation and management structure and procedure for establishing an executive body
V. Qualifications of and procedure for appointing and replacing office holders
VI. Principles of management and use of funds
VII. Procedure for amending the charter
VIII. Procedure in the event of ceasing operations and management of remaining funds
IX. Other business to be regulated by the charter

Article 16 Within thirty days of receiving an application and relevant documents from a social organisation, the registration and management agency must complete its process of investigation. Registration will be approved and a 'social organisation legal entity registration certificate' [*shehui tuanti faren dengji zhengshu*] issued if there are no grounds for exclusion as covered by Article 13 of these regulations, if the preliminary process has been properly completed, and if the charter complies with requirements.

Registration certificates must include the following items:

I. Name
II. Address
III. Objectives, professional area and geographical area of activity
IV. Legal representative
V. Operational budget [*huodong zijin*]
VI. Name of the professional leading unit [*yewu zhuguan danwei*]

If registration is not approved the persons applying must be informed of the decision.

Article 17 From the date of approval of the establishment of a social organisation it will be legally recognised as a legal entity [*faren zige*], and within sixty days of establishment a social organisation must open a file [*bei an*] with the registration and management agency. Within thirty days of receiving the materials for the file, the registration and management agency must issue a 'social organisation legal entity registration certificate'.

The information to be held on file must include the items covered in Article 16 of these regulations, and also the documents of approval in accordance with the law issued by the professional leading unit.

Article 18 The social organisation, as named in the 'social organisation legal entity registration certificate', may apply for an official seal and open a bank account. The social organisation must submit details of the design of the official seal and the bank account numbers for inclusion in the file held by the registration and management agency.

Article 19 If, after establishment, a social organisation wishes to set up a branch or subsidiary [*fenzhi jigou*], or representative agency [*daibiao jigou*], this must be investigated and approved by the professional leading unit; for purposes of registration, the registration and management agency must be supplied with files including the branch or agency name, its area of work, address of premises, and particulars of intended main officers.

Branches and representative agencies of social organisations belong to social organisations and may not be legal entities [*faren zige*] in their own right; they must comply with the rules regarding objectives, area of work, and geographical area as set out in the charter of the social organisation; and implement activities and develop the membership in accordance with the authorised mandate of the social organisation. Social organisation branches must not establish their own branches.

Social organisations must not establish regional branches.

No 4. MODIFICATION OR CANCELLATION OF REGISTRATION

Article 20 If registration particulars or those held on file need to be changed, within thirty days of investigation and approval by the professional leading unit, the social organisation must apply to the registration and management agency for modification of the registration or files. (Hereafter these two kinds of modification are jointly referred to as 'modification of registration'.)

If a social organisation wishes to amend its charter, within thirty days of investigation and approval by the professional leading unit, it must report the changes for approval by the registration and management agency.

Article 21 If any of the following circumstances apply to a social organisation, after investigation and agreement by the professional leading unit, the social organisation must apply to the registration and management agency for cancellation of registration or closing of its file. (Hereafter these two kinds of cancellation are referred to as 'cancellation of registration').

I. The objective of the social organisation has been achieved.

II. Closure of the organisation on its own initiative.
III. Separation of an organisation into discrete groups, or combination with other organisations.
IV. Other reasons for closure.

Article 22 Before a social organisation cancels registration it must, under the guidance of the professional leading unit and other relevant units, establish a receiver group [*qingsuan zuzhi*] to complete winding up [*qingsuan*] operations. In the winding up period, the social organisation may not implement any activities other than winding up.

Article 23 Within fifteen days of completion of the winding up process, the social organisation must undertake cancellation of registration with the registration and management agency. In undertaking cancellation of registration, the organisation must submit an application for cancellation of registration signed by the legal representative person, together with investigation files and winding up report by the professional leading unit. If the registration and management agency approves the cancellation of registration it will issue a confirmation of cancellation and withdraw the social organisation's registration certificate, official seal and accounts.

Article 24 If a social organisation wishes to close a branch or representative agency, the professional leading unit will undertake investigation, approval and subsequent cancellation of registration.

When a social organisation cancels its registration, its branches and representative agencies are simultaneously cancelled.

Article 25 After cancellation of registration of a social organisation, its remaining capital will be dealt with in accordance with relevant national regulations.

Article 26 Establishment, cancellation of registration, or changes in the name, address or legal representative of a social organisation must be publicised [*gonggao*] by the registration and management agency.

No. 5 SUPERVISION AND MANAGEMENT

Article 27 The registration and management agency will have the following responsibilities for supervision and management:

I. It is responsible for the registration and record keeping [*bei an*] with respect to establishment, modification and closure of social organisations.
II. It is responsible for conducting an annual review [*jiancha*] on the social organisation.
III. It is responsible for supervision and review in cases where social organisations fail to comply [*weifan*] with these regulations, and for applying disciplinary sanctions [*xingzheng chufa*] to organisations which fail to comply with these regulations.

Article 28 The professional leading unit will have the following responsibilities for supervision and management:

I. It is responsible for investigating [*shencha*] the social organisation's preliminary application, establishment, modification or cancellation of registration.
II. It is responsible for supervising and guiding the social organisation in observance of the constitution, laws, statutory regulations, national policy, and in developing activities in accordance with their charter.
III. It is responsible for conducting a preliminary stage of the annual review.
IV. It is responsible for helping the registration and management agency and other relevant departments to investigate and deal with illegal activities of social organisations.

V. It is responsible with other relevant departments for guiding the process of winding up social organisations [*qingsuan shiyi*].

Professional leading units may not levy a fee from the social organisations for performing the above services.

Article 29 A social organisation's capital resources must be lawfully obtained; no institution or individual may seize, secretly divide or divert the social organisation's capital.

A social organisation's resources, and income lawfully obtained from activities carried out in accordance with its charter and in accordance with relevant regulations, must be used for the area of work as defined by the organisation's charter and must not be distributed to the membership.

Contributions or donations to social organisations must be used in compliance with the principles and areas of work laid down in the organisation's charter, and in compliance with purposes, methods and timescale as agreed with donors. Social organisations must report to their professional leading unit on the receipt and use of contributions and donations, and must use appropriate means of publicising relevant information to society at large.

Salaries, insurance and social welfare benefits for full time staff of social organisations must comply with relevant regulations for institutional units [*shiye danwei*].

Article 30 Social organisations must comply with the national financial management system and regulations, and accept the supervision of the Ministry of Finance; if an organisation's capital resources also derive from national subsidies or public contributions and donations it must also accept the supervision of the National Audit Office.

Before changing office holders or legal representatives the registration and management agency and professional leading unit must carry out a financial audit of the organisation.

Article 31 Social organisations must submit to their professional leading unit an annual work report for the preceding year by March 31; after preliminary investigation and approval by the professional leading unit, the report must be submitted, by May 31, to the registration and management agency, which will then carry out an annual review. The work report should include the following contents: the organisation's situation in respect of complying with laws, regulations and national policy; its situation in respect of these regulations' registration requirements; activities carried out in accordance with its charter; any changes in membership, administration; financial situation.

The registration and management agency should simplify the contents of the annual review for social organisations which have, in accordance with Article 17 of these regulations, been issued with a 'social organisation legal entity registration certificate'.

No. 6 SANCTIONS

Article 32 If a social organisation engages in deception [*nongxu zuojia*] while applying for registration, or if within one year of receiving the 'social organisation legal entity registration certificate' it does not engage in any activities, then the registration and management agency must cancel the registration.

Article 33 In any of the following cases, the registration and management agency will issue social organisations with a formal warning and instruction to rectify their conduct; it may also stipulate a time frame within which further activities must cease; and may order a change in executives with direct management responsibilities [*zhijie fuze de zhuguan ren*]; in serious cases, registration will be cancelled; if the activities are criminal, criminal sanctions will be applied in accordance with the law.

I. Where the 'social organisation legal entity registration certificate' is obliterated, hired out or lent, or the social organisation's official seal is hired out or lent.
II. Where an organisation's activities go beyond the principles and area of work as defined in the charter.
III. Where supervision and reviews in accordance with the regulations are refused or not accepted.
IV. Where modifications of registration are not carried out in accordance with the regulations.
V. Where branches or representative agencies are established without approval, or where poor management of branches or representative agencies has serious results.
VI. Where organisations engage in profit seeking activities.
VII. Where a social organisation's capital, public contributions or donations are seized, secretly divided or diverted.
VIII. Where relevant national regulations are contravened in the charging of fees, collection or receipt of financial resources, donations or contributions.

Illegal profits and other illegally obtained goods, gained through activities covered in the above regulations, will be confiscated; a fine may also be imposed equivalent to between one and three times the value of illegally gained profits or between three and five times the value of illegally obtained goods.

Article 34 If a social organisation's activities oppose other laws or regulations, it will be dealt with by the appropriate national agencies; if the relevant national agencies consider the social organisation should be closed down, the registration and management agency will cancel the registration.

Article 35 If a social organisation engages in preliminary activities without approval, or if it carries out activities in the name of a social organisation without being registered, or if a social organisation whose registration has been cancelled continues to carry out activities in the name of the social organisation, then the registration and management agency will close the organisation down and confiscate its illegal assets; in criminal [*fanzui*] cases, criminal penalties will be applied in accordance with the law; in non criminal [*shang bu goucheng fanzui*] cases, a public security sanction [*zhi an guanli chufa*] may be imposed in accordance with the law.

Article 36 If a social organisation is instructed to cease its activities within a specified time, the registration and management agency will freeze the 'social organisation legal entity registration certificate', official seal and financial records.
If the registration of a social organisation is cancelled, the registration and management agency will confiscate its 'social organisation legal entity registration certificate' and official seal.

Article 37 If the staff of the registration and management agency or the professional leading unit abuse their powers, fail to act impartially and commit irregularities, or neglect their duty, in criminal cases criminal penalties will be applied in accordance with the law, in non-criminal cases disciplinary sanctions [*xingzheng chufen*] will be imposed in accordance with the law.

No. 7 SUPPLEMENTARY

Article 38 The design of the 'social organisation legal entity registration certificate' is decided by the State Council Ministry of Civil Affairs.

No charge may be levied for conducting the annual review.

Article 39 Social organisations already established before the issuing of these regulations, must apply for registration in accordance with the provisions of these regulations, within one year of these regulations taking effect.

Article 40 These regulations take effect from the date of publication. At the same time, the State Council's 'Regulations on Registration and Management of Social Organisations' published on October 25, 1989 no longer have effect.

Translated by Zhang Yu and Nick Young, February 1999. Translated from announcement in People's Daily 4/11/98. Source: www.chinadevelopmentbrief.com

II

PROVISIONAL REGULATIONS FOR THE REGISTRATION AND MANAGEMENT OF POPULAR NON-ENTERPRISE WORK UNITS[1]

The State Council of the People's Republic of China, Order No. 251 The 'Provisional regulations for the registration and management of popular non-enterprise work units' was passed by the eighth plenum of the standing committee of the State Council on the 25th of September 1998. It is hereby promulgated. It takes effect from the day of promulgation.

Premier Zhu Rongji, 25th October 1998.

1 – GENERAL PRINCIPLES

Article 1 These regulations have been drawn up in order to standardise the registration and management of popular non-enterprise work units, to guarantee their legal rights and interests, and to promote the construction of socialist material and spiritual civilisation.

Article 2 What these regulations refer to as popular non-enterprise work units indicates social organisations carrying out social service activities of a non-profit nature, run by enterprise and institutional work units, social groups and other social forces, and also individual citizens using non-state assets.

Article 3 The establishment of a popular non-enterprise work unit should undergo the examination and agreement of the professional leading and registration should be in accordance with the provisions of these regulations.

Yuwen Li (Ed.), *Freedom of Association in China and Europe: Comparative Perspectives in Law and Practice*, © 2005 Koninklijke Brill NV, Leiden. Printed in The Netherlands, pp. 373-380.

Article 4 Popular non-enterprise work units should respect the constitution, laws, regulations and national policies. They should not oppose the basic principles set out in the constitution, nor should they endanger national unity, security or ethnic unity. They should not harm the national interest nor go against prevailing social morality. Popular non-enterprise work units may not engage in profit seeking business activities.

Article 5 The State Council's Ministry of Civil Affairs and also the civil affairs departments under local Peoples' Governments at all levels above county are the bodies for the management of the registration of popular non-enterprise work units at that level of Government (hereinafter referred to as registration management authorities).

The relevant departments of the State Council and of local Peoples' Governments at all levels above county and organisations authorised by the State Council or local Peoples' Governments at all levels above county shall be the professional leading unit within the ambit of the relevant trade or profession of a popular non-enterprise work unit (hereinafter referred to as professional leading units).

Where laws and administrative regulations have other stipulations regarding the supervision and management of popular non-enterprise work units, these shall be carried out in accordance with the provisions of the relevant laws and administrative regulations.

2 – JURISDICTION

Article 6 Registration management authorities are responsible for the registration and management of popular non-enterprise work units examined and approved by professional leading units at their same level.

Article 7 Where registration management authorities, professional leading units and the popular non-enterprise work units under their jurisdiction are not in the same place, they may entrust the registration management authorities and professional leading units where the popular non-enterprise work unit is located to undertake the work of supervision and management.

3 – REGISTRATION

Article 8 Popular non-enterprise work units applying for registration should meet the following conditions:

I. Examined and approved by the professional leading unit;
II. Having a standard name and the necessary organisational structure;
III. Have the appropriate staff for the activities of their vocation;
IV. Have the appropriate legitimate assets for the activities of their vocation;
V. Have the necessary premises.

The name of a popular non-enterprise work unit should accord with the stipulations of the State Council's Civil Affairs Department, and may not be headed by such words or phrases as 'China', 'All-China', 'Chinese' etc.

Article 9 The applicant for the registration of a popular non-enterprise work unit should provide the following documentation to the registration management body:

I. Letter of application for registration;
II. Document giving the permission of the competent professional body;
III. Proof of use rights for place of business;
IV. Report showing acceptable assets;
V. Basic personal details and identity card of the proposed responsible person;
VI. Draft of the charter.

Article 10 The charter of a popular non-enterprise work unit should include the following items:

I. Name, place of business;
II. Aims and scope of activities;
III. Organisation and management system;
IV. Procedures for the production and recall of legal representatives or responsible persons;
V. Principles for the use and management of assets;
VI. Procedures for the amendment of the charter;
VII. Procedures for ceasing operations and the handling of remaining assets;
VIII. Other business to be regulated by the charter.

Article 11 Within sixty days of receiving full and effective documentation of establishment and application for registration, the registration management authorities should issue a decision on whether or to approve the applicant's registration. Under the following conditions the registration management authorities should not allow registration, and in the case of refusal should must explain the reason to the applicant:

I. There exists evidence showing that the aims or scope of activities of a popular non-enterprise work unit applying for registration are not in accord with the stipulations of Article 4 of these regulations;
II. There has been falsification during application to set up;
III. There already exists a popular non-enterprise work unit in the same administrative district with the same or similar scope of activity, and there is thus no need to set one up;
IV. The proposed legal representative is currently or has previously suffered the criminal penalty of removal of political rights, or does not possess the full ability to engage in civil activities.

V. There are other circumstances forbidden by laws or administrative regulations.

Article 12 The registration management authorities shall register the name, place of business, aims and scope of activities, legal representative or responsible person, starting funds and professional leading unit of those popular non-enterprise work units that obtain permission to register. Moreover, based on their different forms of undertaking civil responsibility in accordance with the law, issue them with either a 'Certificate of registration as a popular non-enterprise work unit (legal entity)', a 'Certificate of registration as a popular non-enterprise work unit (partnership)' or a 'Certificate of registration as a popular non-enterprise work unit (individual).'

Those popular non-enterprise work units that, in accordance with the stipulations of the law and other administrative regulations, have already obtained the appropriate operating license should have their registration procedures simplified by the registration management authority, and should be issued with the appropriate certificate of registration as a popular non-enterprise work unit on the basis of an operating license form the relevant competent department.

Article 13 Popular non-enterprise work units may not set up branch organisations.

Article 14 Popular non-enterprise work units should apply to have seals cut and to open a bank account on the basis of their registration certificate. The popular non-enterprise work unit should report the style of their seal and their bank account number to the registration management authority so that they may be placed on record.

Article 15 Should any of the matters pertaining to the registration of a popular non-enterprise work unit require alteration, they should apply for alteration of their registration by the registration management authority within thirty days of receiving the consent after examination of the professional leading unit.
Should a popular non-enterprise work unit revise its charter, they should report to the registration management authority for approval within thirty days of receiving the consent after examination of the professional leading unit.

Article 16 Those popular non-enterprise work units that disband themselves, subdivide, merge, or that for any other reason need to cancel their registration, should do so through the registration management authority.

Prior to carrying out the cancellation of their registration, popular non-enterprise work units should, under the guidance of the professional leading unit and other relevant authorities, establish a receivership team and complete the winding up of the unit's operations. During this process the popular non-enterprise work unit may not carry out any other activity.

Article 17 The legal representative or responsible person of a popular non-enterprise work unit should cancel their registration with the registration management authority within 15 days of the completion of winding up the unit's operation. When carrying out the cancellation of registration, a letter of application for cancellation of registration, an examination documentation from the professional leading unit and a final winding up report must be submitted.

Those units that are permitted to cancel their registration by the registration management authority will be issued with documentary proof of the cancellation of their registration, and will have their certificate of registration, seals and financial credentials taken away.

Article 18 The registration or cancellation thereof of a popular non-enterprise work unit or their change of name, place of business, legal representative or responsible person should be made public by the registration management authority.

4 – SUPERVISION AND MANAGEMENT

Article 19 The registration management authority has the following supervisory and management responsibilities:

I. Responsible for the establishment, alteration, and cancellation of registrations of popular non-enterprise work units;
II. Conduct an annual review of popular non-enterprise work units;
III. Conduct a supervisory review where there are problems with popular non-enterprise work units fail to comply with these regulations, and apply administrative sanctions to activities of popular non-enterprise work units that fail to comply with these regulations.

Article 20 The professional leading unit has the following supervisory and management responsibilities:

I. Responsible for the investigation of popular non-enterprise work units prior to the establishment, alteration, or cancellation of their registrations;
II. It is responsible for supervising and guiding the popular non-enterprise work units in observance of the constitution, laws, statutory regulations, national policy, and in developing activities in accordance with their charter;
III. Responsible for the annual review of popular non-enterprise work units;
IV. Assist the registration management authority and other relevant departments in investigating and disciplining any illegal activities of popular non-enterprise work units;
V. Jointly oversee the winding down of popular non-enterprise work units with other relevant authorities.

Professional leading units may not levy a fee from the popular non-enterprise work units for performing the above services.

Article 21 A popular non-enterprise work units' capital resources must be lawfully obtained; no institution or individual may seize, secretly divide or divert the popular non-enterprise work unit's capital.

Popular non-enterprise work units' legal income must be used for activities stipulated by the charter of the unit.

Contributions or donations to popular non-enterprise work units must be used in compliance with the principles and areas of work laid down in the organisation's charter, and in compliance with purposes, methods and timescale as agreed with donors. Popular non-enterprise work units must report to their professional leading unit on the receipt and use of contributions and donations, and must use appropriate means of publicising relevant information to society at large.

Article 22 Popular non-enterprise work units must implement a financial management system as per State regulations and accept the supervision of finance departments; those whose source of funds is State financial aid or donations and/or financial aid from society at large should also accept the supervision of auditing organisations.

Before changing office holders or legal representatives the registration and management agency and professional leading unit must carry out a financial audit of the organisation.

Article 23 Popular non-enterprise work units must submit to their professional leading unit an annual work report for the preceding year by March 31; after preliminary investigation and approval by the professional leading unit, the report must be submitted, by May 31, to the registration and management agency, which will then carry out an annual review. The work report should include the following contents: the unit's situation in respect of complying with laws, regulations and national policy; its situation in respect of these regulations' registration requirements; activities carried out in accordance with its charter; any changes in membership, administration; financial situation.

The registration and management agency should simplify the contents of the annual review for social organisations which have, in accordance with Article 12 Section 2 of these regulations, been issued with a registration certificate.

NO. 5 SANCTIONS

Article 24 Those popular non-enterprise work units that whilst applying for registration engage in falsification or attempt to fraudulently obtain registration, or who have their permission revoked by the professional leading unit should have their registration cancelled by the registration management authority.

Article 25 In any of the following cases, the registration and management agency will issue popular non-enterprise work units with a formal warning and instruction to rectify their conduct; it may also stipulate a time frame within which further activities must cease; and may order a change in executives with direct management responsibilities [*zhijie fuze de zhuguan ren*]; in serious cases, registration will be cancelled; if the activities are criminal, criminal sanctions will be applied in accordance with the law:

I. Where the popular non-enterprise work unit's registration certificate is obliterated, hired out or lent, or the social organisation's official seal is hired out or lent.
II. Where a popular non-enterprise work unit's activities go beyond the principles and area of work as defined in the charter.
III. Where supervision and reviews in accordance with the regulations are refused or not accepted.
IV. Where modifications of registration are not carried out in accordance with the regulations.
V. Where branches organisations are established.
VI. Where popular non-enterprise work units engage in profit seeking activities.
VII. Where a popular non-enterprise work unit's capital, public contributions or donations are seized, secretly divided or diverted.
VIII. Where relevant national regulations are contravened in the charging of fees, collection or receipt of financial resources, donations or contributions.

Where the activities listed in the preceding sections produce an illegal operating surplus [*jingying'e*] or illegal gains, this shall be confiscated. They may moreover be fined an amount between twice and three times this illegal surplus or between three and five times such an illegal gain.

Article 26 If a popular non-enterprise work unit's activities oppose other laws or regulations, it will be dealt with by the appropriate national agencies; if the relevant national agencies consider the popular non-enterprise work unit should be closed down, the registration and management agency will cancel the registration.

Article 27 Those who have not registered and engage in the activities in the name of a popular non-enterprise work unit without authorisation, or popular non-enterprise work units that have hade their registrations revoked yet continue to engage in activities in the name of a popular non-enterprise work unit will be disbanded and have their unlawful property confiscated by the registration management authority. Where this constitutes a crime, criminal responsibility should be determined in accordance with the law; where it does not constitute a crime a public security sanction may be imposed in accordance with the law.

1). *Minban fei qiye danwei* is more literally work units that are not enterprises and that are run by the people as opposed to the Party or State.

Translated by Jim Weldon. Source: www.chinadevelopmentbrief.com

III

REGULATIONS FOR THE MANAGEMENT OF FOUNDATIONS

1 – GENERAL PRINCIPLES

Article 1 These regulations have been drafted in order to standardise the organisation and activities of foundations, to protect the legitimate rights and interests of foundations, donors and beneficiaries, and to promote social forces' participation in public benefit enterprises.

Article 2 These regulations when referring to a foundation mean a non-profit legal entity established in accordance with these regulations that employs assets donated by actual persons, legal entities or other organisations for the purpose of engaging in some public benefit enterprise.

Article 3 Foundations can be divided between those that are oriented towards fundraising from the general pubic (referred to below as public fundraising foundations) and those that are not (referred to below as non-public fundraising foundations). Public fundraising foundations are further divided by the geographic scope of their fundraising activities as either national or local public fundraising foundations.

Article 4 Foundations must abide by the constitution, the law, rules and regulations and national policy; they must not endanger national security, national unity or the unity of [China's] nationalities, nor must they transgress social morality.

Article 5 Foundations carry out public benefit activities in line with their charters. They should abide by principles of openness and transparency.

Yuwen Li (Ed.), *Freedom of Association in China and Europe: Comparative Perspectives in Law and Practice*, © 2005 Koninklijke Brill NV, Leiden. Printed in The Netherlands, pp. 381-392.

Article 6 The Ministry of Civil Affairs under the State Council and its departments at provincial, autonomous region and directly administered municipality level are the organs responsible for the registration and management of foundations.

The Ministry of Civil Affairs under the State Council is responsible for the registration and management of the following [types of] foundation and bodies representing foundations:

1. National public fundraising foundations;
2. Foundations who propose to appoint as their legal representatives persons who are not residents of mainland China;
3. Non-public fundraising foundations whose original funds are in excess of CNY 20 million and whose founder applies to establish as a foundation to the Ministry of Civil Affairs under the State Council;
4. Representative bodies in China established by overseas foundations.

Departments of the Ministry of Civil Affairs at provincial, autonomous region and directly administered municipality level are responsible for the registration and management of local public fundraising foundations within their own administrative regions, and also registration and management work concerning non-public fundraising foundations that are not covered under the above article.

Article 7 The professional leading units of foundations or representative bodies of overseas foundations registered with the Ministry of Civil Affairs under the State Council shall be organisations authorised by the ministries under the State Council or by the State Council itself.

The professional leading units of foundations registered with the Ministry of Civil Affairs at provincial, autonomous region and directly administered municipality level shall be organisations authorised by the Ministry of Civil Affairs or by the People's Government at provincial, autonomous region and directly administered municipality level.

2 – ESTABLISHMENT, MODIFICATION AND CANCELLATION

Article 8 The following conditions must be met in order to establish a foundation:

1. It should be established in order to achieve a set public interest objective;
2. The original funds of national public fundraising foundations should be not less than CNY 8 million; the original funds of local public fundraising foundations should be not less than CNY 4 million; the original funds of non-public fundraising foundations should be not less than CNY 2 million and they must retain those funds in their current account;

3. A foundation should have a standard name, a charter, an organisational structure and full-time staff with the appropriate capacity to carry out its [proposed] activities;
4. It must have a fixed place of business;
5. It must be capable of undertaking civil legal liability in its own right.

Article 9 When applying to establish a foundation, the applicant must provide the following documentation to the body in charge of registration:

1. A letter of application;
2. A draft charter;
3. Attested proof of funding and proof of their place of business;
4. A list of names of board members and proof of their identities, and curricula vitae of the persons it is proposed will serve as Chair and Deputy Chair of the Board and as General Secretary;
5. A document attesting to their professional leading units' agreement to the establishment.

Article 10 A foundation's charter must make clear its public welfare status and must not contain any reference stipulating a particular actual person, legal entity or other organisation as beneficiary.

The charter must clearly state the following:

1. The foundation's name and place of business;
2. The purpose for which it was established [Its mission] and the scope of its [proposed] public benefit activities;
3. The amount of its original funds;
4. The composition, professional responsibilities and procedural regulations of its board of directors, the qualifications necessary for a person to serve as a board member and the process under which such a member is appointed and their term of their service;
5. The responsibilities of their legal representative;
6. The responsibilities of their supervisory officials, the qualifications necessary to serve as one, the process whereby they are appointed and their term of their service;
7. The system for producing financial accounts and the system for carrying out audits;
8. The system for the management and use of assets;
9. The conditions under which the foundation can be wound up, the process whereby this would happen and how the assets would be disposed of in such case.

Article 11 The organ in charge of registration should give a decision accepting or rejecting the application to register a foundation within 60 days of receiving in full a valid set of the documentation listed in Article 9 of these regulations. Where the application is accepted, they should issue a 'Certificate of Registration as a Legal Entity for

Foundations'; where the application is rejected they should give written reasons for so doing.

The items to be stipulated in the registration of a foundation include its appellation, place of business, type, mission, scope of public benefit activities, amount of its original funds and its appointed legal representative.

Article 12 Should a foundation wish to establish a branch organisation or representative organisation, it should apply to register them to the organ it originally applied to for its own registration. The application should include documentation stating the appellation, place of business and responsible persons [for the proposed new entity].

The organ in charge of registration should give a decision accepting or rejecting an application of this type within 60 days. Where the application is accepted, they should issue a 'Certificate of Registration of a Foundation Branch (Representative) Organisation'; where the application is rejected they should give written reasons for so doing.

The items to be stipulated in the registration of a branch or representative organisation of a foundation include its appellation, place of business, type, mission, scope of public benefit activities, and its responsible persons.

Branches or representative organisations of a foundation engage in activities under the aegis of their parent organisation and do not have the status of independent legal entities.

Article 13 Overseas foundations seeking to establish a representative body in China should, having secured the agreement of its professional leading unit, provide the following documentation to the organ in charge of registration:

1. A letter of application;
2. Proof of its legal registration overseas and a copy of its charter;
3. Proof of the identities and curricula vitae of the persons it is proposed will act as responsible persons in the representative body;
4. Proof of its place of business;
5. A document attesting to their professional leading units' agreement to the establishment of a representative body in China.

The organ in charge of registration should give a decision accepting or rejecting the application within 60 days of receiving in full a valid set of the documentation listed above. Where the application is accepted, they should issue a 'Certificate of Registration as the Representative Body of an Overseas Foundation'; where the application is rejected they should give written reasons for so doing.

The items to be stipulated in the registration of a representative body of an overseas foundation include its appellation, place of business, scope of public benefit activities, and its responsible persons.

Representative bodies of overseas foundations should engage in public benefit activities that are appropriate for the nature of public benefit enterprises in China. Overseas foundations undertake civil legal liability for the actions of their Chinese representative bodies in accordance with Chinese law.

Article 14 Foundations and representative bodies of overseas foundations should, having completed their registration under these regulations, register with the tax authorities as the law requires.

Foundations and representative bodies of overseas foundations may use their certificate of registration to apply for an organisation registration number, to have official seals cut, and to open a bank account.

Foundations and representative bodies of overseas foundations should submit their organisation registration number, design of their official seal, bank account number and a copy of their tax registration documentation to the registration authorities to be placed on file.

Article 15 Should items in the registration of foundations, their branch organisations or the representative bodies of overseas foundations require modification they should apply to the organ in charge of registration for the changes to be made to their registration.

Should a foundation revise its charter, they should seek the agreement of their professional leading unit and report the revised charter to the organ in charge of registration for ratification.

Article 16 Should any of the following circumstances apply for a foundation or the representative body of an overseas foundation, they should apply to the organ in charge of registration for the cancellation of their registration:

1. They intend to wind up as provided for in their charter;
2. They are incapable of carrying out public benefit activities in line the mission stipulated in their charter;
3. They wish to cease activities for some other reason.

Article 17 Should a foundation wish to close down one of its branches or representative bodies it should process the cancellation of the registration of the branch or representative with the organ in charge of registration.

When a foundation cancels its registration, its branch and representative bodies have their registrations cancelled at the same time.

Article 18 Prior to cancelling its registration, a foundation should establish a liquidation organisation and complete the work of settling its accounts under the guidance of the organ in charge of registration and its professional leading unit.

A foundation should apply for the cancellation of its registration within 15 days of the completion of liquidation. During the process of liquidation the foundation may not carry out any other activities.

Article 19 The establishment, modification and cancellation of the registration of foundations, their branch and representative bodies and the representative bodies of overseas foundations shall be reported to the public by the organ in charge of registration.

3 – ORGANISATION AND STRUCTURE

Article 20 A foundation should establish a board of directors with between 5 and 25 members. Directors' term of service should be stipulated in the charter but a single term must not exceed 5 years. Once a term is served, a director may continue to serve if selected again.

For non-public fundraising foundations established using the assets of a private individual, no more than a third of board members may be close family relations of that individual; for other foundations, close relations may not serve simultaneously as directors.

Directors who receive financial remuneration from a foundation may not make up more than a third of its board members.

A board of directors will appoint a chair, deputy chair and general secretary elected from amongst their membership. The chair of the board is the legal representative of the foundation.

Article 21 The board of directors is the decision making body of a foundation and should carry out their again responsibilities as laid down in the charter in accordance with the law.

The board of directors should meet at least twice a year, with two thirds of directors in attendance as quorum. Decisions must achieve a simple majority of those attending a meeting to be effective.

Decisions concerning the following major items require a two thirds majority of directors attending a meeting to be effective:

1. Revisions to the charter;
2. Election or dismissal of the chair, deputy chair or general secretary;
3. Major fundraising or investment activities as stipulated in the charter;
4. The division or amalgamation of the foundation.

The board of directors should have minutes kept of their meetings which should be read, approved and signed by members in attendance.

Article 22 A foundation should appoint a supervisory official, whose term of service will be the same as a member of the board. Members of the board, their close relatives or financial staff of the foundation may not serve as supervisory official.

The supervisory official will keep check of the financial records and accounts of the foundation in accordance with a process laid down in the charter and monitor the board's compliance with the charter and with the law.

When attending board meeting the supervisory official has the right to question and make suggestions to the board, and should also report on relevant matters to the organ in charge of registration, the professional leading unit and also the tax and auditing authorities.

Article 23 The posts of chair and deputy chair of the board of directors or secretary general should not be taken by persons currently employed by state bodies. The legal representative of the foundation may not at the same time be the legal representative of any other organisation. The legal representative of public fundraising foundations and non-public fundraising foundations whose original funds are of domestic Chinese origin should be a person who is a legal resident of mainland China.

The posts of chair and deputy chair of the board of directors or secretary general should not be taken by persons who because of committing a crime have been put under public surveillance, detained or imprisoned within 5 years of the end of that sentence; nor by those who are currently or have formerly been under sentence of having their political rights removed; nor by those who have served in such posts and had legal culpability at other foundations that were closed down for illegal activities within 5 years of the closure of the said foundation.

Should a board member find there is a connection between their personal interests and the interests of the foundation, they should not take part in decision making related to the matter; nor should a board member, the supervisory official or their close relations have any kind of business dealings with the foundation.

The supervisory official and board members not serving in a full time post at the foundation may not be paid.

Article 24 Residents of Hong Kong, Macau or Taiwan, or foreign nationals serving as chair, deputy chair or secretary general of the board of a foundation or as legal representative of the representative organisation of an overseas foundation must be resident in mainland China for at least three months every year.

4 – MANAGEMENT AND USE OF ASSETS

Article 25 When a foundation engages in fundraising or receives donations it should be in accordance with its mission and the scope of its activities as stipulated in its charter. Representative bodies of overseas foundations may not engage in fundraising or accept donations within China.

Public fundraising foundations when engaging in fundraising should make public the activities for which the money raised is intended to be used and details of how it is to be spent.

Article 26 Foundations, their donors and beneficiaries enjoy tax benefits as stipulated by law and administrative regulations.

Article 27 The assets of a foundation and its other sources of income are protected under the law. No work unit or individual may take a portion or the whole thereof or misuse them in any way.

A foundation should use its assets in accordance with its mission as stipulated in its charter and within the scope of public benefit activities so laid down, donations that are given with an accompanying agreement giving clear instructions for their use must be used in line with the agreement.

If a foundation receives donations in kind that it is impossible to use in accordance with their mission, they may auction or otherwise sell of the items and use the money raised to fulfil the purpose of the donation.

Article 28 A foundation should employ legal, safe and effective means to ensure that their original funds maintain their value or grow.

Article 29 The amount of money spent annually by public fundraising foundations on the public benefit activities stipulated in their charter must not be less than 70% of the previous year's income; non-public fundraising foundations annual expenditure on the public benefit activities stipulated in their charter must not be less than 8% of the surplus from the previous year.

A foundation may not allocate more than 10% of its total expenditure to cover staff wages and benefits and overheads.

Article 30 Should a foundation engage in any grant making activities, it should make public the nature of that activity and the processes for applying for a grant and the selection of grantees.

Article 31 A foundation may draft a contract with a grantee setting out the method of giving the grant, its amount and how it is to be spent.

Foundations have a right to monitor how grants they make are used. If a grantee does not use the grant in the agreed way or if they violate the agreement in any other way, the foundation may cancel their contract with them.

Article 32 Foundations should employ the national unified system of accounting, keep accounts in accordance with the law and establish a full and effective internal system for the monitoring of accounts.

Article 33 Monies left over when a foundation is wound up should be used for public benefit ends as stipulated in the foundation's charter; funds which cannot be used in this way will be donated by the organ in charge of registration to another public benefit organisation with similar aims and objectives to the original foundation. Any such action will be made public.

5 – MONITORING AND MANAGEMENT

Article 34 The organ in charge of registration of foundations has the following responsibilities in regards of monitoring and management:

1. Conduct annual inspections of foundations and representative bodies of overseas foundations;
2. Conduct day-to-day monitoring and supervision of how foundations and representative bodies of overseas foundations carry out activities in line with these regulations and their own charters;
3. Penalise those foundations and representative bodies of overseas foundations whose actions violate the regulations;

Article 35 The professional leading units of foundations have the following responsibilities in regards of monitoring and management:

1. To give guidance and monitor foundations and representative bodies of overseas foundations to carry out public benefit activities in accordance with the law and their own charters;

2. Give preliminary approval to the annual inspections of foundations and representative bodies of overseas foundations;
3. Coordinate with the organ in charge of registration and other law enforcement agencies in the investigation and punishment of any illegal activities by foundations and representative bodies of overseas foundations.

Article 36 Foundations and representative bodies of overseas foundations should submit an annual work report to the organ in charge of registration of foundations before the 31st of March every year and submit to an annual inspection. The annual report should be inspected and approved by the foundation's professional leading unit prior to submission to the organ in charge of registration.

The annual work report should include: a financial report; an audit report by a certified accountant; reports on fundraising activities, donations received and grants made; and any changes to staff or the organisation.

Article 37 Foundations should submit themselves to the supervision of their accounts and tax records by the appropriate authorities in accordance with the law.

Foundations should conduct a financial audit at the end of each term of service of their board or change in the legal representative.

Article 38 Foundations and representative bodies of overseas foundations should make their annual work reports public through media channels stipulated by the organ in charge of registration once that organ has checked and approved the report, to allow public query and monitoring of their work.

Article 39 Donors have the right to make inquiries to a foundation about how their donation was used and how it is being managed and offer opinions and suggestions concerning this. Foundations should respond to such inquires in a timely and truthful fashion.

If foundations violate agreements with donors concerning the use of their donations, the donor has the right to demand the foundation follow their agreement or to ask the courts to revoke the donation and annul the agreement.

6 – LEGAL LIABILITY

Article 40 Anyone who carries out activities in the name of foundations, their branches or representative bodies, or the representative bodies of overseas foundations that have not registered, or who have had their registrations revoked may have their organisation suppressed by the organ in charge of registration and their illegal assets sequestrated. Any such action should be made public.

Article 41 Foundations, their branches or representative bodies, or the representative bodies of overseas foundations that display any of the circumstances listed below will have their registrations revoked by the organ in charge of registration:

1. If they engage in any form of falsification during the application process; or if they have not begun activities in accordance with their charter within twelve months of having their registration approved;
2. If they meet the conditions for cancellation of their registration but do not go through the process for cancellation as laid down in these regulations and continue to carry out activities.

Article 42 Foundations, their branches or representative bodies, or the representative bodies of overseas foundations that display any of the circumstances listed below will receive a warning from the organ in charge of registration and be instructed to cease the said activity; in serious cases their registration may be revoked:

1. Those who do not carry out activities in accordance with their mission or within the scope of public benefit activities as stipulated in their charter;
2. Who engage in any form of falsification in filling out proofs of accounting, in their registered account books and in drafting their financial reports and accounts;
3. Who do not follow regulations when registering or modifying their registration;
4. Who do not meet the public benefit expenditure levels laid down in these regulations;
5. Who do not submit to annual inspection, or whose inspection does not meet requirements as laid down in these regulations;
6. Who fail to fulfil requirements to make information public or who falsify such information.

The organ in charge of registration should ask the tax authorities to demand back payment of any tax remitted for foundations or the representative bodies of overseas foundations that act in any of the ways listed above for the period during which the infringement occurred.

Article 43 Should a foundation's board of directors make decisions that violate these regulations or their own charter and that lead to a loss of the foundation's assets, those directors who took part in the decision should be held responsible for making appropriate reparations.

Should a board member, the supervisory official or any member of a foundation's staff misappropriate or misuse foundation assets they should repay the amount they illegally took. Where there is criminal culpability they should be dealt with accordingly.

Article 44 Should a foundation or the representative bodies of overseas foundations be ordered to cease activities, the organ in charge of registration will seal its registration certificate, official seals and financial documentation.

Article 45 Should staff of the organ in charge of registration or professional leading units abuse their position, fail in their duties, or commit irregularities for personal gain they will be dealt with accordingly where there is criminal culpability. Where the case is not criminal they will be given administrative or disciplinary sanction in accordance with the law.

7 – SUPPLEMENTARY

Article 46 When these regulations refer to the representative bodies of overseas foundations it means foundations established in accordance with the law in foreign countries and also in the Hong Kong and Macau Special Administrative Regions of the People's Republic of China and in the Taiwan region.

Article 47 The format for foundation's registration application letters and annual reports, and models for their official seals will be laid down by the Ministry of Civil Affairs under the State Council.

Article 48 The regulations take effect from the 1st of June 2004. At the same time the State Council's 'Measures for the Management of Foundations' issued on the 27th of September 1988 are annulled.

Foundations and the representative bodies of overseas foundations established prior to these regulations taking effect should apply for a new registration document as stipulated in these regulations within 6 months of them taking effect.

Translated by Jim Weldon, March 2004. Source: www.chinadevelopmentbrief.com

IV

A MODEL OF SIMPLE QUESTIONNAIRE ON DEVELOPMENT AND PROBLEMS OF SOCIAL ORGANIZATIONS IN CHINA

Designed by Dr. Xie Haiding
Translated by Dr. Bi Xiaoqing
CASS Law Institute

Dear Mr. /Ms __________

I am a researcher for the Research Group on "The Legal Aspects of Social Organizations in China" of the Law Institute, Chinese Academy of Social Sciences. The purpose of this questionnaire is to get some basic information about the development of your organization as a basis for making state laws, administrative regulations and policies. This questionnaire will be used only for the purpose of statistical analysis, so please answer all the questions accurately.

Thank you for your support.

Research Group on "The Legal Aspects of Social Organizations in China"
Law Institute, Chinese Academy of Social Sciences
November, 2002

Name of your Organization (Including the English Name): ______________
Address: ____________________ Postal Code: ________________________
Sponsor organization:[1] _______________________
Organization to which your organization is affiliated: ____________________
Number of staff _____________________
Number of CPC members among the full time staff members _____________

1 A sponsor organization is a government or Party organization in charge of supervising and providing guidance to a social organization in its activities.

Yuwen Li (Ed.), *Freedom of Association in China and Europe: Comparative Perspectives in Law and Practice*, © 2005 Koninklijke Brill NV, Leiden. Printed in The Netherlands, pp. 393-401.

Name of respondent: ____________ Name of researcher: ______________
Date of research: __________________ Serial no.:

Instructions:

- Please answer all the questions [in numerical order] so as to avoid any omission.
- For a multiple-choice question, please circle the answer which you think applies to your organization. If your intended answer is not among those provided, please choose "other" and give a brief explanation.
- For each multiple-choice question, please choose only one answer unless otherwise instructed.
- For the questions with blanks, please fill in these blanks according to the actual situation of your organization.
- In some of the multiple-choice questions, one of the answers is followed by an instruction. If you choose such an answer, please continue to answer the questions that follow it according to the instruction.

Part One Basic Information about Your Organization

A. Please fill in the blanks or choose the suitable answers in the following questions.

A1. Date of establishment of the organization (002) ____________

A2. To which of the following spheres does your organization belong? (004)
1. education; 2. public health; 3. culture; 4. science and technology; 5. sports; 6. labor; 7. civil administration; 8. social intermediary services; 9. environment; 10. legal services; 11. foundations; 12. others (please specify).

A3. Your organization is engaged in activities in which of the following fields (you can choose more than one answers)? (005)
1. culture or arts; 2. sports; 3. entertainment; 4. vocational education or training; 5. private primary or secondary school; 6. private colleges or university; 7. investigation or research; 8. old people's welfare home; 9. rehabilitation center; 10. psychological counseling; 11. disaster prevention and relief; 12. poverty relief; 13. environmental protection; 14. animal protection; 15. community development; 16. estate management; 17. employment or re-employment; 18. policy consultation; 19. legal consultation or service; 20. foundation; 21. volunteers association; 22. international exchange or international aid; 23. religion; 24. professional association or chamber of commerce; 25. friendship association; 26. others.

A4. The office of your organization is- (006)
1. borrowed;
2. rented;
3. owned by the organization itself;
4. my organization has no fixed location of office.

A5. Your organization has which of the following equipment (More than one item may be selected)?

equipment	Fixed-line telephones (007)	Computers (008)	Printers (009)	Air conditioners (010)	Cars (011)	others (012)
number						
Date of purchase						
Further explanation (if any)						

A6. Your organization has which of the followings? (More than one item may be selected)

Items	Brochure about your organization (013)	Email (014)	Website or webpage (015)	publications (016)
Further explanation (if any)				

A8. Your organization has which of the followings (More than one items may be selected)?

Charter of the organization	
Congress	
Board of directors	
Executive council	
Secretariat	
Financial department	
Subordinate agencies	
Representative agencies	
Party organizations	
Economic entities	
Membership booklet	

A7. Before holding the current position, the executive director of your organization has held posts in which of the followings organizations/ institutions?

1. administrative organs;
2. state institutions;
3. other social organizations;

4. state or collective enterprises;
5. others.

A7. How are the main managerial personnel in your organization selected?
1. selected and appointed by the sponsor organization;
2. nominated by the leader of the organization and approved by the sponsor organization;
3. chosen through democratic election according to the charter of the organization;
4. no specific rules on the selection of such personnel exist in my organization.

A7. Is there any leadership position in your organization held part-time by the leader of a Party or government organization?

A7. How many staff members does your organization currently have (017) ________

What is the ratio between male and female staff members in your organization? (018) ________

What is the total number of full-time staff members in your organization? (019) ________

How many of them receive salary from your organization? (020) ________

What is the total number of part-time staff members in your organization? (021) ________

How many of them receive remuneration from your organization? (022) ________

What is the total number of volunteers in your organization? (023) ________

On average, how many days/person per month do they work for your organization? (024) ________

A8. Educational backgrounds of the staff of your organization

Education	Junior high school or below (025)	Senior high-school (026)	Secondary specialized school or college for professional training (027)	College or university undergraduate (028)	Master's degree or above (029)
Number of staff members					

A9. Does your organization have permanent members? (030)
1. No 2. Yes

If the answer is "yes", please continue to answer the following questions.

9-1 Total number of the members of your organization (by 30 June 2002) __ _______ (031); number of individual members: _________; number of collective members ___________

9-2 The members of your organization are mainly from _________

(1) In terms of location (032):

1. big cities; 2. medium and small cities; 3. rural areas.

(2) In terms of industry (033): 1. manufacturing; 2. agriculture; 3. ommerce; 4. culture; 5. education; 6. entertainment; 7. transportation; 8. others (please specify) (More than one item may be selected).

(3) In terms of profession (034): 1. workers (not including laid-off workers); 2. peasants; 3. state personnel; 4. leaders of state institutions; 5. owners of large or medium private enterprises; 6. owners of small private enterprises in industry and commerce; 7. leaders of state-owned or collective enterprises; 8. managerial personnel of state-owned enterprises or institutions; 9. ordinary employees in state-owned enterprises or institutions; 10. scholars and teachers; 11. students; 2. laid-off workers; 13. unemployed; 14. private enterprise; 15. law firms; 16. others (please specify).

(4) In terms of gender (035): male/female

A10. Your organization carries out activities ___________

1. within one city, district or county
2. in two or more cities, districts, or counties
3. within one province, autonomous region or municipality directly under the Center Government
4. in two or more provinces, autonomous regions or municipalities directly under the Center Government
5. throughout the country
6. also in Hong Kong, Macao and Taiwan
7. also in other countries.

A11. About how many activities are carried out each year by your organization?

____

A12. What is the total expenditure of your organization in the year 2001 (unit: 10,000 yuan):

< 0.1	0.1-0.5	0.5-1	1-5	5-10	10-50	50-100	100-500	500-1000	> 1000

A13. What are the percentages of the following expenditures in the total expenditure of your organization in the year 2001?

1. personnel (including salaries, bonuses, subsidies and social securities) ________________ %;
2. real estate (housing, water, electricity, gas, heating, etc.) ________ %;

3. office expenditures (all office expenditures except those listed in items 1 and 2 above) ________ %;
4. activities: ________ %;
5. other expenditures ________________ %.

A14. What are the percentages of the following incomes in the total income of your organization in the year 2001?
1. membership fee ________ %;
2. operating income ________ %;
3. allocation of funds or subsidies from the government __________ %;
4. project funds provided by the government ____________ %;
5. financial aids and project funds provided by international organizations, foreign government and other organizations ____________ %;
6. financial aids and project funds provided by enterprises ____________ %;
7. financial aids and project funds provided by other Chinese foundations ____ ________ %;
8. donations collected by the organization ________ %;
9. income from the operation of capitals __________ %;
10. contributions from individual members (other than membership fee) ___________ %;
11. loans ___________ %;
12. surplus from the previous year ________ %;
13. others ____________ %.

A15. The total amount of tax paid by your organization in the year 2001 _________ among which,
1. income tax _____________ %;
2. commodity tax ______________ %;
3. property tax ______________ %;
4. other taxes ______________ %.

A16. What are the main obstacle to the further development of your organization?

Part Two Social Organizations and Law

B. In each of the following questions, several possible answers are given. Please circle the answer (s) which you believe is (are) true; If you have choose more than one answer, please list them in order of priority.

B1. What do you think is the most important reason for the marked increase in the number of social organizations in China since the "reform and opening up"?
1. Competent leadership and management by the Party and the Government;
2. Actual economic benefit resulting from the establishment of and participation in social organizations;

3. Gradual relaxing of legal restriction on the establishment of or participation in social organizations;
4. More and more leisure time enjoyed by the people that enables them to enrich their life by organizing or participating in social organizations.

B2. In which of the following situations do you think the law on social organizations is most relevant to your organization?
1. When establishing the organization;
2. When my organization is carrying out activities;
3. When my organization is involved in a lawsuit against other organizations or individuals;
4. The law is not very relevant to my organization.

B3. In your opinion, which of the following activities of social organizations is unlawful?
1. Engaging in preparatory activities for the establishment of a social organization without approval from the government;
2. Accepting lawful donations without approval from the competent government department;
3. Establishing unincorporated business organizations;
4. Lending the official seal of the organization to others for their use.

B4. In your opinion, the collection of which of the following fees is not unlawful?
1. fees collected by sponsor organizations for the examination of application for, and registration of, the establishment of social organizations;
2. fees collected by sponsor organization for annual examination;
3. fees collected by sponsor organization for assisting relevant government departments in investigating and punishing unlawful acts by social organizations;
4. fees collected by civil administration departments for annual examination of social organizations.

B5. In your opinion, which of the following acts of social organizations are permitted by law?
1. to bring administrative lawsuit in the name of a social organization against a sponsor organization for refusing to register the organization which meets the legal requirements for registration;
2. to bring civil lawsuit in the name of a social organization against other organizations, enterprises or individuals for violation of the property rights of the organization;
3. to file complaints or bring charges or impeachment in the name of a social organization against a sponsor organization or a Party or government organization for unlawful interference in the activities of the organization;

4. to bring administrative lawsuit in the name of an organization against a sponsor organization or other Party or government organs of unlawful interference in the activities of the organization;
5. to bring lawsuit in the name of a social organization against other organizations, state organs, enterprises or individuals for violating the lawful rights and interests of members of the organization;
6. none of the above is permitted by law.

B6. In your opinion, a law on social organization will
1. remove the current chaos in the administration of social organizations;
2. bring about a major development of social organizations in the country;
3. give more autonomy to social organizations;
4. simplify the procedures for the establishment of social organizations;
5. not bring about any substantive change in the country.

B7. If the state is to adopt a law on social organizations, what kind of changes do you expect it to bring about?
1. changes relating to the requirements for the establishment of social organizations;
2. changes relating to the procedures for the establishment or change of social organizations;
3. changes in the system of administration of social organizations;
4. changes relating to the taxation of social organizations;
5. changes relating to the system of annual examination of social organizations;
6. changes in the system of annual examinations of social organizations.

B8. If the state is to adopt a legislation on social organization, you
1. hope that you will be able to participate in the drafting or discussion of the draft law;
2. hope that you will be able to elect a representative to participate in the drafting or discussion of the draft law;
3. hope that your opinion will be taken seriously into consideration in the making of such legislation;
4. do not have any specific idea.

C1. In the past three years, how many times has your organization participated in drafting or discussion of draft legislation?
1. once or twice; 2. three or four times; 3. five to seven times; 4. more than eight times; 5. not at all.

C2. In the past three years, how many policy proposals has your organization put forward to the government? And how many of them have been adopted by the relevant government departments?

C3. In the past three years, on how many occasions has your organization given advice to enterprises? And on how many occasions has it been accepted by the enterprises?

D1. With regard to the following phenomena, please choose one of the answers listed below (after the asterisk sign (*)) according to the actual situation.

(1) a social organization meets all the other conditions for registration except that it cannot find a sponsor organization;
(2) a social organization meets all the other conditions for registration except that the sponsor organization refuses to accept its application for registration;
(3) a social organization meets all the other conditions for registration except that the sponsor organization refuses to approve its application for registration;
(4) a social organization meets all the conditions for registration but the government organ in charge of registration of social organizations refuses to register it;
(5) the sponsor organization collects fees for the examination of the applications for the establishment or the change of registration of social organizations;
(6) the sponsor organization collects fees for the preliminary examination work in the annual examination and verification of social organizations;
(7) the sponsor organization collecting fees on social organizations in other names;
(8) a sponsor organization demands favors from your organizations;
(9) social organizations engage in profit-making activities;
(10) someone uses deception to obtain certificates of registration of social organizations;
(11) someone obtains certificates of registration of social organizations by paying extra money or other things;
(12) a social organization is unable to obtain approval from the sponsor organization for carrying out certain activities;
(13) your organization seldom has any contact with the sponsor organization;
(14) the fund of a social organization is misappropriated by the sponsor organization;
(15) a social organization is banned without having violated any laws or regulations.

* 1. I have never encountered any of the above problems;
2. I have rarely encountered any of the above problems;
3. I have occasionally encountered the above problems;
4. I often encounter the above problems;
5. I almost always encounter the above problems.

V

RELEVANT ARTICLES OF THE DUTCH CIVIL CODE

BOOK II

Title 1 GENERAL PROVISIONS

Article 1

1 The State, the provinces, the municipalities, the water control corporations and all bodies which under the Constitution have the power to issue regulations possess legal personality.

2 Other bodies charged with part of the duties of government possess legal personality only, if this follows from provisions of, or is provided pursuant to, the law.

3 The following articles of this Title, except article 5, shall not apply to the legal persons referred to in the preceding paragraphs.

Article 2

1 Religious associations, their independent subdivisions and bodies in which they are united possess legal personality.

2 They are governed by their own constitution, insofar as this is not contrary to the law. With the exception of article 5, the following articles of this Title shall not apply to them; the same may be applied to them, *mutatis mutandis*, to the extent consistent with their constitution and the nature of their mutual relations.

Yuwen Li (Ed.), *Freedom of Association in China and Europe: Comparative Perspectives in Law and Practice*, © 2005 Koninklijke Brill NV, Leiden. Printed in The Netherlands, pp. 403-434.

Article 3
Associations, cooperatives, mutual insurance societies, companies limited by shares, private companies with limited liability and foundations possess legal personality.

Article 4
1 A legal person is not created in the absence of a deed signed by a *notaris* (notary) or of a certificate of no objection to the extent required by law for its formation. A deed signed by a notary which is not authentic and thus without juridical (*legal*) effect shall only prevent the creation of a legal person if such legal person was to be created by a last will made in such a deed.

2 Annulment (*avoidance*) of the juridical act by which a legal person is created shall not invalidate its existence. The invalidity of the participation of one or more founders of a legal person shall not, of itself, affect the legal validity of the participations of the remaining founders.

3 If there are property, rights and interests in the name of a non-existing legal person, the court shall appoint one or more liquidators on the application of any interested party or of the public prosecution service. Article 22 shall apply, *mutatis mutandis*.

4 The liquidation of the property, rights and interests shall take place in the manner applicable to the liquidation of the professed type of legal person. Persons who have acted as officers or directors shall be solidarily (*jointly and severally*) liable for any obligations which form part of such property, rights and interests and which became exigible (*due*) in the period in which they so acted. They shall, in addition, be liable for any obligations arising from juridical acts performed for such property, rights and interests during such period to the extent that no-one is liable therefor pursuant to the preceding sentence. In the absence of persons who are liable pursuant to the preceding two sentences, the persons who have acted shall be solidarily (*jointly and severally*) liable.

5 If a legal person is subsequently incorporated for the purpose of taking title to the property, rights and interests the court may, upon application, permit that these shall not be liquidated but contributed to such legal person.

Article 5
As regards the law of property, rights and interests, a legal person is equivalent to a natural person, unless the contrary follows from the law.

Article 6
1 Amendments to the articles and by-laws and the dissolution (*winding up*) of the legal person, which must be published pursuant to this Book, may not be invoked against the other party and third parties not aware thereof prior to such publication and, in the

case of an amendment to articles, before the prescribed publication of the amended articles has taken place.

2 The lack of authority of the management or of an officer or director under the articles to represent the legal person in the performance of a juridical (*legal*) act, though otherwise permitted by law, may not be invoked against the other party who was not aware thereof if the restriction or exclusion of the authority of such officer or director was not published in the manner prescribed by law at the time the juridical (*legal*) act was performed. The same applies to the invocation of a restriction on the representative authority of persons other than officers or directors, upon whom such authority is conferred by the articles.

3 A legal person may not invoke the incorrectness or incompleteness of any particulars in the register against any other party who was not aware thereof. A correct and complete registration elsewhere or publication of the articles shall not, of itself, be sufficient evidence that such other party was not unaware of such incorrectness or incompleteness.

4 Save as otherwise provided by law, the other party may not invoke against a legal person any lack of knowledge of a fact published in a manner prescribed by law, unless such publication was not made in every respect in the manner required by law or the prescribed notice thereof was not given.

5 Both aforementioned paragraphs shall not apply to judicial decisions recorded in the *faillissementsregister* (register of bankruptcies) or in the *surséanceregister* (register of suspensions of payments).

Article 7
A juridical (*legal*) act performed by a legal person may be annulled (*avoided*) if, as a result, its object was transgressed and the other party was aware thereof or, without personal investigation, should have been so aware; only the legal person can claim annulment (*avoidance*) on such grounds.

Article 8
1 A legal person and the persons who by virtue of the law and its articles are concerned with its organisation must, in such capacity, conduct themselves in relation to each other in accordance with the dictates of reasonableness and fairness.

2 A rule which binds them by virtue of the law, custom, the articles, by-laws or a resolution shall be inapplicable to the extent that, in the circumstances, it is unacceptable according to standards of reasonableness and fairness.

Article 9
Each officer or director shall be responsible to the legal person for the proper performance of the duties assigned to him. If a matter falls within the scope of responsibility of two or more officers or directors, each shall be solidarily (*jointly and severally*) liable for any shortcoming, unless he proves that it is not attributable to him and that he was not negligent in acting to prevent the consequences.

Article 10
1 The management shall administer the financial condition of the legal person and everything relating to its activities as such activities may require and keep the books, records and other database pertaining thereto in such manner that its rights and obligations can be ascertained at any time.

2 Without prejudice to the provisions in the following Titles, the management shall annually within six months from the end of its financial year prepare a balance sheet and a statement of income and expenditure of the legal person.

3 The management shall retain the books, records and other database referred to in paragraphs 1 and 2 for seven years.

4 The information stored in a database, save for the balance sheet and statement of income and expenditure if recorded in writing, may be transferred to, and stored on, another database, provided such data transmission is correct and complete and the data are available during the entire required retention period and can be converted into legible form within a reasonable period.

Article 10a
The financial year of a legal person shall be the calendar year, unless another financial year has been designated in its articles.

Article 11
Any legal person which, at the time the liability arose, was an officer or director of another body corporate, shall be jointly and severally liable with that body corporate for its liability.

Article 12
The articles of a legal person may disqualify certain persons, their spouses, registered partners, and blood relatives in the direct line, from voting on resolutions in which the legal person grants rights to or waives the obligations of such persons, other than in their capacity as members, shareholders or members of a constituent body.

Article 13
1 A vote is null in the instances in which a unilateral juridical (*legal*) act is a nullity; a vote cannot be annulled (*avoided*).

2 A person without legal capacity who is a member of an association may himself exercise his voting right therein to the extent that its articles do not so prohibit; in all other cases the exercise of the voting right shall vest in his legal representative.

3 Save as otherwise provided in the articles, the ruling pronounced by the chairman at a meeting of a constituent body of a legal person in respect of the outcome of a vote shall be decisive. The same shall apply to the contents of a resolution passed, to the extent that the vote related to a proposal not made in writing.

4 If, immediately after the ruling pronounced by the chairman, its correctness is contested, another vote shall be taken if so desired by the majority at the meeting or, if the original vote was not taken *per capita* or on a poll, by someone present who was entitled to vote. As a result of such new vote the legal consequences of the original vote shall lapse.

Article 14
1 A resolution of a constituent body of a legal person that is contrary to the law or the articles is a nullity, unless another consequence follows from the law.

2 A resolution which is a nullity due to the failure on its adoption to do some prior act required by law or the articles or to notify a person or body other than the constituent body which adopted such resolution, may be ratified by such other person or body. If any condition is imposed for the act which is the subject of the failure, such condition shall also apply to the ratification.

3 Ratification shall no longer be possible after expiration of a reasonable period imposed upon the other person or body by the constituent body which adopted the resolution or by the other party which is the subject of the resolution.

Article 15
1 Without prejudice to any other statutory provision entitling annulment (*avoidance*), a resolution of a constituent body of a legal person may be declared a nullity:
a on the grounds that it is contrary to statutory provisions or provisions in the articles regulating the passing of resolutions;
b on the grounds that it is contrary to the principles of reasonableness and fairness required under article 8;
c on the grounds that it is contrary to any by-laws.

2 The provisions referred to in subparagraph *a* of the preceding paragraph shall not include those containing the conditions referred to in article 14, paragraph 2.

3 Annulment is effected by a decision of the court of the legal person's residence:

a upon the demand against the legal person of a person who has a reasonable interest in the due prestation (*performance*) of the obligation which has not been performed, or

b in proceedings instituted pursuant to a resolution of its management by the legal person itself against the person designated by the interim provisions judge of the court on an application of the legal person made for such purpose; in that case the costs of the proceedings shall be borne by the legal person.

4 If an officer or director makes the application in his own name, the legal person shall apply to the interim provisions judge of the court to designate a person who shall act on behalf of the management in such proceedings.

5 The right to demand annulment of the resolution shall lapse one year from the end of the day on which sufficient publicity of the resolution was given or on which the interested party became aware of the resolution or was notified thereof.

6 A resolution which may be the subject of a claim for annulment under subparagraph *a* of paragraph 1 may be ratified by a resolution to that effect; for such a resolution the same conditions shall apply as those applicable to the resolution to be ratified. The ratification shall not take effect as long as proceedings instituted for the annulment are pending. If the claim is allowed, the avoided resolution shall be deemed to have been passed anew as a result of a later resolution, unless this is contrary to the necessary implication of the resolution.

Article 16

1 An irrevocable decision establishing the nullity of a resolution of a legal person or whereby such resolution is annulled (*avoided*) shall, if the legal person was party to the proceedings, be universally binding, without prejudice to the revocation or to proceedings by third parties to set a judgment aside. Each member or shareholder shall have the right of revocation.

2 If the resolution is a juridical (*legal*) act of the legal person directed at the other party or if it constitutes a condition for the validity of such juridical act, the nullity or annulment (*avoidance*) of the resolution cannot be raised as a defence against such other party if the latter was neither aware nor ought to have been aware of the defect in the resolution. Notwithstanding the foregoing, the nullity or annulment of a resolution to appoint a director or officer or supervisory board member may be invoked as against the appointed person, provided the legal person indemnifies him against any loss if he was neither aware nor ought to have been aware of the defect in the resolution.

Article 17
Legal persons shall be formed for an indeterminate period.

Article 18
1 Subject to compliance with the following paragraphs a legal person may convert itself into another legal type.

2 The following is required for conversion:

a a resolution to convert, passed in accordance with the requirements for a resolution for an amendment of the articles and, save in the case of the conversion of a foundation, adopted with the votes of at least nine-tenths of the votes cast;
b a resolution to amend the articles;
c a notarial deed of conversion embodying the new articles.

3 The majority mentioned in subparagraph *a* of the preceding paragraph is not required for the conversion of a company limited by shares into a private company or *vice versa*.

4 For the conversion of or into a foundation and of a company limited by shares or private company into an association authorisation by the court shall also be required.

5 An application to the court for authorisation to convert can be made only by the legal person on submission of a draft notarial deed. This shall be rejected in any event if any required resolution is a nullity or if proceedings for the annulment (*avoidance*) thereof are pending. It shall be rejected if the interests of persons with voting rights who did not exercise such rights or of any other persons at least one of whom sought the assistance of the court, have been insufficiently respected. If authorisation by the court is required for the conversion, the notary shall state in the conversion deed that such authorisation has been granted to the draft of the deed.

6 After conversion of a foundation it must appear from its articles that its property, rights and interests at the conversion and any proceeds therefrom may only with the consent of the court be applied differently from the manner prescribed prior to its conversion. The same shall apply to the articles of a legal person to the extent that such property, rights and interests and such proceeds were vested in it as a result of a merger or division.

7 The legal person shall file notice of its conversion for entry in the registers in which it was obliged to be and now must be registered or in which, if it is an association, it was registered voluntarily.

8 Conversion shall not terminate the legal existence of a legal person.

Article 19

1 A legal person shall be dissolved (*wound up*)

a by resolution of its general meeting or, if the legal person is a foundation and it is not otherwise provided in its articles, by a management resolution;

b on the occurrence of an event which, pursuant to its articles, results in its dissolution (*winding up*) and which does not constitute a resolution or an act, the object of which is the dissolution (*winding up*);

c after it has been declared bankrupt, either upon termination of its bankruptcy because of the condition of its assets, or by its insolvency;

d if, in the case of an association, a cooperative or a mutual insurance society, there are no longer any members;

e by an order of the chamber of commerce and industry referred to in article 19*a*;

f by the court in the instances provided by law.

2 On the application of the management, an interested party or the public prosecution service, the court shall declare whether a legal person has been dissolved (*wound up*) and the effective date of the dissolution (*winding up*) of the legal person in one of the instances referred to in subparagraph *b* or *d* of paragraph 1. The order shall be universally binding. If the legal person has been registered in a public register, it shall be the responsibility of the clerk of the court to ensure registration in such register of the decision giving such declaratory order when it becomes final and binding.

3 Notice of the dissolution shall be filed for entry in the registers where the legal person is registered; in the instances referred to in subparagraphs *a*, *b* and *d* of paragraph 1, by the liquidator, if there is one, and otherwise by the management; in the instance referred to in subparagraph *c* of paragraph 1, by the *curator* in the bankruptcy; in the instance referred to in subparagraph *e* of paragraph 1, by the chamber of commerce and industry; and, in the instance referred to in subparagraph *f* of paragraph 1, by the clerk of the court concerned.

4 If the legal person no longer has any assets at the time of its dissolution, it shall then cease to exist. In that case the management or, if article 19*a* is applicable, the chamber of commerce and industry shall file notice thereof for entry in the registers where the legal person is registered.

5 A legal person shall continue to exist after its dissolution to the extent required for the purpose of the liquidation of its property, rights and interests. In documents and announcements issued by it, the words '*in liquidatie*' shall be added to its name.

6 On liquidation the legal person shall cease to exist when the liquidation ends. The liquidator or the *curator* in the bankruptcy shall file a notice for entry in the registers where the legal person is registered.

7 The particulars registered in respect of a legal person in the registers on the date on which it ceases to exist shall be kept there for ten years after such date.

Article 19a

1 A company limited by shares, a private company with limited liability, a cooperative or a mutual insurance society registered in the commercial register shall be dissolved (*wound up*) by order of the chamber of commerce and industry in whose district such legal person is registered if the chamber determines that at least two of the following circumstances exist:

a the legal person has not paid the amount due for its registration in the commercial register or for registration of an enterprise belonging to it for at least one year from the due date for payment of such amount;

b during at least one year no directors of the legal person are on record as registered in the register and no entry for registration has been filed or, if directors are registered, one of the following circumstances exists with regard to all of the registered directors:

1 the director has died;

2 for at least one year the director has not been contactable either at the address on record in the register or at the address registered in the municipal population administration or if, for at least one year, no address of the director is on record in such administration;

c the legal person is in default for at least one year in performing its obligation to publish its annual accounts or its balance sheet and notes in accordance with article 394, 396 or 397;

d the legal person has not acted for at least one year upon a summons referred to in article 9, paragraph 3 of the *Algemene wet inzake rijksbelastingen* (General State Taxes Act) on filing a corporate tax return.

2 An association or foundation which does not conduct an enterprise which is registered in the commercial register shall be dissolved (*wound up*) by an order of the chamber of commerce and industry at which the legal person is registered if the chamber has established that a circumstance as mentioned in subparagraph *b* of paragraph 1 exists and the legal person has remained in default for at least one year in paying the amount due for registration in the commercial register concerned.

3 If, on the basis of the information known to it, the chamber determines that a legal person referred to in paragraphs 1 and 2 qualifies for dissolution (*winding up*), it shall notify the legal person and the registered directors, by registered letter sent to their last known address, that it intends to dissolve (*wind up)* the legal person, mentioning the circumstances on which this intention is based. The chamber shall record this notice in the register. If a circumstance as referred to in subparagraph *b* of paragraph 1 exists, the chamber shall ensure the publication of such notice of intent to dissolve in the *Nederlandse Staatscourant* (State Gazette). To the extent that the cost of such publication cannot be met out of the assets of the legal person, such cost shall be for the account of Our Minister of Justice.

4 After expiration of eight weeks from the date of the registered letter the chamber shall issue an order for the dissolution of the legal person, unless, prior thereto it is determined that the circumstances mentioned in the third paragraph do not or no longer exist.

5 The legal person and its registered directors or officers shall be notified of the order.

6 The chamber shall ensure that a notice of the dissolution is published in the *Nederlandse Staatscourant.* Paragraph 3, fourth sentence shall apply *mutatis mutandis.*

7 If, pursuant to article 23, paragraph 1 no liquidators can be appointed, the chamber shall act as liquidator of the estate of the legal person in liquidation, notwithstanding article 19, paragraph 4. On the application of the chamber, the court shall appoint one or more liquidators in its stead.

8 If appeal is instituted against an order referred to in paragraph 4 with the *College van Beroep voor het bedrijfsleven* (Trade and Industry Appeals Tribunal), the chamber shall file notice thereof in its register. A decision on the appeal shall also be recorded. If the necessary implication of the decision is to annul (*avoid*) the order, the chamber shall ensure that notice thereof is published in the *Nederlandse Staatscourant.* During the period in which the legal person had ceased to exist since the order for its dissolution, there is a grounds for extension as referred to in article 320 of Book 3 with regard to the prescription period for rights of action by or against the legal person.

Article 20

1 Upon the application of the public prosecution service the court shall declare that a legal person the activity of which is contrary to public policy shall be prohibited and dissolved (*wound up*).

2 A legal person the object of which is contrary to public policy shall be dissolved by the court upon the application of the public prosecution service. Prior to ordering the dissolution (*winding up*) the court may give the legal person an opportunity within a period to be set by it to amend its object in such a manner that it will no longer be contrary to public policy.

Article 21

1 The court shall dissolve (*wind up*) a legal person, if:

a there are defects in its formation;

b its articles do not comply with the statutory requirements;

c it does not fall within the statutory description of its legal type.

2 The court shall not dissolve a legal person if it has allowed it a given period of time upon expiration of which it is a legal person which complies with the statutory requirements.

3 The court may dissolve a legal person, if it transgresses the prohibitions set in this Book for its legal type or acts to a serious degree contrary to its articles.

4 The dissolution (*winding up*) may be ordered upon application of any interested party or of the public prosecution service.

Article 22
1 The court before which an application for the dissolution (*winding up*) of a legal person is pending may place the property of such legal person, if so demanded, under administration; the order shall set its effective date.

2 In its order the court shall appoint one or more administrators and provide for their powers and remuneration.

3 To the extent that the court does not otherwise determine, the constituent bodies of a legal person may not adopt any resolutions without prior approval of the administrator, and representatives of the legal person may not perform any juridical (*legal*) acts without his cooperation.

4 The order can be amended or withdrawn by the court at any time; the administration ends in any event as soon as the decision on application for the dissolution has become final and binding.

5 The administrator shall file at the registries where the legal person has been registered a notice of the order and of such particulars in respect of himself as are required for a director or officer.

6 A juridical act performed by a legal person prior to the registration, notwithstanding its incapacity on account of such administration, shall nevertheless be valid if the other party was neither aware nor ought to have been aware of the administration.

Article 22a
1 Prior to an application by the public prosecution service for the dissolution (*winding up*) of a company limited by shares or a private company with limited liability the public prosecution service may apply in its application to the court for an order enjoining the shareholders from exercising their power to dispose of, pledge or charge shares with a usufruct until a decision on the aforementioned requisition shall become final and binding.

2 The court shall make its decision after a summary review. Its order shall be made provided that the application for the dissolution is instituted within a period to be set by the court. There shall be no appeal from such order.

3 The order shall be served without delay, if possible on the same day, on the shareholders and the company. The clerk of the court shall ensure the registration of the order in the register where the legal person is registered.

4 Within eight days after the service mentioned in the preceding paragraph the shareholders may commence proceedings to set the order aside. The proceedings to set aside shall not suspend the order, notwithstanding the right of the shareholders to have the President of the court decide the issue in summary proceedings. The proceedings for setting the order aside may not be based on the contention that the shareholder wishes to transfer his shares.

5 The shareholder must be served with the application for the dissolution within eight days after this has been made.

Article 23

1 To the extent that the court has not appointed any other liquidators and the articles do not designate other liquidators, the directors shall become liquidators of the property, rights and interests of a legal person that has been dissolved (*wound up*). The provisions in respect of the appointment, suspension, removal and supervision of directors shall apply to liquidators not appointed by the court, insofar as the articles do not otherwise provide. The property, rights and interests of a legal person that has been dissolved (*wound up*) by the court shall be liquidated by one or more liquidators to be appointed by it.

2 Upon removal by the court of a liquidator, it can appoint one or more other liquidators. If there are no liquidators on the application the court shall appoint one or more liquidators of any interested party or of the public prosecution service. A liquidator appointed by the court shall be entitled to a remuneration to be set by it.

3 A court appointment as liquidator shall take effect on the day after the clerk of the court has informed the liquidator of the appointment; the clerk of the court shall so inform him immediately, if the order for such appointment is enforceable notwithstanding appeal or an action to set the same aside and, otherwise, as soon as it has become final.

4 Every liquidator shall file a notice at the registries where the legal person is registered of his acting in that capacity and of the particulars in respect of himself required for a director or officer.

5 The court may dismiss a liquidator from the date set by it, either at his request or for important reasons, upon the request of a co-liquidator, of the public prosecution service or *ex officio*.

6 The liquidator who is removed shall render account to the persons who continue the liquidation. If his successor is appointed by the court he shall render account to the court.

Article 23a
1 Unless the articles otherwise provide, a liquidator shall have the same powers, duties and liability as a director or officer, to the extent that these are consistent with his duties as liquidator.

2 If there are two or more liquidators each may carry out all activities unless otherwise specified. If there is a difference of opinion between the liquidators the court involved in the liquidation shall decide the issue upon the request of either of them and otherwise the *kantonrechter* (subdistrict court) shall so decide. The court referred to in the preceding sentence may also determine the manner in which remuneration shall be divided.

3 Both the court and the judge delegated by it in respect of the liquidation may give orders required for the liquidation which orders may, but need not be, given in a form immediately enforceable for execution. The liquidator must act in accordance with their directions. There shall be no appeal from such orders and directions.

4 If the liquidator establishes that the liabilities will probably exceed the assets he shall file for a bankruptcy order unless all known obligees when so requested concur to a continuation of the liquidation without bankruptcy.

5 The preceding provisions in this article and articles 23*b*-23*c* shall not apply in the case of a liquidation in a bankruptcy.

Article 23b
1 After satisfaction of the claims of the creditors the liquidator shall transfer any surplus assets of the legal person subject to the liquidation to the parties entitled thereto in proportion to their respective rights under the articles or otherwise to the members or shareholders. If no other person is entitled to such surplus he shall distribute the same to the State which will apply the same to the extent possible in accordance with the legal person's object.

2 The liquidator shall prepare liquidation accounts showing the amount and composition of the surplus. If there are two or more persons entitled to such surplus the liquidator shall prepare a plan of distribution, stating the bases for the apportionment.

3 Insofar as the surplus consists of items other than cash and the articles or the court order do not provide for any direction the following methods may be applied for such apportionment:

a apportionment of part of the surplus to each party so entitled;
b over-apportionment to one of the parties so entitled against payment of the excess value;
c distribution of the net proceeds after sale.

4 The liquidator shall file the accounts rendered and the plan of distribution for entry at the registries where the legal person is registered and, in any event, at the office of the legal person, if there is one, or at any other place in the district where the legal person has its residence. The documents shall be available there for public inspection for two months. The liquidator shall publish a notice in a newspaper stating where and until which date the same shall be available for inspection. The court can order publication in the *Nederlandse Staatscourant* (State Gazette).

5 Within two months after deposit of the accounts rendered and the plan and after such deposit has been published and announced in accordance with paragraph 4, each creditor or party so entitled may institute an action to set the same aside by an application to the court. The liquidator shall publish notice of such instituted action in the same manner as that in which notice was given of the deposit of the accounts rendered and the plan of distribution.

6 Whenever the financial condition justifies the same, the liquidator may make an advance distribution to the parties entitled thereto. After the commencement of the period within which an action to set aside may be made, he shall not so proceed without court authorisation.

7 As soon as the withdrawal of, or a decision on, any action to set the decision aside has become irrevocable, the liquidator shall give notice thereof in the manner in which notice of the action to set the decision aside was given. If the decision alters the plan of distribution, notice of the altered plan of distribution shall also be given in such manner.

8 The liquidator shall tender and deposit for payment any cash funds not disposed of within six months after the last set date on which the same became exigible (*due*).

9 The liquidation shall end when the liquidator is not aware of any further existing assets.

10 After the expiration of one month from the date the liquidation ended, the liquidator shall account for his administration to the court, if it has been involved in the liquidation.

Article 23c

1 If, after the legal person has ceased to exist, a further creditor or party entitled to the surplus comes forward or the existence of an asset is ascertained, the court may, on the application of any interested party, reopen the liquidation and, if necessary, appoint a liquidator. In that event the legal person revives but exclusively for the purpose of the settlement of the reopened liquidation. The liquidator shall have the power to demand repayment from the persons so entitled of whatever amount they received in excess of the amount of their entitlement out of the surplus.

2 During the period in which the legal person ceased to exist there are grounds for extension as referred to in article 320 of Book 3 with regard to the prescription period for rights of action by or against the legal person.

Article 24

1 The books, records and other database of a legal person which has been dissolved (*wound up*) shall be retained for seven years after the legal person has ceased to exist. The depositary thereof shall be the person designated as such in or pursuant to the articles or by the general meeting or, if the legal person was a foundation, by its board.

2 If there is no depositary and if the last liquidator is not prepared to keep the same, a depositary, if possible from amongst the persons who were involved with the legal person, shall be appointed upon the application of any interested party by the subdistrict court within whose district the legal person had its residence. There shall lie no appeal.

3 Within eight days after his custody obligation takes effect, the depositary must notify the registries at which the legal person which has been dissolved (*wound up*) was registered of his name and address.

4 The subdistrict court mentioned in paragraph 2 may, upon application, give authorisation for inspection of the books, records and other database to any interested party, if the legal person was a foundation, and to any further person who shows he has a reasonable interest in such inspection as a former member or shareholder of the legal person or as holder of depositary receipts issued for its shares or as an assignee of such a person.

Article 24a

1 A subsidiary of a legal person is:

a a legal person in which the legal person or one or more of its subsidiaries, pursuant to an agreement with other persons entitled to vote or otherwise, can exercise, solely or jointly, more than one half of the voting rights at a general meeting;

b a legal person of which the legal person or one or more of its subsidiaries is a member or shareholder and, pursuant to an agreement with other persons entitled to vote or otherwise, can appoint or dismiss, solely or jointly, more than one half of the directors or officers or of the supervisory board members, if all persons entitled to vote were to cast their vote.

2 A partnership acting in its own name, for the obligations of which the legal person or one or more subsidiaries is, as a partner, fully liable to obligees, shall be treated as a subsidiary.

3 For the application of paragraph 1, a person who holds the shares for the account of others shall not be deemed to have the rights vested in the shares. A person for whose account the shares are held shall, if such person has the power to determine how the rights are exercised or to obtain the shares for himself, be deemed to have such rights vested in him.

4 For the application of paragraph 1, if a pledgee may determine how the rights, vested in pledged shares, are exercised, he shall be deemed to have the voting rights vested in him, provided that, where shares have been pledged for a loan given by the pledgee in the ordinary course of his business, the voting rights shall be deemed vested in him only if he has exercised the same in his own interest.

Article 24b
A group is an economic unit in which legal persons and partnerships are united in one organisation. Group companies are legal persons and partnerships which are united in one group.

Article 24c
1 A legal person or partnership has a participation or participating interest in a legal person if it or one or more of its subsidiaries, solely or jointly and for its own account, contributes, or causes the contribution of, capital with the object of a lasting relationship with such legal person for the furtherance of its own activities. If one-fifth or more of the issued capital is contributed, the existence of a participation shall be presumed.

2 A legal person has a participation or participating interest in a partnership if it or its subsidiary:
a is, as a partner, fully liable to its obligees for all obligations; or
b is otherwise a partner therein with the object of a lasting relationship with such legal person for the furtherance of its own activities.

Article 24d
When determining the extent to which the members or shareholders vote, are present or represented or to which the share capital is contributed or represented, no account shall be taken of memberships or shares in respect of which the law provides that no vote may be cast.

Article 25
There shall be no derogation from the provisions in this Book except and to the extent that the law so permits.

Title 2 ASSOCIATIONS

Article 26
1 An association is a legal person with members and whose specific object is different from that described in article 53, paragraph 1 or paragraph 2.

2 An association is formed by a multilateral juridical (*legal*) act.

3 An association may not distribute profits among its members.

Article 27
1 Where an association is formed by notarial deed, the following provisions must be observed.

2 The deed shall be executed in the Dutch language. If the association has its registered office in the province of Friesland ("Fryslân") the deed may be executed in the Friesian language. A procuration (*power of attorney*) to enter into such deed must be in writing.

3 The deed shall contain the articles of the association.

4 The articles shall include:
a the name of the association and the municipality in the Netherlands in which it has its registered office;
b the object of the association;
c the obligations which the members owe to the association, or the manner in which those obligations may be imposed;
d the manner of convening general meetings;
e the manner of appointment and removal of the officers;
f the allocation of the surplus of the association upon dissolution (*winding up*), or the manner in which such allocation shall be determined.

5 The notary before whom the deed is executed shall ensure that the deed complies with the provisions of paragraphs 2-4. If he fails to do so he shall be personally liable to the persons who suffered any loss as a result thereof.

Article 28
1 If an association has not been formed pursuant to the first paragraph of the preceding article, its general meeting may pass a resolution to embody the articles in a notarial deed.

2 Paragraphs 2-5 of the preceding article shall apply *mutatis mutandis.*

Article 29
1 Where the articles are embodied in a notarial deed, the officers of the association shall have it registered in the commercial register and shall deposit at the registry an officially certified copy of the deed or an officially certified extract of the deed embodying the articles.

2 Each and every officer shall be solidarily (*jointly and severally*) liable together with the association, for any juridical (*legal*) act by which he binds the association until the filing for deposit of the initial registration.

Article 30
1 Where its articles are not embodied in a notarial deed, an association cannot acquire registered property and cannot inherit under a will.

2 The officers shall be solidarily (*jointly and severally*) liable, together with the association, for debts arising from a juridical (*legal*) act, which became exigible (*due*) during their management. After their resignation they shall, in addition, be solidarily liable for obligations arising from a juridical act performed during their management, to the extent that no person is liable together with the association in respect thereof pursuant to the preceding sentence. No liability shall arise pursuant to one of the preceding sentences for a person not consulted in respect of any juridical act before the same took place and who, becoming aware thereof, refused to accept responsibility as an officer therefor. In the absence of any persons who are liable, together with the association, pursuant to the first or second sentence, the persons who acted shall be solidarily (*jointly and severally*) liable.

3 The officers of such an association may have it registered in the commercial register. Where the articles are recorded in writing, they shall file a copy thereof for deposit at that registry.

4 Where the registration referred to in the preceding paragraph has been made, the person who is bound by virtue of paragraph 2 shall be liable only to the extent the other party shows cause for the assumption that the association will not perform the obligation.

Article 31
Repealed

Article 32
Repealed

Article 33
Unless the articles otherwise provide, admission to membership shall be decided by the management and, if a person is not so admitted, the general meeting may nevertheless still resolve to admit the same.

Article 34
1 Membership of an association shall be personal, unless the articles otherwise provide.

2 Unless the articles of the association otherwise provide, membership shall, where the member is a legal person and ceases to exist as the result of a merger or division, be transmitted to the transferee legal person or, as the case may be, to one of the transferee legal persons in accordance with the description appended to the deed of division.

Article 34a
Obligations can be tied to membership only by or pursuant to the articles.

Article 35
1 Membership ends:
a on the death of a member, unless the articles permit transmission pursuant to the laws of succession;
b by notice of termination by the member;
c by notice of termination by the association;
d by removal.

2 An association may give notice of termination of membership in the instances mentioned in the articles and, in addition, when a member no longer meets the requirements for membership laid down by the articles, and if the association cannot reasonably be required to continue the membership. Such notice shall be given by the management, unless the articles confer such power on another constituent body.

3 Removal may only be ordered if a member acts in breach of the articles, by-laws or resolutions of the association or prejudices the association in an unreasonable manner.

4 Removal is effected by the management unless the articles confer this power on another constituent body. The member concerned shall be notified of the decision and of the reasons on which it is based in writing as soon as possible. Except when the decision has been made under the articles by the general meeting, the member shall have the right to appeal to the general meeting or to a constituent body or third party designated in the articles within one month after having received notice of the decision. The articles may make other provisions for such appeal, provided the term is not set at less than one month. During the period for appeal and pending the appeal, the member shall be suspended.

5 Where membership ends in the course of a financial year, the annual contribution shall nevertheless remain due in full, unless the articles otherwise provide.

Article 36
1 Unless the articles otherwise provide, notice of termination of membership may be given only as at the end of a financial year and with four weeks' notice. The *Algemene Termijnenwet* (Computation of Time Periods (General) Act) shall not be applicable to such period. Membership may, in any event, be terminated by notice as at the end of the financial year following that in which notice is given or, if continuation of membership cannot reasonably be required, immediately.

2 A notice of termination given contrary to the provisions of the preceding paragraph shall terminate membership at the earliest time permitted after the date as at which the notice is given.

3 A member may, in addition, give notice of termination of his membership with immediate effect within one month after having become aware or after having been notified of a resolution restricting his rights or increasing his obligations, in which case the resolution shall not apply to him. The articles may withhold from the members such right to give notice of termination where rights and obligations precisely described therein are changed and, in addition, generally where rights and obligations of a financial nature are changed.

4 Notice of termination of membership with immediate effect may also be given by a member within one month after having been informed of a resolution to convert the association into another legal form or to merge or to divide the same.

Article 37
1 The management shall be appointed from the members. Notwithstanding the foregoing, the articles may provide that non-members may also be appointed officers.

2 The appointment shall be made by the general meeting. Notwithstanding the foregoing, the articles may also provide a different manner of appointment provided each member is able to participate, directly or indirectly, in the voting on the appointment of the officers.

3 The articles may provide that one or more officers but less than one half, shall be appointed by persons other than the members.

4 Where the articles provide that an officer must be appointed at a meeting from a binding list then, by a resolution passed by not less than two-thirds of the votes cast by such meeting, such list may be declared non-binding. The articles may provide that at these meetings at least a certain number of votes must be capable of being cast; such number may not be set higher than two-thirds of the total number of votes that can be cast by the persons entitled to vote.

5 Where, under the articles, an officer is appointed outside a meeting by members or sections, the members must be given an opportunity to propose candidates. The articles may provide that such right shall vest only in a number of members jointly, provided such number is not set higher than one-fifth of the number of members which may participate in the election. In addition, the articles may provide that candidates so proposed are appointed only if they obtain a certain minimum number of votes in their favour, provided such number does not exceed two-thirds of the number of votes cast.

6 An officer may, even if appointed for a specified period, be removed or suspended at any time by the constituent body which appointed him. No order of the court may be issued for reinstatement of the contract of employment between the association and an officer.

7 Unless the articles otherwise provide, the management shall designate from its midst a chairman, secretary and treasurer.

Article 38

1 Save for the provisions of the following article, all members, if not suspended, shall be entitled to attend the general meeting and shall have one vote thereat; a suspended member shall be entitled to attend the meeting at which the resolution to suspend him is on the agenda and may address the meeting in respect thereof. The articles may confer more than one vote on certain members.

2 Unless the articles otherwise provide, the chairman and the secretary of the management or their deputies shall also act at the general meeting in such capacity.

3 The articles may provide that persons who form part of other constituent bodies of the association and who are not members, may vote at the general meeting, provided the number of votes to be cast by them may, in the aggregate, not exceed one half of the number of votes cast by the members.

4 Unless the articles otherwise provide, a person with a right to vote pursuant to paragraph 1 or 3 may give a procuration (*power of attorney*) to vote on his behalf to another person entitled to vote.

Article 39

1 The articles may provide that the general meeting shall consist of delegates elected by and from the members. The method of election and the number of delegates shall be regulated by the articles; each member must be able to, directly or indirectly, participate in the election. Paragraphs 4 and 5 of article 37 shall apply to an election, *mutatis* *mutandis*. Article 38, paragraph 3 shall apply, *mutatis mutandis*, to persons who form part of other constituent bodies of the association and who are not delegates.

2 The articles may provide that certain resolutions of the general meeting shall be subject to a referendum. The articles shall provide for the instances, the period, and the manner in which the referendum shall be held. Pending the outcome of the referendum, the implementation of the resolution shall be suspended.

Article 40
1 All powers of the association not conferred on other constituent bodies by law or the articles shall vest in the general meeting.

2 A unanimous resolution of all members or delegates, even if not present at a meeting, shall have the same force as a resolution of the general meeting, provided it was passed with the advance knowledge of the management.

Article 41
1 The management shall convene the general meeting as often as it shall think fit or when required by law or the articles to do so. The articles may also vest such power in persons other than the management.

2 On the written application of a number of members or delegates entitled to cast not less than one-tenth of the votes in a general meeting or of such lesser number as is provided by the articles, the management shall convene a general meeting within a period of not less than four weeks after the application was lodged.

3 If the application has not been complied with within fourteen days and, unless the articles prescribe another manner of convening the general meeting in such a case, the applicants may then proceed to convene the meeting themselves in the manner in which the general meeting is convened by the management or by making an announcement in at least one daily newspaper, widely read in the place in which the association is established. The applicants may then charge persons other than members of the management with the conduct of the meeting and the preparation of the minutes.

Article 41a
Articles 37-41 shall apply, *mutatis mutandis*, to sections of an association which are not legal persons and which have a general meeting and a management; whatever is provided in those articles in respect of the articles of the association may be provided in by-laws for sections of the association.

Article 42
1 No amendment of the articles of the association may be made other than by a resolution of a general meeting, convened by notice stating that an amendment of the articles

will be proposed thereat. At least seven days' notice shall be given for convening such a meeting.

2 A copy of the proposal, stating the proposed amendment verbatim, must be deposited for inspection by the members at a location suitable for that purpose by the persons who convened the general meeting at which a proposal to amend the articles is to be dealt with, from at least five days before the meeting until after the end of the day on which the meeting is held. The sections which make up the association and the delegates must be notified of the proposal at least fourteen days prior to the meeting, in which case the preceding sentence shall not apply.

3 The provisions of the first two paragraphs shall not apply if all members or delegates are present or represented at the general meeting and the resolution to amend the articles is passed unanimously.

4 The provisions of this article and of the first two paragraphs of the following article shall apply, *mutatis mutandis*, to a resolution to dissolve (*wind up*) the association.

Article 43
1 Unless the articles otherwise provide, at least two-thirds of the votes cast shall be required for a resolution to amend the articles.

2 To the extent that the articles exclude the power to amend, the amendment shall nevertheless be possible by unanimous vote at a meeting at which all members or deputies are present or represented.

3 A provision of the articles restricting the right to amend one or more other provisions may only be amended if a similar restriction is observed.

4 A provision of the articles excluding the right to amend one or more other provisions may only be amended by unanimous vote at a meeting at which all members or deputies are present or represented.

5 If the association has full legal capacity, the amendment shall take effect only upon the drawing up of a notarial deed of amendment. The officers shall deposit an officially certified copy of the amendment and the amended articles at the commercial registry.

6 The officers of an association with limited legal capacity, a copy of whose articles has been deposited at the registry pursuant to article 30, paragraph 3 of this Book, shall also deposit a copy of the amendment and the amended articles at such registry.

Article 44
1 Subject to any restrictions under the articles, the management shall be charged with the management of the association.

2 Only if this follows from the articles, the management has authority to resolve to enter into agreements to purchase, dispose of or encumber registered property or to enter into agreements by which the association commits itself as surety or solidary (*joint and several*) obligor, warrants performance by a third party or undertakes to provide security for an obligation of a third party. The articles may impose restrictions and tie conditions on such authority. The exclusion, restrictions and conditions shall also apply to the authority to represent the association in respect of such acts, unless the articles otherwise provide.

Article 45
1 The management shall represent the association to the extent that the contrary does not follow from the law.

2 The articles may also vest representative authority in one or more officers and may provide that an officer may represent the association only with the cooperation of one or more other persons.

3 Representative authority vested in the management or in an officer shall be unrestricted and unconditional to the extent that the contrary does not follow from the law. A restriction or condition on the representative authority permitted or prescribed by statute may only be invoked by the association.

4 The articles may also vest representative authority in persons other than officers.

Article 46
To the extent that the contrary does not follow from the articles, an association may, on behalf of its members, stipulate rights and, to the extent specifically provided in its articles, enter into commitments for their account. It may claim performance of the stipulated rights of and claim reparation of damage for a member, unless such member opposes the same.

Article 47
In all matters in which the association has a conflict of interest with one or more officers or supervisory board members, the general meeting may designate one or more persons in order to represent the association.

Article 48
1 At a general meeting held within six months after the end of the financial year, unless this period had been extended by the general meeting, the management shall submit

an annual report on the course of business of the association and on the policy conducted. It shall submit the balance sheet and the statement of income and expenditure with notes for the approval of the meeting. These documents shall be signed by the officers and the members of the supervisory board; if one or more signatures is missing, this shall be stated giving the reasons therefor. After expiration of such period every member may commence proceedings against all the officers for the enforcement of these obligations.

2 If there is no supervisory board and if no certificate from an accountant as referred to in article 393, paragraph 1 is submitted to the general meeting in respect of the correctness of the documents, the general meeting shall annually appoint a committee of at least two members who may not form part of the management. The committee shall examine the documents referred to in the second sentence of paragraph 1 and shall report on its findings to the general meeting.
The management must provide the committee for its examination with all information requested by it and show it, if so desired, the cash and valuables and allow it to inspect the books and records of the association.

3 An association which maintains one or more undertakings which must be registered in the commercial register pursuant to the law shall disclose the net turnover of such undertakings in its statement of income and expenditure.

Article 49
1 Each year, within six months after the end of the financial year of an association referred to in article 360, paragraph 3, unless this period has been extended by up to five months by the general meeting on account of special circumstances, annual accounts shall be prepared by the management, which shall be made available for inspection by the members at the office of the association. Within this period the management shall also deposit the annual report for inspection by the members unless the first sentence of article 369, paragraph 6 or article 403 applies in respect of the association. For investment companies which have been issued a licence under the *Wet toezicht beleggingsinstellingen* (Investment Undertakings (Supervision) Act) the period may be shortened by or pursuant to that Act.

2 The annual accounts shall be signed by the officers and members of the supervisory board. If one or more of their signatures is missing, this shall be stated giving the reason therefor.

3 The annual accounts shall be adopted by the general meeting, which the management shall cause to be held no later than one month after the end of the period. Adoption of the annual accounts shall not serve as a discharge and release for a director or supervisory board member, respectively.

4 Article 48, paragraph 1 shall not apply to an association referred to in article 360, paragraph 3. Article 48, paragraph 2 shall apply thereto, provided that the documents referred to therein shall refer to the documents submitted pursuant to paragraph 1.

5 An association referred to in article 360, paragraph 3 may only compensate a shortfall in its required statutory reserves insofar so permitted by law.

6 Our Minister of Economic Affairs may, for important reasons and on application, grant dispensation from the obligation to prepare, present and adopt the annual accounts.

Article 50
An association referred to in article 360, paragraph 3 shall ensure that its annual accounts, as prepared, the annual report and the information to be added pursuant to article 392, paragraph 1 are available at its office from the day of the notice convening the general meeting at which the same are to be considered. The members may inspect the documents there and obtain a copy thereof free of charge.

Article 50a
Articles 131, 138, 139, 149 and 150 shall apply, *mutatis mutandis*, to the bankruptcy of an association the articles of which are embodied in a notarial deed and which is subject to the levy of corporate income tax.

Article 51
In the event of bankruptcy or *surséance van betaling* (suspension of payments) of an association which has been registered in the commercial register, the notices which, by virtue of the *Faillissementswet* (Bankruptcy Act), are published in the *Nederlandse Staatscourant* (State Gazette), shall also be submitted for registration in such register by the person charged with the publication.

Article 52
Insofar as the articles may derogate from the provisions of this Title, such derogation may only be made by articles in writing.

Title 6 FOUNDATIONS

Article 285
1 A foundation is a legal person created by a juridical (*legal*) act which has no members and whose purpose is to realise an object stated in its articles using capital allocated to such purpose.

2 If the authority to fill vacancies in constituent bodies of the foundation is vested in one or more persons by the articles, the foundation shall not, on those grounds alone, be considered as having members.

3 The object of the foundation may not include the making of distributions to any founder or to those participating in its constituent bodies or to other parties, unless, as regards the latter, the distributions have an idealistic or social purpose.

Article 286
1 A foundation must be established by notarial deed.

2 The deed shall be executed in the Dutch language. If the foundation has its registered office in the province of Friesland ("*Fryslân*"), the deed may be executed in the Friesian language. A procuration (*power of attorney*) to enter into such deed must be in writing. The foundation may be established by a last will made by a notarial deed executed in a foreign language; the articles of the foundation must also, in that case, be in the Dutch or Friesian language.

3 The deed shall contain the articles of the foundation.

4 The articles must include:
a the name of the foundation, with the word '*stichting*' as part of its name;
b the object of the foundation;
c the manner of appointment and dismissal of the officers;
d the municipality in the Netherlands where it has its seat;
e the application of the surplus after liquidation of the foundation on a dissolution (*winding up*) or the manner in which such application shall be determined.

5 The notary before whom the deed is executed shall ensure that the articles contain the provisions stated in paragraphs 2-4. On default he shall be personally liable to the persons who suffered any loss as a result thereof.

Article 287
If the articles do not specify a seat, the foundation shall have its seat in the municipality where the notary before whom the deed is executed officiated at the time of the execution of the deed.

Article 288
Repealed

Article 289
1 The officers shall procure registration of the foundation and the surname, forenames and address or last address of the founder or founders registered in the commercial register and shall deposit at the registry an officially certified copy or officially certified extract of the deed of establishment embodying the articles.

2 Each officer shall be solidarily (*jointly and severally*) liable together with the foundation for any juridical (*legal*) act by which he binds the foundation until the filing for deposit of the initial registration.

Article 290
Repealed

Article 291
1 Subject to any restrictions under the articles, the board shall be charged with the management of the foundation.

2 Only if this follows from the articles, the board has the authority to resolve to enter into agreements to purchase, dispose of or encumber registered property or to enter into agreements by which the foundation commits itself as surety or solidary (*joint and several*) obligor, warrants performance by a third party or undertakes to provide security for an obligation of a third person. The articles may impose restrictions and conditions on such authority of the board. The exclusion, restrictions and conditions shall also apply to the authority to represent the foundation in respect of such acts unless the articles otherwise provide.

Article 292
1 The board shall represent the foundation to the extent that the contrary does not follow from the law.

2 The articles may also vest representative authority in one or more officers and may provide that an officer may represent the foundation only with the cooperation of one or more other persons.

3 Representative authority vested in the board or in an officer shall be unrestricted and unconditional to the extent that the contrary does not follow from the law. A restriction or condition on the representative authority permitted or prescribed by statute may only be invoked by the foundation.

4 The articles may also vest representative authority in persons other than officers.

Article 293
The articles of a foundation may be amended by its constituent bodies only if the articles provide for such a possibility. Such an amendment shall be a nullity if not made by notarial deed. The officers must deposit an officially certified copy of such amendment and the amended articles at the registry referred to in article 289 of this Book.

Article 294

1 If the maintenance of the articles in an unamended form would have consequences which, on the establishment, could not reasonably have been envisaged and if the articles do not provide for the possibility of amendment or the persons having the power to amend the same fail to do so, the court may amend the articles on the application of a founder, the management of the public prosecution service.

2 In so doing, the court shall derogate from the existing articles as little as possible and if amendment of the object is necessary it shall designate an object which is related to the existing object. With due observance of the foregoing, the court is empowered, where necessary, to amend the articles otherwise than as applied for.

3 In order to avoid the dissolution (*winding up*) of the foundation on grounds referred to in article 21 or in subparagraph *a* of article 301, paragraph 1, the court may amend the articles duly applying both preceding paragraphs *mutatis mutandis*.

Article 295

A resolution to amend the articles may be annulled (*avoided*) by the court at any time upon the application of the foundation, an interested party or of the public prosecution service, if such an amendment could result in the dissolution (*winding up*) of the foundation on the grounds contemplated in articles 21 or 301, paragraph 1 and such amendment does not lead to conversion. Moreover, article 15, paragraphs 3 and 4 and article 16 shall apply.

Article 296

In proceedings in which an order for the dissolution (*winding up*) of a foundation is applied for on grounds referred to in article 21 or in subparagraph *a* of article 301, paragraph 1, the court may exercise the powers referred to in both preceding articles *ex officio*.

Article 297

1 If there is serious doubt as to whether the law or the articles are observed in good faith or whether the management is properly conducted, the public prosecution service at the court is empowered to request the board for information.

2 If such request is not, or is improperly, complied with, the interim provisions judge of the court may, when so requested, order that the public prosecution service be given access to inspect the books and records of the foundation and that the assets of the foundation be shown to it. No right of appeal or cassation (appeal to the Supreme Court) shall lie against the order of the interim provisions judge.

Article 298

1 An officer who:

a in breach of the provisions of the law or the articles, acts or fails to act, or is guilty of mismanagement, or

b does not, or does not properly, comply with an order made by the interim provisions judge of the court under the preceding article, may be removed by the court. This may take place upon the application of the public prosecution service or of any interested party.

2 Pending the examination of the matter, the court may make provisional arrangements for the management and suspend the officer.

3 An officer who has been removed by the court may not become an officer of a foundation for five years after such removal.

Article 299

Whenever there is no officer on the board or the number of officers falls below that required under the articles and the vacancy is not filled in accordance with the articles, the court may fill the vacancy upon the application of any interested party or of the public prosecution service and, in so doing, the court shall observe the articles as far as possible.

Article 299a

A foundation which maintains one or more undertakings which must be registered in the commercial register pursuant to the law shall disclose the net turnover of such undertakings in its statement of income and expenditure.

Article 300

1 Each year, within six months after the end of the financial year of a foundation referred to in article 360, paragraph 3, unless this period has been extended by up to five months by the constituent body referred to in paragraph 3 on account of special circumstances, annual accounts shall be prepared by the board, which shall be made available for inspection by the members of the constituent body referred to in paragraph 3. Within this period the board shall also make available for inspection to the members of the constituent body referred to in paragraph 3 the information to be added pursuant to article 392, paragraph 1 and the annual report unless the first sentence of article 396, paragraph 6, insofar as it relates to the annual report, or article 403 applies to the foundation. For Investment Undertakings which have been issued a licence under the *Wet toezicht beleggingsinstellingen* (Investment Undertakings (Supervision) Act) the period may be shortened by or pursuant to that Act. Members of the constituent body referred to in paragraph 3 may obtain a copy of those documents without charge.

2 The annual accounts shall be signed by the officers and the persons who constitute the supervisory body. If one or more of their signatures is missing, this shall be stated giving the reason therefor.

3 The annual accounts shall be adopted no later than one month after the term set by the constituent body so empowered under the articles. If the articles do not confer such authority to any constituent body, such authority shall vest in the supervisory body and, in its absence, in the board.

4 A foundation referred to in article 360, paragraph 3 may only compensate a shortfall in its required statutory reserves insofar so permitted by law.

Article 300a
Articles 131, 138, 139, 149 and 150 shall apply, *mutatis mutandis*, in respect of a bankruptcy of a foundation which is subject to the levy of corporate income tax.

Article 301
1 The court shall order the dissolution (*winding up*) of a foundation upon the application of an interested party or of the public prosecution service:
a if the capital of the foundation is wholly insufficient for the realisation of its object and the possibility of obtaining sufficient capital within the foreseeable future by means of contributions or otherwise is unlikely;
b if the object of the foundation has been achieved or can no longer be achieved and amendment of the object cannot be considered.

2 The court may also order the dissolution (*winding up*) of the foundation *ex officio*, simultaneously with the rejection of an application referred to in article 294.

Article 302
Any court decision which has become final and binding and which embodies:
the cancellation, supplementation or amendment of the information in the register,
the amendment of the articles of the foundation,
the change of, or the filling of vacancies on, the board, or
the annulment (*avoidance*) of a resolution for the amendment of the articles
shall be entered in the register referred to in article 289 of this Book at the instance of the clerk of the judicial body before which the case was last pending.

Article 303
On the bankruptcy of, or a *surséance van betaling* (suspension of payments) by, a foundation, the notices which are published in the *Nederlandse Staatscourant* (State Gazette) pursuant to the *Faillissementswet* (Bankruptcy Act) shall be submitted for registration in the register referred to in article 289 of this Book by the person charged with such publication.

Article 304
1 The participants in a pension fund, or a fund referred to in subparagraph *c* of article 631, paragraph 3 of Book 7 shall, for the purposes of the application of article 285 of this Book, not be considered members of a foundation which operates as such a fund.

2 For the purposes of the application of article 285, paragraph 3 of this Book any pension-right distributions or payments arising from an employment contract in which a stipulation referred to in subparagraph *c* of article 631, paragraph 3 of Book 7 has been included shall not be considered to be distributions to founders of such a foundation or to persons who form part of its constituent bodies.

Article 305-307
Repealed

Source: Netherlands Business Legislation Online:
wwww.nblonline.com

SELECTED BIBLIOGRAPHY

250 Chinese NGO's, A Special Report of China Development Brief. 2001. Beijing: China Development Brief.

Almond, Gabriel A. and Sidney Verba. 1989. *The Civic Culture*. Newbury Park: Sage.

An Introduction to Community Interest Companies. 2004. Department of Trade and Industry Document. http://www.dti.gov.uk/cics/pdfs/cicfactsheet1.pdf.

Anheier, Helmut K., Benjamin Gidron, Ralph Kramer and Lester M. Salamon. 1992. *Government and the Third Sector: Emerging Relationships in Welfare States*. San Fransisco: Josey Bass.

Anheier, Helmut K. and Jeremy Kendall. 2001. *Third Sector Policy at the Crossroads*. London: Routledge.

Anheier, Helmut K. and Stefan Toepler. 1999. *Private Funds, Public Purpose*. Dordrecht: Kluwer Academic.

Barber, Benjamin R. 1995. *Jihad vs. McWorld*. New York: Random House.

Beetham, David. 1992. *The Legitimation of Power*. London: MacMillan Education Ltd.

Beugelsdijk, Sjoerd. 2003. *Culture and Economic Development in Europe*. Tilburg: Tilburg University Center Dissertation Series.

Billiet, Jaak B. and Bart Cambré. 1999. "Social Capital, Active Membership in Voluntary Associations and some Aspects of Political Participation". In *Social Capital and European Democracy* edited by Jan W. van Deth *et al*. London: Routledge.

Brook, Timothy and B. Michael Frolic. 1997. "The Ambiguous Challenge of Civil Society". In *Civil Society in China* edited by Timothy Brook and B. Michael Frolic. Armonk: M.E. Sharpe.

Yuwen Li (Ed.), *Freedom of Association in China and Europe: Comparative Perspectives in Law and Practice*, © 2005 Koninklijke Brill NV, Leiden. Printed in The Netherlands, pp. 435-445.

Bureau of Civic Organizations Management of the Ministry of Civil Affairs (ed.). 1996. *Handbook for Administrative Work on Social Organizations.* Internal Document.

Bureau of Civic Organizations Management of the Ministry of Civil Affairs (ed.). 2000. *Collected Recent Regulations and Policy Concerning the Administration of Civic Organizations.* Internal Document.

Burger, Ary and Paul Dekker. 2000. *The Nonprofit Sector in the Netherlands.* The Hague: Social and Cultural Planning Office. www.scp.nl/english.

Burger, Ary, Paul Dekker, Tymen van der Ploeg and Wino van Veen. 2001. *The Nonprofit Sector in The Netherlands.* Working Document 70. The Hague: Social and Cultural Planning Bureau.

Chambers, Simone. 2002. "A Critical Theory of Civil Society". In *Alternative Conceptions of Civil Society* edited by Simone Chambers and Will Kymlicka. Princeton: Princeton University Press.

Charity Commission Corporate Plan 2003-06. 2003. Charity Commission. http://www.charitycommission.gov.uk/spr/pdfs/corpplan03.pdf.

Chen, Jianfu.1999. *Chinese Law: Towards an Understanding of Chinese Law, Its Nature and Development.* The Hague: Kluwer Law International.

Chen, Jinluo and Wang Jianqin. 2003. *Theoretical and Practical Research on Chinese Social Organisations.* Research Centre on NPO Law at the Law School of Peking University.

Chen, Jinluo. 1997. *Legislation for and Administration of Social Organisations.* Beijing: falü chubanshe.

Chen, Sixie. 2002. "The Current Situation and Future, A Comment on the Current Legislation concerning Social Organisations in China". In *Global Law Review* Summer 2002.

Cohen, Jean L. And Andrew Arato. 1992. *Civil Society and Political Theory.* Cambridge: MIT Press.

Communication on Promoting the Role of Voluntary Organisations and Foundations in Europe. 1997. http://europe.eu.int/comm/enterprise/library/lib-social_economy/orgfd_en.pdf.

Connolly, William. 1984. *Legitimacy and State.* Oxford: Blackwell Ltd.

Dekker, Paul and Andries van den Broek. 1998. "Civil society in comparative perspective". In *Voluntas* 8 (1).

Dekker, Paul, Peter Ester and Henk Vinken. 2003. "Civil Society, Social Trust and Democratic Involvement". In *The Cultural Diversity of European Unity* edited by Wil Arts *et al.* Leiden/Boston: Brill 2003.

Dekker, Paul. 2004. "The Netherlands: From private initiatives to nonprofits and back?". In *The Third Sector in Europe* edited by Adalbert Evers and Jean-Louis Laville. Cheltenham (UK): Edward Elgar.

Dekker, Paul. 2002. "On the Prospects of Volunteering in Civil Society." *Voluntary Action* 4 (3).

Deng, Guosheng and Gong Huixian. 2004. "Volunteer Help, Civil Charity: First Aid Association for Traffic Accidents in Huludao City". In *Chinese Non-government Public Sector* edited by Wang Ming *et al.* Beijing: Tsinghua daxue chubanshe.

Deng, Guosheng and Wang Ming. 2001. "Xiang Yang Children Development Center". In *Case Study on China's NGOs, UNCRD Research Report Series No. 43* edited by Wang Ming, *et al.* Beijing: UNCRD.

Denning, Lord Alfred Thompson. 1979. *The Discipline of Law*. Chinese translation by Yang Baikui *et al.* 1999. Beijing: Falü chubanshe.

van Deth, Jan W. 1997. "Introduction". In *Private Groups and Public Life* edited by Jan W. van Deth. London: Routledge.

Dijk-Van der Ploeg. 2002. *Of Association and Foundation, Cooperative and Mutual Society*. 4th ed. Deventer: Gouda Quint.

Dickens, Charles. 2003. *Bleak House*. London: Penguin Classics.

Dooyeweerd, Herman. 1979. *Roots of Western Culture*. Toronto: Wedge Publishing Foundation.

Duoji, Cairang. 1998. "Actively Foster, Improve Management, Promote the Healthy Development of Civil Society Organisations". In *A Selection of Recent Regulations and Policies Concerning the Administration of Civil Society Organisations* edited by Bureau of Civic Organisations Management of the Ministry of Civil Affairs. Internal Document.

Du, Jie. 2004. "The Rise of Women's Organisations". In *Governance in China* edited by Jude Howell. Lanham: Rowman & Littlefiled Publishers.

Evers, Adalbert and Jean-Louis Laville. 2004. "Defining the Third Sector in Europe". In *The Third Sector in Europe*, edited by Adalbert Evers and Jean-Louis Laville. Cheltenham: Edward Elgar.

Fan Baojun. 1996. "See the Trend Clearly, Liberate Thinking, Open up a New Situation in our Country's Social Organisation Work – speech to the National Conference on Social Organisation Work". In *Handbook for Administrative Work on Social Organizations* edited by the Bureau of Civic Organsations Management of the Ministry of Civil Affairs. Internal Document.

Fernando, Jude L. and Alan W. Heston. 2000. "NGOs between States, Markets and Civil Society". In *Civil Society and the Third Sector* edited by He Zengke. Beijing: Shehui kexue wenxian chubanshe.

"Freedom of Association East and West: Current Law and Practice in Helsinki Signatory Countries". 1989. *Report of US Helsinki Watch Committee*. New York: Helsinki Watch.

Freedom of Association: Digest of Decision and Principle of the Freedom of Association Committee of the Governing Body of the ILO. 1996. Geneva: ILO.

"Freedom of Association: The Question of NGO Registration". 1998. *OSCE Human Dimension Implementation Meeting, October 1998, Background Paper 5*. Warsaw, Poland: OSCE-ODIHR.

Frolic, B. Michael. 1997. "State-Led Civil Society". In *Civil Society in China* edited by Timothy Brook and B. Michael Frolic. Armonk: M.E. Sharpe.

Frolic, B. Michael. 2003. "Reflections on Civil Society and Human Rights". In *Bridging the Global Divide on Human Rights, A Canada – China Dialogue* edited by Errol P. Mendes and Anik Lalonde-Roussy. Aldershot: Ashgate.

Gao, Bingzhong. 1999. "The Concept of Legitimacy – Understanding the Emergence of the Third Sector". In *System and Development – Legal Environment for the Third Sector* edited Su Li *et al.* Hangzhou: Zhejiang renmin chubanshe.

Gao, Bingzhong. 2001. "The Rise of Social Organizations and their Problems of Legitimicy". In *Chinese Social Organizations at a Crossroads* edited by China Youth Development Foundation and Committee on Development Research on Foundations. Tianjing: Tianjing renmin chubanshe.

Ge, Yunsong. 2000. "On the Establishment of Social Organisations Under Chinese Law". *International Journal for Not-for Profit Law* (2) 3. www.icnl.org/journal/vol2iss3/ar_chinalaw.htm.

Ge, Yunsong. 1999. "The Legal System on the Third Sector". In *The Regulatory System and Development – The Legal Environment for the Third Sector* edited by Su Li *et al.* Hangzhou: Zhejiang renmin chubanshe.

Gellner, Ernest. 1996. *Conditions of Liberty: Civil Society and its Rivals.* 2nd ed. London: Penguin.

Graf Strachwitz, Rupert. 1994. *Stiftungen nutzen, führen und verwalten – ein Handbuch.* Frankfurt/Main: Campus.

Habermas, Jurgen. 1976. *Legitimation Crisis.* London: Heinemann Educational Books.

He, Zengke (ed.). 2000. *Civil Society and the Third Sector.* Beijing: Shehui kexue wenxian chubanshe.

Heerma van Voss, Lex. 2002. "A History of Progress Towards Freedom of Association". Paper presented at the Seminar on Legal Aspects of Social Organizations, organised by the Institute of Law of the Chinese Academy of Social Sciences. Beijing.

Ho, Peter. 2001. "Greening Without Conflict? Environmentalism, NGOs and Civil Society in China". In *Development and Change* 32 (5).

Hodgkinson, Virginia A. 2003. "Volunteering in Global Perspective". In *The Values of Volunteering* edited by Paul Dekker and Loek Halman. New York: Plenum.

Hondius, Frits W. and Tymen J. van der Ploeg. 2000. "Foundations". In *International Encyclopedia of Comparative Law* Volume XIII.

Hooghe, Marc. 2003. "Voluntary Associations and Democratic Attitudes". In *Generating Social Capital* edited by Marc Hooghe and Dietlind Stolle. New York: Palgrave.

Howell, Jude. 2003. "Women's Organisations and Civil Society in China". *International Feminist Journal of Politics* 5 (2).

Hupe, Peter L. and Lucas C.P.M. Meijs. 2002. *Hybrid Governance – The Impact of the Nonprofit Sector in the Netherlands.* The Hague: Social and Cultural Planning Office.

Jessurun d'Oliveira, H.U. 1990. "Group Actions in Civil Procedure". In *Netherlands Reports to the Thirteenth International Congress of Comparative Law in Montreal 1990* edited by E.H. Hondius and G.J.W. Steenhoff. The Hague: The Asser Institute.

Ji, Weidong. 1998. "The One Inevitable Error of the Critics". In *State and Society* edited by Zhang Jing. Hangzhou: Zhejiang renmin chubanshe.

Jia, Xiejing. 2004. "Trade Associations in Wenzhou". In *Chinese Non-government Public Sector* edited by Wang Ming. Beijing: Tsinghua daxue chubanshe.

Jin Dongsheng. 2004. "The Current Situation of Preferential Tax Policies for China's NPOs and Some Problems". Paper presented at the Conference on Tax Reform Concerning NPOs, organised by the Research Centre for NPO Law Studies at Peking University.

Kang, Xiaoguang. 2001. "Chinese Social Organisations in the Era of Transition". In *Chinese Social Organisations at a Crossroads* edited by China Youth Development Foundation and Committee on Development Research on Foundations. Tianjin: Tianjin renmin chubanshe.

Kang, Xiaoguang. 1999. *Shifts in Power – Changes to the Distribution in Power in China in Transition.* Hangzhou: Zhejiang renmin chubanshe.

Kateb, George. 1998. "The Value of Association". In *Freedom of Association* edited by Amy Gutmann. Princeton: Princeton University Press.

Kymlicka, Will. 1998. "Ethnic Associations and Democratic Citizenship". In *Freedom of Association* edited by Amy Gutman. Princeton: Princeton University Press.

Korpi, Walter. 1983. *The Democratic Class Struggle.* London: Routledge and Kegan Paul.

Li, Jianjung. 2004. "Development of Trade Associations in Transitional China". In *Chinese Non-government Public Sector* edited by Wang Ming. Beijing: Tsinghua daxue chubanshe.

Li, Yong and Qiao Shengqan. 2002. "The History, Presence, and Future of Social Organizations in China". In *Collection of Papers for the Seminar on Legal Aspects of Social Organizations* issued by the Institute of Law of the Chinese Academy of Social Sciences. Beijing.

Lin, Yansheng. 2000. "Keep our Eyes on Stabilising the Overall Situation, Improve Management and Guidance, Promote the Healthy and Orderly Development of Civil Society Organisations. In *Collected Recent Regulations and Policy Concerning the*

Administration of Civil Society Organizations edited by the Bureau of Civic Organizations Management of the Ministry of Civil Affairs. Internal Document.

Liu, Zuoxiang. 2002. "The Roots in Basic Human Nature of the Right to Freedom of Association". Paper presented at the Conference on Legal Aspects of Social Organisations held by the Institute of Law of the Chinese Academy of Social Sciences.

Lu, Yiyi. 2003. *The Limitations of NGOs: A Preliminary Study of Non-governmental Social Welfare Organisations in China.* London School of Economics. www.lse.ac.uk/collections/ccs/publications/iwp/iwp13.htm.

Luxton, Peter. 2001. *The Law of Charities.* Oxford: Oxford University Press.

Ma, Changshan.1992. "Brief Discussion of the Legal Status of China's Social Organisations and how to Restrain the Tendency for them to Become Instruments of Official Administration". *Politics and Law* 3.

Ma, Changshan. 1993. "A Discussion of the Right to Freedom of Association in China". *Politics and Law* 5.

ten Napel, H.-M.Th.D. 2002. "A Dutch Taliban?". In *De multiculturele samenleving en het recht* edited by N.F. van Manen. Nijmegen: Ars Aequi.

Nesbitt-Larking, Paul and Alfred L. Chan.1997. "Chinese Youth and Civil Society". In *Civil Society in China* edited by Timothy Brook and B. Michael Frolic. Armonk: M.E. Sharpe.

Newton, Ken. 2001. "Social Capital and Democracy". In *Beyong Tocqueville* edited by Bob Edwards, Michel W. Foley and Mario Diani. Hanover: Tufts University Press.

Nowak, Manfred. 1993. *U.N. Covenant on Civil and Political Rights: CCPR Commentary.* Kehl am Rhein, Strasbourg, Arlington: N.P.Engel.

Olson, Macur. 1982. *The Rise and Decline of Nations.* New Haven: Yale University Press.

Olsen, Marvin E. 1982. *Participatory Pluralism.* Chicago: Nelson Hall.Olsen.

Ou, Guangyuan. 2000. "Explore a New Way of Managing Social Organizations for a New Era, Serve Social Stability and the Construction of the Two Civilizations". In *Collected Recent Regulations and Policy Concerning the Administration of Civil Society Organizations* edited by the Bureau of Civic Organizations Management of the Ministry of Civil Affairs. Internal Document.

Ovey, Clare and Robin White. 2003. *Jacobs and White, The European Convention on Human Rights.* Oxford: Oxford University Press.

Parry, Geraint, George Moyser and Neil Day. 1992. *Political Participation and Democracy in Britain.* Cambridge: Cambridge University Press.

Pérez-Díaz, Victor. 1993. *The Return of Civil Society*. Cambridge: Harvard University Press.

Perrow, Charles. 2001. "The Rise of Nonprofits and the Decline of Civil Society". In *Organisational Theory and the Nonprofit Form* edited by Helmut K. Anheier. London: Centre for Civil Society, London School of Economics.

Picarda, Hubert. 1999. *The Law and Practice Relating to Charities*. 3rd ed. London: Butterworths.

van der Ploeg, Tymen J. 1999. "A Comparative Legal Analysis of Foundations: Aspects of Supervision and Transparency". In *Private Funds, Public Purpose* edited by Helmut K. Anheier and Stefan Toepler. New York, Dordrecht: Kluwer Academic.

van der Ploeg, Tymen J. 1992. "Changing Relationships between Private Nonprofit Organisations and Government in The Netherlands". In *The Nonprofit Sector in the Global Community* edited by Kathleen McCarthy. San Fransisco: Josey Bass.

Private Action, Public Benefit. 2002. UK Government's Strategy Unit Report Chapter 2. Cabinet Office. http://www.number-10.gov.uk/su/voluntary/report/downloads/strat-data.pdf.

Putnam, Robert. 1993. *Making Democracy Work*. Princeton: Princeton University Press.

Putnam, Robert 2000. *Bowling Alone*. New York: Simon & Schuster.

Qi, Bingwen (ed.). 2001. *The Management, Building, and Development of Civil Society Organisations*. Jinan: Shandong daxue chubanshe.

Qin Hui. 2001. "From Traditional Civic Public Welfare Organisations to a Modern 'Third Sector'- Certain Questions in the Comparative History of Public Welfare in China and the West". In *Chinese Social Organisations at a Crossroads* edited by the China Youth Development Foundation and Committee on Development Research on Foundations. Tianjin: Tianjin renmin chubanshe.

Reichert, Bernhard. 1999. *Manual of Association and Organisation Law*. Neuwied: Luchterhand.

Rousseau, Jean-Jacques. 1913. *The Social Contract and Discourses*. Translated by G.D.H. Cole. London: J.M. Dent.

Rueschemeyer, Dietrich. 1998. "The Self-organisation of Society and Democratic Rule". In *Participation and Democracy in East and West* edited by Dietrich Rueschemeyer, Marilyn Rueschemeyer and Björn Wittrock. Armonk: M.E. Sharpe.

Salamon, Lester M. 1997. "Introduction". In *The International Guide to Nonprofit Law*, edited by Lester M. Salamon. New York: John Wiley & Sons, Inc.

Salamon, Lester M. and Helmut K. Anheier, *et al*. 1999. *Global Civil Society*. Baltimore: The John Hopkins Center for Civil Society Studies.

Salamon, Lester M. and Helmut K. Anheier. 1992. *In Search of the Non-profit Sector: The Question of Definition*. Baltimore: John Hopkins University Institute for Policy Studies.

Sauter, Gerhard Schweyer. 1990. *The Registered Association*. 14th ed. München: Beck.
Seifart, Werner and Axel von Campenhausen. 1999. *Handbuch des Stiftungsrechts*. 2nd ed. München: Beck.

Selle, Per and Kristin Strømsnes. 2001. "Membership and Democracy". In *Social Capital and Participation in Everyday Life* edited by Paul Dekker and Eric M. Uslander. London: Routledge.

Sheng, Hongchao and Wang Ming. 2001. "Low Voltage Electrical Apparatus of Yueqing City". In *Case-Study on China's NGOs, UNCRD Research Report Series No. 43* edited by Wang Ming *et al.* Beijing: UNCRD.

Silk, Thomas. 2000. *Public Welfare in Asia and Related Laws and Regulations*. Beijing: Zhongguo shehui kexue chubanshe.

Silk, Thomas. 1999. *Philanthropy and Law in Asia: A Comparative Study of the Nonprofit Sector in Ten Asia Pacific Societies.* San Fransisco: Jossey Bass Publishers.

Skocpol, Theda. 1999. "Advocates without members". In *Civic Engagement in American Democracy* edited by Theda Skocpol and Morris P. Fiorino. Washington D.C.: Brookings Institution Press.

Sprengel, Rainer. 2001. *Statistics on the Nature of German Foundations, A Research Report*. Berlin: Maecenata.

Stoeber, Kurt. 1997. *Manual of Association Law*. Köln: Schmidt.

Stolle, Dietland. 2001. "Getting to Trust". In *Social Capital and Participation in Everyday Life* edited by Paul Dekker and Eric M. Uslaner. London: Routledge.

Su, Li *et al.* 1999. *The Regulatory System and Development – The Legal Environment for the Third Sector*. Hangzhou: Zhejiang renmin chubanshe.

Sun, Bingyao. 1994. "Township Social Organisations and China's Grassroots Society". *Chinese Journal of Social Sciences* 9.

Tao, Chuangjin. 2004. "China's Civil Society in the Field of Market Economy". In *Chinese Non-government Public Sector* edited by Wang Ming. Beijing: Tsinghua daxue chubanshe.

Tao, Heshan. 2001. *Civic Groups and Innovations in the Political System – Research into the Main Actors in China's Modernisation*. Nanjing: Nanjing daxue chubanshe.

Tamir, Yael. 1998. "Revisiting the Civic Sphere". In *Freedom of Association* edited by Amy Gutman. Princeton: Princeton University Press.

The Commission and Nongovernemental Organisations: Building a Strong Partnership. COM (2000) 11 def. 128.1.00.

The Netherlands in an European Perspective. 2001. The Hague: Social and Cultural Planning Office. www.scp.nl

The Strengthening of the Role of Associations and Foundations in Europe. 1997. Report of the European Commission. COM (97)0241-C4 0546-96.

de Tocqueville, Alexis. 1969. *Democracy in America*. Garden City, New York: Anchor Books. Chinese translation by Dong guoliang, 1988.

Tong, Lei. 2000. "The Way of Grass-roots Organisations' Cooperation – 'Friends of Green'". In *UNCRD Research Report Series No. 38* edited by Wang Ming *et al.* Beijing: UNCRD.

van Til, Jon. 2001. *Growing Civil Society*. Bloomington: Indiana University Press.

Verba, Sidney, Kay Lehman Schlozman and Henry E. Brady. 1995. *Voice and Equality*. Cambridge: Harvard University Press.

Versteegh, C.R.M. 2003. *De Goede Doelstichting*. Utrecht: Lemma.

Walzer, Michael. 2002. "Equality and civil society". In *Alternative Conceptions of Civil Society* edited by Simone Chambers and Will Kymlicka. Princeton: Princeton University Press.

Wang Ming, *et al.* (eds). 2000. "Case Study on China's NGOs". In *UNCRD Research Report Series No. 38*. Beijing: UNCRD and Tsinghua University NGO Research Centre.

Wang, Ming, *et al* (eds). 2001. "Case Study on China's NGOs". In *UNCRD Research Report Series No. 43*. Beijing: UNCRD and Tsinghua University NGO Research Centre.

Wang, Ming, *et al.* 2001. *Reform of China's Social Organizations – from a Government Choice to a Social Choice*. Beijing: Shehui kexue wenxian chubanshe.

Wang, Shaoguang. 2001. "Theory and Practice – An Overview of the Third Sector in Different Countries". In *Chinese Social Organizations at a Crossroads* edited by China Youth Development Foundations and Committee on Development Research on Foundations. Tianjin: Tianjin renmin chubanshe.

Wang, Shaoguang and Hu Angang. 1998. "The Decline and Consequence in Capacity of the Chinese Government's Ability to Derive?" In *State and Society* edited by Zhang Jing. Hangzhou: Zhejiang renmin chubanshe.

Wang, Shijie and Qian Duansheng. 1997. *Comparing Constitutions*. Beijing: Zhongguo zhengfa daxue chubanshe.

Wang, Ying *et al.* 1993. *An Intermediate Level of Society – Reform and China's Social Organisations*. Beijing: Zhongguo fazhan chubanshe.

Warren, Mark E. 2001. *Democracy and Association*. Princeton: Princeton University Press.

White, Gordon. 1993. "Prospects for Civil Society in China: A Case Study of Xiaoshan City". In *The Australian Journal of Chinese Affairs*. January 1993 (29). www.jstor.org.

Wu, Yuzheng. 2004. *Legal Aspects on Social Organizations*. Beijing: Shehui kexue wenxian chubanshe.

Wu, Zhongze and Chen Jinluo (eds.). 1996. *Social Organisations Management Work*. Beijing: Zhongguo shehui chubanshe.

Xia, Baolong. 2000. "Serve the Overall Situation, Support Reform, Vigorously Explore New Ways of Conducting Social Organisations Work". In *Collected Recent Regulations and Policy Concerning the Administration of Civil Society Organizations* edited by the Bureau of Civic Organizations Management of Ministry of Civil Affairs. Internal Document.

Xia, Yong. 2001. *Towards An Age of Rights*. Beijing: Zhongguo zhengfa daxue chubanshe.

Xiang, Biao. 1998. "Mobilisation, the Marketisation of Traditional Networks, and Non-state Spaces". In *State and Society* edited by Zhang Jing. Hangzhou: Zhejiang renmin chubanshe.

Xie, Haiding. 2002. "Several Hot Issues on Studying China's Social Organisations in Recent Years". In *Global Law Review*, Summer 2002.

Xu, Ruixin. 1998. "Explanation on a Few Key Issues Relating to Administration of Social Organizations". In *A Selection of Recent Regulations and Policies Concerning the Administration of Civil Society Organisations* edited by the Bureau of Civic Organisations Management of Ministry of Civil Affairs. Internal Document.

Xu, Ruixin. 1996. "An Explanation of Several Major Issues in Social Organisations Management". In *Handbook for Administrative Work on Social Organizations* edited by the Bureau of Civic Organizations Management of Ministry of Civil Affairs. Internal Document.

Xu, Yongguang. 2001. "The Current Situation of the Third Sector in China and Our Tasks". In *Chinese Social Organisations at a Crossroads* edited by China Youth Development Foundation and Committee on Development Research on Foundations. Tianjin: Tianjin renmin chubanshe.

Xu, Yongguang. 2001. "Foreword to the 'China Third Sector Research Yearbook'". In *Chinese Social Organisations at a Crossroads* edited by the China Youth Development Foundation and Committee on Development Research on Foundations. Tianjin: Tianjin renmin chubanshe.

Yang, Hua. 1991. *Documentary Account of the Dramatic Changes in Eastern Europe*. Beijing: Shijie zhishi chubanshe.

Yang, Xiaomin, Zhou Yi. 2000. *China's Work Unit System*. Beijing: Zhongguo jingji chubanshe.

Young, Nick. 2001. "Searching for Civil Society". In *250 Chinese NGO's, A Special Report from China Development Brief*. Beijing: China Development Brief.

Yu, Keping. 2002. "The Rise of Chinese Civil Society and its Significance for Governance". In *The Rise of Chinese Civil Society and Changes in Governance* edited by Yu Keping *et al.* Beijing: Shehui kexue wenxian chubanshe.

Yu Keping. 2002. "China's Rural CSOs and Changes in Governance". In *The Rise of Chinese Civil Society and Changes in Governance* edited by Yu Keping *et al.* Beijing: Shehui kexue wenxian chubanshe.

Yu, Keping. 2000. *Governance and 'Good Governance'*. Beijing: Shehui kexue wenxian chubanshe.

Zhang, Jing (ed.). 1998. *State and Society*. Hangzhou: Zhejiang renmin chubanshe.

Zhang, Lianzhen. 2000. "Actively Explore Social Organisation Reform, Work Hard in the Service of the Whole Province's Economy and Society". In *Collected Recent Regulations and Policy Concerning the Administration of Civil Society Organizations* edited by Bureau of Civic Organisations Management of Ministry of Civil Affairs. Internal Document.

Zhang, Xiaoshan *et al.* 2002. *Linking Farmers and the Market – Research into Chinese Farmer's Intermediary Organisations*. Beijing: Zhongguo shehui kexue chubanshe.

Zhao, Xiumei. 2000. "Investigation on Environmental NGOs in Beijing". In *UNCRD Research Report Series No. 38* edited by Wang Ming *et al.* Beijing: UNCRD.

Zu, Yuqing. 2002. "Analysis of the Current Situation of Social Organisations' Development in Shenzhen". In *Global Law Review* Summer 2002.

INDEX

www.ingramcontent.com/pod-product-compliance
Lightning Source LLC
LaVergne TN
LVHW010631300926
849162LV00001B/118